THE BEHAVIOR SURVIVAL GUIDE FOR KIDS

HOW TO MAKE GOOD CHOICES AND STAY OUT OF TROUBLE

Tom McIntyre, Ph.D.

Edited by Marjorie Lisovskis

free spirit
PUBLISHING®
Works for kids®

Library of Congress Cataloging-in-Publication Data
McIntyre, Thomas, 1952–
    The behavior survival guide for kids : how to make good choices and stay out of trouble /
    Thomas McIntyre.
       p. cm.
      ISBN 1-57542-132-1
      1. Problem children. I. Title: How to make good choices and stay out of trouble. II. Title.
HQ773.M35 2003
649'.153—dc21
                                                                      2003004565

For privacy reasons, the names of the kids and teachers who are quoted in this book and included in its stories have been changed.

The study referenced in "It's Tough to Be a Kid with BD" (pages 11–12) was conducted by B. Behre, T. McIntyre, and K. Rogers (1993) and is reported in "They Tell Me I'm Crazy: Student Responses to Being Labeled Behavior Disordered," *Perceptions*, 27(4), 12–13.

"20 Adults You Might Talk To" (page 45) is adapted from "Adults Who Can Help" in *How to Take the Grrrr Out of Anger* by Elizabeth Verdick and Marjorie Lisovskis (Minneapolis: Free Spirit Publishing, 2002), pp. 24–25. Used with permission.

Cover and interior book design: Marieka Heinlen
Assistant editor: Douglas Fehlen
Illustrations: Chris Sharp
Photograph: Cindy Huang
Index: Kay Schlembach

10 9 8 7 6 5 4 3 2 1
Printed in Canada

Free Spirit Publishing Inc.
217 Fifth Avenue North, Suite 200
Minneapolis, MN 55401-1299
(612) 338-2068
help4kids@freespirit.com
www.freespirit.com

The following are registered trademarks of Free Spirit Publishing Inc.:

FREE SPIRIT®
FREE SPIRIT PUBLISHING®
THE FREE SPIRITED CLASSROOM®
SELF-HELP FOR KIDS®
SELF-HELP FOR TEENS®
WORKS FOR KIDS®
HOW RUDE!™
LEARNING TO GET ALONG™
LAUGH & LEARN™

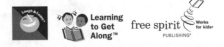

DEDICATION

While I was writing this book, I thought a lot about the students I used to teach who had behavior disorders. We learned many things from each other. So I want to dedicate this book to them.

I also want to dedicate the book to my wonderful family, who have always supported me. My new wife Cindy has joined them in making my life fun and rewarding.

THANK YOU

Even though my name is on the front of this book, it's important to let you know that I was part of a team. Many people helped me to write the book. I would like to thank them:

Thanks to Ms. Dorota Koczewska and her students who have behavior disorders. Many of the quotes from kids came from their class.

Other teachers like Ms. Kirstin Larson and Mr. John Schmidt read the book before it was finished. They told me ways to change the book to make it even better. Dr. Beth Russell, a principal, also reviewed the book and gave me good ideas. So did Ms. Denise Poston, a researcher and parent of a kid who has been working on making good choices. Another helper was Ms. Debra Carlson, who works with parents of kids who have behavior disorders.

The person I worked with the most was Margie Lisovskis, the editor of this book. This hard-working and funny lady helped me to write things better so that you could understand them well. She also gave me some great ideas to use in the book.

Other people at Free Spirit Publishing worked to make this book a good one, too. Judy Galbraith, Free Spirit's president, came up with the idea for the book and asked me to write it. Douglas Fehlen found lots of information that I needed and worked with Ms. Lisovskis to help me write a better book. The wonderful cover was drawn by Marieka Heinlen, who also designed the pages inside. An artist named Chris Sharp drew the cartoons.

Now I want to thank **YOU** for reading the book! Good luck to you as you work hard to make your life better.

CONTENTS

FORMS TO COPY AND USE

MEET DR. MAC

Hi! I'm Tom McIntyre (Mack-in-tire). I have worked in schools with lots of kids who have behavior disorders (BD). Today, I am a professor at Hunter College in New York City. I teach teachers how to work better with kids who have BD. I visit these teachers' classrooms and talk with their students. The teachers and students call me Dr. Mac. ("Dr." stands for "Doctor." In my case, this doesn't mean that I practice medicine. "Doctor" is also a title for people who go to college for eight years so that they can get a doctoral degree.) I have a Web site that helps parents and teachers work well with kids who are trying to manage their behavior better. It is called "Dr. Mac's Amazing Behavior Management Advice Site."

When I have free time, I like to hike in the woods where there's peace and quiet. If I'm looking for excitement, I paddle my kayak on river rapids.

—DR. MAC

HOW THIS BOOK CAN HELP YOU

- Do you get in trouble a lot (even though you try to do the right thing)?

- Do you have problems following the rules in school and at home?

- Do you have a hard time sitting still or staying in one place?

- Do you have problems learning because you can't stop thinking about your feelings?

- Do you hit people or yell at them when you're angry or upset?

- Do you have trouble making friends and keeping them?

- Do you sometimes feel really sad?

- Do you feel bad about who you are and the things you do?

- Have you stopped trying to behave well because you don't think you can?

If you said **YES** to any of these questions, this book is for you!

HAVE YOU BEEN GIVEN A BEHAVIOR "LABEL"? This book can help you if you have been given a label like BD, EBD, SED, or anything else that has to do with behavior. (You'll read more about these labels a little later.) To keep things simple, I use the term BD in the book. But the ideas fit kids with other behavior labels, too. Look for answers in this book to questions like these:

- Why do kids with BD have trouble making good choices?

- What can kids with BD do about having it?

- Why don't teachers, parents, and other kids understand kids with BD?

- How can kids with BD make things better for themselves?

WHAT IF YOU DON'T HAVE A BEHAVIOR "LABEL"? Maybe behavior is a problem for you even though you don't have a label like BD. This book can help you, too. It's full of ideas for learning to take charge of your own behavior so you can get along better with teachers, other kids, and parents.

Kids live in many kinds of families. Maybe you live with one or two parents. Maybe you live with a foster parent, stepparent, guardian, or an adult relative. This book usually says *parents, family adults,* or *adults at home.* When you see these words, think of the adult or adults you live with who take care of you.

That's why this book is called *The Behavior Survival Guide for Kids.* "Survival" is when you keep going and make it through a tough experience. The book will talk about challenges a lot because that is what you face—challenges. These new challenges are like hurdles that runners jump over in some of their races. You will be jumping over new hurdles, behavior hurdles. Getting over these hurdles can help you to win in the race of life.

This book won't clear up all problems. But if you use its suggestions, it can make things **BETTER** for you in many ways. It can help you understand BD better. It can give you ideas for making school and home better places to be. It can help you form better friendships. It can help you make better choices and feel better about yourself.

HOW TO USE THIS BOOK

You can read this book a little at a time, or from start to finish. Or you can just read parts that are most interesting to you.

CHAPTERS 1, 2, AND 3 talk about the label "BD." Here you'll find information about what it means to have a label like BD, or ED, or EBD, or SED, or some other set of letters. (This book uses BD. But it is meant for you no matter which label you may have. You will find more about labels in Chapter 1.) You'll learn about the reasons some kids have BD. You'll read about the law that says schools are supposed to help kids with BD. You'll find out some ways schools work to do this.

CHAPTERS 4–12 focus on helping you take charge of your behavior. You'll learn many skills for handling your strong feelings and dealing with difficult people. You'll read and try ideas to help you get fair treatment from teachers. You'll learn ways to make and keep friends and get along at home, too.

IN THE BOOK you will also find:

- Stories and quotes from real kids. These kids have faced challenges because they have BD. (Their names have been changed for privacy reasons.)

- "It's Your Turn" questions. You can think or write about the questions. Or you can talk about them with someone else.

- "Idea!" boxes. These suggest things you can do to help you make changes.

- "A Challenge for You" activities. These will give you practice trying out new skills.

- Forms you can copy and use to keep track of your goals and progress.

- Words you may need to know highlighted in **bold** type. Most of these words are explained the first time you read them. All of them are defined in the glossary on pages 148–153.

- A list of books, organizations, and Web sites for learning more about many of the book's topics.

- The index, an alphabetical list of words and page numbers. It is helpful if you want to find something very specific. For example, maybe in Chapter 10 you'll read about making a "sandwich." What if you don't remember what that's about? You can look for "sandwich" in the index. The index will tell you the page numbers where the "sandwich" skill is explained. Then you can turn to those pages and read all about it.

Idea!

Keep a notebook or journal while you read this book. Use it to draw or write in. You can do the activities in it or record thoughts, feelings, and experiences that come to mind. Maybe you'll have an idea to send to me!

WRITE TO DR. MAC

After you're done reading *The Behavior Survival Guide for Kids,* please write to me. Let me know about the behavior challenges you have faced and how this book helps you. Tell me some ideas you have for dealing with behavior challenges. You can send a letter to me at this address:

Tom McIntyre
c/o Free Spirit Publishing
217 Fifth Avenue North, Suite 200
Minneapolis, MN 55401-1299

I like email, too! You can reach me that way at:

help4kids@freespirit.com

My best wishes go out to you. Keep believing in yourself. And keep working on facing your challenges. If you do, someday you'll be able to look back and be really proud of the changes you've made.

—DR. MAC

THE SIX GREAT GRIPES OF KIDS WITH BD

1. Nobody tells me what BD is all about. It makes me worry a lot. I wonder if something is wrong with me.

2. Teachers, parents, and other kids don't like me for who I really am. The behavior keeps them from seeing the real me.

3. I don't have many friends.
   —OR—
   I wish that I had better friends who acted nicer.

4. Kids tease me. They call me names and make fun of the things I do.

5. People only tell me when I'm doing things wrong. Even when I do the right thing, sometimes people don't notice.

6. It's really hard to change my behavior. I'm so used to acting in a certain way that I forget to use better ways.

Chapter 1

WHAT IS BD?

"BD is a label. I don't like it. But at school, I'm learning ways to behave better." —Julio, 11

WHAT DOES BD MEAN?

THAT'S A GOOD QUESTION. BD stands for **behavior disorder.** (This is the "official" language.) It means that teachers and other adults think your behavior is getting in the way at school. It is keeping you from learning as well as you could. It

Words in **bold** type are explained in the glossary on pages 148–153.

is keeping you from getting along well with others. The school is using special ways to help you learn to make better choices in class. The behaviors teachers are trying to teach you will also help you in other ways. They'll help you get along better with your family and other kids. These new ways of acting will help you later, too. They'll help when you go to junior high or high school. They'll help you get a good job (and keep it). They'll even help you be a good parent when you are an adult.

YOU MIGHT HEAR OTHER TERMS. There are different names for the many types of behavior problems. Professionals who work with kids who have BD don't all agree on what labels to use—even when they're talking about the same kid! Doctors use different names than teachers. Teachers use different labels than **psychologists**. Even different schools will use different labels. The students have the same behavior, but it's called different things in different places. For example, students could be labeled BD in one part of the country. But if they move to another part of the country, the label might change to **ED, EBD, SED,** or some other term used in that place. (You'll find the official meanings for these labels in the glossary.) For this book, I chose to say BD because that's the term many teachers and books use.

IF IT WERE UP TO ME, EVERYONE WOULD USE THE LABEL "CC." CC would mean **choice challenged.** That is because the **challenge** for all kids with BD is to learn to make better choices. Choices about which behaviors to show at school, at home, and in other places. Choices about which words and actions will help them get along with teachers, parents, and other kids. Choices that will help them enjoy life more.

You will find *"It's Your Turn"* all through this book. You might want to think or write about the questions and ideas in these boxes on your own. Or maybe you'll talk about them with a teacher, family adult, classmate, or friend. It's up to you.

It's Your Turn

• **What good choices did you make in the last couple of days?**

You can be proud of those. Tell yourself, "Hey, great job!"

• **Which choices were not so good because they caused problems? What could you have done instead?**

Practice that better choice right now. Really! Pretend that you are back in that situation. Then say or act out the right behavior. This practice will help you remember to make better choices in the future.

It's important to know that being labeled BD is not a punishment. You were given the label BD because teachers want you to be a success in life. They want to be sure you get special help to make better decisions.

It's also important to remember that being labeled BD can mean different challenges for different kids. Not everyone has BD in the same way.

- Some kids with BD have problems obeying rules or following directions.

- Other kids find it hard to sit still or pay attention.

- Some have trouble making friends.

- Others are very shy or sad.

- Some kids have to work on telling the truth.

- Some kids have one of these challenges, or two or three of them. Some may have all of the challenges. It just depends.

Idea!

Think about a behavior challenge you have—a situation where you often make the wrong choice about what to say or do.

- What is **ONE** better thing you can do the next time you are in that situation?

Talk about this with your parent or a friend you trust. Or think about it on your own.

Promise yourself that you will do that one better thing next time. Write your promise in your notebook or journal. Then do your best to keep it.

WHAT BD DOES **NOT** MEAN

It is hard to explain what BD means. But there are some things that it definitely does *not* mean.

BD DOES NOT MEAN YOU ARE "BAD." Yes, sometimes people may call you "bad." They are very upset at a behavior they have seen. They wish you had made a better choice. But it is not right to call you a bad person.

A better thing for them to say would be, "You are a good kid, but the behavior is bad and it needs to stop." Or, "I like you, but I don't like that behavior." The reason you're making wrong choices is because you *learned* wrong choices or because you are *feeling* bad—it is **NOT** because *you* are bad. But you can learn to make better choices and handle your feelings better. As you do this, people won't get so darn upset and say terrible things like this to you. Your smart behavior choices might even help other people see their own bad behaviors and wrong choices!

BD DOES NOT MEAN YOU ARE "CRAZY." People who are "crazy" have no control over what they do. You have control over many behaviors. And you will learn to have control over other ones soon. When people see someone make wrong choices about behavior, they sometimes use words that hurt—words like "crazy," "weird," "loco," and "nuts." As you learn to make better choices about your behavior, you won't hear those angry, hurtful words so often. It will take time before people know that you have really changed your ways forever. So you'll have to make the right choices for quite a while before people notice.

BD DOES NOT MEAN YOU ARE "RETARDED." In most schools, having BD means that you take part in **special education (special ed).** Some kids think that everyone in special classes is **retarded.** That is not true. Kids are in special ed for many reasons, but very few of these kids are retarded. People who are retarded learn very slowly. And they can't learn many things because of a problem in their brain. But you get special help because of your behavior, not because your brain is slow. If it feels like you're learning too slowly, this is probably because you need to make better choices about listening, following directions, and working on assignments. You might have a **learning difference (LD)** as well. This is true for some kids with BD, but not all. (You can read more about that in Chapter 2.)

It's Your Turn

- **What hurtful things have people said to you? Why do you think they said those things?**

- **Have you figured out a helpful thing to say or do when someone says mean things to you? If so, what do you do?**

IT'S TOUGH TO BE A KID WITH BD

That's the truth! Years ago, I did a study with two other teachers. We asked a group of kids who were labeled BD a few questions. One question was:

"How do other kids react when they find out you're in special education?"

Here are some of the answers we got:

"Some of them laugh and I get angry."

"They tease me."

"Some kids understand and some don't."

"They think I'm slow or stupid, but I'm not. That's why I'm quiet about it."

"They think that I'm bad or crazy."

"They start calling me names."

Another question we asked was:

"How do you feel about being labeled BD?"

These were some kids' replies:

"I feel hurt inside of me."

"I don't think they should label anymore."

"I feel embarrassed because kids make fun of me."

"I feel dumb."

"It stinks."

Like most kids with BD, you probably wish you didn't have it. Teachers and other adults tend to get upset about it. Other kids sometimes make fun of you or don't want to be friends with you. Plus, changing the way you behave in different situations is really hard. It can seem easier to just keep acting in the same old ways.

Even when you try the different ways, those ways sometimes don't feel right because they are new to you. People don't always give you the reaction you want from them, either. They might not notice how you're trying to change. Or maybe they notice, but they don't let you know this. Your challenge is to keep believing that if you make better choices, things will get better for you as time goes on.

It's Your Turn

- Have you ever made the right choice, but no one noticed—or people still treated you badly? What happened?

- What did you do then?

- What is a helpful thing you can say or do the next time something like this happens?

Remember . . .

It's no fun to be labeled. But if you are, you can get special help at school. In fact, there may be many people working to help you with behavior challenges in and out of school. And you can do your part to work on changing how you act at certain times. As you keep working, things will slowly improve for you. Getting along at school, with other kids, and at home will become easier. You will find that you like yourself a lot more. That may be the best thing of all!

Chapter 2

DIFFERENT KIDS, DIFFERENT CAUSES FOR BD

"I lose my temper a lot and want to scream. My mom just yells back. But now my foster parents and teachers are helping me to take responsibility. I don't want to let BD mess up my life." —Anne, 13

Do all kids with BD have the same behavior challenges? Nope! There are many different types of BD. There are many different reasons why kids have BD. And there are many different ways that adults help the kids to make better choices.

It's difficult to really be sure about the exact cause of a kid's BD. Still, it's usually possible to get a pretty good idea in most cases. This chapter talks about some common reasons why kids have BD. As you read, think about which reasons sound like they apply to you. You might find just one that fits your experience, or you might find more.

If you don't have the label BD, you can still read this chapter. It can help you think about some of the reasons you could be making wrong choices.

1. KIDS WHO NEED TO LEARN HOW TO MAKE GOOD CHOICES

Parents and other adults want kids to do well. But sometimes they don't know the best ways to help kids make the right choices about behavior. Other times, they try to teach kids the right ways to behave, but the kids don't catch on or don't learn them well. Sometimes, too, kids have learned to make wrong choices from adults who make wrong choices.

This means more problems when the kids come to school. Kids who haven't learned to make good choices have trouble getting along. They don't have the behaviors they need to follow school rules, learn well in class, or make new friends. Teachers try to help kids with BD make better choices.

The challenge for these students is to work hard to learn new and better ways of acting.

RODNEY

Rodney liked sports and enjoyed working on bicycles with his older brother. But he had problems making friends. He tried to talk and play with other kids, but he did things that they didn't like. He called them nasty names. He said things that he thought were funny, but that really weren't nice. He just didn't know how to meet people and make good impressions. Instead of liking Rodney, other kids stayed away from him. Rodney asked his teacher for help.

The teacher worked on helping Rodney become the type of person people like. Rodney and the other students took lessons in **social skills.** They learned about new ways to act. They practiced the ways together. Rodney worked very hard. He quickly learned ways to make friends and be liked by others. He made new friends slowly—not as fast as he would have liked to. Even though Rodney had better social skills, some of the other kids still didn't want to be friendly with him because he was in a special class.

MORE

Rodney didn't give up. He worked hard to follow rules and improve his grades. He kept getting better at making good choices. When he had been doing well for many months, he was allowed to take science and social studies in the regular class. (He already took art and gym with the regular education teachers.) Then other kids got to spend more time with Rodney. They saw that he was fun to be with and could be a good friend. It took patience and hard work, but over time Rodney made lots of new friends. Learning to make better choices made a big difference in Rodney's life.

2. KIDS WHOSE BRAIN CHEMICALS ARE MIXED UP

Chemicals in the brain help people to think and make decisions. Some kids have too much of one chemical or too little of another. This can make different things happen. It might make the kids move around a lot. It might make them feel really sad, or get very mad at things that don't get others upset. It might make them see and hear things that are not really there. You probably know labels for some brain chemical mix-ups. For example, maybe you have (or know someone who has) a label like **ADD** or **ADHD**.

Doctors sometimes give medicine to help with these kinds of conditions. The medicine helps the brain make the right amount of each chemical. This helps kids to slow down, concentrate better, learn more, and make better choices.

"My doctor switched me to a new medicine. Now I only have to take one pill each day. It helps, but I still need to tell myself to slow down, pay attention, and think."
—Shawna, 9

The challenge for these students is to remember to take their medicine. The students may also have learned some wrong behavior habits. So these kids often need to learn some new ways to act around teachers, friends, and family members, too.

3. KIDS WHO LEARN IN A DIFFERENT WAY

Some kids have trouble learning the things that teachers teach in school. These kids may have a **learning difference (LD)**. Some people say LD means a **learning disability.** It's true that kids with LD have problems learning, but usually this is because they learn in a different way from many of the other students. For example, some kids with LD have trouble reading, but they learn really well if the teacher explains things and they listen instead of read. Or some kids may have trouble doing math, but they're great at reading. They just have a learning difference.

When kids with LD struggle with something that's really hard for them, they may get mad at themselves. Or they might get mad at the work or at the teacher. They may start to act up. They might do things like rip up the paper or say, "I am not going to do this work." One ten-year-old student slammed books shut and told teachers "No!" when they asked him to read out loud. He would yell at the teacher, "I'm trying, but these books are too hard!" Teachers can get pretty upset about behavior like this. (Remember, it might seem like they're

mad at the student, but it's really the behavior they don't like.) If the problems with learning go on, these kids may give up and not even try to do the work anymore.

The challenge for these students is to tell teachers that the work is hard and that they need special ways to learn better. Students with LD can work with their special ed teachers to figure out how they learn best. Then they can explain this to their regular teachers and to other adults who help them with learning. These students may also have to study more than other kids. This can be frustrating! The ideas in this book can help kids with LD make good behavior choices. Then wrong words and actions won't get in the way of the progress they are making with their learning.

4. KIDS WHO WANT ATTENTION

> "Calvin and I like to get on other kids' nerves when they're trying to work. It's fun to get them upset with us." —Ted, 10

Sometimes parents and teachers don't tell kids when they are doing things right. These adults think that kids should "just behave." They forget that we all like to be noticed when we are doing the right thing. If kids don't hear nice things very often when they work hard or do well, they may try to get attention in other ways. They might act up to get *some* kind of attention, even if it's not the good kind.

Sometimes, students act up to get attention from other kids. They like the laughs they get or the things other kids say. Even if the other kids get annoyed instead of laughing, it feels good to be noticed. So these students keep using wrong behavior. They think it helps them fit in and feel important with classmates and friends.

The challenge for these students is to learn better ways to get noticed. It can seem nice to get attention for wrong behaviors, but usually kids who do this don't really feel very good about it inside. They know it feels better to get attention for **positive** reasons.

5. KIDS WHO FEEL ANGRY AND WANT TO GET BACK AT SOMEONE

Some students want **revenge** when someone else makes them mad. They try to hurt the other person. They may tell rumors. They may yell awful things at the person or hit the person. Or they may do some other behavior that really only makes things worse.

> "If anyone laughs at me, I kick their butt."—Dante, 12

The challenge for these students is to learn how to control angry feelings and choose better ways to deal with strong emotions. Schools can help these students with **counseling** and with lessons in **anger management.**

Some schools also help students stop being mad at each other with ways like **peer mediation** and **conflict resolution.** This book will help as well. It will show you some helpful ways to deal with anger. It will give you lots of ideas for getting along better with other people, too. (For help handling anger right now, turn to Chapter 5, pages 49–59.)

6. KIDS WHO FEEL BAD ABOUT THEMSELVES

Some kids don't like who they are. This can happen because of one of the reasons you read about already, or maybe for another reason. When kids don't feel good about themselves, they sometimes make poor choices. They might say or do bad things to themselves. They might avoid doing things or being with others. They might pick friends who make bad choices and then get in trouble with them.

The challenge for these students is to build their **self-esteem** so that they feel better about themselves. Building self-esteem can make it easier to choose right decisions instead of wrong ones. This book can help you improve your self-esteem and make more good choices. Teachers and counselors have ways to help kids improve their self-esteem, too.

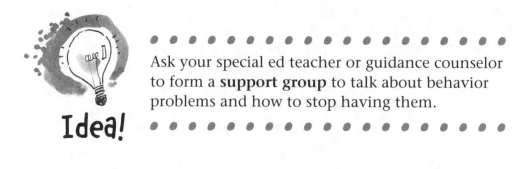

Ask your special ed teacher or guidance counselor to form a **support group** to talk about behavior problems and how to stop having them.

Idea!

MARIA

Maria didn't feel good about who she was. She was very shy and cried a lot. When her teachers would ask her what was wrong, she didn't really know what to tell them. Her mother gave permission for the school to have a psychologist talk with Maria and give her some tests. The psychologist thought that things would get better if Maria talked with a counselor a couple of times each week.

Sometimes Maria talked alone with Miss Brown, the counselor. Other times, a few other kids with the same kinds of problems were there. They would talk about the things that were happening at home and school that made them unhappy. They also worked on ways to feel better. Maria liked to meet with Miss Brown and the other kids. They understood her problems. They gave her words to explain to other people how she felt.

Over time, Maria smiled more in school. She played more with the other kids and could concentrate on her schoolwork. The problems at home and school didn't go away like magic, but she was able to handle them better.

Think about the six different reasons why kids have behavior problems:

1. Some kids never learned to make good choices.

2. Sometimes the chemicals in the brain are mixed up.

3. Some kids learn in a different way than most people.

4. Some kids want attention.

5. Some kids feel angry and want to get back at someone.

6. Some kids feel bad about themselves.

- Why do you think you sometimes make bad choices?

- What challenges do you have to remember to work on?

Remember . . .

There is *one* way that BD kids *are* the same. *All* kids with BD—including you—have great **potential.** This means that it is possible for you to stop having so many behavior problems. With hard work, you can change your way of acting. By using the ideas in this book, and the suggestions of your teachers and counselor (if you have one), you can make changes. You can become a kid other students like, one who gets along well in school. Really. **Yes—really!**

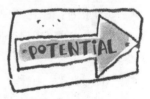

Chapter 3

WHY AM I IN A PROGRAM FOR KIDS WITH BD?

"Mrs. Vang is my special class teacher. She knows how to teach me. I know what to do in her class. In the regular class, things are harder to figure out." —Adam, 10

Before 1975, many schools did not want to teach kids with BD. If students didn't follow the rules or if they made poor choices, the schools could kick them out. If parents wanted their children with BD to go to school, they would have to use their own money to pay a special school to teach them. In 1975, a new law was passed. Today, that law is named **IDEA.** Here are some important things the IDEA law says:

- All kids, no matter what kind of problems they have, must be allowed to go to school.

- All kids must be taught in the kind of classes that help them to learn best.

- Students with behavior problems must have their own special school program that will help them learn and behave

better. That program is written in a long report called an **IEP.**
Each student who is part of IDEA has his or her own IEP.

• The school must use the best ways it knows to help kids with certain kinds of **special needs** learn better and make good choices.

In other words, schools must give you the help you need to make
better decisions about behavior.

How DID THE SCHOOL DECIDE THAT I HAVE BD?

IDEA says that teachers should get help for kids who have behavior
that:

• keeps them from learning **OR**

• keeps other kids from learning **OR**

• keeps the teacher from being able to teach

Before you got the label of BD,
a teacher noticed that you were
having problems making good
choices about your behavior. The
teacher and some other adults at
school talked about ways to help
you make good choices and show
positive school behavior. The
teacher tried these ways, but they
didn't work very well. So another
group of adults called the **IEP team** had to decide if you needed special education to learn better ways to act in school. People on the team
collected lots of information from adults who know you. They also
asked your parent or parents if they could meet with you and give
you some tests. Someone from the team may have come into your
classroom to watch you for a while. This was so the person could see

> **Remember,** you may have a different
> label than BD. Pages 7–8 tell some of
> the other labels. If you have an IEP and
> are in a special class or program to help
> you with your behavior, the information
> here applies to you. If you don't have
> an IEP or a special class, skip this chap-
> ter and check out Chapter 4.

how well you followed directions, paid attention, got along with other kids, and did your work.

Collecting all of this information helped the IEP team to do two things:

- Understand why the **inappropriate** behavior was happening.
- Figure out ways to help you make better choices.

Then the team invited your parent or guardian to a meeting to talk about how to help you learn and behave better. After this, the team wrote your long IEP plan.

WHAT IS IN MY IEP?

All kids with special needs have an IEP plan in their school folders. Your plan tells your teachers how to teach you best and help you make choices that will bring success in school and life.

What Your IEP Says

The law says that the IEP must tell:

- what the tests and talks found out
- how well you are learning and behaving in school right now
- what type of classroom will help you learn best
- goals for learning and behavior that teachers think you can meet in one year
- ways to decide if you have met those goals

For kids with BD, a special behavior plan **(BIP)** is placed at the back of the IEP. Your BIP tells teachers the ways that should be used to help you make better decisions. It must include positive ways to help you make better choices. These ways are called **PBIS.** Your PBIS can't just be punishments for bad choices. (There may be some of these in your IEP, though.) They have to include ways to change your behavior that treat you well when you make good choices. There also need to be ways to treat you with respect if you make a bad decision. For example, one of your PBIS might be that you get a reward or prizes for meeting goals. Another might be that you work in a group with other kids. There you learn the skills you need to beat BD.

Once your first IEP has been written, the IEP team meets at least once each year to talk about how you have been doing at meeting your goals. When the team meets, they change the IEP, or make a new one, to keep helping you meet more goals. Sometimes kids come to the IEP meeting if their parents or guardians invite them.

You might not like your plan or the fact that you are in special education. But remember: People who care about kids and know how to help them worked very hard to find the best ways to help you.

RASHID

Rashid had trouble sitting still. He also did things without thinking first. He didn't mean to break the rules or stop the lesson. But he just couldn't seem to help it. He also talked with other students when he was supposed to be working.

For the last two months, Rashid has been taking a pill before he comes to school. He takes another one later in the day. The medicine helps him sit still and think before he acts. He also carries a point card with him. His special class teacher gives him points for his behavior. So do the art teacher, the gym teacher, the bus monitor, the playground supervisor, and the lunchroom attendant. When he earns enough points, Rashid gets a reward like extra time in the learning center or on the computer. This point system is part of Rashid's IEP.

The point card makes Rashid want to do well. He tries hard to follow the rules. And he's doing great. His teacher, Mr. Dradi, is thinking that maybe Rashid is ready to go to the regular classes for one or two subjects. Mr. Dradi will decide in a few weeks if he should tell the IEP team that Rashid is ready for this.

It's Your Turn

- What goals does your IEP say you are supposed to be working on?

- What positive ways (PBIS) are your teachers using to help you?

- What would you like to have changed in your IEP?

Idea!

- Do you have questions about your IEP or about being in special education because of BD? Then be sure to talk to your special education teacher, your counselor, or an adult at home.

- Do you think that there are better ways to teach you to make good choices? Talk to some of these people about your ideas.

WHY AREN'T I IN THE REGULAR EDUCATION CLASS?

Some kids with BD spend all day in the regular education classroom. Other kids with BD spend all day in a special classroom or special ed school. Some kids with BD have a mix of special and regular classes.

WHEN KIDS WITH BD ARE IN THE REGULAR CLASS FOR THE WHOLE DAY, they usually still get some help from a **consultant teacher** or **paraprofessional** who works in the room. Or maybe these kids go to see a counselor a couple of times a week to talk. The law says that kids with special needs have to be in the regular education classroom as much as they can handle well. This is called **inclusion.**

KIDS WITH BD WHO AREN'T IN A REGULAR CLASSROOM ALL THE TIME are often in a **self-contained classroom.** This is a room where these students go to school for all (or most) of the day. Sometimes it is called a special class. Students in special classes might go to regular education classes for one or two subjects. Usually they start with art or gym. If they do well in those classes, they will get a chance to go into more regular classes.

If you are in a special class, your special ed teacher helps you learn ways of doing things that will help you succeed in school. These ways help you learn better and make smart decisions. They can also help you to make friends easier. If you learn these things well, you will be able to spend more time in the regular classroom. How much time? That depends on how well you are making choices.

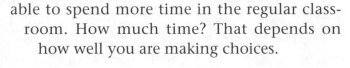

STEPS TO SUCCESS

TO GET INTO REGULAR CLASSES, you have to work hard and make good choices while you are in the special classroom. This is the **ONLY** way to get into the regular classroom. Once you do, you have to keep working hard and making good decisions if you want to stay there.

MORE ABOUT RODNEY

You first read about Rodney in Chapter 2 (pages 15–16). Rodney was in a special class because he had BD. He worked hard to follow rules, improve his grades, and make good decisions about his behavior. After many months, Rodney was allowed to go to the regular classroom for gym, art, science, and social studies.

Rodney wanted to be in the regular classes all the time. He kept working hard in his special class and his regular classes. He made an effort to obey the regular teachers' rules and complete all the work. He was polite even when one of the teachers wasn't so nice to him. He kept getting along better and better with other kids. He earned respect from the teachers.

After another year, Rodney only had to see his special ed teacher for fifteen minutes each morning. He and the teacher would check his homework. They would talk about his plan for the rest of the day. Then Rodney went to regular classes. He learned about all the good things that happen when people make smart choices.

CHANGES TAKE TIME AND PATIENCE. It took Rodney a long time to go from a special class to mostly regular classes. He had to work hard and be patient. At first, this might sound discouraging. Slow changes are often the best kind, though. With slow change, you have a chance to learn and practice new behaviors step by step.

You have time to get used to each new experience you have to deal with. It's easier to make small changes, one by one, than to try to do one big change all at once. You need to get comfortable with your new behavior. Your teacher needs to see that the changes you're making are real. Each thing you accomplish—like getting to go to a regular class for one subject, or figuring out how to get along with a certain teacher—brings progress. You'll keep getting small rewards on the way to the big one.

It's Your Turn

- If you are in a special class, how do you feel about being in it?

- Do you spend time in a regular class, too? If so, what do you like about it? What don't you like? Why?

- What goals do you have in your class or classes? What are you doing to work on them?

WHAT IF I DON'T WANT TO GO BACK TO REGULAR CLASSES?

Some kids with BD don't want to go back to the regular classroom. They are happy in the special class. They learn well there. They get lots of attention, and they get along with others. They remember when they did not do well in the regular class. Some are afraid that other kids will tease them. They worry that the work will be too hard. They don't know if they will get the help they need in the regular class.

TYRONE

Tyrone never liked being labeled BD. He wanted to be in a regular class. When he started his special all-day class, he hated it. But after a couple of months, he was starting to like it in a lot of ways. He liked the way the teacher (Mrs. Mercado) and the assistant teacher (Mr. White) treated him. He was learning quicker, too. He still wanted to get back to the regular classroom, though. So he worked hard to change his behavior. He worked at this for almost two years. His behavior improved slowly all the time.

Then, partway through sixth grade, Mrs. Mercado said she had good news. She told Tyrone that the IEP team was talking about moving him back into the regular classroom. When Tyrone heard this, he had mixed feelings. Yes, he wanted to go back to regular classes. That was the dream that he had worked so hard for. But he liked being in Mrs. Mercado's class. Without help from Mrs. Mercado and Mr. White, could he keep making good choices? Could he do the work? Would kids in the regular class be friends with him? Would they make fun of him?

Tyrone hadn't even moved to a regular class, but he was very worried about it. Then he started to mess up. He began picking on weaker kids. He showed up late for class. He stopped doing his assignments. He began getting in trouble in the hallways, too. His teachers were confused. So was Tyrone.

Mr. White and Mrs. Mercado talked with Tyrone about why he was making so many bad choices all of a sudden. They asked if he really wanted to go into regular ed. He said he didn't know anymore. He told them that he was scared in some ways.

Talking about things helped Tyrone handle the stress and make sense of what was going on. He saw that he was comfortable in the special class. He didn't know how things would go outside of it. The teachers explained that he would only be in two classes to start. If things were going okay, then he could

MORE

be in more later. Mrs. Mercado would talk with the teachers about the special ways (from the IEP) to help Tyrone do well. Mr. White would still check in with him and talk with him about his behavior. It wasn't going to happen all at once. Tyrone would be able to try out regular ed in small steps.

Today, Tyrone is in regular classes full time. He still sees his counselor twice a week. He is even asked to talk to other kids who are getting ready to go back into regular ed. He tells them what it's like. He offers tips about things that will help them succeed.

Yes, it can be scary to move into a regular classroom when you've been away so long. Like Tyrone, you might worry that kids will tease you. You might think that the teachers won't understand the best ways to help. Sometimes these things can happen. But not too often. And if you are ready to be in regular ed, you are ready to deal with problems that sometimes happen.

"Mrs. Erdahl tries to help me do better in the regular class. We talk and practice things. She has a favorite saying: 'A ship is safe in the harbor, but that's not what ships are for.' She is helping me leave her special ed harbor and sail to regular ed." —Gina, 10

Once you have learned ways to be a success in school, it is time to try them in the regular class. The IEP team knows that you are ready to be there. Your new teachers have been told about the ways that help you learn and make good choices. And there's one really great thing about moving into a regular class: With so many more kids, you have more chances to make new friends.

8 Tips for Feeling More at Ease in a Regular Class

1. Ask to meet your new teacher before you start the class.

2. Whenever you see the teacher, say hi in a friendly way.

3. Say hi to the other kids in the class. Especially be sure to do this to the nice kids, the shy kids, and those who sit near you.

4. Ask for help when you need it, but try to do the work first.

5. Say thank you to the teacher when you leave the regular class.

6. Keep in touch with your special education teacher. Make a plan together for how you can do this.

7. Expect a few "bumps in the road." Maybe at first you will feel uncomfortable or have trouble getting along in the regular class. If this happens, talk to the regular teacher, your counselor, or your special education teacher.

8. Give the regular class a try for at least two weeks. That will help you tell if you are ready to be in a regular class yet or not.

Remember . . .

Sometimes all the "official" stuff can seem like a big hassle—labels, special classes, IEPs, goals to work on. You have to deal with different people and work on tough changes. These are the challenges you face. There was once a time when kids with BD couldn't get good help at school. But now, being in a special program can help you get the support you need in order to succeed in school. Be patient with yourself and other people. Believe in yourself and don't give up! You CAN make the changes that will help you reach your goals.

Chapter 4

FOUR SMART CHOICES FOR DEALING WITH FEELINGS

> "I don't like having BD. It keeps me out of classes, and other kids don't want to be around me. That hurts a lot. Sometimes, I get really angry and want to hurt those kids back. I get mad at myself, too. I hate BD. It's messing up my life." —T.J., 12

BEING A KID WITH BD IS TOUGH. I'm sure I'm not telling you anything you don't already know. You're under a lot of pressure to behave well. The work of trying to be good all the time can cause a lot of **stress.** Other people always seem to be telling you what you did wrong, or what you should be doing. Teachers, parents, and other kids may not see things the same way you do. When you make poor choices, people can get mad or decide they don't want to be around you. You might feel angry at people, at the choices you've made, and at yourself. You might feel **frustrated** or hurt, too.

With so much pressure, you can get pretty unhappy. This happens to many kids with BD. If it happens so much that you're sad all the time, it is called **depression.** And maybe sometimes you just want to be left alone. It can seem like no one understands or cares about you. You might find that you're confused about your own feelings and behavior.

SO WHAT CAN YOU DO WHEN THE STRESS PILES UP? First, know that the feelings you have are okay. It's okay to feel sad or hurt or angry sometimes. It's also okay to have other strong, upset feelings—even if you don't know what exact feeling you have at the moment. Second, know that you always have choices about how to *deal* with strong emotions. You can learn to make smart choices instead of bad ones.

HOW CAN I TELL THE DIFFERENCE BETWEEN A BAD CHOICE AND A SMART ONE?

There's usually an easy way to tell the difference:

- Bad choices bring on more stress and more bad feelings. They make things worse than they were.

- Smart choices get rid of the stress and bring better feelings. They make things better.

Bad Choices

People who make bad choices when they have strong feelings often do it in one of these ways:

ACTING WITHOUT THINKING. Someone who does this feels the emotion and just says or does something right away. This isn't really a choice because the person does not think about what to do. But with practice, this person can learn to think before acting.

THINKING IN A NEGATIVE WAY. Sometimes people think, but they don't think in helpful ways. Instead, they think about the stressful thing over and over. Their emotions keep getting stronger and stronger. Finally, a person in this situation will feel ready to burst. Then the person acts up.

LOSING CONTROL. Kids who make no decisions or bad ones about handling emotions lose control. They do things like:

- hit themselves or others
- throw things (or destroy them)
- curse or say bad things to themselves or others
- refuse to do work or follow directions
- walk out of class

Some kids cry when their emotions get too strong. This is a lot better than doing something wrong. But these kids can learn to make choices that will work better than crying.

You Always Have a Choice

You can choose whether to let something bother you. And you can choose how *much* you'll let it bother you. The amount of stress you feel, and how you react to it, depends on how much attention you decide to give it. It depends on whether you make bad choices or smart ones.

What happens when you act on your feelings without thinking about how to handle them? You let your feelings control you. And what if you keep thinking about someone or something until it makes you burst out with bad behavior? You give others power over you.

YOU'RE SMARTER THAN THAT!

You don't want to be "controlled" in these ways. All you need to do is learn the ways to handle your emotions and make good decisions when stress starts to build up. No, it's not easy to make smart choices when your feelings get really strong. Yes, it takes practice to learn new and better ways to help yourself. But **YOU CAN DO IT!**

Smart Choices

When your feelings build up, it's important to talk to yourself about what's happening. You need to figure out whether you really want some person or thing to give you stress and cause you to make bad choices. Then you can decide how to deal with the situation and ease the stress.

There are many ways to help deal with your feelings and make better choices. Here are five important ways:

1. **BUILD YOUR SELF-ESTEEM SO THAT YOU LIKE YOURSELF BETTER.** Then things won't bother you as much.

> This chapter will explain the first four ways to make smart choices.

2. **TALK WITH SOMEONE YOU TRUST.** The person can listen and help.

3. **WRITE, DRAW, OR PAINT.** Use writing or art to express how you feel. Doing this can help you understand your feelings and think about how to handle them.

4. **CHILL OUT OR GET MOVING!** Relaxation and exercise can go a long way to ease strong feelings.

5. **STOP, THINK, CHOOSE, AND THINK AGAIN.** Getting in the habit of doing these steps can help you through many tough times.

> **Chapter 5** explains the fifth way.

Read about each of these ways. Decide which ones would work best for you. Then try them out.

IMPORTANT!

Everybody feels angry, sad, stressed, and even depressed sometimes. Sometimes these feelings are extra-strong for kids with BD. The ideas in Chapters 4 and 5 can help. But maybe you have strong, upset feelings all the time. Or maybe you feel like hurting yourself or someone else. Maybe you're afraid someone else is going to hurt you. If any of these things are true for you, get help right away. Here are three ways to get help:

• Talk to an adult you trust.

• Look in the Yellow Pages under Crisis Intervention.

• Call the toll-free National Youth Crisis Hotline at 1-800-448-4663.

SMART CHOICE #1
BUILD YOUR SELF-ESTEEM

Kids with BD want to get rid of it right away. But getting rid of BD takes time and hard work. The BD can make kids feel bad about themselves. Sometimes their **self-esteem** is low. Often they forget about the good things they do and how they are getting better at making good choices. It's important for kids with BD to remember these positive things. Be proud of what you do well! Also, take pride in the things you are doing better now than before.

It's Your Turn

Make a list of things you do well (or are getting better at doing). What things about YOU should you take pride in?

Do "Pride and Progress" Exercises

It's important to take **pride** in things that you do well. It's also important to notice when you are getting better at doing things. That shows **progress.** You can remember to notice those strong skills you have and keep getting better at others. How? By doing "pride and progress" exercises each day. These aren't exercises for your body (even though those can help self-esteem, too). They are exercises for your mind. The "pride" part lets you notice things you like about yourself. The "progress" part lets you notice smart choices. Here's how to do these exercises. (They're fun!)

IN THE MORNING

1. Start the day by talking to yourself. Look in the mirror and give yourself a big, happy "Good morning!" (Or maybe a simple thumbs-up.)

2. Say **one** thing you like about yourself. (After a few days, say two or three things.)

3. Tell yourself the ways that you're improving. Brag to yourself.

4. Set a goal for today. Tell yourself the good choice you will make today.

5. Imagine the times during the day when it might be hard to meet your goal. Think of people and places that might lead you to wrong choices. Think about what you will say and do to be sure you meet your goal.

DURING THE DAY

1. Think about your goal every time you enter a new room. Think about it before you enter the bus or hallway or playground, too. Get yourself ready to do well.

2. Compliment yourself during the day. Congratulate yourself for doing well on meeting a goal in a class. You don't have to do this in a mirror. You can say it in your head. Be sure to say something nice to yourself when you make a right choice anytime during the day.

AT NIGHT

1. End the day with "mirror talking" again. Look in the mirror and report on how well you did.

2. Talk about the times when you made good choices today. Smile. Give yourself a thumbs-up or high five.

3. Talk about the times when things went wrong. Don't let these things bother you again. Just make a report. What bad choices did you make? Don't blame others. You have to learn to make good choices even when other people do things you don't like. What mistakes did **YOU** make?

4. Think about the choices you **should** have made when things went wrong.

5. Promise to do things better tomorrow. Set a goal (or two) for the next day. (You'll say the goal again tomorrow morning when you get ready for school.) Say "Good night" and get a good night's sleep.

Pride and progress exercises feel good. They also make your mind stronger so that things bother you less. Then it won't hurt so much if people tease or **criticize** you. The stress from hard work and trying to behave better won't be so strong. When you know and remember the good things about yourself, you'll be able to fight BD better.

Do these exercises each morning and night. On the weekends, set goals for getting along better at home and with the people in your neighborhood. Take pride in your progress. Of course, you'll still make mistakes. But you are getting better at working with people and handling frustration. If you mess up, be honest about it and work on your goals again. **Never give up.** You'll get there.

DAVID

David is working on self-esteem with his counselor, Mr. Jones. He asks David to say something good about himself. David says, "I'm great at computer games."

"Anything other than those games?" Mr. Jones asks.

"I'm good at taking care of the dog and fixing things that break."

The counselor says, "Great. The games show that you have good attention and good eye-hand coordination. Helping with the dog and fixing things show responsibility, patience, and caring. What goal are you working on?"

"Asking before taking something," says David.

"How are you doing at meeting your goal?" asks Mr. Jones.

"Sometimes I remember, but I still forget, too," says David.

Mr. Jones tells David that remembering the goal some of the time shows progress: It's better than not remembering at all. He says that David is starting to make better decisions. The counselor reminds David to think of the goal before going into each classroom. He also reminds him to do his pride and progress exercises.

At home that evening, David walks to his bedroom mirror and looks in it. He feels strange about talking to the mirror. He thinks, "This is stupid." But he wants to make better decisions and handle stress better. He has trouble looking at himself. But each time his head drops down, he looks up again. Finally, David says hi in a soft voice. Then he goes through all the nighttime steps.

It's Your Turn

Practice "mirror talking" with another person who knows what it is. You might have to explain it first. Have the person watch and listen while you do it. Ask the person to tell you how you did. Try it again. Do it better this time.

Start a "Helping Habit"

Have you ever noticed how good you feel when you do something that makes another person happy? Giving a helping hand to others is a great way to start building your own self-esteem. Make it a habit! We often think of habits as bad things. But it's **GOOD**—for others and for you—when you get into a "helping habit."

SANDRA

Sandra's elementary school is two blocks from the middle school. In the hall at school, Sandra noticed a man and woman. They were talking, looking around, and pointing in different directions. They seemed lost. Sandra asked if they needed help. They looked relieved. The woman asked, "Which way is the middle school office?" Sandra told her they were in the wrong building. She gave them directions to get to the middle school. They thanked her. Then Sandra turned to go to her classroom. She felt good that she'd been able to help these people.

MO AND TINA

Mo and Tina saw Mrs. Hassett's car pull up into the parking lot behind their apartment building. There were lots of bags and boxes in the car. They put away the cards they'd been trading and walked toward Mrs. Hassett. They offered to help her bring the things into her apartment. "Thank you," their neighbor said. Bringing the items up to the apartment earned Tina and Mo another thank you. They also got a slice of homemade pie! Afterward, Mo and Tina both felt proud about being good neighbors. Helping out took only a few minutes, but the good feeling lasted a lot longer.

The stories about Sandra, Mo, and Tina show that there are easy ways to be helpful. You can look for chances to show kindness to others in the school, at home, and in your neighborhood. Do good deeds for no reason. Notice how you feel about yourself when you do this.

Here are some "kindly" things you might do. You can probably think of more:

- Volunteer when your teacher asks for someone to pass out papers or clean off the board.

- Notice someone who seems lonesome or left out. Say hi and talk for a minute. Invite the person to sit with you during lunch.

- Listen when a friend is mad or sad.

- Surprise your sister (or brother) by making her (or his) bed.

- Send a card or an email to your parent, uncle or aunt, grandparent, or cousin.

- Give someone a hand with a heavy backpack.

- When you sit down in class, smile at the person next to you and say hi.

Idea! In your journal or notebook, make a large calendar page. Make the box for each day large enough to write a few words inside. Each night, write down one nice thing that you did for someone that day. If you can't remember anything, think of something that you can do for your family right now. Can you wash some dishes, take out the trash, or fold some clothes? Once you do that thing, write it in that date's box. Start thinking about something nice you can do for someone tomorrow. Don't forget to compliment yourself each day for your kindness to others!

SMART CHOICE #2 TALK WITH SOMEONE YOU TRUST

JESSIE

Jessie had trouble making smart choices when her feelings got really strong. If things went well at home in the morning, she was all smiles. She would be in a great mood when she came to school. But there were things in Jessie's life that sometimes caused a lot of stress or pressure. When she had troubles at home, she would come to school upset. She would act up in class and sometimes hurt others. The teachers punished Jessie for doing these things. Then she would get even more upset and act worse.

The IEP team thought Jessie should talk with a school counselor. The counselor helped Jessie understand her feelings better. She talked with the counselor about the strong emotions she felt. She wanted to make better choices so she wouldn't get in trouble and feel bad. The counselor helped her figure out ways to cope at angry moments. Jessie talked to the teacher in her special class, too. The teacher decided to work with Jessie (and the other kids with BD) on anger management. They practiced better ways to act when their feelings got to be too much.

Over time, Jessie made more smart choices. And she made fewer poor choices when she was under stress. She got better at dealing with strong feelings. As she did this, things improved a little at home. But not much. Even so, Jessie became a lot better at handling her feelings and making the right choices when there was pressure.

When a person can't talk with someone about being angry or sad, those feelings can stay around. Often, they get stronger. The person keeps feeling confused, hurt, or mad. It's hard to enjoy doing things or being with people. It's hard to do school work and follow directions. It's hard to think about anything but those bad feelings.

Teachers care about you. They want to help you deal better with your feelings. Many schools also have counselors who are trained to help kids talk about feelings. If you would like to talk with a counselor, ask your teacher to introduce you. You can do this even if you're not sure how you're feeling or what to say. Counselors can help you make sense of things and feel better.

A friend who really cares about you can be another helpful person to talk to. If you have a friend like this, that's great. It can still be a good idea to find an adult to talk things over with as well. If your school doesn't have a counselor, maybe you can talk to a grown-up at home. Or maybe there's another adult you can talk to. It should be someone you trust to listen to your feelings, offer some good advice, and keep things private.

20 Adults You Might Talk To

1. a parent
2. a stepparent
3. a foster parent
4. an aunt
5. an uncle
6. a grandparent
7. a counselor
8. a teacher
9. a coach
10. a principal
11. a doctor
12. a nurse
13. your friend's parent
14. a neighbor you know well
15. a scout or club leader
16. a leader at your place of worship
17. a psychologist or therapist
18. a social worker
19. a sitter
20. a family friend

or maybe your dog (just kidding)

Idea!

Think of some people you know who might be good "counselors"—people you would trust to listen to you and talk about feelings. For each person you think of, ask yourself:

- Am I comfortable talking honestly with this person about myself?

- Is the person wise?

- Does the person listen well?

- Can I trust the person to keep our conversation private (or only share it with adults who can help)?

If the answers to the questions are all yes, this may be a good person to talk to. In your notebook or journal, make a list of the adults and friends who can be "counselors" when you need help with feelings.

SMART CHOICE #3
WRITE OR DRAW

If you don't have someone to talk to about feelings (or just don't want to talk), there are ways that can help you to sort things out. One way is by writing in your journal or notebook. You could write something short, or something long. You could write a poem or a song. You could write a letter to yourself or someone else. You could write a story. Or you could write words that describe how you feel or how you'd like to feel.

Maybe writing isn't your "thing." You can also draw pictures that show how you feel. If you find a trustworthy person (or finally feel like talking), you can show the person your drawings. This will help him or her understand what you are going through.

SMART CHOICE #4
CHILL OUT OR GET MOVING!

Sometimes, even when we try our best to manage our emotions, they can start to get out of control. Maybe you're working on some of the ways you read about in this chapter, but you're not really good at using them yet. (You will be, with more practice.) In the meantime, what can you do if you really start to get mad, hurt, or sad?

Just stop what you're doing and *relax*. Take some deep breaths through your nose. Breathe **D-E-E-P-L-Y.** Then let out the air in a "Whoosh!" Think of some nice things. You might think of being with friends. Or about a trip you took to a favorite place, or doing your favorite activity. See if you can move your hands, arms, and head in a slow, relaxed way. Your arms and neck should feel like wet noodles. If they feel stiff, start taking those deep breaths again. Think those good thoughts. Calm yourself down until you are ready to get back into the situation that got you upset. Just before you do, congratulate yourself on controlling your feelings.

whoosh!

It's Your Turn

Practice the breathing and the positive thinking you just read about. If it helps, lie down and close your eyes to get used to breathing slowly to relax. With practice, you'll be able to relax sitting or standing in other situations, too.

Sometimes you may be too worked up to relax. If that happens, get moving! Exercise may seem like the opposite of relaxing. But it is another good way to help with strong feelings. If you're in a sad or bad mood, exercise can help you feel better. It's also a great way to let out strong feelings like anger and frustration. You don't have to keep your feelings inside you till you feel like you want to burst. Instead, you can help them "escape" as you run, jump, do push-ups, shoot baskets, ride a bike, or even dance.

Remember . . .

It's important to feel good about who you are and learn to be in control of your feelings. Building your self-esteem can help you to make better choices. So can talking to people who can help, writing or drawing, relaxing, and getting exercise. When you make those better choices, you'll be on your way to overcoming your behavior challenges.

But wait, there's more!
Read Chapter 5 for one more smart choice that can help you take charge of your feelings and how you handle them.

NEXT TURN ANOTHER SMART CHOICE

ANOTHER SMART CHOICE FOR DEALING WITH FEELINGS

"I'm not fighting like before or cursing at the teachers. I've calmed my attitude down." —Amber, 12

Sometimes what you do to try to make things better doesn't work. At other times, you might choose to keep quiet, but you still feel upset. You might feel very angry at someone. You might be frustrated at not being able to do something well. You might be sad because someone did or said something that hurt you. You might want to hurt the person back. You feel the stress building up. These are the times when it's easy to make a wrong choice about behavior.

In Chapter 4 you learned four smart choices for handling your feelings at such times. But what if the situation calls for something different? You might not be home in front of a mirror. There may not be someone there **RIGHT NOW** who you trust to listen and understand. You might not be able to write or draw or relax or get moving. That's when it's time for another smart choice. It's called "Stop, Think, Choose, and Think Again."

SMART CHOICE #5
STOP, THINK, CHOOSE, AND THINK AGAIN

When you're in a tough situation and feeling upset, you need a plan. How can you keep from doing things that will probably make the situation even worse? How can you avoid a bad decision? Follow these four steps:

STOP. The first thing is to be sure that you don't do anything you'll **regret.** Tell yourself, "Stop!" Don't do anything! Don't say anything! Just stand or sit and be quiet.

"Regret" means you did something, but later you wish you hadn't—and now it's too late to take it back.

THINK. The next thing to do is calm down and think about what's going on. This can help you sort things out and make better choices. To do this kind of thinking, use **self-talk**—talk to yourself.

Ask yourself, "What is the problem?" Think about different ways to handle it. Each way is a possible choice. For each choice, think about what could or will happen. Ask yourself:

"Will I get what I want with this choice?"

"Will it make things better or worse?"

"Will everyone feel respected?"

"Will I be proud of my actions later?"

"Will it keep me out of trouble?"

CHOOSE. After thinking about the different things you could do right now, choose the one that has the **MOST** good reasons with the **FEWEST** chances of getting you in trouble or making things worse.

THINK AGAIN. After you have followed your choice, think again. Ask yourself:

"Did my choice work the way I thought it would? Why or why not?"

"Should I do the same thing again?"

"What's another good choice I could make to help with this problem?"

Keeping Calm Can Help

You always have a choice about what you decide to do. Your decision will depend on the situation.

PAULO

Paulo looks at the worksheet his teacher just gave to him. Miss O'Hara said it was easy. Even so, Paulo doesn't remember what to do. He tries to figure it out, but he gets frustrated. He remembers the right thing to do when he gets stuck: He asks for help. But Miss O'Hara says, "Keep going. You can do it."

This bothers Paulo. Miss O'Hara thinks Paulo ought to be able to do it, but Paulo can't remember how. He wonders if he is dumb. He tries again. The work just doesn't make sense. The stress gets even stronger. He keeps thinking about how Miss O'Hara didn't help him. Then Paulo makes a bad choice. He

MORE

yells out, "I can't do this stuff! I need help!" Instead of giving him help, Miss O'Hara gives him a warning. And she tells Paulo to get back to work.

Paulo is about to curse at his teacher. But then he remembers "Stop, Think, Choose, and Think Again." He has practiced doing this in his special class and on his own. He **STOPS** himself. He knows swearing will get him punished. He says silently to himself, "Calm down. Think about what to do."

Then Paulo **THINKS.** The first thing that comes to his mind is to rip up the paper. That would show how angry he is! But he knows it will get him punished. (And how can he learn the stuff if the paper is ripped up?) Then he thinks about walking out of the room. He could go see Mrs. Lee, the special ed teacher who always helps him. But if he walks out now, he'll get in trouble. Paulo keeps trying to figure out how to handle this situation.

After thinking some more, Paulo **CHOOSES** what to do. He decides to put his name and the date at the top of the paper. He pretends to work. When the bell rings for lunch, he hands in the paper.

At lunch, Paulo **THINKS AGAIN** about what happened. He knows Miss O'Hara didn't like the way he yelled in class. He also worries about what she will do when she sees that Paulo didn't complete the work. He doesn't know how to get the help he needs. He decides to visit Mrs. Lee. He gets a pass to do this during recess. She says she will talk to Miss O'Hara about the learning help Paulo needs. Paulo says he will stick with his choice to stay calm and polite.

MORE

The next day, Paulo apologizes to Miss O'Hara for yelling out in class. Miss O'Hara smiles and says, "That's okay. Just don't let it happen again."

Paulo is disappointed. He thinks, "This isn't fair. Where's my apology?" He wants to tell the teacher, "You should say you're sorry, too." Paulo keeps thinking about this. He feels the stress build up. Then he remembers to tell himself to "Stop!" He goes to his desk. He starts to use self-talk again to keep from saying something wrong. Getting in trouble isn't worth it.

Did you notice how Paulo stayed cool even when he was frustrated? He didn't get the help or the apology he wanted from Miss O'Hara. But he kept himself out of trouble just the same. He stopped. He thought about ways to act. He made choices about what to do. He found some help from Mrs. Lee. And he decided to just forget that Miss O'Hara didn't apologize. Heck, if she needed to learn better manners, that was her problem—not his. Paulo did the right thing. He should congratulate himself for staying calm, being polite, and making good choices.

MALI

Mali and Linda are friends most of the time. But Linda sometimes does things that aren't very nice. She sometimes tells Mali's secrets to others. Once in a while at lunch, Linda sits with the popular kids and ignores Mali. At times, she blames things on Mali. Then Mali gets punished instead of her. When Mali finds out about these things, she becomes really angry! She yells at Linda and threatens her. One time she even threw things at Linda. When this happened, the teacher saw it. Mali got in trouble and was sent to the principal.

Mr. Redcloud, the school's counselor, is working with Mali to help her handle her anger better. He gives her and some other students lessons in

MORE

anger management. It has taken awhile, but Mali is making progress. Now, when Linda is not such a good friend, Mali remembers to **STOP** and **THINK.** She says, "I'll talk with you later. I have something I need to do right now." Using calm words is a smart **CHOICE** for Mali. Linda apologizes when she hears Mali's words. She knows she has hurt her friend. Later, Mali **THINKS AGAIN.** She plans more things she can do and say in other situations that start to get her mad. She is also thinking about ways she can talk to Linda about their friendship. She wants to be friends, but not if Linda keeps hurting her.

Mali made a plan for what to say in situations that happened a lot. She thought ahead about some words she could use.

Idea!

Ask your special education teacher or school counselor to start an **anger management** group to help kids keep from making bad choices when they get mad. (Page 162 tells where schools can find a list of books to help kids with anger and conflict management.)

Using "Ready Replies"

When it comes to figuring out what to say, there are good and bad choices. The bad ones are angry words like insults. They make the situation worse. The good ones give you the chance to defend yourself without making things worse. Good choices show respect. They leave some room to solve the problem. You can think of these good responses as "ready replies." They are helpful words you can plan ahead for when you need them.

Here are some examples of wrong words kids with BD might be tempted to say, and ready replies they could plan to say instead:

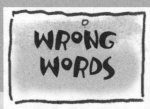

TO A TEACHER

- "I don't get this stuff because you don't teach it right! How come I got stuck with such a crummy teacher?"

- "Could you please explain it again? Or could you help me during lunch?"

TO ANOTHER KID

- "If you think I'm so stupid, why don't you go sit some-where else? You're the one who's stupid!"

- "You can move somewhere else if you want. But I'm not stupid, and I don't like to be called that."

TO A FAMILY ADULT

- "Why don't you ever notice when I do something *right?* I hate you!"

- "I wish you'd also notice when I do something right. I make lots of good decisions, too."

A Challenge for You

Read the challenge and look at the choices. Think about what might happen if Sam uses each one. Choose the ones that let him handle the situation without causing more problems or getting in trouble. Write down the numbers. (When you're done, you can compare your choices to the solutions on pages 154–155.)

When you see **"A Challenge for You,"** get out your pencil and notebook. These fun exercises will help you practice the new skills you're learning.

CHALLENGE: A couple of boys pass by Sam. They say a bad thing about his mother. Which choices are smart ones for Sam?

1. Sam says something nasty about their mothers.

2. Sam says, "I don't play the mother insult game."

3. Sam chases and hits one of the boys.

4. Sam thinks, "They can't be talking about my mom. She's super!" He ignores them.

5. Sam thinks, "That really hurts. I hate when they say these things. But if I get upset, they'll do it more. I'm going to walk away."

6. Sam says, "Come on guys, quit talking about others and worry about yourselves."

7. Sam says nothing. Later, he talks with his friend Louis about how much it hurts to hear these things.

8. Sam says, "You've got the wrong mom," and keeps walking.

It's Your Turn

Think of a time when someone said something mean or upsetting to you. Maybe the person called you a name. Or maybe somebody made fun of you for being in special ed.

- What did you do? Did you just stay quiet? Did you say something angry back?

- What ready reply could you have said instead?

Plan to use that ready reply the next time this happens!

Idea!

Think about hard situations that sometimes happen for you in school. For each situation, come up with a ready reply you can say. Write them in your notebook or journal. (If you want, copy and use the "Ready Replies" planning form on pages 60–61.) Practice them. You could do this alone in front of the mirror. Or you could practice with a friend, your special ed teacher or counselor, or someone in your family. Then, the next time something happens that usually leads to problems, you'll be prepared!

Thinking About Solutions

When you're using "Stop, Think, Choose, and Think Again," ready replies are things you can **CHOOSE**. They give you one way of making a choice that won't hurt—and might help. Often, you will have to think of some other solutions to problem situations.

JASMINE

Jasmine moved to her new school from another part of the country. She said some words in a different way than the kids in her new school—like "y'all" instead of "you all" and "mah" instead of "my." Some of her new classmates said she had an accent. Jasmine didn't like to hear this. The kids laughed at her and made fun of the way she talked.

Jasmine wanted to shout: "What a bunch of jerks!" But before she did this, she stopped herself. She thought, "I don't want to cause trouble. And I don't want to make things worse at my new school." So Jasmine made a smart choice: She decided not to say anything back. But Jasmine kept thinking about those comments. She felt really hurt by them. She cried about them a lot when she was by herself. At school, Jasmine felt lonely. She was embarrassed to talk. At home, she felt sad and angry. She realized it was time to think again about how to handle her situation. She had done the right thing when she chose not to yell at the kids and call them names. But she needed to do something else, too.

Jasmine thought that if she spoke more like the other kids, the teasing would probably slowly stop. She decided to pay attention to how people at her new school said things. When she was alone, she started practicing the new ways to talk. Soon, she could say some things in two different ways. That felt good. Plus, she was getting in the habit of speaking more like the other kids when they were around.

This seemed to work some of the time. Quite a few of the kids stopped teasing. But there were still some kids who remembered the old way Jasmine had spoken. They kept picking on her about it. In her special class, Jasmine and the other students had been learning about good and bad replies. She thought about a good reply (ready reply) she could say the next time someone teased her. In front of the mirror, she practiced smiling and saying it: "Yeah. We say things in different ways where I come from. I want to learn your way, too. How do you say that word here?"

Jasmine also decided on what to do if some kids kept teasing her anyway and she felt bothered. She would ask her teacher to please do something to stop these comments.

It's Your Turn

Practice "Stop, Think, Choose, and Think Again." Find someone you trust and like. Have the person say or do some things that you sometimes get mad about. Practice each step. Talk together about how different choices might work. Write some of the good ideas you have in your notebook or journal. Next time you're really in a situation like the one you practiced, try doing one of the choices you figured out.

Remember . . .

Everybody gets angry and upset. It's normal. When your feelings are really strong, it's easy to make the wrong choices. But you can handle things a better way! "Stop, Think, Choose, and Think Again" is a skill that can help you do this. Practice, keep trying, and don't give up! I can't promise this skill will make your life perfect. But I CAN promise that things will be better for you. **Honest!**

READY REPLIES

Make some copies of this planning form to keep in your desk, notebook, or locker. Keep some at home, too. Use a form each time you want to plan ahead about what to say in a tough situation.

FOR NOW

1. What is one thing people say or do that you don't like? Write it here:

_____

_____

_____

_____

2. What ready reply can you say next time someone says or does that thing? Write your ready reply here:

_____

_____

_____

_____

FOR LATER

After you have tried using the words you planned, answer questions 3–6.

3. Did your reply help the situation?   _____ Yes   _____ No

4. If YES, that's great! Keep that ready reply in mind. Use it again!

MORE ➤

5. If NOT, what was the problem?

_____ I got the words wrong.

_____ I should have used a different voice.

_____ The person didn't listen to what I said.

_____ The person made fun of what I said.

_____ Other (write the problem here):

_____

_____

_____

_____

6. If there was a PROBLEM, what can you say or do next time? Write how you'll change what you say:

_____

_____

_____

_____

_____

_____

_____

_____

Chapter 6

THREE SURVIVAL SKILLS FOR DEALING WITH DIFFICULT PEOPLE

"I found out that kids picked on me to see me react. But since I started ignoring the comments that used to make me mad, things are getting better." —Trina, 9

It's really hard to control your feelings around "difficult" people. Difficult people can do lots of irritating things. How do you keep from getting upset?

FIRST, remember those smart choices from Chapters 4 and 5.

SECOND, think about what **YOU** can control. Can you control what other people say or do? No. Can you control how you respond? **YES.** You decide what you say, do, or tell yourself. You might feel hurt or angry about what someone says. But no one can "make" you yell, hit, or say awful things back. If you do something mean or hurt someone back, you aren't staying in charge of your own actions. That means you're letting someone else take charge of you.

That old way of reacting can get you into trouble. It's not a smart choice. It won't help you feel good about yourself. It won't help you get along with other kids or adults. And it won't let **YOU** take control.

So don't give your power away to others. Instead, use the power you have to help yourself! There are lots of ways to stay in charge. Many kids have learned smart choices to make when others do things that aren't right. You can learn them, too. This chapter will show you three powerful skills you can use to deal with people who are difficult. Practice these skills and get in the habit of using them. They'll help you **survive** and take control in all kinds of tough situations.

1. IGNORE MEAN WORDS AND ACTIONS

Sometimes, the best thing to do is to ignore nasty comments and other kids' bothersome behavior. This is easy to say, and hard to do. But you can do it. How?

STOP YOURSELF BEFORE YOU MAKE A BAD CHOICE. Cool yourself down with **self-talk.** (You can read more about self-talk in Chapter 5, pages 50–51.) While you ignore others, it helps to tell yourself things like this:

> "This isn't worth getting excited about."
>
> "It's all over now. Just let it go out of your mind and get on with life."
>
> "She's trying to get me in trouble. I'm not falling for that trick."
>
> "Forget about it. I'm not going to let him take over my brain."

Ask yourself, "What else can I think about?" Maybe you'll think about what you should be doing right then. Or about a song or game you like. Or just about something nice.

DON'T TAKE IT PERSONALLY. When people say or do something mean or unkind, understand that **THEY** have a problem. They are filled with bad feelings. Why let this become a problem for you, too? Don't let someone else's wrong choice take up space in your head. Shut your mind to it. If someone keeps bothering you, call the teacher over. Tell the teacher how you are trying to ignore the person. Say that you could use some help.

KEEP AT IT. When you first ignore someone, the person is probably going to do more of the same thing. You'll have to keep ignoring the behavior. This will be hard. The person may say and do more mean things to get you to pay attention. Keep ignoring this. Sooner or later, the person will think, "Hmmm, this doesn't work anymore." Then the person will finally stop. But if you give in and say "Shut up" or "Stop," you're giving the person control. Then you'll just keep having problems in the future.

Ignoring means **NO** attention at all. None. This includes not rolling your eyes, making faces, or giving dirty looks. You just want to put on a calm face and go about your business.

IMPORTANT! Ignoring may not always be a smart choice if the difficult person you're dealing with is an **authority figure.** Often, ignoring a teacher or parent will just get you in trouble. Instead, you can use the next two survival skills in this chapter. Chapters 7–8 and 10–11 also have lots of ideas to help you solve problems with teachers and family adults.

It's Your Turn

• What are some things you can do or think about when someone is trying to upset you?

• What are some ways you can stay calm and ignore the person?

After you think of some ways, have someone you trust say or do unkind or annoying things to you. Practice the new ways of staying calm and ignoring these things.

2. BE ASSERTIVE

Sometimes you need to tell others that you don't like what they have done. Maybe the teacher blamed you for something that wasn't your fault. Maybe your parent told you to do something you don't think you should have to do. Maybe another student took something of yours without asking. When these things happen, it's time to be **assertive.**

PEOPLE WHO ARE ASSERTIVE SPEAK UP, IN A STRONG BUT POLITE WAY. They don't use a harsh voice or angry words. They don't try to solve problems by shouting, fighting, or saying awful things about someone else. (Shouting and angry words make things worse, not better.) And assertive people don't keep quiet about what really matters to them. If something's important, they stick up for themselves.

KENDRA

Kendra walked into the lunchroom. She saw her close friend Tanya sitting with a group of girls. Kendra started to walk to their table. Then one of the girls said loudly, "Oh no. Here comes Kendra." The girl also said something mean about Kendra's clothes and hair. All the girls laughed—even Tanya. Kendra was shocked and hurt that her friend laughed. She turned away, walked to another table, and sat down. She started to think of something nasty to say to those girls—especially Tanya.

Just then, Kendra remembered to "Stop, Think, Choose, and Think Again." She asked herself, "What should I do?"

At first, more mean ideas came into Kendra's mind. Maybe she could say nasty things to the girls before lunch was over. That might feel good for a minute. But then what would happen? They might pick on her more. Maybe she could get her brother and his friends to threaten the girls. That would scare them! But it would also get her brother and his friends in trouble. The girls might fight back. The students might end up in trouble with the principal.

MORE

They'd want to get back at Kendra. And Kendra would a bigger one.

Kendra thought, "I could just be quiet and try to forget ab. she thought again. Ignoring those girls was probably smart. Bu. Tanya? Why had Tanya laughed? Was she trying to fit in? Or didn't to be friends anymore? Kendra *did* want to try to stay friends with Tar. Kendra decided she couldn't ignore what Tanya did.

She wondered if she could try to talk to Tanya later, alone. She could ask he. why she laughed. She could hear what Tanya had to say, and tell her that the laughing hurt. She could do this without yelling or being mean. This would be assertive. Both girls could try to sort things out and feel better about things.

They did talk. Tanya said she felt awful about how she acted. She had done it to be accepted by the other girls. Kendra and Tanya talked about ways to keep it from happening again.

BEING ASSERTIVE IS SMART. Assertive people have a better chance of getting what they want. That's because they say what they mean clearly and strongly, but they don't attack the other person. Think about it: You don't win an argument when you "beat" someone by proving the person is wrong. That only makes you enemies. You win when you get the person to see things your way. In fact, then you **BOTH** win. You both feel okay about things.

A Challenge for You

Read the challenge and look at choices 1, 2, and 3. Also read results A, B, and C. Match the letter for the result that would probably happen to the number of the choice. Write your answers on a piece of paper, or in your notebook. (When you're done, you can compare your choices to the solutions on page 155.)

CHALLENGE: For weeks, a bully has pushed Jake around. Finally, Jake shoves him back. The hallway monitor sees this. He scolds Jake and takes him to the principal's office. The principal gives Jake detention. Jake thinks that this punishment is unfair. Here are three ways Jake could react. Which one is assertive and tries to solve the problem with respect?

1. Jake could yell at the principal. He could shout, "You should punish the hall monitor for catching the wrong kid!"

2. Jake could tell the principal why he pushed the other kid. Then he could ask, "Is there something the school can do to protect us from bullies? Could we start a 'no-bullying' program like they have at my cousin's school?"

3. Jake could lower his head, say nothing, and take the punishment.

Which is the most likely result of each choice?

A. Later, the bully laughs at Jake and threatens him. Every time Jake walks by the hallway monitor, he sternly reminds Jake to behave.

B. The principal gets upset and gives Jake more detention.

C. The principal says, "I'll look into it." Later, she calls the boy who was bullying into her office.

3. SAY "I" INSTEAD OF "YOU"

People don't like to be told that they are doing wrong things. They don't like to hear "You're wrong!" or "You're being mean!" They hear that blaming word **"YOU."** Then they get angry, or angrier. This doesn't help make anything better.

Here's a way to be assertive when you talk, without criticizing or blaming: Tell how you feel by using the words **"I," "me,"** and **"my"** instead of "you."

Below are some things people say to others. The "you-talk" statements use the word "you." The "I-talk" statements use "I," "me," or "my." Which ones would you want somebody to say to you?

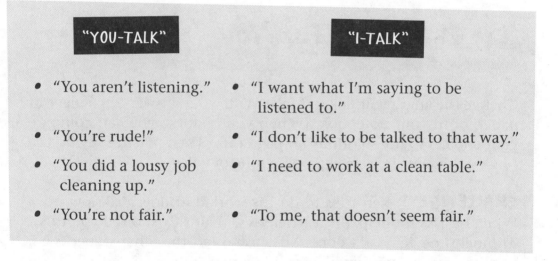

"YOU-TALK"	**"I-TALK"**
• "You aren't listening."	• "I want what I'm saying to be listened to."
• "You're rude!"	• "I don't like to be talked to that way."
• "You did a lousy job cleaning up."	• "I need to work at a clean table."
• "You're not fair."	• "To me, that doesn't seem fair."

Can you see how I-talk avoids making others upset? That's because it doesn't blame someone for what's happening. It simply says how a situation affects the person who's talking. Using I-talk lets you be assertive. It lets you **speak up,** in a **strong but polite** way, without using a harsh voice or angry words.

Along with I-talk, you can also use the words **"we"** and **"us."** For example, you and your sister might ask your parent, "We'd really like to finish watching our program before we do the dishes. Would that be okay?" You and some other kids in class might say to your teacher, "We're hoping we can have more time during class to finish our project. Okay?"

I-talk can be tricky to do at first, especially when you're upset with someone. Once you get the hang of it, it's easier. Keep in mind the number one rule of I-talk: Never, NEVER, **NEVER** use the word "you."

Sometimes, it's just natural to say "you." Sometimes, you might feel like you want to blame the other person. But how will that help you get what you want? The important thing is to solve a problem or avoid it, not make things worse. So instead of blaming, be assertive and use I-talk.

A Challenge for You

Change the angry you-talk to I-talk. Write your answers on a piece of paper, or in your notebook. (When you're done, you can compare your choices to the solutions on page 155.) Then practice saying the I-talk statements in a strong, polite tone of voice.

CHALLENGE 1: Ken tries to do his work, but doesn't know how. When he asks for help, his teacher says, "I already showed you this." At lunchtime, Ken isn't done. Mrs. Travis lets the other students go. But she says to Ken, "You'll be eating lunch with me today while you do the work." Ken yells out, "You witch! You're the one who ought to be doing the work. You know how and I don't! You're mean and you never help anybody."

CHALLENGE 2: Maggie's watch has a broken wristband. During a test, she puts the watch on her desk. She wants to keep track of how much time is left. She finishes early and leaves her desk to hand in her

MORE

test. She asks for a pass to go to the bathroom. When she returns to her desk, the watch is gone. Kevin is looking at her and smiling. Maggie yells out, "Mr. Tess, Kevin stole my watch!" Kevin says that he didn't do it. Maggie says, "Yes you did. I saw you smiling. You're a thief!"

CHALLENGE 3: Tim and Sasha are working on a project together. They have to write their report on the computer. Sasha starts writing the paper while Tim goes to the library for a book they need. When he returns, he reads what Sasha wrote. He says, "What are you doing? You're writing it all wrong. You're not supposed to start by telling what we think. First we have to write about all the other possible answers and why they were wrong. You're going to make us late handing in the project."

CHALLENGE 4: Mr. Cannon is mad at the class for acting up, and he takes away next week's field trip. Ira talks with the other students during lunch. He tells them that they have to stand up to Mr. C. When they return to class, Mr. C. tries to start the lesson. He tells the class to take out their science books. Ira says, "You're not getting any work until you give the field trip back. You can talk all you want, but you'll be talking to yourself." Mr. C. says he will give out punishments to students who don't get out their books. Most of the students get their books from their desks. Ira and a few others don't. They get detention.

Idea!

Notice when other people use you-talk. In your notebook or journal, write down blaming statements that you hear people use. Change those statements to I-talk. Keep noticing you-talk and thinking about I-talk. This is a good way to help yourself get used to naturally using I-talk.

It's Your Turn

Practice being assertive with somebody. Have the person pretend to be someone who does something you don't like. Think of a way to stick up for yourself in a strong, polite way. Use I-talk, and be careful not to speak in a harsh voice.

Remember . . .

You will really have to be strong to stay with your new and better choices. Things that happen in school and at home will challenge you. They can make you think about going back to the old ways of acting. Other kids will try to get you to make bad choices. Sometimes things won't seem fair. You may want to yell, or blame, or argue. Don't do it! Instead, ask yourself: "Is this a good choice? Is it going to help me become the person I want to be?" Stay assertive. **Take charge of your behavior!**

Chapter 7

WAYS TO HELP YOURSELF MAKE GOOD CHOICES IN SCHOOL

"I like to say funny things about the lesson when teachers are teaching. Usually the other kids laugh. Some teachers laugh, but others don't. It depends on the teacher. Knowing when it's okay to say funny things and when it's not isn't easy." —Malik, 14

Many kids with BD don't like school (or some parts of it). After all, it's not fun or rewarding to be in a place where the teachers and kids get upset with you. But these things can change. You can learn "tricks" that have helped other kids with BD. This chapter tells about some of those tricks. They are ways to help you make better choices in class. If you use them, things will get better for you in school. Then you'll find that you like being there more of the time.

BE PREPARED

When you get ready to go into your classroom, think about what behaviors you need to show in there to be a success. Remind yourself to do them.

REUBEN

Reuben enters the school building. On the way to school, he has been thinking about his goal for the day. Now he gives himself one more reminder. He hangs up his jacket and gets things out of his backpack. Then he starts to talk with one of his friends. The teacher tells everyone to sit down and listen to the announcements. Reuben goes to his seat and listens to the voice coming over the speaker. Next to the speaker box is the list of class rules. He looks at them and sees that he is already doing two things right: The first rule is "Be ready to learn." Reuben is ready. He has his notebook and pencil out on the desk. The second rule is "Be quiet when the teacher is talking." The teacher on the speaker isn't his classroom teacher, but it's a teacher just the same. And Reuben is being quiet. He looks at the other class rules. He reminds himself to raise his hand if he wants to say something during class. If Reuben can keep following the rules, he'll have a good day at school and learn a lot.

Did you notice that Reuben thought about how to act before he went into class? He also looked at the class rules before the lesson began. These are ways Reuben has learned to be prepared for school.

PATTY

Patty gets scolded by the teacher for talking to a friend during the lesson. Darn! Patty was trying so hard to follow the rules, but she just forgot for a minute. She reminds herself of what she's supposed to do: Listen while the teacher is teaching. Patty says, "Oops. I'm sorry, Mr. Chen." She puts her eyes on him and listens to what he is saying.

How could Patty have stayed out of trouble? Thinking about the rules she needed to follow would have helped her. But everyone makes mistakes sometimes. After her first mistake, Patty thought about the rules. In this way, she prepared herself to do better.

It's Your Turn

- Think about your usual classroom (or classes). Now think of the rules and expectations there. What behaviors should you remind yourself to use before you go into the room?

- Think about other classes and places at school. What rules do you need to remember for:

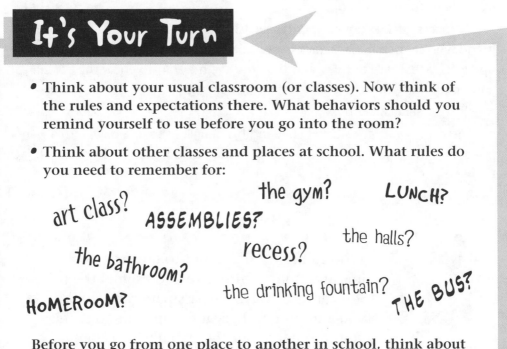

art class?   ASSEMBLIES?   the gym?   LUNCH?

recess?   the halls?

the bathroom?

HOMEROOM?   the drinking fountain?   THE BUS?

Before you go from one place to another in school, think about the rules for the new place. Get yourself prepared to follow the rules.

ASK FOR HELP FROM OTHERS

You can ask other kids to stop you if they see you make a bad choice about behavior. This can be a good way to make your chances of success stronger. Just be sure to ask people you trust. And when they remind you, don't act mad at them. Remember that they're helping you do the right thing. Just nod "yes" and then show the right behavior. Thank your helpers after class.

JACK

"Why do you keep doing that?" Jack's teacher said in an angry voice. "Stop it now." Jack took his pencil out of his mouth. He got caught chewing it again. It's so hard for him to stop.

At recess, Jack asked his friend Lakeesha to help him. Lakeesha was a good friend who sat behind Jack. Jack knew Lakeesha could see him bring the pencil up to his face. He said, "Hey Keesh. If you see me start to chew my pencil, can you poke me once so I stop? I gotta quit doing it."

"Sure," said Lakeesha.

Later that day, Jack started chewing his pencil. Lakeesha gave him a gentle poke, and he stopped. She stopped him another time later. After school, Jack thanked her.

Idea!

Who can remind you not to do wrong behaviors at school? Think of a good signal the person can use. Maybe a classmate can look at you and pull on his ear or tap your arm. Tell your teacher about the signal, too. When teachers know what's going on, they won't get upset if someone gives you the signal.

FIVE "TRICKS" TO HELP YOU TRACK YOUR PROGRESS

Sometimes it helps to keep track of how you are doing at stopping a wrong behavior or choosing a better one. This chapter explains five "tricks" you can use to do this.

1. Keep a Goal Record

A goal record lets you see your progress on making good choices. Page 84 has a "Goal Record" form that you can use. Here's how to use your form:

- **FIRST, COPY THE FORM** at school (ask permission) or at the library. You can make two or three copies if you want to work on more than one behavior. But working on one is a good start.

- **AT THE TOP** of the copied form, write your goal for the week. This is a behavior you'd like to show more often in class.

- **ON THE SIDE** of the form, write the parts of your school day. These are places you are at different times—like in the picture below.

- **EACH DAY,** notice how you did in each time or place on the form. For each part of the day, give yourself a "grade" from 0 to 3. (3 is the best—it means you've met your goal.) You might have the teacher or a friend rate you, too. That will help you see if you are noticing your behavior really carefully.

Carry your goal record around in your backpack, or keep it in your desk. Mark it each day for a week. At the end of the week, take a look at how you did. Congratulate yourself for good behavior choices. Then ask yourself how you're doing in the "big picture." Should you set a new goal that is harder to do? Should you practice the same goal again? Should you set an easier goal? Once you decide, start the next week using a new form.

You can make your own form if you want. It should include your

This form is for an elementary student. Every kid will fill out a form in a different way. It depends on what grade you are in and what you do in school each day.

GOAL RECORD

My goal for the week:
Keep my hands to myself

Scoring Key
0 Forgot goal or made bad choice   2 Did my goal behavior pretty often
1 Did my goal behavior a little bit   3 Met my goal!

ACTIVITY	M	T	W	Th	F
Entering room	2	0	2		
Start of class	1	2	2		
Large group activities	1	1	1		

weekly goal and space for tracking your behavior all during your school day. Your school or teacher might have a special goal record form, too.

2. Use Plus (+) and Minus (−)

Here's another trick to help you notice your behavior during the day. Think of something that could remind you to notice your behavior. This is your own personal signal. It could be anything that happens at least a few times during a class. It might be a clock tick. (You don't have to hear every one, just a few.) It could be someone saying the teacher's name. It could be hearing someone going by in the hallway. It could be the bell or the sound of the pencil sharpener. Also have a sheet of paper ready. The paper should be just for noticing behavior.

Whenever you hear your signal, think about your behavior right at that moment. If you were doing the right thing in the classroom, write a plus (+) sign. If you were making a wrong choice, write a minus (-) sign. (You don't have to hear every one of the signals. But when you *do* hear the signal, check your behavior.)

At the end of the day, count the plus and minus signs. Every day, try to have MORE plus signs and FEWER minus signs.

3. Beat Your Previous Best

Bad habits can be hard to stop. We are so used to doing them! They become almost automatic. Sometimes it's best to try to break them in steps. One way to do this is with a system for making small improvements. Make a copy of the "Beat Your Previous Best" form on page 85. Cut out one card. (Save the rest to use later.) Think of a wrong behavior choice that can be counted. (Examples are using curse words or saying an answer without being called on.)

Keep your card with you. Check off a box each time you show that bad behavior choice. For behaviors you do a lot, look at the card at the end of the class period. (For example, look at it when science or math is over for the day.) For behaviors you don't do as often, look at the card at the end of the day. Count how many times you showed the wrong behavior. Now set a goal: Do the behavior **one less time** during the next class period or day. Repeat this the next period or next day. When you meet your new goal, set a new one of again doing it one less time.

Bit by bit, the behavior will disappear.

TRY THIS FUN EXERCISE!

Are habits hard to break? You bet. Impossible? No way! It's difficult to change, but you can do it. This exercise will prove it:

1. Cross your arms over your chest.

2. Look at your hands. Which hand is on top of the other arm? Which hand is tucked under?

3. Uncross your arms and cross them again . . . but this time, **switch** the way you place your hands.

4. Keep trying until you can do it!

4. Set and Reach Small Goals

Some people think that it is better to give attention to **positive** behavior, not bad choices. There is something called **shaping** that helps students to do this. It lets them reach a big behavior goal by breaking it down into little goals. With shaping, you set small goals. Each time you meet a small goal, you set another small goal. Each small goal gets you closer to the bigger behavior goal. The small goals add up. Soon, they lead you to reaching the big goal that you wanted to accomplish. You build better behavior one small goal at a time.

Here are the steps you can follow to make a **shaping plan.** You can copy the "Shaping Plan" form on page 86 and use that if you want. Do these on your own or with help from a teacher, family grown-up, or friend:

1. **SET A BIG GOAL.** Set your goal for a smart behavior choice you want to make. Ask yourself, "What behavior do I want to show in class?" This is your big goal. Write it down. Write down the **GOOD** behavior you **WANT** to show.

2. **LOOK AT HOW YOU'RE DOING RIGHT NOW.** Ask yourself, "How am I doing on meeting that goal right now?" Write down how well you have shown the behavior this week. Then move to the small goals.

3. **SET A SMALL GOAL.** Look at what you wrote for "How I'm Doing Now." Think of a small thing you can do that is a little bit better than how you are doing right now. This is your first small goal. Write it down. Be sure it says what you **WILL** do in class or at home (*not* what you *won't* do). It doesn't have to be a big change—just a small improvement.

4. **SET OTHER SMALL GOALS.** Think of another little goal. This goal should be harder to do than the first small goal. Write it down. Keep writing other small goals. Each one should be slightly harder than the one before it. Each goal should get you closer to the big goal you wrote.

5. **START TRYING TO MEET THE FIRST SMALL GOAL.** At the start of the day, look at your first small goal. Work to meet that goal today.

6. **SEE HOW YOU DID.** At the end of the day, think about how you did. Did you meet the small goal? Congratulate yourself! Then decide if you should try the same one again tomorrow, or try to meet the next small goal on your list. If you didn't meet the goal, think about it again. Ask yourself, "Should I try for the same goal again tomorrow? Or should I think of a smaller goal?"

7. **CHOOSE YOUR NEXT SMALL GOAL.** Maybe you'll try for the first small goal again. Maybe you'll go on to the next small goal.

What if you think you need a smaller goal? Try to think of one that is easier to do but will still make you work a little.

8. **KEEP WORKING ON THE SMALL GOALS.** Work on them one at a time. Each time you feel ready, move to the next, bigger goal.

It's a good idea to get your teacher's approval to do things this way. Most teachers will be happy to help you with your plan. They would like to see you improve.

Here is an example of a shaping plan:

SHAPING PLAN

BIG GOAL: Finish and hand in my math homework.

HOW I'M DOING NOW: I don't finish my math homework, so I don't turn it in.

Small Goal 1: Hand in the homework sheet with my name and the date at the top.

Small Goal 2: Do Small Goal 1 AND do one of the math homework problems.

Small Goal 3: Do Small Goal 1 AND five of the problems.

Small Goal 4: Do Small Goal 1 AND all the even-numbered problems.

Small Goal 5: Do Small Goal 1 AND all the problems except for one.

Small Goal 6: Do Small Goal 1 AND all the problems.

Small Goal 7: Keep doing Small Goal 6 for 2 weeks.

Small Goal 8: Start a new shaping plan. The BIG GOAL will be to get more problems correct on my math homework.

Small Goal 9:

Small Goal 10:

5. Make a Contract with Your Teacher

You've probably heard of contracts before. They are written agreements between people. Sports players have contracts. They get paid a certain amount of money to play for a team. Music groups and singers have contracts. They agree to perform at a certain time and place. Then they'll get a certain amount of money.

Kids can set up contracts with teachers to get a reward for doing something in school. (Rewards at school probably won't be money!) The kids get the reward if they do what they agreed to do. (Kids can also have contracts at home with parents.) If you would like to make a contract, you'll have to bargain with the teacher. You'll promise to do something the teacher wants you to do. For example, your teacher might want you to be on time for class. The teacher will promise to give you a reward if you do *exactly* what you agree to do in your contract.

Here are the steps to follow to make a contract:

1. Set up a meeting with the teacher.

2. Have the teacher tell you what behavior she or he would like to see you do. Or suggest a behavior yourself.

3. Tell the teacher what reward you would like to have. It could be a class duty. It could be more time on the computer. It could be a free lunch, a baseball cap . . . whatever. You might want to have a list of rewards ready, in case the teacher doesn't agree to some of your ideas.

4. With the teacher, talk about how much you have to do to get a certain reward. Figure it out together. Make a deal.

5. Write down your agreement. This is your contract. Be very exact about **how much** you must do and **when** you will do it. Also write:
   • exactly what the reward will be
   • who will decide that you have done what the contract says you will do
   • a date when the two of you will meet again to see how the

contract is working (so you can redo the contract if something isn't fair)

- a place to sign and date the contract

6. Now it's time for you and the teacher to sign the contract. You might want to get a witness to sign it, too. The witness will help decide if you and the adult are being fair and obeying the rules in the contract.

You will find a contract form on page 87. You can photocopy the form to use if you want. Your teacher might have a different contract form, too. Or the two of you could make one up together.

It's Your Turn

- Think of a behavior you want to work on changing in school. Which of the ideas in this chapter might help you change to a better behavior?

- Talk with your teacher about what way could work best for you. You might even do two ways at once. For example, maybe you'll do a shaping plan. Then you could use plus and minus to help you reach the goals.

Remember . . .

School will be a much nicer place to be if you can choose good behavior. It helps to have a few different "tricks" for doing this. Give the ideas in this chapter a try. See which ones work best for you. As you get used to using the ideas, **you will make progress.** You will start to make better behavior choices more often. Then you'll learn more, enjoy class more, and get along better with teachers. There are more tips for getting along better with your teachers (and other adults) in Chapter 8.

GOAL RECORD

My goal for the week:

_____

Scoring Key

0 Forgot goal or made bad choice **2** Did my goal behavior pretty often
1 Did my goal behavior a little bit **3** Met my goal!

ACTIVITY	M	T	W	Th	F

BEAT YOUR PREVIOUS BEST

To learn how to use these cards to beat your previous best, see pages 78–79.

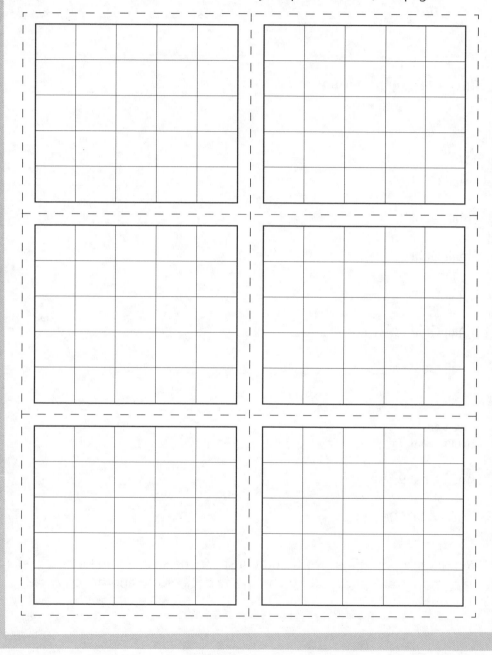

SHAPING PLAN

BIG GOAL: _____

_____

HOW I'M DOING NOW:_____

_____

Small Goal 1: _____

Small Goal 2: _____

Small Goal 3: _____

Small Goal 4: _____

Small Goal 5: _____

Small Goal 6: _____

Small Goal 7: _____

Small Goal 8: _____

Small Goal 9: _____

Small Goal 10: _____

You might not have 10 small goals. Just use the spaces you need. If you have more small goals, add them on the back or use another copy of the form.

CONTRACT

This is an agreement between _____ and
                                                    (student)

_____.
               (teacher)

AGREEMENT

The student will do this:_____

_____

If the student does what is written, the teacher will do this: _____

_____

CONDITIONS OF AGREEMENT

1. _____

2. _____

3. _____

4. _____

This contract is in effect as soon as it is signed. The teacher and student

will review it on _____.
                               (day/date)

SIGNATURES

Student: _____

Teacher: _____

Witness: _____

Date: _____

Chapter 8

WAYS TO GET ALONG BETTER WITH TEACHERS

"I've started showing respect to teachers more. I try not to argue with them or bother them while they're teaching." —Juana, 10

Did you know that you (yes, YOU) can help teachers be nicer to you? It's true. You can do things to help teachers treat you better. This chapter gives you some ways to do this.

SAY NICE THINGS TO TEACHERS

Make teachers notice you at times when they're not busy or upset. Then they get to say something positive to you. This is a great way to help teachers see you in a "better light." Say hello in a clear, pleasant voice. Put a smile on your face, too. Add the teacher's title and name ("Mrs. Mufti," "Mr. Tate"). This gives your greeting a personal touch. It also gives teachers the respect they like.

Once you're comfortable saying hello, add comments and compliments. Say something nice about the teacher's class. You can even compliment the teacher's clothes. Or you can remark on something the teacher has done:

"Hey, Mr. McGee. How are you doing today? It was fun to do that experiment yesterday. Are we doing another one tomorrow?"

"That was a great speaker you got for career day, Ms. Silmon."

"Mrs. Marco, I did just what you said would work, and it did. That was good advice."

"Nice tie, Mr. B."

People like to hear nice things about themselves. They usually like the people who say these things. So give teachers compliments. Then they will probably start to be nicer to you.

Try to say nice things that you *really mean.* Most people can tell when a compliment is fake. If the teacher thinks you don't mean it, you won't get the results you want.

It's Your Turn

- Pick a teacher you don't know well or have had problems with. Say hi and notice the result. Even if nothing changes after one hello, don't give up. Try saying it every day for three days, or even for a week. See what happens.

- Think of a teacher who you would like to treat you better. (It might be the one you've been saying hi to.) Make a plan. Think of what comments and compliments you'll say. When will you say them? Practice with someone first. That way you'll feel more confident when you say them to your teacher. Keep at it. See what happens after a few days.

LET TEACHERS TEACH

One of the main reasons kids get a behavior label is because they keep teachers from teaching. It makes sense to avoid arguing with teachers. Let's face it. They have a lot of power. They can give kids lots of punishments (and rewards). Plus, the IEP team will ask your teachers if you are beating BD and making good choices. You want your teachers to tell the team good news. So let teachers teach. **That's their job.** That's what they're paid to do.

Really listen if they stop the lesson to tell you something. They are trying to let you know what is the right thing to do right now. Some teachers do this in a friendly way. Others don't always say it very nicely. In that case, ignore the unfriendly tone and listen to the words.

But what if you have a good point? What if you really want to say something? Save it until later when the lesson is over. If you think the teacher is wrong, speak with him or her about it in private. Wait until free time, or recess, or lunchtime, or after class. Right now, just say "Okay" and follow the directions. That will keep you out of trouble.

Later, if your concern still seems important, you can ask the teacher for a moment to talk with you. When you do talk, speak politely. Don't argue. (Arguing won't get you what you want.) Instead, try using a question or making a request with a "sandwich." These are the next two things you'll read about in this chapter.

Idea!

Think of a teacher who sometimes gets mad about your behavior. Make a deal with yourself to say "Okay" to everything this teacher tells you to do tomorrow. After class, think about how you did. Try to do even better the next day.

MAKE SUGGESTIONS WITH QUESTIONS

Suppose you don't like an assignment the teacher gave you. Refusing to do it will **NOT** help. It also won't help to say **negative** things, like "This stinks" or "This is stupid." And it definitely won't help to say rude things, like "I'm not doing this stuff" or "Do it yourself!" These are sure ways to get in trouble.

Instead, be **assertive:** Use a strong, polite voice to say what's on your mind. Use the word "I" instead of "you." (This is called I-talk. You can read more about it on pages 69–70.) Then suggest another way of doing things. How? By asking a question. No one likes bossy people. That's why it's important to ask, not demand.

LUCI

Mr. Rivera told Luci, "Please read aloud starting at the top of page 85." Luci had problems reading. She wanted to think of an excuse so she didn't have to read, but she tried to read it, and stumbled through. The other kids giggled and whispered. Luci was really embarrassed, especially when the teacher stopped her. He said, "That's enough, Luci. Bob, please read that part again." Luci felt foolish—and mad. But even though it was hard, she kept quiet.

After class, Luci went to the teacher. She said to him, "Mr. Rivera, I have problems with reading. Could you tell me the day before which parts I'm going to read out loud? I'll practice it at home so I read it well the next day."

Mr. Rivera thought Luci had a good idea. He agreed to tell her ahead of time. He showed her a part to prepare for the next day.

Luci was embarrassed and upset in class. But she still made good choices. She waited for the right time to talk to the teacher. When they talked, she was assertive. She made a suggestion by asking a question. As a result, she got the help that she needed. And her teacher saw that Luci was able to work politely with him.

Like Luci, you can ask (not tell) about what you want. You can give a reason why it would be a good idea. Here are two examples of ways to try to get help. They show the difference between telling and asking.

"I'd learn more if I did it on the computer."

This is a way of telling, not asking. It sounds bossy. Teachers don't like to be told how to teach.

"Ms. Cobb, would it be okay to do it on the computer? That way I can add diagrams and show my ideas better."

This time the student gives a suggestion in the form of a question. She gives the reason for asking the question, too. Plus, she uses the teacher's title ("Ms.") and name ("Cobb"). Teachers like this. It shows respect.

When you make suggestions with questions, you won't always get your way. But you'll have a better chance.

It's Your Turn

Turn these orders into questions:

- "Let me do the project with Tony."

- "It would work better to use paint instead of chalk."

- "Give me the scissors so I can cut this out."

MAKE A "SANDWICH"

Got a gripe that's so important you can't just say "Okay" right now? If so, put it between two nice comments.

1. Start off by saying something that will please the teacher. It could be a nice comment about the class. Or it could be a compliment about how the teacher teaches.

2. Next, tell what the problem is. Try not to make it a bossy or whiny complaint. Instead, say the important thing you want in a way

that's assertive. You can even make a suggestion with a question when you do this. The main thing is to be friendly and show respect.

3. Finish quickly with another nice remark. It can be the same nice thing as before, or something new. It might be another compliment. It might let the teacher know how you have been helped. It might be a thank you.

Think of these three steps as making a request sandwich. The nice things are the two pieces of bread. The important thing you want (your request) is the peanut butter or turkey that goes in the middle. Here are the three parts of a request sandwich:

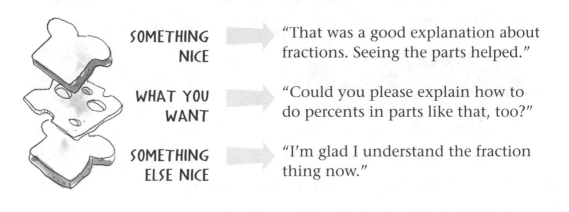

SOMETHING NICE → "That was a good explanation about fractions. Seeing the parts helped."

WHAT YOU WANT → "Could you please explain how to do percents in parts like that, too?"

SOMETHING ELSE NICE → "I'm glad I understand the fraction thing now."

Here's the whole sandwich, put together:

"That was a good explanation about fractions. Seeing the parts helped. Could you please explain how to do percents in parts like that, too? I'm glad I understand the fraction thing now."

Here are three different ways students talk to teachers. In each case, the student has something important to say or ask. Which is a sandwich?

> "This is stupid. We did this last year. Why do we have to do this stuff again?"

You probably figured out that this isn't the sandwich. It doesn't start with something nice. In fact, there's nothing nice anywhere.

> "I think it would be better if we did it like we did last year. That was fun. It isn't going to be any fun this way."

This says that last year was fun. But it doesn't start with a compliment. And it ends with a complaint. It's not the kind of thing a teacher will be glad to hear.

> "The way you explained it made it really easy, Mr. Hill. It reminded me of what we learned last year. I was wondering: If we can prove that we know this stuff, could we learn something else instead? That would be great, 'cause the way you teach new stuff makes it interesting."

This starts with a compliment: It tells the teacher he helped the student learn. The message in the middle is friendly, and it doesn't sound like complaining. But it tells the teacher what the student wants. Then it ends with another compliment. What teacher wouldn't like to hear this?

A Challenge for You

This is a challenge in two parts. Do it in your notebook, one part at a time. (When you're done, you can compare your ideas to the solutions on page 156.)

CHALLENGE 1: Here are the three parts of a request sandwich. Put them in the right order.

> "But I think a zero grade is unfair. I couldn't do the paper last night because I left my notebook at Paula's. Could I please turn it in after lunch? That's when I'll see her so I can get it back."

> "Miss Lange, I agree with you that it is important to do my schoolwork."

> "I really enjoyed doing the report on Ben Franklin, and learned a lot. I think you'll like the paper if you take it late."

CHALLENGE 2: Aron is known for being late to class a lot. His goal this week is to get to class on time. He enters the door to class as the bell is ringing. He thinks that he is on time. Mr. Hunter says, "You're late. Go to the office and get a late pass." Aron gives a surprised look. Mr. Hunter says, "You have to be in your seat when the bell rings. Go to the office." Aron doesn't want to miss any of the class. And he will if he goes to the office. He wants to explain this to Mr. Hunter. Write a request sandwich for Aron.

USE "BEHAVIOR MOD"

Have you ever heard of **behavior modification?** It is a scientific way of changing the way people act. Sometimes it's called **behavior mod.**

There are scientists who study why people do what they do. They found out that if people get a reward for doing something, they show more of that behavior. The reward makes them want to do it again. It's nice to get a reward (like a prize, a thank you, or a smile).

When teachers reward you for good behavior, they're using behavior mod. They're helping you change (modify) your behavior. You can even use this on yourself. In Chapter 7, you learned tricks for tracking your progress in changing behavior. These are ways to use behavior mod.

And guess what? You can use behavior mod with teachers, too. Yes, really! You can decide on a behavior you'd like your teacher to use with you. You can "reward" the teacher for using it.

Think of all the things students can do that are rewarding to teachers. They can pay attention. They can do their assignment. They can say "Okay." They can ask good questions about the lesson. They can say nice things about the class. They can follow rules and directions.

"REWARD" YOUR TEACHER. So how do you help teachers be nicer and more helpful to you? Reward them when they do things you like! This doesn't mean giving teachers prizes. It means letting them know when **their** teaching is helping **you** learn. For example:

- When your teacher teaches an interesting lesson, nod your head and pay attention.

- When a teacher speaks nicely to you, smile and be nice, too.

- Maybe your teacher gives you fun projects or lets you do interesting computer activities. Tell the teacher how much you enjoy doing those things.

- Maybe the teacher explains things well. Say, "Thanks. Now I get it."

- Some teachers like to tell jokes. If yours does, smile or chuckle.

These are all ways to reward the behavior you like. Then you'll probably see more of that behavior in the future.

HELP YOUR TEACHER DO NICE THINGS. Sometimes you'll have to help teachers do the nice things in the first place. Then you can reward that behavior when they show it. For example, you can ask for help in a polite way:

> "Mr. Smith, I did the first two questions. How does it look so far?"

> "I think I'm finished. Is this how you wanted it?"

It's probably best to ask these types of questions two or three times during a class. (Any more might annoy the teacher.) And it's even better when you mention something from the lesson before you ask for the help:

MARK

During math, Mark was having some problems when he tried to regroup numbers. He raised his hand to call the teacher over. Mark said, "Mrs. Petty, I remember that you said to borrow from the tens column. But can I borrow more than one ten?"

Mark showed Mrs. Petty that he was listening. He did this first, before he asked the question. (Teachers like that.) Mrs. Petty nodded and said, "I'm glad to know you listened, Mark. You may need to borrow from the tens column. You can't borrow more than one ten, though." Mark was happy he got this nice response from Mrs. Petty. He smiled at her and said, "Okay, I get it. Thanks."

If you try Mark's approach, remember to get attention in the right way. Raise your hand and wait. Don't get out of your seat or interrupt a teacher who's working with other kids. Wait until he or she is done. Then, when you have the teacher's attention, use a strong and polite voice.

5 Steps to Using Behavior Mod with a Teacher

1. **Choose a teacher** who you would like to see be nicer or more helpful to you.
2. **Think about a behavior** you want the teacher to do more often.
3. **Figure out what you'll do** to encourage the behavior. Maybe you'll reward it each time it happens. Or maybe you'll first find ways to help the teacher do nice things.
4. **Think of rewards** the teacher will like. You might use compliments, smiles, saying "Okay," or other things. You can use a different nice thing each time the behavior happens.
5. **Try out your plan.** Give it time to work. Notice ways of helping and which rewards work best.

IMPORTANT!

What if you have a teacher who treats you badly? What if there's a teacher who's NEVER nice or fair no matter what you do? Or one who says mean things, or just won't help you? Talk to your special ed teacher about this. Or talk to the school counselor. If you don't find help at school, talk to your parent, guardian, or another adult. Keep looking until you find an adult who can help you with this problem. Also ask an adult if you need help learning skills to get along with teachers. (For a list of adults to talk to, see page 45.)

USE YOUR SKILLS TOGETHER

In this chapter and earlier ones, you've learned lots of ways to get along better at school. You read about how a special class can help you. You also learned ideas for spending more time in the regular classroom. You found out how important it is to build your self-esteem. You practiced how to "Stop, Think, Choose, and Think Again." You learned about being assertive and using I-talk. You read that it's important to be prepared and ask for help when you need it. You learned ways that will help you change your behavior and help your teachers want to treat you nicely.

Often the information and skills you are learning can work together. As you get used to using each idea, you'll find that you do some things without having to think too hard first. You will also find that you are using the skills together to help yourself. That's how it is for Nina:

NINA

Nina gets a stern warning from Miss Tan for talking to Will. Nina was just doing something funny with the pencil that Will lent to her. She was going to get right to work. She doesn't like how the teacher spoke to her. It sounded mean. Nina wants to say something mean back.

She stops herself and remembers the goal she set for herself that morning: Say "Okay" to whatever the teacher says. So Nina says "Okay." But she can't stop thinking that Miss Tan treated her wrong. Nina keeps imagining things she could have said back. She feels angry, like things aren't fair.

Nina doesn't like these feelings. They make her want to explode. She remembers the self-talk that she is practicing with the school counselor. She thinks to herself: "Stop! Cool down. Think. If I say those things, I'll get in trouble. But I want to let Miss Tan know how I feel about this."

Nina thinks about what she can do. Finally, a good idea comes to mind. "I know! I'll talk with Miss Tan when I'm leaving class. I'll tell her that I didn't like

MORE

the way she spoke to me. I'd better be careful though. I want her to treat me better. So I've got to show respect when I say what's on my mind."

Nina thinks some more and plans what she will say. She decides to say: "Miss Tan, I apologize for goofing around when I was getting a pencil. I like your class and I was going to get right to work. I'll try not to do that again. But if I make a mistake, could you just call my name next time? I promise to figure out what I'm supposed to be doing. Then I'll do it right away because I like what we're learning here."

After class, Nina says the words she planned. Miss Tan looks a little surprised. She says, "I'll think about it, but you have to remember to behave, right?" That's not quite what Nina wanted to hear. But she says "Okay." (That's her goal, remember?) She's pretty sure Miss Tan is thinking about doing something different next time. That's all that Nina really wants. Even if the teacher won't admit it, Nina has made a difference. She did it in a strong, positive way. And she kept out of trouble.

A Challenge for You

Think of the ideas you have learned in this book. Which of those ideas did Nina use? List them in your notebook. You may want to read the story again, making your list as you read. When you're done, compare your list to the one on page 156.

Many teachers are already nice to kids. Treat these teachers well, too. Be friendly and helpful. Cooperate in their classes. Reward their nice behavior that makes school a better place for you. Then they'll know you appreciate them. That way, they'll keep being nice.

It's usually easy to show this kind of respect to teachers who treat you well. It can be harder to show it to the ones who don't. For those teachers who seem not-so-nice, look for times when they **do** treat you well. (They probably do this once in a while.) Smile and do what they ask. Tell them how it makes you want to work for them. With time, they will probably start to treat you better more often.

Even if they don't, keep trying. And keep working to make good behavior choices yourself. You won't always have the teachers you have today. But you will always be you. **YOU** are the person who wants to feel better and have a better life. That means you need to take charge of your behavior.

Remember . . .

It's good to know ways to help your teachers help you. This can make a big difference in how you get along at school. But don't forget, the best way to change how teachers treat you is by changing your own behavior. When you make good choices, you and your teachers will get along better. You'll want to work harder for them, and they're likely to treat you nicer, too!

Chapter 9

WAYS TO MAKE
AND KEEP FRIENDS

"I wish I had better friends. I want friends who act right and help me stay out of trouble." —Jerome, 13

We all want people to like us. We want friends we can trust. Having good friends makes life at school and home more fun. But for many kids with BD, it's not easy to make friends. Other kids don't always want to be friends. They don't like the behaviors and choices they often see kids with BD make. You're working on making better choices. If you keep at it, this shouldn't be a problem much longer. But sometimes kids with BD haven't learned the ways to make and keep good friends. This chap-ter has tips for being friendly so that others will want to be your friend. It also has ideas for finding friends who are right for you.

SAY NICE THINGS TO OTHERS

When you notice things you like about other people, say something nice. Look for chances to give compliments or say thank you. Depending on what is happening, you might say things like:

"That was a good answer."

"Your project really looks great."

"That joke you made was funny."

"Thanks for lending me a pen."

"I like your shirt!"

Why say nice things? Because people like to hear good things about themselves. Don't you? When you first try this, others may not be nice back to you. They need to know you truly mean well. They probably aren't used to hearing you say these things. They may remember when you teased them or made mean remarks. (No one likes that.) You have to show them a "new you," and keep showing it. Don't give up! In time, they'll see that you want to be a real friend.

Idea!

Ask your special ed teacher about having **social skills** lessons. These lessons let kids practice how to get along better with others. Social skills will help you make and keep friends. Page 162 tells where schools can find lessons to use.

ASK PEOPLE ABOUT THEMSELVES

When you're around other kids, ask them questions to get them talking. (Do this with adults, too.) You can ask them what they like to do for fun. Ask them which teams, bands, books, hobbies, or TV shows they enjoy. When they start to tell you about what they like, listen closely. Then you can ask them more questions about what they said. You can tell them what YOU think, too—in a friendly way. Try to keep the conversation going. There are lots of ways to do this. You might ask them why they like doing those things. Or ask how they got interested in them. A conversation involves both people. Be sure that both of you have a chance to say things back and forth.

Sometimes it can seem hard to just start a conversation with a kid at school. One idea is to try it first with people you know a little bit. Pick someone who will probably be friendly back to you. For example, you could ask a neighbor about himself. You could ask a relative. This could be someone your own age, or younger, or older.

JODY

Jody never knew what to say to relatives when they came over. One morning she found out that her uncle was coming to visit. Jody wondered how to get a conversation going. She thought about what her uncle liked to do. She knew one thing: He liked to fish. Jody thought of some questions to ask about that. She remembered that she had heard an ad for fishing gear on the radio. That gave her some ideas about questions she could ask.

After saying hello, Jody asked her uncle, "How's fishing?" Her uncle said, "Pretty good."

Jody thought of one of the questions she'd planned. "How do you know what time of day to fish?" she asked. Her uncle said it depended. The fish he liked to catch usually bit early in the morning.

Hearing that, Jody thought of another question: "What kind of fish do you like to go after?" Jody's uncle said he liked to fish for bass. That let Jody ask

MORE

how her uncle knew what bait or lures to use. They talked for half an hour. Jody's uncle invited her on a fishing trip. After hearing so much about fishing, she thought that sounded fun.

What can talking to adult relatives have to do with making friends? Lots. Friends come from many places. You may want to make friends your own age at school. But don't forget that neighbors and relatives can be friends, too. People of different ages can be friends—or at least friendly! Like Jody, you might find that you can have fun with people you didn't know you would enjoy. Also like Jody, you can try out conversation skills with people you already know.

It's Your Turn

- Are there some people you would like to talk with? Think of things they enjoy.

- Think of some questions you could ask them about what they like to do.

- If you know what they like, try to learn a little bit about it before you see them. You could find information in a magazine or library book. You could look on the Internet.

GIVE A HELPING HAND

Chapter 4 talks about how starting a "helping habit" can build your self-esteem (pages 42–43). Helping others is also a way to make friends. Remember a time when you had a big job to do and someone helped you out? Remember how it made the job easier? It was nice of that person, wasn't it? Helpful people are liked by others. Be helpful to everyone you **like** and **respect** (or think you want to get to know). Offer to help others when it looks like they could use a hand. Assist them when they are busy. Volunteer to share a chore.

Also tell teachers that you'd like to help with events they are planning. Maybe there's going to be a school dance. Maybe the class is doing a play or music program. If you offer to help get ready for these things, you'll get to work with other kids. This can be a good way to get to know new people and show that you want to make friends. You will have things in common. You'll have a chance to talk about those things.

Another idea for getting to know others is to become an expert in something. An expert knows a lot about a certain thing. If you know things that other kids like to talk and learn about, they'll come to you for help and advice. What would you like to become an expert about? Comics? Pet care? Sports rules?

You want others to see the changes you are making. Helping out can be a good way to show people at school that you are changing your behavior. You can show this to people in your neighborhood, too.

DANTRELL

Dantrell wanted friends to do things with around his street. But there was a problem. Dantrell had BD. He was known for getting into trouble. Some of the parents didn't want him to play with their kids. Dantrell felt awful about this. He was working hard to make better choices. His special ed teacher suggested that he try helping out some of the parents. That way, they would see that Dantrell was really changing his behavior.

MORE

Dantrell started offering to carry in groceries. He opened the door for people when they went in and out. He picked things up for people if they dropped them. Word about "the new Dantrell" started to spread around the neighborhood. A couple of the parents started being nice to him. After a while, they let him come over and play with their kids.

Idea!

Think of some younger kids who live in your neighborhood. Become their **mentor:** Ask their parents if you can help them out with their schoolwork (with their dad or mom nearby). If you see these kids around the neighborhood, say hello. Help them learn to do good things that you know how to do. Show them how to be a friend. Remember to be patient and kind with the children. Be sure to only teach them good things and how to make smart choices. One of the best ways to learn the new ways is to teach them to others.

"I like playing with little kids. They like how I teach them things when I'm a referee for their games." —Talika, 12

TAKE PART IN ACTIVITIES

A great place to find new friends is in an after-school club or other organized group. There you can get to know others **outside of class.** You'll meet kids who like to do the same things you do. People who share the same interests often make good friends.

Activities for Making Friends

SPORTS (SCHOOL OR COMMUNITY)

baseball or softball
basketball
in-line skating or skateboarding
soccer
football
track or cross-country
skiing or snowboarding
hockey
tennis
swimming
volleyball
wrestling
gymnastics

CLASSES AND LESSONS FOR KIDS

acting
dancing or singing
skating
guitar or another instrument
martial arts like karate
yoga
woodworking
baby-sitting
swimming
sailing, canoeing, or kayaking
fishing
juggling
cooking

SCHOOL CLUBS AND GROUPS

foreign language club
computer club
chess club
science club
book group
school yearbook
school newspaper
band, orchestra, or chorus
drama
writers' group

COMMUNITY GROUPS

Scouts
Boys and Girls Clubs of America
YMCA, YWCA, YHA
youth group at a place of worship
4H
after-school programs
summer programs

What if you're not sure how to join something? Or how to find a group?

FIRST, THINK ABOUT WHAT YOU WANT TO DO. This will help you figure out what to look for.

- What would you like to **know more** about? The way computers work? How to become a cheerleader? The secrets of great coaches? Why airplanes fly?

- What would you like to **learn** to do? Fish? Skate? Knit or sew? Cook? Turn cartwheels?

- What do you wish you could do **with someone else?** Take care of animals? Ride bikes? Write a TV script?

- What sounds **fun?** Playing games? Doing stuff with little kids? Talking about books or movies? Planning a school party?

THEN THINK OF WHAT GROUPS YOU KNOW ABOUT. These might be at your school. They might be activities in your community that you've seen or heard about. You might already go to a youth center, park, or place of worship. Often these are places where there are things going on.

LOOK FOR AN ACTIVITY THAT YOU WOULD LIKE. Look on the bulletin board and in the school yearbook. Look in your local newspaper. Many schools, towns, cities, and counties have Web sites. The sites tell about clubs, lessons, sports, and other things people can do. Your school or library may have a computer you can use. Also talk to students, teachers, and other kids and adults. Ask for their suggestions.

VISIT THE GROUP OR FIND OUT HOW TO JOIN IN. If you want, ask someone you know to help you find an activity. Be brave and give it a try!

It's Your Turn

Think about an activity you could do to meet people and make friends. If you want, use your notebook to list ideas and make plans. Decide on an activity. Then find out what you need to know in order to join in. Most groups don't require you to have special skills. They just want interested people.

CHOOSE FRIENDS CAREFULLY

Everyone wants good friends. They make us laugh. They do things with us. They let us know that we are okay. But often kids with BD have some friends with too many **negative** behaviors. These friends do and say things that are mean or embarrassing. They hurt people's feelings and get in trouble. Sometimes they are good to be around, but other times they aren't. You know if you have friends like these. They make things hard for you at times. You get into trouble with them.

When friendships are negative, it's time to find some new friends. This isn't always easy to do. You may be used to spending time with "problem" friends. They will want you to keep hanging out with them. Plus, to get good friends, you'll have to be on your best behavior. You'll have to make smart choices. It's worth it!

5 Things GOOD FRIENDS Do

Here are some things good friends do. Kids who do these things are the kind of people **YOU** want to be friends with:

1. **Good friends can be counted on.** They call when they say they will. They keep secrets that their friends tell them. They listen and give good advice.

2. **Good friends are loyal.** They stand up for their friends when others say bad things about them. They don't make their friends feel left out.

3. **Good friends share.** They share time and do things together. They share feelings, too.

4. **Good friends show respect.** They play fair and take turns. They're good sports who make a game fun for everyone. They like their friends for who they are. They say nice things. They don't tease in a mean way. If they disagree, they talk about it and work together to solve the problem.

5. **Good friends help each other.** They help their friends learn to do things. They cheer them on. They talk with them. They also help their friends find trusted adults to talk to about problems.

It's Your Turn

- Think of someone who's a **GOOD FRIEND.** What makes him or her a good friend?

- Which qualities do you have that make **YOU** a good friend?

- What could you work on so you could learn to be a better friend?

- Do you have any "problem" friends? What can you do to find better friendships?

Remember . . .

Maybe you have lots of good friends already. Maybe you don't yet, but you are trying to make some new ones. Even if this is hard at first, you can do it! Use the ideas in this chapter. Also use the skills you've learned for getting along with adults. Talk and listen. Show respect. Be assertive. These things can all help you in your friendships.

You are learning lots of ways to change your behavior. You are working on making good choices. One really good choice is to decide to *make* good friends and to *be* a good friend. The skills for making and keeping friends will also help you be a *success in life.*

Chapter 10

WAYS TO HELP THE ADULTS AT HOME HELP YOU

> "My mom talks to me. She tells me that I need to be good. She tries to help me make better decisions." —Evelyn, 9

Ahhh. It's great to be home . . . or is it? Sometimes the grown-ups at home (and the kids, too) don't understand the challenges of BD. When kids make good and bad choices, family adults might not react like teachers do. They don't know how hard it can be to make the right decisions. Some parents think their BD kids should make smart choices every time. Sometimes they don't know how hard their kids are working to do this. Sometimes they forget to pay attention to the good choices their kids make.

> **Remember,** when you read about *family adults, parents,* or *adults at home,* think of the adult or adults who live with you and take care of you. This might be one or two parents, stepparents, foster parents, guardians, relatives, or others. It's different for each kid.

And they get mad when kids still make some bad ones. Some of these adults think that the kids are just being lazy. Maybe they even think kids are making bad choices on purpose.

Some parents are very good at helping their kids make better choices. Others haven't learned the best ways to do this. Read what these kids say about how adults at home try to help them behave better:

"They punish me. I can't watch TV or play video games. They won't let me go places."

"My stepmom does homework with me to make sure I get it done."

"With my new foster parents, I get to go see my grandfather if I have a good week."

"My dad tells me I need to be good."

"My mom's boyfriend tells my mom to 'get tough' with me. He's always yelling at me and bossing me around. When I do what he says, he tells me that I did it wrong. That makes me mad. Sometimes I ignore him and walk away. Sometimes I get so upset that I yell back at him. That really gets me in trouble."

"I live with my grandma. She loves me a lot and does nice things for me. But when I make mistakes, she gets really mad and says I'm no good. It really hurts me when she says these things. I get afraid she won't let me stay with her anymore. Then I try to do nice things for her. But she stays mad for a long time."

You're trying to make good choices. It feels pretty darn bad when the grown-ups you live with don't understand this. It's easier to change when others help you. But sometimes kids with BD don't have much help at home. They have to work on making better choices all by themselves. You **CAN** make changes yourself. That is something to be very proud about. As you do, you can start to help family adults help **YOU.** This chapter will give you ways to do that. It has ways to help no matter how well or not-so-well the adults handle things right now. The ideas can also help you get along better with others at home, like sisters and brothers.

USE TALKING AND LISTENING SKILLS

Many kids with BD have problems talking about things with the grown-ups at home. Remember the skills you've been practicing, like I-talk (Chapter 6) and request sandwiches (Chapter 8). People listen when others talk to them in a nice way. This shows respect. Help people at home (the adults *and* the kids in your family) understand what you're doing or how you're feeling. Do this by talking to them in a polite and friendly way. When they answer you, listen to what they say. Then you'll understand what they're thinking, too.

ALWAYS LOOK FOR SOLUTIONS. Remind yourself that yelling and arguing don't help solve problems. They usually make problems worse. When people argue, they get mad. They may get so mad that they say really mean things. Also, with an angry argument, no one can listen very well. Maybe you and your mom or dad get upset with each other. Maybe you yell at each other. Then no one listens to the other person. The grown-up doesn't think about what you are trying to say. You don't think about how the adult feels. When people don't work together, nothing changes. The same arguments happen over and over. **Fighting can't help** make things better. **Talking can.**

USE I-TALK. It's hard to keep calm and talk nicely when people don't agree with you. It takes some practice, too. But, it's worth it! Try to talk about what happened and how everyone feels about it. Don't blame others. That keeps them from listening to you. Instead, use I-talk (pages 69–70) to explain how you feel and what you want. (If the others use you-talk, do your best not to notice. They may not know about I-talk like you do.) Together, talk about how to solve the problem (so it doesn't happen again, or happens less). Work on solutions. Then do your part to make things better.

WHAT IF TALKING DOESN'T SEEM TO WORK? You could ask (nicely), "What would you like me to do to solve the problem?" Listen to what your parent (or brother or sister) would like you to do. Decide if you could do it. If it sounds like a good choice, do it. If it doesn't, see if you can think of another idea that would be okay with everyone. Ask if you could do that instead. Later, be sure to let the other person know that you did what you said you would.

These things are easy to say, but not so easy to do. Adults may want perfect behavior. **Hey, nobody's perfect!** But you are working hard on making better choices. Explain how you are working to do this. You might even have to tell about a time when you *did* make a better choice. That might help family grown-ups notice your smart choices more. Tell them you'll keep working to improve. Say you'll do this because you want to get along better and stay out of trouble. You can also tell them you want **them** to feel good and proud about **you.** Tell them you are working hard to make all these good things happen.

If trying to talk nicely doesn't work, show this book to the grown-ups at home. Point out the ideas you have read about for working better together. Tell them how the book is helping you meet your challenges.

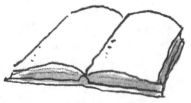

IMPORTANT!

Talking nicely can help you avoid arguments. But what if adults at home yell and fight with you no matter what you do? What if a grown-up's anger is out of control? If the fighting is really bad or you are scared or unhappy at home, talk to another grown-up. Ask this person for help. See the list of adults to talk to on page 45.

ASK FOR HELP WITH YOUR GOAL

Tell the adults at home what behavior goals you are working on. Ask them to watch for those behaviors. Ask them to notice and say something nice when you do the right things. Ask them to remind you when you should be making a better choice. When they remind you, say thank you. Be sure to do that better thing **right away.** Then they will know that you really are trying to make a change.

Idea!

Find someone to play the part of an adult at home. Practice talking to the person about your goals and asking for help with them.

Ask What the Grown-Ups Want You to Do

Many adults tell kids what **NOT** to do. ("Don't do that!") It would be better for them to tell kids what they **DO want them to do.** If your parents tell you what to stop doing, be polite and ask them to say it in a different way. Ask them to tell you exactly what they would like you to do. They might answer, "Be good" or "Stay out of trouble." If they do, ask them to tell you the actions they want to see you show. Then you'll know exactly what behaviors they expect.

Ask for "Sandwiches"

Remember the request sandwich you read about in Chapter 8 (pages 93–95)? Request sandwiches let you put your request between two nice things. Request sandwiches are a great way to ask adults to do something *you* want *them* to do. Here's another sandwich idea: a **compliment sandwich.**

Ask adults at home to use a compliment sandwich to talk to you about things *they* want *you* to do. Explain (nicely) how they can use three steps:

1. Ask or give you a reminder.

2. Tell you one thing they like about you. (This is the compliment.)

3. Remind you again.

The reminders are like the two pieces of bread in a sandwich. The compliment is like the cheese or tuna fish that goes between them. If grown-ups can use a sandwich like this, you'll know what to do right now. You will also hear a **good thing** about yourself.

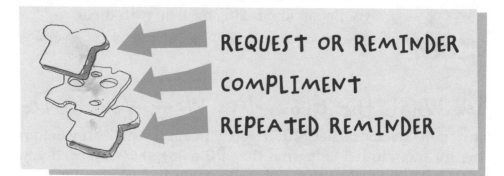

REQUEST OR REMINDER

COMPLIMENT

REPEATED REMINDER

Here is an example. Can you find the compliment between the two reminders?

"Swearing isn't allowed at home. I've noticed how much nicer you've been talking, and I really appreciate that. Please remember not to use swearwords, though."

You can also ask for a **request sandwich.** (It's the one that starts and ends with nice things. The request or reminder comes in the middle.) That way you'll hear nice things about yourself twice! You'll do the right thing (or figure out how to make things better). Then your parent might use a request sandwich again next time. Here's an example:

SOMETHING NICE ➡ "You were really playing nicely with your brother at first. Thanks for being such a good brother."

REMINDER ➡ "But remember that he's a lot smaller than you. It really hurt him when he got tackled so hard."

SOMETHING NICE AGAIN ➡ "I know you'll be gentle with him from now on, just like you were doing before."

What will you do when you hear this? Apologize and play nicely with your brother again, of course!

So ask parents and other adults to use a "sandwich" when they want you to do something. If you want, show them the examples of request and compliment sandwiches in this book. Ask them in a friendly way. You could use your own request sandwich to do this:

> "It helps when you remind me to make good choices. Could you please tell me what I'm doing right, too? Like in this book? That would be great. Thanks for reminding me."

You can give sandwiches to other family members, too. You can give them to sisters, brothers, cousins, and visitors. After all, everybody likes to hear nice things about themselves. Plus, people are more likely to do what you want when you ask nicely. This almost always works a lot better than unfriendly words or a mean voice.

A Challenge for You

This is a challenge in two parts. Do it in your notebook, one part at a time. (When you're done, you can compare your ideas to the solutions on page 156–157.)

CHALLENGE 1: Read the statements. Which one is a request sandwich? Which is a compliment sandwich? Which one is just a complaint?

1. "The dirty dishes are in the sink and it's your turn to do them. Be sure to do a super job on them just like you did last time. Do them now please."

2. "You forgot to take out the garbage again. What's your problem? It's the only chore we ask you to do."

3. "I remember how great your room looked yesterday. But right now it looks like a tornado was in there. I know you'll make it look super again before dinner."

CHALLENGE 2: You are trying to put together a really hard jigsaw puzzle. Your sister wants to help you, but she puts pieces in the wrong places. She is breaking parts of the puzzle that you have put together, too. You feel upset. But you remember to use a sandwich and a nice voice to get her to stop. She is trying to help you, but you don't want the puzzle messed up. Make your own sandwich for this situation. It can be a compliment sandwich or a request sandwich.

TAKE A TIME-OUT

How can you avoid making bad choices when you get mad? Take a time-out. Stop yourself from doing anything wrong. Instead, say in a calm voice, "I need to be alone for a little bit." Then leave and go to a place where you can be by yourself. Go to your room. Go to the bathroom. Take a walk.

While you're alone, work on a solution. Instead of just being mad, try to think of a way to make things better. Think about what you will say or do the next time you see the adult (or kid) you have a problem with. **If you did some things wrong,** take responsibility for them. Apologize and promise to do better. **If it's not your fault,** can you think of way to say what you need with I-talk? Can you think of a way to make a sandwich? Can you think of some things to suggest so the problem won't happen in the future? Think of how you will suggest things in a nice way so that everyone works together to solve the problem.

ALI

Ali lived with his mom. He knew she loved him. But his BD had made lots of problems for her. Ali was working hard on getting along better at home. He tried to show respect and talk nicely. He saw some small changes. His mom was nicer to him sometimes. Ali felt happy to see how his smart choices made his mom smile.

He wanted to get something nice for her birthday. He told Mr. Hill, who owned the corner store. Mr. Hill said he would pay Ali to run errands. Ali helped Mr. Hill every day after school for two weeks. He made enough money to buy his mom some new cooking utensils. She was a great cook, but her utensils were bent and scratched. Even though she said they still worked just fine, Ali knew she would like new ones. So Ali went to a department store and bought some. He used the money he'd earned helping Mr. Hill. The clerk gave him a box for the new utensils. Ali decorated the box and made a card. He was excited about the gift.

MORE

On his mom's birthday, Ali handed her the gift. "Happy Birthday!" he said. She smiled and opened the box. Then her smile turned to a frown. "Where did you get the money to buy these?" she asked in an angry voice. "Did you take it from my drawer?"

Ali was very hurt and angry. He started to feel like screaming and hitting. But he knew that would make things worse. He tried to start telling his mom how he bought the gift. But she said, "Don't lie to me!" She wouldn't listen. So Ali took a deep breath. Tears came, but he said as calmly as he could, "I worked hard for those. Right now I'm gonna go to my room. Okay?" Mom said, "Yes. You get to your room now till I'm ready to deal with you!"

Ali sat on the bed and squeezed his pillow. He thought, "This is really unfair." He had wanted to surprise his mom. He had done the right thing and earned money for the present. But she thought he had stolen it. Even when she'd said this, Ali had made smart choices. He had stopped to think. He had used I-talk. He had taken a time-out. But Mom hadn't noticed any of that. In between his upset feelings, Ali tried to think about what to do next. How could he solve the problem?

He knew his mom would cool down after a while. She always did. He decided to wait until they both felt calmer. That night, his mom went out with a friend. In the morning, Ali went to school. He made good choices there. But he kept thinking about things at home. The next night, Ali's mom came home from work. She asked, "Ali, where did you get the money for my present?" He told her how he earned the money. He said she could ask Mr. Hill if she wanted to. He said all this in a respectful way. And he could tell that his mom believed him and felt bad. She said, "It's hard for me to learn to trust you, Ali. I'm happy about how you earned the money. And I like my gift a lot." Then she started to fix supper. Ali saw that she was using the new utensils.

Ali felt better. He started to think about more ways he could try to make things better at home.

It's Your Turn

Think about a time when you were arguing and no one was really listening to the other person. Pretend that it is happening again. This time, imagine taking a time-out to handle things better.

- What words could you use before you leave the room?

- Where could you go to be by yourself?

- What solution could you suggest when you talk to the person later?

- What words could you use to suggest your plan? (Remember respect, I-talk, and sandwiches!)

SET UP A POINT SHEET TOGETHER

Want a good way to remind adults at home to pay attention to the good things you do? And to remind yourself to do them? Try using a point sheet. You may already use a point sheet at school. There, point sheets have the goals for how you should behave in class. Here, you can have a point sheet with goals for good ways to act at home.

You and your parent or guardian could set two or three goals for you to work on at home. Write them down on a form to use for a week. You can copy the "Score Points at Home" form on page 125. Each week, you can use a new copy of the form. Every day, look at the goals together. Decide how many points, 0–3, you earned for each goal for the day. (3 means you remembered something every time and did a really good job.) Agree on what the reward will be. Also agree on a number of points that will earn it.

At the end of the week, add up your points. If you earned your reward, enjoy it! Make a new point sheet with some different goals for the next week.

SCORE POINTS AT HOME

Scoring Key
0 Forgot goal or made bad choice   2 Did my goal behavior pretty often
1 Did my goal behavior a little bit   3 Met my goal!

MY GOALS FOR THIS WEEK

Goal 1: Respect family

SUN	MON	TUES	WED	THURS	FRI	SAT
2	3	2	3	3	2	2

Goal 2: Remove dishes from room

SUN	MON	TUES	WED	THURS	FRI	SAT
2	3	3	3	2	3	3

Goal 3: Do chores without reminder

SUN	MON	TUES	WED	THURS	FRI	SAT
2	1	1	2	3	3	2

MY REWARD

Reward: Trip to Burger Bob's

If you didn't quite earn your reward, try again for another week. Keep trying to improve a little bit at a time.

Here's one other idea: You could look with a family grown-up at the "Five 'Tricks' to Help You Track Your Progress" (starting on page 76). They are ideas for school, but you could use some of the same ways at home. With the adult, figure out some ways to track your progress at home. Work together to make things better.

Remember . . .

Sometimes the folks at home forget (or don't know) about how hard you are working to change your behavior. Be sure to tell family adults about smart choices you have made. Use the nice ways you have learned to remind them that you are trying to improve. Keep using the ideas in this chapter. If you do, little by little things at home are likely to get better.

Don't expect things to change right away. And don't expect home to be perfect. (Remember, you're not perfect. And your family isn't, either.) No matter what, you can feel good that you're showing respect and making better decisions. Give yourself a BIG pat on the back for that!

And then . . . **keep reading.** The next chapter has more ideas for making home a happier place to be.

SCORE POINTS AT HOME

Scoring Key

0 Forgot goal or made bad choice   **2** Did my goal behavior pretty often
1 Did my goal behavior a little bit   **3** Met my goal!

MY GOALS FOR THIS WEEK

Goal 1: _____

SUN	MON	TUES	WED	THURS	FRI	SAT

Goal 2: _____

SUN	MON	TUES	WED	THURS	FRI	SAT

Goal 3: _____

SUN	MON	TUES	WED	THURS	FRI	SAT

MY REWARD

Reward: _____

Points needed for reward: _____

Chapter 11

MORE IDEAS FOR FEELING GOOD AT HOME

"I like being at home. I can relax and just be myself. I can do what I want. I don't have to worry about a teacher watching me all the time." —Lena, 12

When you're home, you want to be relaxed and comfortable. You want to take a break from the hard work in school. In other words, you want to feel "at home." It's hard to do this if you are having trouble getting along with people in your family. In Chapter 10, you read about ways to talk and listen to family adults. You found ideas for asking them to help you in positive ways. This chapter has some other "tricks" you can do to make things better at home. These are ideas that will help you:

- Show grown-ups at home the good choices you are making.

- Solve problems with the adults and kids in your family.

- Treat people the way you want them to treat you.

- Take care of yourself so you feel healthy and strong.

All of these ways can help **YOU** make home a happier place to be.

TELL FAMILY ADULTS ABOUT YOUR GOOD CHOICES

Sometimes people forget to notice the good things that others do. They need to be reminded. That can be true with adults at home. Sometimes they only seem to notice bad choices, not smart ones. It's important to make fewer wrong choices. It's also important to help people at home notice the good things that you do.

Remember, when you read in this chapter about *family adults, parents,* or *adults at home,* think about the grown-up or grown-ups **YOU** live with.

Tell your parents when you do good things and make smart choices. If they don't show that they are happy, ask them what they think about your good choice. If you still don't hear what you want, give yourself credit just the same. You did well and you know it. That's the **most important** thing.

BE SURE YOUR TEACHERS SHARE GOOD NEWS

Parents and guardians of kids with BD often hear a lot more bad news than good news. Your parents have probably been asked to come to school to talk about when you made a poor choice. It is hard for them to hear this kind of news. They want you to do well. They need to hear more good things about you. Here are some ways to make sure this happens:

- Ask your teachers to tell your parent or guardian when you are doing better at making good choices. Ask your classroom teacher and your special teacher, too. Ask them to make a phone call home or send notes with you when you've made lots of good decisions during the day.

- Ask grown-ups from home to ask your teachers for **good news.** They can explain that they want to help with problems, but want to hear about **Progress,** too. They can ask to talk about things that you have been doing better than before. That will remind teachers to say good things about you. Parents need to hear those good things. You can also ask your parents to tell your teacher about **smart choices** you have made at home. Then your teacher will hear more good things about you, too.

- Remind your parents to ask about the **FBA (functional behavior assessment).** This is something all schools use with BD kids. They use it to figure out why kids sometimes make wrong choices and mis-behave. The school does an FBA for each  student who has BD. People at your school did this to see why you were making bad choices. After the school figured this out, they wrote a **BIP (behavior intervention plan).** It told how they were going to help you find better ways to behave. Your parents or guardians need to know what's in the FBA and BIP. That way, they'll know why you were making poor choices and what the school is supposed to do to help. Then they can think of ways to help you make better choices at home, too.

MAKE A PLAN TO SOLVE PROBLEMS

What things seem to cause problems again and again at home? Is it doing your homework? Remembering to do your chores? Getting in arguments with your brothers or sisters? Think about what thing causes problems over and over again. Make a plan to handle the prob-lem better. Then put the plan into action. Later, think about if your plan worked or not. If it worked, keep doing it. If it didn't work, think of a new plan and try it.

Renee has a problem doing her homework. She forgets to bring it home a lot. Other times, she brings it home but plays first, eats dinner, and then watches TV. By the time she thinks about doing the homework, she is feeling too tired. She knows that the teacher will be upset and give her a zero. She knows that her foster mom, Bev, will find out and be mad. She and Renee will probably have a big fight. Renee sees that getting her homework done can help her get along better at home.

What plan can Renee make to be sure that she gets it done each day? She needs to do two things:

1. **REMEMBER TO BRING THE HOMEWORK HOME.** To do this, Renee might put a big reminder note where she'll see it. She could put it in her folder or pocket. She could tape it right inside her desk or locker. Maybe she could hook the note to her key ring. Renee could also ask her teacher or a friend to remind her each day. She could ask the teacher and kids in her special class for ideas for ways to remember, too.

2. **PLAN AND TAKE TIME TO DO IT.** Having a set time to study every day can really help. Maybe Renee could do the work right after school. Maybe she'd rather play for an hour and then study. She might decide to do half the homework right after school, and half right after dinner. She could reward herself with a favorite TV show. The main thing she'll need to do is figure out a time and stick to it as much as she can.

When you think about it, Renee has lots of choices that could be good ones. Often there is more than one way to solve a problem. Sometimes, too, it takes more than one person to solve (and also to make) the problem:

TOM AND DINO

Tom and his brother Dino argued a lot about which TV show or video game should be on the screen. They'd grab the remote control, yell, and fight. Their dad would come in and turn off the TV. Then neither of them got to watch or play.

Tom decided to see if he and Dino could try a plan to solve this problem. He took the TV schedule from the newspaper. The two boys looked at what was going to be on TV later. They joked and tried to make deals about which shows to watch that night. After a while, they agreed on some shows and times. (They didn't always get their first choice. They each had to give in a little.) They circled the choices. They even remembered to leave the TV free for their dad at news time.

Coming up with a plan for computer games was harder. First they agreed that they would take 15-minute turns. But sometimes that was too short a time. The game was just getting going when it was time to stop. They had to find a better plan. They decided what to do if one of them couldn't stop at the 15-minute mark: The player could keep going for up to 10 minutes more. At that point, the person **MUST** stop the game. The other person would then get 10 minutes of extra time the next time he played. They made a chart to keep track of how many minutes they "owed" each other.

It's Your Turn

Think of something that keeps causing arguments at home. Follow these steps:

1. Think of all the ways you can that could help solve the problem. Write some of your ideas in your notebook. Be sure to think about some of the ideas and skills you practiced with Chapters 4–10.

2. Choose an idea to try. Make a plan for solving that problem.

3. Try it out and decide if it was a good plan or not.

If your plan doesn't work, go back to your other ideas. Try another plan. Keep working on solving the problem.

DO KIND THINGS FOR NO REASON

Want to hear more good things about yourself? And feel better about **YOU?** One good way is to do nice things for others—even things you don't *have* to do. When you've got some free time, think of something nice you can do for somebody in your family (or a neighbor). Anytime you're not really busy, look around for something nice to do for someone you like. It will feel great to do a good deed, even if the other person never finds out who did it. You can take pride in making someone happy.

Sometimes, your good deed won't make someone happy. Maybe the person you helped doesn't like part of what you did. What can you do? Ask for a "sandwich." (Read about sandwiches on pages 117–119.) Or ask (in a nice way): "Did you see that I was trying to help you?" Let's hope the person sees that you meant to be a big help. If not, say, "I'm sorry you didn't like what I did. I wanted to help." But don't give up on doing nice things for people. Most of the time, people are glad to be treated kindly.

SAY "THANKS"

Another way to make things better at home is to notice the nice things other people in your family do. Isn't it great when someone cooks the meal? Wasn't it helpful of your big brother to get that game you wanted off the top shelf? Wasn't it nice that your younger cousin drew a picture for you? Weren't you glad to be allowed another five minutes to play outside? Say **"Thanks."** Tell people who are nice to you what you like about what they did.

Here's another idea. Maybe you forgot to say thank you to someone who did something nice for you. When will you see the person again? Remind yourself to thank the person. You could even write it in a note.

TAKE CARE OF YOURSELF

What does taking care of **YOU** have to do with changing your behavior? Lots! When you are healthy and feel strong, many things become easier to do. It can be easier to think, make good choices, and solve problems. Really! Here are six important things you can do to take great care of yourself:

1. **EAT RIGHT.** Candy, snacks, soda and other "junk food" can taste pretty good, but did you know that they make it harder to think? Healthy food actually helps your brain. It helps your emotions. It helps you think clearly. Make a promise to yourself to eat more of the healthy stuff. Ask if you can have vitamins, too. Take them every day. Start skipping junk food more often. (Or eat less of it when you do have it.) **Your brain will thank you** by helping you make better decisions.

2. **TAKE YOUR MEDICINES.** Sometimes kids with BD have medications to help even out the chemicals in their brain. When the chemicals are working right, kids find it easier to slow down or think more clearly. If you have medicines to help you with your BD, be sure to take them. Follow the exact directions from the doctor. Taking your "meds" is important for making better choices.

3. **KEEP YOUR APPOINTMENTS.** Many kids with BD have regular appointments with people who work to help them. These people might be counselors, social workers, childcare workers, doctors, or others. They are adults who have had special training so they can help kids. It's important to show up for appointments. Let these good people help you solve problems and make good decisions.

4. **FIND A HOBBY TO DO AT HOME.** A hobby is a great way to get your mind off of teachers and parents for a while. Start a collection. You could collect stamps, bottle caps, pennies with different dates, rocks—anything that's interesting to you. Or think of something you would like to learn about or do. Choose something that makes you happy and is a good choice. Would you like to know

more about how car engines work? If so, become an expert! Read about cars. Search the Web for information. Watch car races on TV. Build model cars. See if you can go to an auto show.

Maybe you could earn some money to spend (or save) for your hobby. You could collect soda cans and bottles to return to the store. You could put up signs telling others that you will cut grass, run errands, or clean windows. You could shovel snow in the winter or water plants in the summer. But before you decide on a job, be sure to talk it over with grown-ups at home. They will tell you if the job is a safe one for you.

5. **FIND A PLACE TO RELAX.** Everyone needs some quiet time alone once in a while. Maybe you already have a spot at home where you go to daydream, read, or just be still. If not, think about where you can go. You could lie on your bed. You could rest in a corner or chair in the living room or bedroom. Maybe you'll sit in the closet for a while. Or find a tree outdoors to sit down beside. Find a spot where you feel comfortable and at ease. (It might be the time-out place you planned in Chapter 10.) When you need a quiet break, go to your place. Take a little time to breathe deeply and relax.

6. **KEEP WORKING ON YOUR SELF-ESTEEM.** It's important to remember all the **good things** about yourself. Be proud of the things you do well and the smart choices you make. Notice the things you are doing better now than before. Keep doing your pride and progress exercises and the "mirror talking" that you read about in Chapter 4 (pages 39–40). Doing these things will remind you of your good qualities and all the progress you are making.

Remember . . .

You can't control everything that goes on at home (or school), but you can make a **BIG** difference. Your choices can make things better or worse. They can make it easier or harder to get along with other people. So work hard on making good choices and getting along at home. If you do, home will feel like a better place to be. Not only that, but it will be easier to make better choices at school. When you try your best at both home *and* school, you'll beat BD even quicker. **You've got power! Use it well.**

Chapter 12

SEVEN WINNING WAYS TO WORK TOWARD POSITIVE CHANGE

"You know what BD means? Bad Decisions! I used to have a nasty attitude about everything. I finally listened to what my grandpa always said to me: 'If you're gonna have an attitude, at least make it a good one.' Things are better for everyone now that I'm in charge of my behavior." —Anton, 11

There isn't much about the BD label that kids like. But there is one good point: It lets you know that it is time to make changes in your life. In this book, you've read many quotes about making changes (like the one above). All of the quotes are from kids with BD. All of the kids who said these things know how tough it is to make good choices and improve behavior. Did you notice how many kids felt good about the choices they have made?

- It feels great to know you can keep making progress.

- It feels great to look forward to middle school or high school knowing that you can join activities, make friends, and learn new things.

- It feels great to take charge and make your own life better.

Some kids with BD don't want to try so hard. They like to think that their problems will be over when they grow up and leave school. They think that when adults aren't telling them what to do, everything will be okay. But that's not true. In fact, these kids are very wrong.

Adults have lots of responsibilities. For example, they have to hold a job. They have to show up at work almost every day. (More days than school!) They always have to be on time. They have to follow their boss's directions and do their jobs well. And they have to get along with the other workers. Gee, it sounds a lot like school, doesn't it? Yep, school prepares you for your future in many ways.

That's why it's so important to learn to make smart choices now, not later. What happens when kids with BD leave school without learning to make better choices? They face lots of problems. They are more likely to get in big trouble and end up in jail. They usually make less money than other people. They have problems getting along with girlfriends, boyfriends, husbands, wives, kids, bosses, people they work with, and friends. These are facts from research studies that have been done.

Your future starts now! How well you do in the future depends on the choices you make today. In the other chapters in this book, you learned ways to make smarter choices. This chapter is about getting a positive attitude. It gives ideas to help you get and keep a "mindset" that will make you a success.

1. REMEMBER THE GOLDEN RULE

There's an old saying that is heard all over the world:

> *"Do unto others as you would have them do unto you."*

This is known as the **golden rule.** It means that we should treat others the way that we would like to be treated. You can't expect to *get* respect unless you *give* it, too.

Here's another old saying: "What goes around comes around." Can you figure out what that means? Think of it this way: What you send out to others is what usually comes back to you. If you shout at others, do they usually smile and say something nice in return? Well, they might (if they remember the golden rule). But more often they probably shout back. If you treat others badly, will you get the respect you want? Most likely not.

Prove your **inner strength** by refusing to treat others in a bad way. Show respect to other people even if they forget *their* manners. You can still stick up for yourself in that firm-but-kind (assertive) way you learned about in Chapter 6. Remind yourself to act the way you want others to act toward you. Keep your behavior "golden."

2. TAKE RESPONSIBILITY FOR YOUR ACTIONS

Everyone makes bad choices now and then. The challenge for kids with BD is to keep working on making fewer.

BEFORE YOU ACT, ask yourself: "Will my action make things better?" **Better** means that everyone feels respected and listened to. Your friends stay your friends. You keep out of trouble, look mature, and can be proud of your behavior.

WHEN YOU DO CHOOSE A WRONG BEHAVIOR, it's important to "own up" to it. This means you admit to making a bad choice. It means you know that you have control over your behavior. And it means that you're able and willing to change it. You take responsibility for what you do!

Sometimes people say, "He made me do it" or "She made me angry." Those are excuses. Someone who blames others gives control to others. When that happens, the person will probably keep making the same bad choices in the future. So don't blame others for bad choices you make. Only **YOU** control your behavior. You decide how to act.

YOU'LL STILL MAKE SOME MISTAKES, even when you are good at making choices. We all make mistakes. What then? Admit it. Try to make things better. Avoid the mistake in the future.

These are things that others respect. If you mess up, apologize. Say, "I goofed. I'm sorry." Say you didn't really mean it, or that you wish you'd done something else. Later, think of why it was wrong and what you should have done instead. Then practice the right way to do it so that you'll remember next time.

What if you make a mistake, really didn't mean to do it, apologize, and still get yelled at? You could have this ready reply ready: "I admitted that I was wrong and said it won't happen again. I mean that." (Did you notice the I-talk?) Of course, now you'll really have to be sure that you don't do it again. (Or stop yourself quickly if you start to make that bad choice again.) Then people will see that you are truly changing your behavior.

3. DON'T USE BD AS AN EXCUSE

Some kids with BD use their label as an excuse for making poor choices. They say things like:

"I'm sorry, but you gotta understand. I can't help myself . . . I have BD."

Yes, changing is difficult. But it will happen faster if you take responsibility for your choices (good ones *and* bad ones). You can get better at making smart choices. Change excuses like "I can't help it" to words like:

"It's up to me to make smart choices and work hard. That way I can get rid of the BD label."

On pages 146–147 is a form you can copy called "Taking Responsibility for Choices." Use the form to help you figure out how to own up to a wrong choice you have made, fix things if possible, and do better in the future.

It's Your Turn

- Think of a time when you did something wrong, but said you didn't do it (or blamed someone else). Pretend that you are back in that situation. Act it out with a teacher or a friend. This time, take responsibility. **What will you say?** You can give a short excuse, but be sure that you say that *you* were wrong and won't do it again.

- After that, think of what you would do in that situation if it happened again today.

Idea!

Apologize to someone you have caused a problem with. Practice your apology ahead of time. Before you go, think of something friendly you could do to make things better. Maybe you can give the person something you made, or do something nice for her or him.

4. BE PATIENT AND PERSISTENT

You are used to doing things in certain ways. Change will take time. Be patient with yourself. And be **persistent**—keep trying. It will also take time for others to believe that you are really serious about changing your ways. You'll have to keep making good choices for a long time before people say, "Gee, this kid has changed." Then *they'll* change the way they act toward you. In the meantime, be patient with these people, too. You will keep working on better behavior. They will start to notice.

5. LEARN FROM EXPERIENCE

Everything that happens to you can teach you something. Every mistake has a lesson in it, a lesson about life and choices. Take a moment when you are feeling calm after upsetting situations. Ask yourself what you can learn from these experiences. Think about what better choices you will make next time. Your **self-talk** can go something like this:

"I made a mistake. Mistakes happen. What can I learn from this experience so that I don't make the same mistake again? Maybe I ought to practice the right thing right now. Or I can practice it in my head."

6. THINK ABOUT YOUR FUTURE

You know that right now you are preparing for your future. School prepares you for being an adult. Activities outside of school prepare you, too. You get an education about things like math, reading, and writing. (These are things you need to know to be good at just about any job.) You learn how things work. You learn to follow directions so that work is done right and everyone stays safe. You learn to team up with other people, solve problems together, and get things done. Right now, you may even be learning about something that could lead to a future job that you will like to do. That's great!

Maybe you're nine, or eleven, or thirteen years old. These are all good ages for thinking about your adult career. Have you thought about what jobs you might want to do someday? Veterinarian? Restaurant owner? Lifeguard? Counselor? Bus driver? Teacher? Music store manager? Lawyer? Computer Technician?

Don't know? Think about the kinds of things do you like to do. For example:

- Maybe you enjoy drawing. Cartoonists, architects who plan buildings, graphic artists who design things like logos and charts, and clothing designers are all people who draw in their work.

- Maybe you enjoy a sport. It's not just those star players who have careers in sports. So do coaches, team managers, game officials, and reporters.

- Maybe you really like animals. Some animal lovers work in zoos and at animal shelters. Others become marine biologists, dog or horse trainers, or professional pet-sitters.

Start to notice and learn about jobs. Ask different people you meet about their work. See if you could spend a few hours with someone on the job. Or volunteer at workplaces that interest you. (Ask a teacher or family adult to help you figure out how to do this.) Find out how different workers chose their jobs. See who likes (and doesn't like) what jobs. Ask why people do or don't like what they do.

It's Your Turn

In your notebook, start a list of jobs that sound interesting to you. Then choose a job (for example, police officer or piano teacher). Or choose a job area (for example, crime prevention or music). Do some research about the job or job area. Use books and magazines, the Internet, or videos about careers. Also talk to real workers who have those jobs. Learn things like this:

• What do the workers do every day on the job?

• What do they need to be able to do so that they can do their job well?

• What did they need to learn in school to do that job well? Read? Write? Do math? Be polite? Work well with others?

Maybe you know exactly what you want to do as an adult. Maybe you have no idea yet. (If this last is true for you, don't worry. You will figure this out in time.) Either way, working to change your behavior is important for that future. The main reason people get fired from jobs isn't because they can't do the work. Most people can be trained to do the job. The main reason is because they don't behave in a safe way, follow directions, and get along well with others at work. So, the work you're doing now to make smart choices is getting you ready for any job you'll do later in life.

7. Know that you CAN beat BD

The road out of BD is a long and hard one. It's filled with bumps, detours, and roadblocks that may distract you from your goal. You have to work hard as you travel along the way. You have to keep trying and never give up. **YOU CAN DO THIS!** If you believe in yourself and how you *can* change, you will complete your journey. The rewards make it worth the trip! Keep your eye on your goals. Notice your progress. If you stumble, pick yourself up, dust yourself off, and move forward again. Each step brings you closer to a bright future.

Read what some kids with BD said about the progress they have made:

"I'm calming down quicker when I get angry. I get back to activities sooner."

"I've learned to control my temper better. I'm in charge of what I do now. I listen more to what people try to tell me."

"My teacher is proud of how I've changed my behavior."

"I'm working on showing more self-control. I'm trying to do better at following directions and not talking when the teacher is teaching."

"I've learned to read and to behave better."

"I'm proud of my behavior grades that keep getting better because I'm meeting my goals."

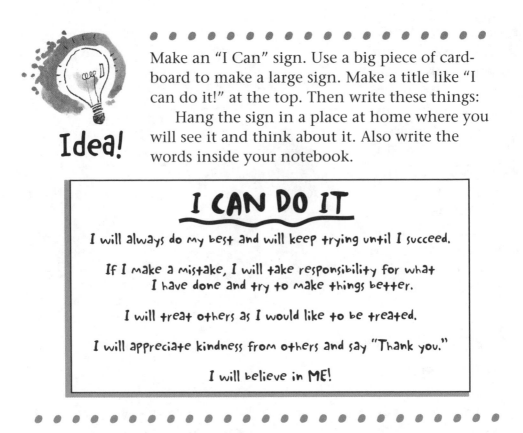

Idea!

Make an "I Can" sign. Use a big piece of cardboard to make a large sign. Make a title like "I can do it!" at the top. Then write these things:

Hang the sign in a place at home where you will see it and think about it. Also write the words inside your notebook.

I CAN DO IT

I will always do my best and will keep trying until I succeed.

If I make a mistake, I will take responsibility for what I have done and try to make things better.

I will treat others as I would like to be treated.

I will appreciate kindness from others and say "Thank you."

I will believe in ME!

A Challenge for You

Here are your last questions to think about:

1. What makes a smart choice different from a bad choice?

2. How are the results of smart choices different from the results of bad ones?

In your notebook, list some of the things that tell you when you've made a good (smart) choice. (When you're done, you can compare what you wrote with some of the possible answers listed on page 157.)

Remember . . .

You've read about many ideas in this book. It contains lots of skills, tips, and information you need to succeed in making better choices. The challenge for you now is to choose some ideas that you read and try them. Then come back and try a few more. Keep trying out new ways to make better choices. You'll find that you're learning more, making new and better friends, and getting along better with your teachers and family. You really, truly will.

Thanks for reading this book. You've learned a lot. You've probably already started to make some changes. Keep making those important changes. And keep believing in yourself!

While I was writing this book, a student told me: "My teachers keep telling me I can do anything if I work hard enough. I like that they believe in me." **I believe in YOU.** I know that if you're reading this book, it means you are serious about making your life better. I would like to hear from you about how you're making smarter choices. Write to me at help4kids@freespirit.com.

—DR. MAC

TAKING RESPONSIBILITY FOR CHOICES

Copy and use this form when you have made a wrong choice at school, at home, or somewhere else.

FIRST, ask yourself these questions:

1. What wrong choice did I make? _____

_____

_____

_____

2. What happens when this rule is broken? _____

_____

_____

_____

3. Would I like to be treated the way I treated
the person or people involved? Explain: _____

_____

_____

_____

MORE ➤

4. What was I trying to do or get when I chose the wrong behavior? Did my choice get me what I wanted? _____

_____

_____

_____

5. How could I get what I wanted in a way that wouldn't hurt anyone or get me in trouble? _____

_____

_____

_____

SECOND, decide what to do now to make things better. Check one or two choices. Then DO them!

☐ Apologize to _____

☐ Write a note to _____

☐ Do something nice for _____

☐ Make an appointment to talk with _____

☐ Do nothing right now, but remember to make the right choice from now on.

☐ Practice the right choice right now.

☐ Something else: _____

_____

GLOSSARY

This part of the book explains the words that were shown in **bold** type in each chapter.

ADD (attention deficit disorder): This label is given to kids who have lots of trouble paying attention. Doctors sometimes prescribe medicine for kids with ADD. The medicine helps the kids concentrate better.

ADHD (attention deficit hyperactivity disorder): This label is given to kids who have lots of trouble sitting still and paying attention. Doctors sometimes prescribe medicine for kids with ADHD. The medicine helps the kids slow down and concentrate better.

anger management: Being able to control angry feelings is important. Counselors and teachers sometimes meet with groups of students who need to learn and practice ways to handle anger better. Counselors or psychologists may sometimes work on this with students individually, too. There are books with lessons and activities that adults can use to teach kids how to manage their anger better. Page 162 tells where adults can find a list of some of these books.

assertive: People who are assertive speak up, in a strong but polite way. You are assertive if you say what's important to you *and* treat the other person with respect.

authority figure: This is an adult who is in charge of keeping kids safe and helping them make good choices. Teachers, principals, counselors, parents, guardians, and police officers are examples of authority figures.

BD (behavior disorder): This is one of the labels given to kids whose behavior keeps teachers from teaching and keeps other kids and themselves from learning. Kids who need to learn to follow school rules or the directions of teachers might have this label. Different schools use different labels. So some kids with similar problems might be labeled ED, EBD, SED, or something else.

behavior modification (behavior mod): This is a scientific way of changing the behavior of people. When teachers or parents reward you for good behavior, they're using behavior mod. They're helping you change (modify) your behavior.

BIP (behavior intervention plan): This is a part of the IEP (individualized education program) that tells teachers the positive things they should do to help students with BD make better choices.

challenge: A challenge is something hard to do, but worth working at. When you are challenged, it means that you have to work hard to accomplish something.

choice challenged (CC): Kids who are "choice challenged" need to work hard to make better decisions (choices) about how to behave.

conflict resolution: When kids are angry with each other, it's important for them to figure out how to solve their problem without getting violent. Counselors and teachers sometimes meet with groups of students who need to learn and practice ways to solve problems together. There are books with lessons and activities that adults can use to teach kids how to resolve conflicts in helpful ways. Page 162 tells where adults can find a list of some of these books.

consultant teacher: This is a teacher who is trained to help kids with BD. Consultant teachers travel from school to school. They work with kids and also help teachers learn better ways to work with students who have BD.

counseling: This is a kind of help from a specially trained adult called a *counselor*. The counselor is trained to help kids understand their problems better. He or she also helps kids figure out what to do about those problems.

criticize: To criticize means to tell someone that she or he isn't doing something right. When a person judges what another person does in this way, it's called *criticism*.

depression: Depression means feeling really sad most of the time. A person who is *depressed* feels sad, down, or bummed out most or all of the time. (Being sad sometimes or for a few days is usually not the same as being depressed.)

EBD (emotional or behavioral disorder): This is one of the labels given to kids whose behavior keeps teachers from teaching and keeps other kids and themselves from learning. Kids who need to learn to follow school rules or the directions of teachers might have this label. Different schools use different labels. So some kids with similar problems might be labeled BD, ED, SED, or something else.

ED (emotional disturbance): This is one of the labels given to kids whose behavior keeps teachers from teaching and keeps other kids and themselves from learning. Kids who need to learn to follow school rules or the directions of teachers might have this label. Different schools use different labels. So some kids with similar problems might be labeled BD, EBD, SED, or something else.

FBA (functional behavior assessment): This is a part of the IEP (individualized education program) that tells the school why a student sometimes makes wrong choices and misbehaves. The FBA helps adults at school decide what ways to help the student improve his or her behavior. They use the FBA to make a BIP (behavior intervention plan).

frustrated: When you're frustrated, you feel upset. You might get frustrated when people or things get in the way of something you want to do. *Frustration* happens when someone or something keeps you from reaching a goal that you want to achieve. If you're frustrated, you probably feel angry. You feel like you just can't do what you want or need to do. Some people feel like they're going to burst.

IDEA (Individuals with Disabilities Education Act): IDEA is the "special ed law" in the United States. It says that schools must do the right things for students with disabilities. With this law, the word "disabilities" includes kids with behavior disorders. IDEA says that schools must give these students the help they need to make better choices in school.

IEP (individualized education program): All students who are part of IDEA (Individuals with Disabilities Education Act) have their own IEP in their school records. This includes kids labeled with a behavior disorder. The IEP is a plan that tells how a student is doing in school, what she or he will learn during the school year, and how teachers will help the student reach goals. For kids with BD, the IEP also has a part called the BIP (behavior intervention plan). The BIP tells what behaviors they need to work on. The BIP also tells teachers positive ways to teach the new behaviors.

IEP team: This is a group of adults that decides if a student needs special education to learn and behave better in school.

inappropriate: When a behavior is wrong, it is called inappropriate. It is the wrong behavior in a certain time or place. Inappropriate behavior happens when someone makes a bad choice. Good choices result in *appropriate* behavior.

inclusion: Inclusion means having students with all kinds of special education needs in the regular classroom. Different kids are included for different amounts of time and different subjects. As students improve in making good choices, they are included in the regular classroom for more of the school day.

LD (learning difference, learning disability): This is a label given to kids who don't always learn as easily or in the same way as most of the other students. Kids with LD need special help with some kinds of learning.

mentor: A mentor knows how to make good choices. It's a person who teaches others how to make good choices, too.

negative: This means not-so-nice, or bad. "No" is a negative word. Wrong behavior is negative behavior. The opposite of negative is *positive*, which means good, or nice.

paraprofessional: This is a person who is trained to help teachers do their jobs. Different paraprofessionals have different jobs and duties. Sometimes they work with kids who have BD in the regular or special classroom.

PBIS (positive behavioral interventions and supports): For kids with BD, there is a part of the individualized education program (IEP) called the behavior intervention plan (BIP). The BIP lists the positive ways that teachers are supposed to use to help BD students to make better choices and behave better. These ways are called PBIS (positive behavioral interventions and supports).

peer mediation: Some schools train kids to help other kids end their battles. This formal system where kids help other kids solve problems is called peer mediation. *Peers* are people from the same age group or place. At school, you and the other students are peers. A peer mediator is a student who is trained to help both sides listen to each other and find a way to end the argument.

persistent: Being persistent means continuing to work at something that is hard to do. When you keep trying and working, you *persist*.

positive: This means nice, or good. "Yes" is a positive word. Good behavior is positive behavior. The opposite of positive is *negative*, which means not-so-nice, or bad.

potential: Potential means the possibility for doing well. Your potential is what you can be and what you can do if you work hard to make good decisions.

psychologist: A psychologist is trained to study the mind and how it works. Psychologists know how to find out what's bothering kids. They ask questions about feelings and what is happening. They have kids do things that will help discover what the problem is. Then the psychologists (and others) help kids to solve the problems.

retarded: This is a label for people who learn very slowly and can't learn some things because of a problem in their brain.

revenge: Revenge means getting back at someone. Some kids want revenge when they get mad at someone. So they try to hurt the other person or make him or her feel bad, too. Revenge makes things worse between people, not better.

SED (seriously emotionally disturbed): This is one of the labels given to kids whose behavior keeps teachers from teaching and keeps other kids and themselves from learning. Kids who need to learn to follow school rules or the directions of teachers might have this label. Different schools use different labels. So some kids with similar problems might be labeled BD, ED, EBD, or something else.

self-contained classroom: This is a classroom where kids in special education go to school for all (or most) of the day. Sometimes a self-contained class is called a "special class." Students with BD might be in a self-contained classroom all, most, or some of the time. Often they go to a regular education classroom for one or two subjects. If they do well in those classes, they will get a chance to go into a regular classroom more of the time.

self-esteem: Self-esteem is how you feel about yourself. People who like themselves have *high self-esteem*. People who don't feel good about themselves have *low self-esteem*. Teachers and counselors have ways to help kids improve their self-esteem.

self-talk: The things you think and say silently to yourself are self-talk. When people think to themselves about ways to stay calm, keep out of trouble, and make good decisions, they are using *positive self-talk*. They are telling themselves smart ways to handle a difficult situation.

shaping: With shaping, you build a good behavior in steps. You set small goals to get you to a big behavior goal. Each time you meet a small goal, you set another small goal. Each small goal gets you closer to the bigger behavior goal. The small goals lead you to reaching the big goal that you want to accomplish.

shaping plan: This is a kind of plan you write down. You write your big goal and how you're doing with that goal now. Then you write the small goals you will work on in order to meet your big goal.

social skills: These are skills people need to get along with other people. Someone with good social skills gets along well with others. Kids with poor social skills have trouble making friends. They also have problems doing the right thing when they are talking or working with others. Some schools hold special classes or groups where students learn social skills. There are books with lessons and activities that adults can use to teach these skills. Page 162 tells where adults can find a list of some of these books.

special education (special ed): This is the term for the special classes and other kinds of help that schools give to students with special needs. The students have behavior problems, learning differences, or physical disabilities.

special needs: These are needs that cause kids to be in special education. Kids with BD have special needs. They need to learn to choose better behavior and actions so they can learn and get along in school.

stress: Stress is the pressure or tension you feel sometimes in your mind or body. When you feel tense or upset, you are under stress.

support group: This is a group that meets with a counselor or another specially trained adult to talk about a problem or challenge. Some kids with BD meet in a support group with a counselor. They talk about their behavior problems and how they're doing when it comes to making better choices.

survive: This means to keep going and become stronger when things are difficult. *Survival* skills (like the ones you learn in this book) can help you keep going and succeed. They can help you get along with teachers, other kids, and adults at home even though you are challenged with BD.

SOLUTIONS TO SOME OF THE CHALLENGES AND QUESTIONS

Page 56

Sam's Smart Choices

2. Sam's words tell the boys that he knows about insulting mothers. He also shows that he is too mature (grown up) and cool to get involved in the "game."

4. Sam thinks his mom is great. He realizes that this is what's important. His self-talk helps him to not get involved defending his mom. He doesn't get trapped in a war of words. He remembers to stop and think before choosing what to say.

5. Sam has hurt feelings, but he stops, thinks, and chooses. He controls himself. That is a very mature response. He sees that if he falls into the boys' trap, the insults will continue or get worse.

7. Sam chooses a good way to handle his feelings. He shares his problem with a friend to feel better. Someday he'll listen when his friend has a problem.

8. Sam defends his mom and then leaves. He doesn't want to show the behavior that makes trouble for him. His ready reply lets him stand up for his mom without getting in a fight.

Sam's Poor Choices

1. Sam does what the boys want him to do: He gets into a war of words. It's a war he probably can't win. What happens? He acts like the kids who are making him feel bad. He says things that he hates to hear. That doesn't make sense.

3. Sam shows the others that the insults upset him. Now the boys will say those insults again. Sam will probably get sent to the principal, too. He'll probably be punished for hitting others.

What About Choice 6?

It's hard to know how this choice will work. It could be a strong, friendly response. It could also seem bossy. It depends on how Sam says the words and how he looks when he speaks. *How* you say and do things can be just as important as the words you use.

Page 68

1. B
2. C (choice 2 is an assertive response)
3. A

Page 70–71

These answers show one way to change the you-talk to I-talk. There are lots of ways to do this, so your answers might be different. That's okay. Just be sure NOT to use the word "you" to tell people they are wrong.

Challenge 1

"Mrs. Travis, I've tried again. I guess I just forgot what to do. Could I please have help on one problem so I can remember what to do on the rest of them?"

Challenge 2

When Maggie sees that her watch is gone, she can say: "My watch is missing. Did anyone borrow it?"

If no one says anything, Maggie can go quietly to the teacher and say: "Mr. Tess, my watch was on my desk and now it's gone. Could you please help me find out if someone took it?"

Challenge 3

"Sasha, weren't we supposed to start by writing about the answers that are wrong? And tell why they're wrong? I've got the dates and places we needed for the beginning of the paper. How can we get them in there?"

Challenge 4

Ira can speak for the other kids if they agree. He can talk to Mr. C. as he enters class instead of at science time: "Hey, Mr. C. We talked about the way we acted earlier today, and we were wrong. But we were really looking forward to the trip. Is there anything we can do to earn the trip back?"

Page 96

Challenge 1
In this sandwich, the request (the middle of the sandwich) is highlighted in *italics:*

"Miss Lange, I agree with you that it is important to do my schoolwork. But I think a zero grade is unfair. I couldn't do the paper last night because I left my notebook at Paula's. *Could I please turn it in after lunch?* That's when I'll see her so I can get it back. I really enjoyed doing the report on Ben Franklin, and learned a lot. I think you'll like the paper if you take it late."

Challenge 2
There are lots of ways Aron could make his request sandwich. Yours will probably be different from the one here. That's okay. Just be sure to start and end with something nice. Remember to make your request firm and friendly. In this sandwich, the request (the middle of the sandwich) is highlighted in *italics:*

"Mr. Hunter, I don't want to miss the explanation. I really like doing your projects, and I don't want to miss the instructions. *Could I please have another chance and stay here now?* Next time I'll know I'm supposed to be in my seat, not just in the room. I'm glad you explained that to me."

Page 101

- Nina remembered her goal.
- She used "Stop, Think, Choose, and Think Again."
- She showed respect.
- When she spoke, she used assertive I-talk.
- She made a request sandwich.

Page 120

Challenge 1
1. Compliment sandwich
2. Complaint
3. Request sandwich

Challenge 2
Here is one possible compliment sandwich. The compliment (the middle of the sandwich) is highlighted in *italics:*

"I don't want anyone doing this puzzle without asking me. Please ask first *like you do before coming in my side of the room. It's been great since you started doing that.* So please ask me before you work on my puzzle."

Here is one possible request sandwich. The request (the middle of the sandwich) is highlighted in *italics*:

"It's nice that you want to help with the puzzle. I want to keep the part that's already done, though. Otherwise the pieces get messed up. *I need you to ask me if you want to do this puzzle.* You do a good job of asking before you go in my part of the bedroom, so I know you can do a good job about the puzzle, too. Thanks."

Page 144

Here's Dr. Mac's list of things that tell you when you've made a smart choice:

- You stay out of trouble in school and get along better with teachers.
- You learn more in school because you're listening and paying attention.
- You hear people say nice things about you.
- You make more friends—the good kind.
- You become a better friend.
- You stay out of trouble with the police and other adults.
- You feel happier at home.
- You get along better with people in your family.
- You feel better about yourself.
- Your future looks brighter.

AND SOMEDAY, when you get really good at making smart choices . . .

- You won't be labeled BD anymore.

What other ones did you think of?

RESOURCES FOR YOU

Books

Look for these books at the library or bookstore. If a book isn't on the shelf, the librarian or store clerk can find or order a copy. You can also visit libraries and bookstores on the Internet.

Basic Social Skills for Youth: A Handbook from Boys Town (Boys Town, NE: Boys Town Press, 1992). This small book covers eight social skills that are really important for you to know. Find out why it's important to follow instructions, show respect, and notice the feelings of others.

The Best of "Brakes": An Activity Book for Kids with ADD edited by Patricia Quinn and Judith M. Stern (Washington, DC: Magination Press, 2000). Here is a book that teaches you about ADD and its challenges. You'll find games, puzzles, activities, and tips for coping with problems.

Cliques, Phonies, and Other Baloney by Trevor Romain (Minneapolis: Free Spirit Publishing, 1998). Being left out by a clique (a group of kids) can really hurt your feelings. This book tells why cliques exist, how they work, and how to cope. Learn ways to boost your confidence and make friends who really care about you. Trevor Romain also wrote a helpful and funny book about bullying. It's called *Bullies Are a Pain in the Brain.*

Dealing with Bullying by Marianne Johnstone (New York: Rosen Publishing, 1996). This book explains why bullies act the way they do and offers tips for dealing with them.

Don't Be a Menace on Sundays! by Adolph Moser (Kansas City, MO: Landmark Editions, 2002). Stay safe and out of trouble with this book. It's full of ideas for avoiding violence. You'll learn about violence on TV, in movies and video games, and in your own school and community. Also check out *Don't Feed the Monster on Tuesdays!* (a book on self-esteem), *Don't Rant and Rave on Wednesdays!* (controlling anger), and *Don't Tell a Whopper on Fridays!* (telling the truth).

Help! My Teacher Hates Me by Meg Schneider (New York: Workman Publishing, 1994). Find out how to get along better with teachers and other adults at school. Also learn ways to improve your grades and solve lots of school problems.

How Kids Make Friends: Secrets for Making Lots of Friends, No Matter How Shy You Are by Lonnie Michelle (Buffalo Grove, IL: Freedom Publishing, 1995). We all deserve friends we can trust. Here you'll find ideas for making friends, feeling confident, and thinking of things to talk about.

How to Handle Bullies, Teasers, and Other Meanies by Kate Cohen-Posey (Highland City, FL: Rainbow Books, 1995). This book is about teasing, name-calling, prejudice, anger, and conflict. It gives lots of positive ways to deal with difficult situations.

How to Take the GRRRR Out of Anger by Elizabeth Verdick and Marjorie Lisovskis (Minneapolis: Free Spirit Publishing, 2003). Everybody feels angry at times. The key is learning how to manage anger. This book uses humor and teaches tricks and skills that can help.

Kids' Random Acts of Kindness by the editors of Conari Press (Berkeley: Conari Press, 1994). Read real stories from kids who have done kind, helpful things. Learn how you can make a difference in your school and community, too.

Learning to Slow Down and Pay Attention: A Book for Kids About ADD by Kathleen Nadeau and Ellen Dixon (Washington, DC: Magination Press, 1997). This book can help you at school and at home. Find cartoons, games, and activities that teach you about ADD and ways to handle it.

School Power: Study Skill Strategies for Succeeding in School by Jeanne Shay Schumm (Minneapolis: Free Spirit Publishing, 2001). This book helps you to be your best in the classroom. Find hints and checklists for taking notes, writing papers, taking tests, and staying organized as you work on projects.

Sibling Rivalry: Brothers and Sisters at Odds by Elaine Landau (Brookfield, CT: Millbrook Press, 1994). "Sibling rivalry" means problems between kids in families. Read kids' own true stories about this challenge. Find advice for making good choices when conflicts occur.

Sometimes I Like to Fight, But I Don't Do It Much Anymore by Lawrence Shapiro (King of Prussia, PA: The Center for Applied Psychology, 1995). Read about Douglas, a boy whose fighting gets him into trouble at school and with his friends. He learns how to control his anger with the help of a counselor and a friendship group. Also look for *Sometimes I Drive My Mom Crazy, But I Know She's Crazy About Me.* It's a book by the same author for kids with ADHD.

Stick Up for Yourself! Every Kid's Guide to Personal Power and Positive Self-Esteem by Gershen Kaufman, Lev Raphael, and Pamela Espeland (Minneapolis: Free Spirit Publishing, 1999). This is a book with lots of great tips on how to be assertive. It can help you feel good about yourself and be firm and polite with others.

Stress Can Really Get on Your Nerves! by Trevor Romain and Elizabeth Verdick (Minneapolis: Free Spirit Publishing, 2000). Did you know that stress can make your stomach hurt or your head ache? Some stressed people have trouble paying attention and sitting still, too. This book can help you deal with stress and become stronger.

The Survival Guide for Kids with LD by Gary Fisher and Rhoda Cummings (Minneapolis: Free Spirit Publishing, 2002). Find out why some kids have problems learning in certain ways. You'll also discover many ideas for overcoming learning challenges.

Too Old for This, Too Young for That! Your Survival Guide for the Middle-School Years by Harriet S. Mosatche and Karen Unger (Minneapolis: Free Spirit Publishing, 2000). Middle school brings lots of changes. School gets harder. Home life and friendships sometimes do, too. This book offers tips just for middle-school kids. Find ways to set goals, make good choices, and take charge of your life.

What Do You Know About Manners? A Funny Quiz for Kids by Cynthia Mac-Gregor with Christine Zuchora-Walske (Minnetonka, MN: Meadowbrook Press, 2000). Is it ever okay to interrupt someone? When should you apologize to a parent, teacher, or classmate? Find the answers to these questions and many others in this fun book. People will be complimenting you on your good manners in no time!

What Do You Really Want? How to Set a Goal and Go for It! by Beverly K. Bachel (Minneapolis: Free Spirit Publishing, 2001). Setting goals can help you succeed in school, ease stress, and boost your self-esteem. This book is a step-by-step guide that makes setting goals easy and fun.

You and the Rules in Your Family by Lea MacAdam (New York: Rosen Publishing, 2001). This book explains why families need rules. It looks at why rules can lead to arguments or conflict. You'll find good ideas for talking about and dealing with rules. There's also advice for getting along with parents.

Web Sites

Kidscape *(www.kidscape.org.uk)*. This Web site offers a lot of great advice for dealing with bullies. Also find tips for making friends and getting along with difficult people.

KidsHealth *(www.kidshealth.org)*. This site offers lots of information on different issues facing kids today. You'll find ways to handle feelings, get along with others, deal with tough situations, and stay healthy and safe. Also learn where to turn for more help if you need it.

Organizations

These are all national organizations. You can visit their Web sites, write, or call for more information. (Phone numbers beginning with "800" and "888" are free to call. The others may cost money. Check with an adult before calling the numbers that are not free.) You can also look in the phone book for a club or group near you.

Big Brothers Big Sisters of America • 230 North 13th Street • Philadelphia, PA 19107 • 1-888-412-2447 • *www.bbbsa.org*
Sometimes having an adult friend can make all the difference as you try to improve your behavior. This organization arranges adult mentors for kids. On the Web site, click on "Enroll a Child or Youth" to find out how to contact a group near you.

Boys and Girls Clubs of America • 1230 West Peachtree Street NW • Atlanta, GA 30309 • (404) 487-5700 • *www.bgca.org*
Want to become friends with other kids and adults in your neighborhood? These clubs have all kinds of activities that are both fun and educational. If you're looking for a little support as try to be your best, this is a great resource for you.

Boy Scouts of America • P.O. Box 152079 • Irving, TX 75015 • (972) 580-2000 • *www.scouting.org*
Scouting is a great way to try new things, learn to make good decisions, and make friends. It's fun, too.

Girl Scouts of the USA • 420 Fifth Avenue • New York, NY 10018 • 1-800-478-7248 • *www.girlscouts.org*
In Girl Scouts, you can build skills for succeeding in school and at home while enjoying fun activities and events.

YMCA of the USA • 101 North Wacker Drive • Chicago, IL 60606 • 1-800-872-9622 • *www.ymca.net*
The "Y" has gyms and sports activities. It has fun learning activities and day camps, too. You can join a class, go swimming, or play sports. The YMCA is for boys and girls.

WHAT ABOUT RESOURCES FOR GROWN-UPS?

Teachers and parents want to help you learn to behave better and make good choices. There are lots of books and lessons that can help them understand the best ways to do this. I have made a list of these resources. Tell the adults in your life about this list. They can find it on the Internet at my Web site *(www.behavioradvisor.com)* and my publisher's Web site *(www.freespirit.com)*.

INDEX

Other Great Books from Free Spirit

You're Smarter Than You Think
A Kid's Guide to Multiple Intelligences
by Thomas Armstrong, Ph.D.
No longer are teachers asking about students, "How smart are they?" Instead, they're asking, "How are they smart?" In clear, simple language, this book introduces Howard Gardner's theory of multiple intelligences. Kids learn how they can use all eight intelligences in school, expand on them at home, and draw on them to plan for the future. Resources point the way to books, software, games, and organizations that can help kids develop the eight intelligences. Recommended for all kids, their parents, and educators. For ages 8–12.
$15.95; 192 pp.; softcover; illus.; 7" x 9"

Stick Up for Yourself!
Every Kid's Guide to Personal Power and Positive Self-Esteem
Revised and Updated
by Gershen Kaufman, Ph.D., Lev Raphael, Ph.D., and Pamela Espeland
Realistic, encouraging, how-to advice for kids on being assertive, buildin relationships, becoming responsible, growing a "feelings vocabulary," ma good choices, solving problems, setting goals, and more. For ages 8–12.
$11.95; 128 pp.; softcover; illus.; 6" x 9"

Teacher's Guide
For teachers, grades 3–7. *$19.95; 128 pp.; softcover; 8½" x 11"*

How to Do Homework Without Throwing Up
written and illustrated by Trevor Romain
This book features hilarious cartoons and witty insights that teach important truths about homework and positive, practical strategies for getting it done. For ages 8–13.
$8.95; 72 pp.; softcover; illus.; 5⅛" x 7"

Stress Can Really Get on Your NERVES!
by Trevor Romain and Elizabeth Verdick
More kids than ever feel worried, stressed out, and anxious ev day. This book is a helping hand for those kids. Reassuring wo silly jokes, and light-hearted cartoons let them know they're n the only worry-warts on the planet—and they can learn to ma their stress. For ages 8–13.
$9.95; 104 pp.; softcover; illus.; 5⅛" x 7"

To place an order or to request a free catalog of SELF-HELP FOR KIDS® and SELF-HELP FOR TEENS® materials, please write, call, email, or visit our Web site:

Free Spirit Publishing Inc.
217 Fifth Avenue North • Suite 200 • Minneapolis, MN 55401-1299
toll-free 800.735.7323 • local 612.338.2068 • fax 612.337.5050
help4kids@freespirit.com • www.freespirit.com

Praise for *Birdman:*

"A blood-curdlingly creepy debut thriller . . . [Hayder's] graphic imagination knows no bounds."   —*Publishers Weekly*

"A writer in touch with her dark side and a major new talent."
     —*The Guardian* (UK)

"[An] assured and excellent thriller . . . Caffery . . . is a likeable and credible hero, and Hayder tells the story in convincing but flesh-creeping detail—it is hard to believe that this is her first crime novel."   —*Sunday Times* (UK)

"[A] top-notch debut thriller, a deftly plotted assault on the nerves. . . . *Birdman* preys on the reader's expectations expertly. . . . Graphic, disturbing, splendidly readable."   —*Kirkus Reviews*

"With enormous confidence, and in just a few pages, she manages to create a character with the sort of rounded complexities that many writers take books to develop."   —*New Statesman* (UK)

"A terrific thriller. There are twists and turns in this case that should defy the most ardent armchair detective."
     —*Melbourne Herald Sun*

BIRDMAN

MO HAYDER

Grove Press
New York

First published in 1999 by Doubleday a division of Random House Inc.

Printed in the United States of America

ISBN: 978-0-8021-4612-0
e-Book ISBN: 978-0-8021-9449-7

Grove Press
an imprint of Grove/Atlantic, Inc.
841 Broadway
New York, NY 10003

Distributed by Publishers Group West

www.groveatlantic.com

12 13 14 15   10 9 8 7 6 5 4 3 2 1

Acknowledgments are due to everyone at AMIP Thornton Heath, especially DSupt D. Reeve and PC M. Little. Also Iain West of the Forensic Pathology Department, Guy's Hospital, Dr. Elizabeth Wilson and Doug Stowton of the Forensic Science Services, Zeno Geradts, and pathologist Ed Friedlander, University of Health, Missouri, all of whom were professional and supportive beyond the call of duty.

A special mention to DCI Steve Gwilliam for his patience and help.

For their friendship and their faith in me: Jimmy Brooks, Karen Catling, Rilke D., Linda Downing, Jon Fink, Jo Goldsworthy, Jane Gregory, Dave and Deborah Head, Patrick Janson-Smith, Sue and Michael Laydon, Doreen Norman, Lisanne Radice, Sam Serafy, and Simon Taylor. Thank you also to Caroline Shanks, who saved my life years ago, to Mairi Hitomi, who continues to do so, to my truly outstanding and wonderful family (the most educated and resourceful bunch of people I have ever encountered), and, most of all, to Keith Quinn.

Birdman

One

NORTH GREENWICH. Late May. Three hours before sunup and the river was deserted. Dark barges strained upstream on their moorings and a spring tide gently nosed small sloops free of the sludge they slept in. A mist lifted from the water, rolling inland, past unlit chandlers, over the deserted Millennium Dome and on across lonely wastelands, strange, lunar landscapes—until it settled, a quarter of a mile inland amongst the ghostly machinery of a half-derelict construction yard.

A sudden sweep of headlights—a police vehicle swung into the service route, blue lights flashing silently. It was joined moments later by a second and a third. Over the next twenty minutes more police converged on the yard—eight marked area cars, two plain Ford Sierras and the white transit van of the forensic camera team. A roadblock was placed at the head of the service route and local uniform were detailed to seal off riverside access. The first attending CID officer got onto Croydon exchange, asking for pager numbers for the Area Major Investigation Pool and, five miles away, Detective Inspector Jack Caffery, AMIP team B, was woken in his bed.

He lay blinking in the dark, collecting his thoughts, fighting the impulse to tilt back into sleep. Then, taking a deep breath, he made the effort—rolled out of bed and went into the bathroom, splashing water onto his face—*no more Glenmorangies in standby week, Jack, swear it now, swear it*—and dressed—not too hurried, better to arrive fully awake and composed—now the tie, something understated—*CID don't like us looking flashier than them.* The pager, and coffee, lots of instant coffee—with sugar but not milk, no milk—and above all, *don't eat, you just never know what you're going to have to look at*—drank two cups, found car keys in the pocket of his jeans and, bolted awake now on caffeine, a rollup between his teeth, drove through the deserted streets of Greenwich to the crime scene, where his superior, Detective Superintendent Steve Maddox, a small, prematurely gray man, immaculate as always in a stone-brown suit, waited for him outside the construction yard—pacing under a solitary streetlight, spinning car keys and chewing his lip.

He saw Jack's car pull up, crossed to him, put an elbow on the roof, leaned through the open window and said: "I hope you haven't just eaten."

Caffery dragged on the handbrake. He pulled cigarettes and tobacco from the dashboard. "Great. Just what I was hoping to hear."

"This one's well past its sell-by." He stepped back as Jack climbed out of the car. "Female, partly buried. Bang in the middle of the wasteland."

"Been in, have you?"

"No, no. Divisional CID briefed me. And, um—" He glanced over his shoulder to where the local CID officers stood in a huddle. When he turned back his voice was low. "There's been an autopsy on her. The old Y zipper."

Jack paused, his hand on the car door. "An *autopsy?*"

"Yup."

"Then it's probably gone walkabout from a path lab."

"I know—"

"A med student prank—"

"I know, I know." Maddox held hands up, stalling him. "It's not really our territory, but look—" He checked over his shoulder again and leaned in closer. "Look, they're pretty good with us usually, Greenwich CID. Let's humor them. It won't kill us to have a quick look. Okay?"

"Okay."

"Good. Now." He straightened up. "Now you. How about you? Reckon you're ready?"

"Shit, no." Caffery slammed the door, pulled his warrant card from his pocket and shrugged. "Of course I'm not ready. When would I ever be?"

They headed for the entrance, moving along the perimeter fence. The only light was the weak sodium yellow of the scattered streetlamps, the occasional white flash of the forensic camera crew floods sweeping across the wasteland. A mile beyond, dominating the northern skyline, the luminous Millennium Dome, its red aircraft lights blinking against the stars.

"She's been stuck in a bin-liner or something," Maddox said. "But it's so dark out there, the first attending couldn't be sure—his first suspicious circumstances and it's put the wind up him." He jerked his head toward a group of cars. "The Merc. See the Merc?"

"Yeah." Caffery didn't break step. A heavy-backed man in a camel overcoat hunched over in the front seat, speaking intently to a CID officer.

"The owner. A lot of tarting-up going around here, what with the Millennium thing. Says last week he took on a team to clear the place up. They probably disturbed the grave without knowing it, a lot of heavy machinery, and then at oh one hundred hours—"

He paused at the gate and they showed warrant cards, logged on with the PC and ducked under the crime scene tape.

"And then at oh one hundred hours this A.M., three lads were out here doing something dodgy with a can of Evostick and they stumbled on her. They're down at the station now. The CSC'll tell us more. She's been in."

Detective Sergeant Fiona Quinn, the crime scene coordinator, down from the Yard, waited for them in a floodlit clearing next to a Portakabin, ghostly in her white Tyvek overalls, solemnly pulling back the hood as they approached.

Maddox did the introductions.

"Jack, meet DS Quinn. Fiona—my new DI, Jack Caffery."

Caffery approached, hand extended. "Good to meet you."

"You too, sir." The CSC snapped off latex gloves and shook Caffery's hand. "Your first. Isn't it?"

"With AMIP, yes."

"Well, I wish I had a nicer one for you. Things are not very lovely in there. Not very lovely at all. Something's split the skull open—machinery, probably. She's on her back." She leaned back to demonstrate, her arms out, her mouth open. In the half-light Caffery could see the glint of amalgam fillings. "From waist down is buried under precast concrete, the side of a pavement or something."

"Been there long?"

"No, no. A rough guess"—she pulled the glove back on and handed Maddox a cotton face mask—"less than a week; but too long to be worth rushing a 'special.' I think you should wait until daylight to drag the pathologist out of bed. He'll give you more when he's got her in the pit and seen about insect activity. She's semi-interred, half wrapped in a dustbin liner: that'll've made a difference."

"The pathologist," Caffery said. "You sure we need a pathologist? CID think there's been an autopsy."

"That's right."

"And you still want us to see her?"

"Yes." Quinn's face didn't change. "Yes, I still think you need to see her. We're not talking about a professional autopsy."

Maddox and Caffery exchanged glances. A moment's silence and Jack nodded.

"Right. Right, then." He cleared his throat, took the gloves and face mask Quinn offered and quickly tucked his tie inside his shirt. "Come on, then. Let's have a look."

Even with the protective gloves, old CID habit made Caffery walk with hands in pockets. From time to time he lost sight of DS Quinn's flagged forensics torch, giving him moments of unease—this far into the yard it was dark: the camera crew had finished and were shut in their white van, copying the master tape. Now the only light source was the dim, chemical glow of the fluorescent tape the CSC had used to outline objects either side of the path, protecting them until AMIP's exhibits officer arrived to label and bag. They hovered in the mist like inquisitive ghosts, faint green outlines of bottles, crumpled cans, something shapeless which might have been a T-shirt or a towel. Conveyor belts and bridge cranes rose eighty feet and more into the night sky around them, gray and silent as an out-of-season roller coaster.

Quinn held a hand up to stop them.

"There," she told Caffery. "See her? Just lying on her back."

"Where?"

"See the oil drum?" She let the torch slide over it.

"Yes."

"And the two reinforcing rods to its right?"

"Yes."

"Follow that down."

Jesus.

"See it?"

"Yes." He steadied himself. "Okay. I see it."

That? That's a body? He'd thought it was a piece of expanding foam, the type fired from an aerosol, so distended and yellow and shiny it was. Then he saw hair and teeth and recognized an arm. And at last, by tilting his head on one side, he understood what he was looking at.

"Oh, for Christ's sake," Maddox said wearily. "Come on, then. Someone stick an Inci over her."

Two

BY THE TIME the sun had come up and burned off the river mist, everyone who had seen the body in the daylight knew that this was no medical school prank. The Home Office duty pathologist, Harsha Krishnamurthi, arrived and disappeared for an hour inside the white Incitent. A fingertip search team was corralled and instructed, and by noon the body was being freed from under the concrete.

Caffery found Maddox in the front seat of B team's Sierra.

"You all right?"

"There's nothing more we can do here, mate. We'll let Krishnamurthi take over from here."

"Go home, get some kip."

"You too."

"No. I'll stay."

"No, Jack. You too. If you want an exercise in insomnia you'll get it in the next few days. Trust me."

Caffery held his hand up. "Okay, okay. Whatever you say. Sir."

"Whatever I say."

"But I won't sleep."

"Fine. That's fine. Go home." He gestured to Caffery's battered old Jaguar. "Go home and *pretend* to sleep."

The image of the rich-yellow body under the tent kept pace with Caffery, even when he got home. In the new whitish light she seemed more real than she had last night. Her nails, bitten and painted sky blue, curled inward to the swollen palms.

He showered, shaved. His face in the mirror was tanned from a morning near the river; there were new sun crinkles around his eyes. He knew he wouldn't sleep.

The accelerated promotion of new blood in the Area Major Investigation Pool: younger, harder, fitter, he recognized the resentment coming from the lower ranks and understood the small, grim pleasure they took when the eight-week standby rota circled back to B team, coinciding neatly and nastily with his first case duty.

Seven days, twenty-four-hour standby, wakeful nights: and slam straight into the case, no time to catch a breath. He wouldn't be at his best.

And it was looking like a complex one.

It wasn't only the location and lack of witnesses that muddied it; in the morning light they had seen the black ulcerated marks of needle tracks.

And the offender had done something to the victim's breasts that Caffery didn't want to think about here in his white-tiled bathroom. He toweled his hair and shook his head to free the water in his ears. *Stop thinking about it, now. Stop letting it chase its tail round your head.* Maddox was right, he needed to rest.

He was in the kitchen, pouring a Glenmorangie, when the doorbell rang.

"It's me," Veronica called through the letter box. "I'd've phoned but I left my mobile at home."

He opened the door. She wore a cream linen suit and Armani sunglasses tucked in her hair. Shopping bags from

Chelsea boutiques clustered around her ankles. Her postbox-red Tigra convertible was parked in the evening sun beyond the garden gate and Caffery saw she was holding his front door key as if she had been on the point of letting herself in.

"Hello, sexy." She leaned in for a kiss.

He kissed her, tasting lipstick and menthol breath spray.

"Mmmmm!" She held his wrist and drew back, taking in the morning's suntan, the jeans, the bare feet. The bottle of whisky dangling between his fingers. "Relaxing, were you?"

"I was in the garden."

"Watching Penderecki?"

"You think I can't go in the garden without watching Penderecki?"

"Of course you can't." She started to laugh, then saw his face. "Oh, come on, Jack. I'm *joking*. Here." She picked up a Waitrose carrier bag and handed it to him. "I've been shopping—prawns, fresh dill, fresh coriander and, oh, the *best* muscatel. And this—" She held up a dark green box. "From Dad and me." She raised one long leg like an exotic bird and rested the box against her knee to open it. A brown leather jacket nestled in printed tissue. "One of the lines we import."

"I've got a leather jacket."

"Oh." Her smile faltered. "Oh. Okay. Not to worry." She closed the box. They were both silent for a moment. "I can take it back."

"No." Jack was instantly ashamed. "Don't."

"Honestly. I can swap it from stock."

"No, really. Here, give it to me."

This, he thought, kneeing the front door closed and following her into the house, was the Veronica pattern. She made a life-altering suggestion, he rebutted it, she pushed out her lower lip, bravely shrugged her shoulders, and immediately he became guilty, rolled onto his back and capitulated. Because of her past. *Simple but effective, Veronica.* In the six short months they'd known each other, his worn, comfortable home had been transformed into something unfamiliar, crammed with scented plants and labor-saving gadgets, his wardrobe bulging with clothes he would never wear: designer suits, hand-stitched jackets, silk ties, moleskin jeans, all courtesy of her father's Mortimer Street importing company.

Now, as Veronica made herself at home in his kitchen—the windows open, the Guzzini buzzing, peanut oil sizzling in bright green pans—Jack took the whisky onto the terrace.

The garden. Now there, he thought, unstoppering the Glenmorangie, there was perfect proof that the relationship was on a tilt. Planted long before his parents had bought the house—full of hibiscus, Russell lupins, a gnarled, ancient clematis—he liked to let it grow each summer until it almost blocked the windows with green. But Veronica wanted to trim, prune and fertilize, to grow lemongrass and capers in painted pots on the windowsills, make garden plans, talk gravel paths and bay trees. And ultimately—once she'd repackaged him and his house—she'd like him to sell up, leave this, the little South London, crumbly-brick Victorian cottage he was born in, with its mullioned windows, its tangled garden, the trains rattling by in the distance. She wanted to give up her token job in the family business, move out of her parents' and get started on making a home for him.

But he couldn't. His history was embedded too deeply in this quarter acre of loam and clay to pull it out on a whim. And after six months of knowing Veronica, he was sure of one thing: he didn't love her.

He watched her through the window now, scrubbing potatoes, making butter curls. At the end of last year he had been four years in CID and slacking—treading water, bored, waiting for the next thing. Until, at an out-of-control CID Halloween party, he realized that wherever he turned, a girl in a miniskirt and strappy gold sandals was watching him, a knowing smile on her face.

Veronica triggered in Jack a two-month-long hormonal obsession. She matched his sex drive. She woke him at 6:00 each morning for sex and spent the weekends wandering around the house in nothing but heels and sorbet-bright lipstick.

She gave him new energy, and other areas of his life began to change. By April he had Manolo Blahnik kitten-heel marks in his headboard and a transfer to AMIP. The murder squad.

But in spring, just as his drive toward her faltered, Veronica's agenda swerved. She became serious about him, started a campaign to tether him to her. One night she sat him down and in serious tones told him about the big injustice in her life, long before they had met: two of her teenage years taken from her by a struggle against cancer.

The ploy worked. Brought up short, suddenly he didn't know how to finish with her.

How arrogant, Jack, he realized, *as if you not leaving might be compensation. How arrogant can you get.*

In the kitchen she tucked her thin, asymmetric chin down onto her chest, her tongue between her teeth, and ripped a sprig of mint into shreds. He poured a shot of whisky and swallowed it in one.

Tonight he would do it. Maybe over dinner—

It was ready in an hour. Veronica switched all the lights on in the house and lit citronella garden candles on the patio.

"Pancetta and broad-bean salad with rocket, prawns in honey and soy sauce, followed by clementine sorbet. Am I the perfect woman or what?" She shook her hair and briefly exposed expensively cared-for teeth. "Thought I'd try it out on you and see if it'll do for the party."

"The party." He'd forgotten. They'd arranged it when they thought that ten days after standby week was a good, quiet time to throw a party.

"Lucky *I* haven't forgotten, isn't it?" She pushed past him, carrying the Le Creuset piled with baby new potatoes. In the living room the French windows were open onto the garden. "We're eating in here tonight, no point in opening the dining room." She stopped, looking at his crumpled T-shin, the dark feral hair. "Do you think you should dress for dinner?"

"You *are* joking."

"Well, I—" She unfolded a napkin on her lap. "I think it'd be nice."

"No." He sat down. "I need my suit. My case has started."

Go on, ask me about the case, Veronica, show an interest in something other than my wardrobe, my table linen.

But she staned pushing potatoes onto his plate. "You've got more than one suit, haven't you? Dad sent you that gray one."

"The others're at the cleaner's."

"Oh, Jack, you should have said. I could have picked them up."

"Veronica—"

"Okay." She held her hand up. "I'm sorry. I won't mention it again—" She broke off. In the hallway the phone was ringing. "I wonder who that is." She speared a potato. "As if I couldn't guess."

Caffery put his glass down and pushed his chair back.

"God," she sighed, exasperated, putting the fork down. "They've got a sixth sense, they really have. Can't you just let it ring?"

"No."

In the hallway he picked up the phone. "Yeah?"

"Don't tell me. You were asleep."

"I told you I wouldn't."

"Sorry to do this to you, mate."

"Yeah, what's up?"

"I'm back down here. The governor's okayed bringing in some equipment. One of the search team found something."

"Equipment?"

"GPR."

"GPR? That's—" Caffery broke off. Veronica pushed past him and walked purposefully up the stairs, closing the bedroom door behind her. He stood in the narrow hallway staring after her, one hand propped up against the wall.

"You there, Jack?"

"Yeah, sorry. What were you saying? GPR, that's ground-probing something?"

"Ground-probing radar."

"Okay. What you're telling me is—" Caffery dug a small niche in the wall with his black thumbnail. "You're telling me you've got more?"

"We've got more." Maddox was solemn. "Four more."

"Shit." He massaged his neck. "In at the deep end or what?"

"They've started on the recovery now."

"Okay. Where'll you be?"

"At the yard. We can follow them down to Devonshire Drive."

"The mortuary? Greenwich?"

"Uh-huh. Krishnamurthi's already started with the first one. He's agreed to do an all-nighter for us."

"Okay. I'll see you there in thirty."

Upstairs, Veronica was in the bedroom with the door shut. Caffery dressed in Ewan's room, checked once out of the window for activity over the railway at Penderecki's—nothing—and, doing up his tie, put his head around the bedroom door.

"Right. We're going to talk. When I get back—"

He stopped. She was sitting in bed, the covers pulled up to her neck, clutching a bottle of pills.

"What are they?"

She looked up at him. Bruised, sullen eyes. "Ibuprofen. Why?"

"What are you doing?"

"Nothing."

"What are you doing, Veronica?"

"My throat's up again."

He stopped, the tie extended in his left hand. "*Your throat's up?*"

"That's what I said."

"Since when?"

"I don't know."

"Well, either your throat's up or it isn't."

She muttered something under her breath, opened the bottle, shook two pills into her hand and looked up at him. "Going somewhere nice?"

"Why didn't you tell me your throat was up? Shouldn't you be having tests?"

"Don't worry about it. You've got more important things to think about."

"Veronica—"

"What *now*?"

He was silent for a moment. "Nothing." He finished knotting the tie and turned for the stairs.

"Don't worry about me, will you?" she called after him. "I won't wait up."

Three

TWO-THIRTY A.M., Caffery and Maddox stood silently staring off into the white-tiled autopsy suite: five aluminum dissecting stations, five bodies, unseamed from pubis to shoulders, skin peeled away like hides, revealing raw ribs marbled with fat and muscle. Juices leaked into the pans beneath them.

Caffery knew this well: the smell of disinfectant mingling with the unmistakable stench of viscera in the chill air. But five. *Five.* All tagged and dated the same day. He had never seen it on this scale. The morticians, moving silently in their peppermint-green galoshes and scrubs, didn't appear to find this unusual. One smiled as she handed him a face mask.

"Just one moment, gentlemen." Harsha Krishnamurthi was at the farthest dissecting table. The corpse's scalp had been peeled from the skull down to the squamous cleft of the nose, and folded over so the hair and face hung like a wet rubber mask, inside out, covering the mouth and neck, pooling on the clavicle. Krishnamurthi lifted the intestines out and slopped them into a stainless-steel bowl.

"Who's running?"

"Me." A small mortician in round glasses appeared at his side.

"Good, Martin. Weigh them, run them, prepare samples. Paula, I'm finished here, you can close up. Don't let the sutures overlap the wounds. Now, gentlemen." He pushed aside the halogen light, lifted his plastic visor and turned to Maddox and Caffery, gloved, splattered hands held rigidly out in front. He was handsome, slim, in his fifties, the deep-polished wood-colored eyes slightly wet with age, his gray beard carefully trimmed. "Grand tour, is it?"

Maddox nodded. "Have we got a cause of death?"

"I think so. And if I'm right, a very interesting one too. I'll come to that." He pointed down the room. "Entomology'll give you more—but I can give you approximates on all of them. The first one you found was the last one to die. Let's call her number five. She died less than a week ago. Then we jump back almost a month, then another five weeks and then another month and a half. The first one probably died Decemberish but the gaps are getting closer. We're lucky: not too much in the way of third-party artifacts—they're pretty well preserved."

He pointed to a sad loose pile of blackened flesh on the second dissecting table.

"The first to die. Long bones tell me she hadn't even turned eighteen. There's something that looks like a tattoo on her left arm. Might be the only way we can ID her. That or odontology. Now"—he held up a crooked finger—"appearance on arrival: I don't know how much you saw in the field, but they were all wearing makeup. *Heavy* makeup. Clearly visible. Even after they've been in the ground this long. Eye shadow, lipstick. The photographer has it all covered."

"Makeup, tattoos—"

"Yes, Mr. Maddox. And, thinking along those lines, two had pelvic infections, one a keratinized anus, plenty of evidence of drug use; endocarditis of the tricuspid valves. I don't want to jump to conclusions—"

"Yes, yes, yes," Maddox muttered. "So we're saying they're toms. I think we already guessed that. What can you tell us about the mutilations?"

"Ah! Interesting." Krishnamurthi edged in next to a cadaver, beckoning them to follow. Caffery thought, not for the first time, how like a side of hung meat the unskinned human body is. "You can see what I've done is to bring the second TA incision in tight, missing the one our offender did and avoiding the breasts so I could biopsy the incisions and get a look inside to see what's going on in there."

"And?"

"Some tissue has been removed."

Maddox and Caffery exchanged glances.

"Yes. It's roughly consistent with a standard beta mark breast reduction procedure. Stitched up, too. I suppose it's significant that your offender hasn't bothered with this decoration on the smaller-breasted victims."

"Which ones?"

"Victims two and three. And let me show you something interesting." He beckoned them to where a mortician was stitching up the crumpled torso he'd taken the intestines from. "The nail scrapings look dismal—and the very strange thing is I can't find any signs of a struggle. Except on this one. On victim number three."

They gathered around the corpse. It was small, as small as a child, and Caffery knew that for this accidental resemblance, rational or not, she would be set aside in the team's considerations.

"She weighed in at forty kilos, that's not much more than six stone." Reading Caffery's mind, Krishnamurthi said, "But she wasn't an adolescent. Just very petite. Perhaps that's why the breasts were not mutilated."

"The hair color . . . ?"

"Hair dye. Hair degrades very slowly. That aubergine color—it won't have changed much since death. Now, look."

He pointed a wet black finger at a scattered pattern on the wrists. "It's difficult to distinguish from the normal lesions of decomposition, but these are actually ligature marks. Antemortem. And a gag around here on the face. On the ankles too, chafing, bleeding. The others died as cool as ice; they just"—he held out his hand and mimed cresting a summit— "just *tipped* over the edge there. Like falling off a log. But this one—this one's different."

"Different?" Caffery looked up. "Why different?"

"This one struggled, gentlemen. She fought for her life."

"The others didn't struggle?"

"No." He held up his hands. "I'm coming to that. Just bear with me, okay?" He rolled aside a triple-beam balance and moved on to the congested, swollen body of the first victim discovered. "Now." He looked up, waiting for Maddox and Caffery to follow. "Now, then. This we'll call number five. Dreadful state, really. No doubt the head injury was postmortem, done by heavy machinery. Your guess of the bulldozer sounds about right. Gives us big problems identifying her. Our best hope's prints, although there again we encounter problems." He lifted up a hand and gently pushed the skin back and forward. It moved, jellied and thick, like the skin on a pudding.

"See that slippage? Not a hope in hell of getting a straight dead set. What I'll have to do is flip the skin off and print." He lowered the hand. "She was a user, but her death was instantaneous, not an OD, none of the usual esophageal and tracheal artifacts, no pulmonary edema." He rolled the body gently onto its side and pointed to a greenish collection on the buttocks. "Most of what you're seeing is putrefaction. But under it you can see black blood pricks?"

"Yes."

He rolled the body back. "Scattered hypostasis. She was moved after death. There's more on her arms—even, rather unusually, in her ankles."

"Unusually?"

"You'd see that in a hanging victim. Blood drifts downward into the feet and ankles."

Caffery frowned. "You said the hyoid's intact."

"It is. And from what's left of the neck I can guarantee this was not a hanging."

"Well?"

"She was in a standing position for some time. Postmortem."

"*Standing?*" Caffery said. "Standing?" The image made him uneasy. He turned to Maddox, expecting explanation—an easy reassurance. But it wasn't there. Instead Maddox narrowed his eyes and shook his head. *I don't know,* he was saying. *Don't look at me for every answer.*

"Maybe she was propped up," Krishnamurthi continued. "I can't see any whitish areas to indicate how—the putrefaction is too advanced—but she might have been suspended under her arms, or wedged somewhere so she was upright. Some time soon after death, when the blood was not yet viscid." He paused. "Mmmmhm. I missed that."

"What is it?"

He bent in and gently tweezered something from the scalp. "Good."

"What's that?"

"A hair."

Caffery leaned in. "A pubic hair?"

"Maybe." Krishnamurthi held it to the light. "No. That's a head hair. Negroid. It won't be any use for DNA except mitochondrial, there's not enough follicle on it." He carefully bagged the hair and handed it to the mortician for labeling. "I've already pulled some blond hairs off three of the victims. They're on their way to Lambeth." He moved to the next table. "Number two. She died fourteen or fifteen weeks ago. Five eight, age maybe thirty. The fingers are desiccated, but we'll still get a good dead set; there's an excellent chelation tissue builder on the market. Gelatin. Swells the tips up. Normally for that we'd take the hands off and do it at Lambeth, but"—he leaned in to Maddox—"since the fuss over the *Marchioness* I've stopped taking hands off. Do it right here in the pit, awkward or not."

He moved on to the next table, where a large white carcass lay, cracked down the center and unfurled. A cobwebbing of silvery white fascia shimmered between the blue ribs. The bleached blond hair had been wetted and smoothed back off the clean forehead. The throat, too, was split wide, revealing a glimpse of a milky cord. "Victim four, gentlemen."

Caffery lightly touched the ankle. "Good." A tattoo, surprisingly clear, centimeters above the tarsal bone. Bugs Bunny. Trademark green-topped carrot.

"You say no OD artifacts?"

"That's correct. No trauma either."

"So how did they die?"

Krishnamurthi held up a stained finger and smiled slowly. "That's where I've got an idea. Look at this." He gently inserted his fingers into the neck cavity, carefully opening the throat wider, inching aside the trachea and esophagus, until the spinal column showed slippery and gray. "This man is so clever, but not as clever as I am. If you drain off enough cerebrospinal fluid from down here"—he straightened and tapped his lower back—"instant death, hardly a mark. Even your standard lumbar puncture has to be done very, very carefully; take too much of that stuff and whoopee, your patient hits the deck. Now, these subjects've got about the right amount of CSF in the spine and no puncture wounds on the back. So I'm wondering if he cut out the middleman and went direct"—he nudged the calibrated scalpel in the opening between the vertebrae and carefully excised a small amount of the white myelin caul—"to the brain stem itself."

"The brain stem?"

"That's right." Krishnamurthi made a second incision and bent in to look. "Hmmmm." He carefully manipulated the scalpel and muttered to himself. "No, I'm incorrect." He frowned and looked up. "This wasn't done by *removing* CSF."

"No?"

"No. But there *has* been something invasive here. You see, Superintendent Maddox, the brain stem is a very delicate structure. You would only have to get a needle in the medulla oblongata, wiggle it about, and every physiological function would crash to a halt—just as we're seeing with these subjects."

"Instant death."

"Exactly. Now, I'm not seeing the extensive damage you'd expect with that, but it doesn't mean something wasn't *injected* in there. It wouldn't have mattered what—even water could do it. Subject's heart and lungs would have simply stopped. Instantly."

"And you say that except for number three none of them struggled?"

"That's what I said."

"Then how?" Caffery rubbed his temples lightly. "*How* did he keep them still?"

"My guess is once you get stomach, blood and deep-tissue analysis back from toxicology you'll find something had them tranquilized." He cocked his head. "One would have to assume they were semiconscious when that needle went in."

"Right." Caffery folded his arms and tilted back on his heels. "Lambeth needs to test for alcohol, Rohypnol, barbs, mazis. And those—" He nodded to a victim's forehead. About a centimeter below the hairline he could make out a horizontal line of faint ocher marks. "Those things on her head."

"Yes, odd, aren't they?"

"They all have them?"

"All except number four. They extend all the way around the head. Almost a perfect circle. And they've a very distinctive pattern: a few dots, then a slash."

Caffery bent a little closer. *Dot dot dash. Someone's joke?* "How were they made?"

"No idea—I'll work on it."

"How about this suture material?"

"Yes." Krishnamurthi was silent for a moment. "It's professional."

Caffery straightened up. Maddox was looking at him with clear gray eyes over his mask. Caffery raised his eyebrows. "Now, isn't *that* interesting?"

"I didn't say the *technique* was professional, gentlemen." Krishnamurthi peeled off his gloves, tipped them into a yellow biohazard bin and crossed to a sink. "Just the material. It's silk. But the incision didn't extend to the xiphoid process. Pretty crude. The beta breast incision, that's the classic surgery technique taught in med school." He picked up the yellow bar of reen soap and lathered his arms. "He's taken the fat from almost the right place, and the incision is very clean, done with a scalpel. But the stitching—not professional. Not professional at all."

"But if I guessed our offender had a grasp on the rudiments, you'd say—?"

"I'd say you had a point. A good point. He was able to find the brain stem, which is remarkable." He rinsed his hands and pulled off the visor. "Well. Do you want to see what he did before he sewed them back up?"

"Yes."

"This way."

Drying his hands, he led them into an anteroom where the small mortician was chewing gum and cleaning the intestines at a porcelain scrub sink: holding them under a tap and rinsing the contents into a bowl. He carefully inspected the inner and outer linings, checking for corrosion. When he saw Krishnamurthi he laid the intestines to one side and rinsed his hands.

"Show them what we found inside the chest cavities, Martin."

"Sure."

He tucked the gum in his cheek and picked up a large stainless-steel bowl covered in a square of brown paper. He removed the paper and held the bowl out.

Maddox bent in and jerked his head back as if he'd been slapped. "Jesus." He turned away, pulling a clean, monogrammed handkerchief from his suit pocket.

"Show me?"

"Sure." The assistant held the bowl out and Caffery gingerly peered over the edge.

In the stinking stew at the bottom of the blood-spattered bowl, five tiny dead shapes huddled together as if trying to keep warm. He looked up at the mortician. "Are they what I think they are?"

The mortician nodded. "Oh yes. They're what they appear to be."

Four

CAFFERY GOT TO BED at 4:00 A.M. Next to him Veronica slept solid and unruffled, snoring delicately. If her throat was up it meant swollen glands. Swollen glands meant the resurfacing of the Hodgkin's, the return of the deadly lymphoma.

Timing, Veronica, perfect timing; almost as if you knew.

At 4:30 A.M. he finally fell into a shallow, fitful sleep, only to come awake again at 5:30.

He lay staring at the ceiling thinking about the five corpses in Devonshire Drive.

Something in their injuries was significant to the killer: the marks on the heads—*Something he had made them wear? Bondage paraphernalia?*—were absent only on victim four. None of the victims had been raped; there were no signs of forced penetration—anal, oral or vaginal—and yet using an omniprint blue light, Krishnamurthi had pointed out traces of semen on the abdomens. Combined with the mutilation to the breasts of three of the women, and the lack of clothing, Caffery knew they were looking for the force's nightmare, a sexual serial killer, someone already too ill to stop. And what lodged hardest in his head, refusing to leave, were the five bloodied shapes in the bottom of a stainless-steel bowl. Whichever way he turned those followed him.

When he knew he wasn't going to sleep again, he showered, dressed and without waking Veronica drove through early morning London to B team's HQ.

B team, sometimes called Shrivemoor after the street they were based in, shared a functional red brick building with Four Area's Territorial Support Group, the TSG. The exterior was anonymous, but the traffic fatalities statistics displayed in an unlit box outside had given the public the impression that this was a functioning police station. Eventually a sign had appeared outside the garage entrance warning people not to walk in here with their everyday problems. Go to a normal police station, there's one just down the road, it said.

By the time Caffery arrived the sun had climbed over the terraced thirties houses, schoolchildren were being ushered into Volvos. He parked the Jaguar—something else Veronica wanted him to trade for a newer, shinier version.

"*You could sell that and get something really nice.*"

"*I don't want something really nice. I want the car I've got.*"

"*Then at least let me clean it.*"

He swiped his entrance card and climbed the stairs, past the TSG's fifteen armored Ford Sherpas parked in their own spilled oil. In AMIP's rooms the fluorescent lights were on—four database indexers, all women, all civilians, sat at their desks, tapping away.

He found Maddox in the office, fresh from breakfast with the chief superintendent. Over Earl Grey and bran muffins at Chislehurst golf club, the DCS had set out a game plan.

"He's slapped a moratorium on the press." Maddox seemed weary; Jack could see he hadn't slept. "Any female officers or civilians who find the case distressing can apply for transfer, and—" He straightened a pencil so that it lined up exactly with the other objects on his desk. His lips were colorless. "And he's giving us reinforcements—the whole of F team bumped over here from Eltham."

"Two teams on a case?"

"Yup. The guv's worried about this one. Really worried. Doesn't like Krishnamurthi's diminishing time periods. And—"

"Yes?"

Maddox sighed. "The hair Krishnamurthi pulled off that girl? The *black* hair?"

"He found blond hairs too. With toms, trace evidence is misleading."

"Right, Jack, right. But the chief's got Stephen Lawrence fever—all he can see are human rights groups in the shadows, razor blades in his mail." Someone knocked and Maddox reached for the door with a grim look on his face. "He distinctly does *not* want our target to be black."

"Morning, sir." Detective Sergeant Paul Essex, with his usual air of good-natured dishevelment—tie unknotted, sleeves rolled up to reveal his huge red forearms—stood in the doorway holding up an orange National Identification Bureau docket. "NIB."

"Prints?"

"Yup." He swiped thinning fair hair back from his big, flushed forehead. "Victim five was kind enough to get herself on the prostitute register. One Shellene Craw."

Caffery opened the docket. "These were indexed on the tom register." He looked up at Maddox. "Funny they never found their way to missing persons, isn't it?"

"Meaning someone chez Craw has a lot of explaining to do."

"Namely one, uh, Harrison." He handed him the docket. "Barry Harrison. Stepney Green."

"Fancy putting him top of your shopping list today?" Maddox said.

"Will do."

"And, Essex, mate, I believe you're family-liaison officer this case. Am I correct?"

"You are, sir. Specially selected for my tenderness."

"Then you'd better go with Caffery. Someone might need your tender shoulder to cry on."

"Will do. And, sir, this came." He passed a length of computer feed paper to Caffery. "From the Yard. The operation name—Operation Alcatraz."

Caffery took the paper, frowning. "Is that a joke?"

"No."

"Okay. Get on to them and have it changed. It's not appropriate."

"Why?"

"Birdman. The Birdman of Alcatraz. Haven't you seen the PM prelims?"

"I only just got here."

Maddox sighed. "Our offender left us a little gift on the victims."

"*Inside* the victims," Caffery corrected, folding his arms. "Inside the rib cage, sewn in next to the heart."

Essex's face changed. "Nasty." He looked from face to face, waiting for the follow-up. Maddox cleared his throat and looked at Caffery. Neither spoke.

"Well?" Essex opened his hands, frustrated. "*What?* What are we talking about here? What did he leave?"

"A bird," Caffery said eventually. "A small bird. A cage bird, probably a finch. And that doesn't go any further than the team. You hear?"

Five

Y 10:00 A.M. NIB had another match on the prints. Victim number two was one Michelle Wilcox, a prostitute from Deptford. Her files were transferred from Bermondsey to Shrivemoor that morning as Caffery and Essex drove through the Rotherhithe Tunnel to interview Shellene Craw's boyfriend. It was a fresh, sparkling day. Even the East End rushing past the car seemed alive, the poor, grimy London trees vivid with leaves.

"This Harrison character." Paul Essex looked out across the oaks on Stepney Green past a row of blond-bricked Georgian houses—freshly painted, the pride of their bond-salesman owners—to Harrison's red brick Victorian tenement: blackened by years of pollution, forgotten by the march of gentrification. "I *know* you don't think he's our offender."

Caffery stopped the car and pulled on the handbrake. "Of course not."

"So what *do* you think?"

"Dunno." He wound up the window, got out of the car and was about to close the door when he hesitated and put his head back inside. "Our offender's got a car, that's certain."

"He's got a car. Is that it?" Essex heaved himself out of the Jaguar and slammed his door. "Haven't you got a better theory than *He's got a car?*"

"No." He spun the car keys on his fingers and pocketed them. "Not yet."

In Harrison's building the lift was broken, so they climbed the four flights of stairs, Caffery stopping once in a while to let Essex catch up.

Maddox had explained Paul Essex to Caffery early on. *"Every team's got to have a joker. In B team we've got Essex. Likes geeing the lads up—swears he gets home at night and slips into a baby doll to do the hoovering. It's bullshit of course—go along with it, but still take him seriously. Truth is he's solid, the cornerstone . . ."*

And slowly Caffery was starting to believe in the innate goodness of this dray horse of a man. He took his cues from the way women treated Essex: like a wounded old bear—they flirted and teased him, sat on his lap and lightly slapped him for his jokes. But maybe they secretly understood that he operated from an emotional baseline deeper than their capabilities; at the age of thirty-seven DS Essex still lived alone. This awareness brought Caffery moments of guilt for the ease and lightness of his life compared to Essex's. Even now the physical inequalities proved themselves: Caffery reached Harrison's cool, ready; Essex dragged himself the last few steps to stand panting at the top, sweating and red-faced, pulling on his shirt collar and tugging at his trousers where they stuck to his legs. He took several minutes to recover.

"Ready?"

"Yup." He nodded, wiping his forehead. "Go on."

Jack knocked on Harrison's door.

"What?" The voice from inside the flat was sleepy.

Caffery bent down to the letter box. "Mr. Harrison? Barry Harrison?"

"Who wants to know?"

"Detective Inspector Caffery." He shot a look at Essex. They could smell marijuana. "We'd like a few words."

A hiss, and the sound of a body rolling out of bed. Then a tap running, a toilet flushed and the door opened, the safety chain neatly bisecting a face—bulbous blue eyes and a patchy beard.

"Mr. Harrison?" He flashed his card.

"What's up?"

"Can DS Essex and I come in?"

"If you tell me why, yeah." He was thin and freckled, naked from the waist up.

"We'd like to talk to you about Shellene Craw."

"She's not here, mate. Hasn't been for days." He started to shut the door but Caffery leaned his shoulder into it.

"I want to talk *about* her, not *to* her."

Harrison eyed Caffery and then Essex as if deciding who'd come out best in a scrap. "Look, she and me, we're finished. If she's in trouble, I'm sorry, but we weren't married or nothing, see, so I ain't responsible for her."

"We won't keep you, sir."

"You don't give up, do you?"

"No, sir."

"Oh for fuck's sake." The door closed and they heard the safety lock being unhooked. "Let's get it over with, then. Come on, come on."

Harrison's living room was small and grubby, opening on one side to a balcony and on the other to a kitchen dotted with pallid spider plants, KFC boxes. The floor was scattered with cigarette papers and tobacco.

Caffery sat, uninvited, on a blue PVC chair near the window and folded his arms.

"When did you last see Shellene, Mr. Harrison?"

"Dunno. Coupla weeks."

"Any more specific?"

"What's she got into now?"

"A couple of weeks, is that a week or a month?"

"Can't remember." Harrison pulled on a T-shirt and took a cigarette pack from his jeans. He stuck a Silk Cut between clenched teeth and retrieved a disposable lighter from the floor. "It was after my birthday."

"Which is?"

"May tenth."

"She was living here, wasn't she?"

"You're fucking good, you are."

"What happened?"

"I dunno, do I? She did a runner. Went out one night and never come back." He tensed his hand and smacked its heel across the other palm, letting it shoot away toward the window. "But that was Shellene for you. Left half her crap in the bedroom."

"Have you still got it?"

"No. I was, you know, so pissed off I chucked it—her stripping stuff and that."

"She was a stripper?"

"On her good days. But with Shellene it's always borderline hooking. Catch her fucking Arabs in Portland Place, did you?"

"Did you report her missing?"

Harrison clicked his tongue sarcastically. "Missing? Missing what? A conscience?"

"She left her stuff here, didn't you wonder?"

"Why would I? When she moved in here it was with just her makeup, ghetto blaster, a few syringes, y'know, the usual."

"Did you wonder if something had gone wrong?"

"No." He shook his head. "No. We were near our end anyway. It weren't no big surprise to me when she never come back that night . . ." His voice trailed off. He looked from Essex to Caffery and back again. "Hey," he said, suddenly nervous. "What're you getting at here?" When neither replied, something dawned in Harrison's eyes. He hurriedly lit the cigarette, inhaling deeply. "I'm not going to want to hear this, am I? Come on. You better say it quick. What is she? *Dead* or something?"

"Yes."

"Yes, what?"

"Dead."

"God." The blood drained from his face. He dropped onto the sofa. "I should have guessed. I should've guessed the moment I saw you. A fucking overdose."

"Probably not an overdose. Probably looking at an unlawful killing."

Harrison stared at Caffery without blinking. Then, as if he could protect himself from the words, his hands went up to his ears. Pale pink needle tracks were visible on the white forearms.

"Jesus," he forced out. "Jesus, I can't—" He sucked hard on the Silk Cut, his eyes watering. "Wait there," he said suddenly, leaped up and disappeared into the corridor.

Caffery and Essex looked at each other for a moment. They could hear him shuffling around in the bedroom, drawers being opened. Essex spoke first.

"Didn't know. Did he?"

"No."

They were silent for a moment. Someone below had woken and was firing up the stereo. Trance, the sort of thing Caffery had heard a thousand times interviewing around clubs when he was in CID. He shifted in his seat. "What the hell's he doing in there?"

"I don't know . . ." Essex trailed off. "Jesus, you don't think—?"

"Shit." Caffery jumped up and in the hallway slammed the flat of his hand against the bedroom door. "Don't fucking shoot up on me, Barry," he shouted. "Can you hear me? Don't fucking do it. I'll have you for it."

The door opened and Harrison's face appeared, immobile. "You can't do me for jellies. They're prescription. Before the ban." Holding the inside of his left elbow, he pushed past them into the living room. Caffery followed, swearing softly.

"We need to speak to you. We can't do it if you're ripped to the tits."

"I'm more use to you on it than off. I'll be clearer."

"Clearer," Essex muttered, and shook his head.

Harrison dropped himself onto the sofa and pulled his knees up, wrapping his arms around his calves in a strangely girl-like way. "Spent most of my time with Shellene stoned." He tilted his head back. For a moment Caffery thought he was going to cry. Instead he tightened his mouth and said, "Okay. Tell me. Where was she?"

"Southeast."

"Greenwich?"

Caffery looked up. "Yeah. How d'you know?"

Harrison dropped his arms and shook his head. "She was always hanging around there. Most of her work was down there. And when? When did it happen?"

"We found her yesterday morning."

"Yeah but, you know—" He coughed. "When did she—"

"About the time you last saw her."

"Shit." Harrison sighed. He lit another cigarette and pulled on it, dropping his head back, exhaling smoke toward the ceiling. "Go on, then, let's get it over with. What d'you want to know?"

Caffery sat on the sofa arm and fished his notepad out of his jacket. "This is a statement, all right, so tell me now if you're too off your face to do it." When Harrison didn't reply, Caffery nodded. "Okay, I'm taking that as a go-ahead. DS Essex here is our family-liaison officer. He'll be the one you contact whenever you deal with us. He's going to stay with you after I've gone, go through the statement with you, ask you to help us contact Shellene's family. We want details till they're coming out of our ears: what she was wearing, what makeup she used, what underwear she had on, did she prefer *EastEnders* or the *Street*." He stopped. "And I suppose it's a waste of time him getting you in to see a CDT counselor? Stop you turning your veins into pebbles?"

Harrison put his hand to his head. "Jesus."

"Thought so." He sighed. "Now, do you know where Shellene was going that night?"

"One of her pubs. She had a gig."

"Name?"

"Dunno. Ask her agent."

"Who is?"

"Who is Little Darlings."

"Little Darlings?"

"Not well named, trust me on that. It's Earl's Court way."

"Okay. And any other names? Anyone she hung out with?"

"Yeah." Harrison stuck the Silk Cut between his teeth. "There was Julie Darling, agent." He counted the names off on his fingers. "And the girls. Pussy—funny how there's always a Pussy, isn't it? And Pinky and Tracy or Lacey or some shite, Petra and Betty, and that—" He slammed his hands down on his knees, suddenly angry. "That makes six, and that is the sum total of what I knew about Shellene's life, and you tell me that you're surprised I never reported her missing, like I *knew* or something, you *bunch* of fucking wankers."

"Okay, okay. Take it easy."

"Yeah yeah, yeah." He was exasperated. "I'm taking it easy. Fucking easy." He turned and stared out of the window. No one spoke for a moment. Harrison gazed out at the roofs of the Mile End Road, the greenish domes of Spiegelhalter's emporium high in the blue. A pigeon landed on the balcony and Harrison shucked his shoulders, sighed and turned to Caffery.

"Okay."

"What?"

"You better tell me now."

"Tell you what?"

"You know. Did the cunt rape her?"

The sun had put Caffery into a better mood by the time he got to Mackelson Mews, Earl's Court. He found the agency easily:"Little Darlings" on the door in peeling gold stick-on letters.

Julie Darling was a small woman in her mid-forties, shiny dyed-black hair cut in a neat page, her nose improbably tiny on the taut face. She was dressed in a strawberry-pink velour jogging suit and matching high-heeled mule slippers and she held her head up and back as if balancing an invisible glass as she led Caffery through the cork-tiled hallway. A white Persian cat, disturbed by Jack's presence, scampered ahead of them into an open doorway. Caffery heard a man's voice speaking to it in the depth of the room.

"My husband," Julie said expressionlessly. "I got him in Japan twenty years ago." She closed the door. Caffery had a brief glimpse of a huge man in a vest, seated on the edge of a bed, scratching his stomach with the lugubriousness of a walrus. The room was lit dimly by the sun coming through a crack in the curtains. "American air force," she whispered, as if that explained why he wouldn't be joining them.

Caffery followed her into the office: a low-ceilinged room, brilliant sunlight coming through two small leaded windows. A bee buzzed in the window boxes, and beyond them a red E-type Jaguar basked in the sun. Somewhere in the mews someone was practicing arpeggios on a piano.

"Well."Julie sat at her desk, crossed her legs and regarded him thoughtfully. "*Caffery*. Now, there's a name. Are you Irish?"

He smiled. "Probably, generations back. County Tyrone via Liverpool."

"Dark hair, dark blue eyes. Typical Irish. My mother always warned me off the Irish boys. *'If they're not stupid they're dangerous, Julie.'*"

"I hope you listened, Miss, uh, *Darling*."

"It's my real name."

"Yes." He put his hands in his pockets and looked up at the low ceiling. It was covered in glossy publicity photographs, countless faces staring down at him. "I'd like to hear what you can tell me about—" He stopped.

Under a smiling blond face the name was printed. Shellene Craw.

So that's what you looked like.

"Shellene Craw was on your books?"

"Ah, so it's Shellene you want. This is no big surprise, Inspector. She owes me two months' commission. Two hundred quid. And now she brings you to my door, asking about what? Drugs, I suppose?"

"I don't think you'll be getting your money." He sat down and placed his hands on the desk. "She's dead."

Julie didn't miss a beat. "I could have told you that was coming—she was an overdose waiting to happen. The clients complained. Said she had needle marks on the inside of her thighs. Put the punters off. Ho-hum, two hundred quid. I'm going to guess she didn't leave it to me in her will."

"When did you last hear from her?"

"Week before last. Then she didn't turn up to a gig last Wednesday, didn't call." She paused, lightly drumming her nails on the desk. "I lost that venue right off."

"Where?"

"Nag's Head. Archway."

"And what was the last place she *did* turn up?"

"Um . . ." Julie leaned forward in her seat and, licking a finger, flicked through a large loose-leaf file. He could see a seam of gray hair along her parting, the scalp very pink underneath. "There." She tapped a page. "She must've turned up to the Dog and Bell because I didn't hear from them. That was a lunchtime gig, last Monday."

"The Dog and Bell?"

"Trafalgar Road. That's in—"

"Yes, I know." Caffery's skin tingled minutely. "It's east Greenwich." The construction yard was less than a mile away. He started a new page in his notebook. "Did Shellene work on her own that day?"

"No." She tilted her head and looked at him carefully. "Are you going to tell me? *Was* it an overdose?"

"There was another girl on the show?"

Julie looked at him for a moment, her mouth twitching slightly. "Pussy Willow. She only does Greenwich shows."

"Has she got a real name?"

"We all have real names, Mr. Caffery. It's only the very saddest of punters that believe our mommies and daddies really call us Frooty Tootie or Beverly Hills. Joni Marsh. She's been with me years."

"Have you got her address?"

"She won't like it if I give it out. Specially to the pi—" Julie stopped herself, and smiled slowly. "Specially to a detective."

"She won't know."

She gave him a narrow look and scribbled an address down on the back of a business card. "She shares with Pinky. Used to be on my books too. Becky, she's called, now that she's stopped."

"Thank you." He took the card. The air force husband was coughing up phlegm in the bedroom.

"Do you have a girl on your books called Lacey?"

"Nope."

"Betty?"

Julie shook her head.

"And does the name . . ." He looked at his notes. "The name Tracy ring a bell?"

"No."

"Petra?"

"Petra? Yes."

Caffery looked up. "Yes?"

"Yes, I—Petra. Funny little thing."

He raised his eyebrows. "*Little?*"

"Small I mean." She gave him a dirty look. "We're not child pornographers, Mr. Caffery. I mean one of the strippers. She pulled a fast one on me too, and me thinking I was a good judge of character."

"She disappeared?"

"Off the face of the planet. I wrote to her hostel. Never got a reply, of course." She shrugged. "She didn't owe much so I let it drift. You put these things down to experience, don't you?"

"When was this?"

"Christmas. No, early February, because we'd just come back from Majorca."

"Drugs?"

"Her? No. Wouldn't touch them. The others, yes. But not Petra."

"When you say she was small—"

"Tiny bones. Like a little bird. And skinny with it."

He shifted uncomfortably in the narrow chair. "Do you remember the last gig she did?"

Julie gave him a long, thoughtful look, then slowly, woodenly, turned to the book. "Here." She ran her finger across the page. "January twenty-fifth. The King's Head. Wembley."

"Did she ever do the Dog and Bell?"

"All the time. Her hostel was in Elephant and Castle. Joni knows her." She licked her finger and flicked the page over. "Odd," she said faintly. "She did the Dog and Bell the day before the King's Head. The day before she disappeared."

"Okay. I need her address."

"Look." Julie sat back and placed her hands on the desk. "Tell me now what's going on."

"And a photo of Petra."

"I *said* what's going on?"

He nodded at the ceiling. "And that one of Shellene."

She sniffed loudly and retrieved a file from under the desk. She flipped through it, pulling out two head-and-shoulders of Shellene and one badly lit full-length color shot of a brunet in a fishnet leotard, and held the photos out to Caffery without looking at him.

Petra wasn't pretty. She had very small features, dark eyes and the determined triangular chin of a street urchin. The only makeup she wore was a dark pencil outline on her mouth. Caffery held the picture so it caught the sunlight and looked at it for a long time.

"What is it?"

He looked up. "Did she dye her hair?"

"They all do."

"It looks—"

"Purple. Yeah, awful, isn't it? I told her not to."

He dropped the picture into his Samsonite, thinking of the childlike corpse lying in the Greenwich morgue; the only one who had resisted death, the only one who had been re-strained. He closed the briefcase, embarrassed by a sudden rush of feeling for a poor anorexic, bound, gagged and fighting for her life.

"Thank you for your help, Mrs. Darling."

"Are you going to tell me what Petra's got to do with Shellene?"

"We don't know yet."

Julie said suddenly, "She's dead too, isn't she? Little Petra."

The two of them regarded each other across the table for a long time. Caffery cleared his throat and stood.

"Mrs. Darling, please don't speak about this to anyone. It's very early days of the investigation. We appreciate your help." He held his hand out, but she declined it.

"Will you tell me more when you can?" She looked very pale under her blue-black bob. "I'd like to hear what happened to poor little Petra."

"As soon as we know ourselves," Caffery said. "As soon as we know."

Six

A MIP RELIES HEAVILY on the Home Office Large Major Enquiry System, the cross-checking database known by its acronym: HOLMES. The pivot in any team is the HOLMES "receiver"—the officer who collates, extracts and interprets the data. At Shrivemoor that person was Marilyn Kryotos.

Caffery had liked Marilyn instantly. Plump and languorous, she drifted through the day, talking in her low, quirky voice about her kids, their pets, their illnesses, their small triumphs and their knee scrapes. The universal mother, Kryotos seemed to deal with a murder in the same resigned way she'd deal with a dirty nappy—as if it were a faintly unpleasant, but correctable, fact of life. It pleased him that her first choice of companion in the team was Paul Essex: as if their friendship endorsed Caffery's own judgment of the pair.

Jack encountered Marilyn that evening when he returned to Shrivemoor with his notes. She was carrying "action" dockets from the Senior Investigating Officer's room to the incident room and he knew immediately something had her ruffled.

"Marilyn." He leaned toward her. "What's up? The kids?"

"No," she hissed. "It's bloody F team. They're moving in and driving me loony toons. They want this, they don't want that. The latest is that they want a separate bloody office, like they're better than us or something." She pushed dark hair out of her eyes. "The CS's got a hair up his bum about this case and he's making *us* suffer for it. I mean look, will you, Jack, just *look* at this place—it's not big enough for one investigation team, let alone us *and* them."

Caffery saw what she meant—taking his notes in to the indexers, he had to push past unfamiliar faces in the incident room. The F team officers all wore crisp shirts and ties, many of them with fresh-from-the-cellophane creases. That pride in their clothing would wear thin after a week of fifteen-hour shifts, he knew.

"Scuse me, mate." Someone caught his arm. A sharp-faced man, shorter than Caffery, tanned, with pale blue eyes and a slim little unbroken nose. His yellow hair was slicked into a gleaming shield curved over his head. He wore a crisp, bottle-green suit and was carrying two more in a dry cleaner's bag over his shoulder. "You got somewhere I can hang these?"

Caffery found Maddox in the SIO's office, signing overtime forms. He threw the car keys on the desk.

"The Dog and Bell."

"I'm sorry?"

"The Dog and Bell. It's a pub in east Greenwich."

Maddox leaned back in his chair and looked at him carefully. "Well?" He opened his hands. "What are you thinking?"

"A Q&A. I'd want to look at any regulars with medical connections."

"That'll get the press hopping. They won't stick to the moratorium if we open our mouths in public. I'll run it by the chief, but no." He shook his head slowly. "I think he'll say no. Not yet. You must've got other leads?"

"Names. A possible ID on victim three."

"Okay, so get Marilyn to divvy those up. What's the most promising one?"

"Joni Marsh. Working the Dog and Bell the day Craw disappeared."

"Right, you take that tomorrow. But take someone else with you, for God's sake. You know how these women can be." A knock on the door and Maddox sighed. "Yeah? What?"

"Mel Diamond. DI Diamond, sir."

"Come in, Mr. Diamond. Come in."

The yellow-haired inspector came in, shucking his suit sleeves down so they covered his cuffs. "Evening, sir." He ignored Caffery and extended his tanned hand to Maddox, briefly flashing a micro-thin wristwatch. "You won't know me, but I know you. From the Met boat club. Sir."

Maddox paused a moment, his small face unresponsive.

"Chipstead," Diamond prompted.

"Good Lord." Maddox came out from behind the desk and shook his hand. "Of course, of course. I know the face. So"—he leaned against the desk and folded his arms, looking Diamond up and down—"you're the lucky DI who's joining us. Welcome to Shrivemoor."

"Thank you, sir." His voice was fractionally too loud for the small office, as if he was used to being listened to. "All the way from tranquil Eltham."

"We'll be putting you straight in: you and your men on the knock tomorrow. Do a three-mile diameter. That okay with you?"

"It'll have to be okay, won't it? The guv wants us on routines, backup to the real team."

Maddox paused. "Yes, there's not much," he said carefully. "Not much we can do about it, Mr. Diamond. I'm sure you're aware of that."

"Well, of course," he said. "Of course I'm aware. And I have absolutely *no problem* with it. No problem at all. If it's okay by the governor it's okay by me—that doesn't need saying." He nodded. Then, as if to draw a line under the issue, he smiled, waved a hand in the direction of the photos on the walls and said, "Nice boat. She yours?"

"Yes." Maddox was hesitant.

"She's a Valiant."

"Yes she is, indeed she is."

"Good boats, Valiants. Some find them a bit tubby, but I like them. Marvelous cruisers too."

"Yes, well." Maddox was warming now. "Hate to say it but the Americans usually come up trumps with cruisers. Mammoth indulgence, of course."

"A cutter won the Met's Frostbite run this year." Diamond's tongue moved inside his mouth. "It wasn't by any chance . . . ?"

"Yes." Maddox nodded modestly. "Yes, indeed."

Standing against the wall, his arms folded tightly, Caffery was surprised to find himself irritated by this exchange. As if the benefit of Maddox's support and affability was his exclusive right, not something to be switched on a whim to another DI. Irrational though it was—*he's not your father, Jack, you don't have any rights to him*—he was angered to see Maddox this vulnerable to flattery, and when DI Diamond grinned, delighted:

"Good God, good God. Just wait till I tell my mates who I'm working with."

Caffery turned away and quietly left the room.

Seven

THAT EVENING Jack sat at his desk in Ewan's room, gazing at the Windows 98 clouds on the screen. The upper branches of the old beech at the foot of the garden cast shifting, coppery shadows on the wall above him. He didn't need to turn and look to know how the new leaves almost concealed the rusting nails, deep in the flesh of the tree, and the few mossy planks: the remains of the tree house which he and Ewan had crouched in as kids, shouting to the roaring trains in the distance below.

Sometimes, in his solitariness, Jack strained to remember how it was, how *he* was. Before. He had an image of a child, lighter than a breath, nothing to stop him from floating away over the rooftops into the blue air.

And then—that day. Recollected as a set of jerky scenes spliced carelessly together, slightly grainy, as if he'd cheated and taken the memories not from real life but from a spool of eight-millimeter film tucked somewhere in the back of his parents' attic.

It was mid-September, windy and sunny, and the dried planks of the tree house creaked as the beech, still soft and green with summer sap, bowed in the wind. Jack and Ewan had clashed. They had found four floorboards in a skip; Ewan wanted to build a watch platform in the southernmost branches of the tree so he could see the trains swaying down the line from Brockley station. Jack wanted the platform at the north end so he could look off down the track at the misty bridges of New Cross, see the faces on the city workers as they traveled home with their *London Evening News*.

Jack—an exasperated eight-year-old on a short fuse—shoved his older brother hard against the tree trunk. Ewan's response was ferocious and startling: he recovered his balance, extended sturdy arms and bulldozered, screaming, into Jack. "I'm telling, I'm telling." Spittle flew from his mouth. "I'm telling Dad."

Jack was caught off balance, sent reeling to the edge of the tree house, coming to a halt half on, half off the deck, his shorts ripped by a nail, legs dangling, the thumb on his left hand trapped between two planks. Pain made him furious.

"Tell, then, you bastard! Go on. Bloody tell."

"I will." Ewan settled into resentful guilt. His eyebrows closed together, his bottom lip pushed out. "I hate you, you scum. Bloody, bloody, *fucking* scum."

He turned and clambered down the rope ladder, his face closed in angry concentration, and dropped into the railway cutting. Swearing loudly, Jack freed his thumb, pulled himself back into the tree house and lay there, breathing slowly, his throbbing hand sandwiched between his bare knees, angry and exasperated.

Beneath the tree house, where the banks of the cutting flattened into a wide band of undergrowth, the brothers had created a network of paths for their games, each route meticulously explored, mapped, named: a trampled cobweb spiraling out in the bindweed. As Jack watched from the tree house, Ewan chose the southern path, the one dubbed the "death trail" because it skirted by a rusting immersion heater—"*See*

that, Ewan? That's an unexploded bomb. A V2 probably."
His clean dark head bobbed a few times above the undergrowth, the mustard T-shirt flashed. He reached the clearing
they called camp 1, beyond which lay the DMZ, demilita-
rized zone, the lethal V2 and land of the gooks.

Jack lost interest. Ewan sulked too easily. It tired him.
Angry and in pain, he slid down out of the tree and went
inside to complain about the black and yellow half-moon
bursting under his thumbnail.

Afterward it was the tree house which cut their mother more
deeply than anything. Caffery could see her now, a thought
or memory having halted her oven cleaning or washing-up,
to send her stiffly into the garden, where she would stand,
staring at the tree, pink rubber gloves dripping suds into the
grass. The last place she'd seen her son.

And then the half-hysterical, helpless outbursts to her
husband. *"Explain that tree house, Frank; if it's still there,
then why isn't he? Explain it, Frank! Tell me."*

And Jack's father would cover his ears and sink into the
armchair, the sports pages bunching up on his lap, unable to
tolerate his wife's anguish, until one day he snatched up a ball
peen hammer and marched out into the mud and rain still
wearing his checkered slippers.

Caffery had crept up to this very room and stood wobbling on the bed so he could reach the window and watch
the wood cracking, slats dropping to the ground, the mud
splatters on his mother's tights as she stood sobbing on the
churned-up lawn.

And then, through the bare branches of the trees, on the
other side of the railway cutting he saw someone else.

Ivan Penderecki. Pale, meaty arms propped on his decom-
posing back fence, gray rain and a distant smile on his face.

Penderecki stood for twenty minutes or so, the house behind him silhouetted against the rain clouds. Then, as if he'd

been filled to the brim with satisfaction, he turned and silently walked away.

To Caffery, eight years old, small nose pressed against the
steamy glass, that was the proof he'd needed of the inconceiv-
able and the unvoiceable. The thing the police said was an im-
possibility because *"we've searched every house in the area,
Mrs. Caffery; we're going to extend the search of the railway
cutting; past the New Cross Bridge . . ."*

Caffery knew, in the organic, instinctive way a child
knows things it has never been told, that Penderecki could
show the police exactly where to find Ewan.

The Cafferys gave up the battle in Jack's twenty-first year.
They moved back to Liverpool, selling him the house for a
nominal sum in return, he understood, for never having to
see his face again. Jack the antagonist, the difficult one, the
one who wouldn't obey, be quiet, sit still. *The one they would
rather have lost.* They never said the words, but he saw them
in his mother's face when he caught her staring at his thumbnail. The ruby-black bruise had refused to grow out—proof
in his mother's eyes of her second son's intent to remind her
of that day forever. Ewan's disappearance had done more
than simply diminish Jack in his mother's eyes. He knew that
even now she was waiting, somewhere in the sprawling Liverpool suburbs, for what? For him to find Ewan? For him to *die*
too? Caffery didn't know how much she needed from him—
what compensation she wanted from him for being the one
who was left behind. Now and then, in spite of Veronica and
the women who'd come before her, he found himself almost
crippled by loss and loneliness.

So he took his energy into a high-velocity sprint up the
Met's ranks. Penderecki's name was the first thing he plugged
into the police national computer. And there he found the
truth.

John (Ivan) Penderecki, convicted pedophile, two sentences served in the sixties before coming to live in the same inner-London streets as Jack and Ewan Caffery.

On the shelves in the study—still "Ewan's room—lined up and color-coded, stood twelve box files, each crammed with scraps of paper, cling-film-wrapped John Player cartons, faded Swan Vesta boxes containing paper clips, a rusted nail, a scrap of a burned gas bill, the trivial facts of Penderecki's life collected over twenty-six years, by Caffery, boy detective and obsessive. Now he was committing the contents of the files to digital memory.

He put on his glasses and opened the database.

"At it again?"

He started. Veronica was standing in the doorway, arms crossed, head on one side. She smiled. "I've been watching you."

"I see." He took his glasses off. "You let yourself in."

"I wanted to surprise you."

"Have you had the tests?"

"No."

"It's Monday. Why not?"

"I was at the office all day."

"Your father wouldn't let you leave?"

She frowned and massaged her throat. The crocus-yellow jacket was cut low enough to reveal the tattooed point on her sternum. A memento of the radiotherapy in her teens. "There's no need to get angry."

"I'm not angry. Just concerned. Why not go to casualty? Now."

"Calm down. I'll call Dr. Cavendish tomorrow. Okay?"

He turned back to the screen, biting his lip, trying to be intent on his work, wishing for the hundredth time he had never given Veronica the front door key. She watched him from the doorway, half sighing, pushing her hair behind her ears, running her nails along the door frame, the discreetly expensive rings and bracelets—the best way a father knew to show love for his daughter—jingling softly. Caffery knew she wanted him to watch her. He pretended not to notice.

"Jack," she said eventually, coming over to the chair, lifting a swatch of his dark hair, running her thumb across the exposed skin, "I wanted to talk about the party. It's only a few days away." She crawled onto the chair and folded herself against him like oil, mouth to cheek, hands tangling in his hair, her left leg cocked over the chair arm. Her hair tickled his neck. "Jackie? Yoo-hoo. Can you hear me?" She pressed her fingers into his face, her fingers that always smelled of menthol and expensive perfume, and wiggled herself against his groin.

"Veronica—" He was starting a reluctant erection.

"What?"

He disentangled himself. "I want an hour here."

"Oh God," she groaned, climbing off. "You're sick, you know that?"

"Probably."

"Obsessive-compulsive. You'll die in this place if you're not careful."

"We've discussed this."

"This is the twenty-first century, Jack. You know, new starts, onwards and upwards." She stood in the window and stared out at the garden. "In our family we were brought up to move away from our roots, better ourselves."

"Your family's more ambitious than me."

"Ambitious than *I am*," she corrected.

"Yes. And give a shit more than me."

"More than *I do*."

"God."

"What?"

He put his glasses down and rubbed his eyes. Candy-bright tropical fish cruised across the screen. Thirty-four years old and he still couldn't bring himself to tell this woman he didn't love her. After the tests, and after the party—*coward, Jack, you coward*—if the tests were okay, that would be easy. Then he'd tell her. Tell her it was over. Tell her to give him back the keys.

"What is it?" she said. "What've I said now?"

"Nothing," he said, and went back to his work.

Eight

IT WAS THE SORT of overhead sun that induced head-aches and shrank shadows to dense borders around ob-jects. Caffery kept the windows open as they drove but Essex complained so much about the heat, made such a show of running his fingers under his collar and billowing out his shirtfront, that Caffery gave in; when they parked they both locked their jackets in the boot of the Jaguar and walked down Greenwich South Street rolling up shirtsleeves.

Number 8 turned out to be two floors of a Georgian house above a junk shop.

"Harrison remembered what Craw was wearing," Essex said as they ducked inside the small doorway on the left. "Clear plastic sandals with pink glitter in the heels, black tights, a miniskirt and he *thinks* a T-shirt." He leaned on the intercom. "Sounds my sort of woman."

"How're her parents taking it?"

"Like they don't give a shit. They're not coming down to London, can't find the train fare. '*She were a right little prossie, Sergeant, if that's any help,*' is Mum's idea of helping the police."

The metallic intercom box suddenly crackled to life, making them both jump. "Who is it?"

Caffery took his sunglasses off and leaned into the intercom. "Detective Inspector Jack Caffery. Looking for Joni Marsh."

A few moments later the door opened and a slim, chestnut-haired girl looked out at them. In her late twenties, he guessed, but the long hair, the sensible flat leather shoes on tanned feet and a short, sky-blue corduroy pinafore dress lent her a college-girl freshness.

He held up his warrant card. "Joni?"

"No." Paintbrushes stuck out of the two pinafore pockets, making her look as if she'd been interrupted in art class. An art class at an expensive girls' school. "Joni's upstairs. Can I help?"

"You are?"

She gave a slight smile and extended her hand. "Becky. Rebecca, I mean. Joni and I share."

Caffery shook her hand. "Can we come in?"

"I, that is, we—" She looked embarrassed. "Well—no. Not really. I'm sorry."

"We want to ask some questions, about someone Miss Marsh knows."

Rebecca pushed her fringe away from her green eyes and stared past them into the street as if she expected they'd come with snipers trained on the doorway. "It's a bit—it's a bit awkward." She had a very soft voice, educated, listenable, a voice that could stop other conversations with a whisper. "Can't we speak out here?"

"We're not interested in the blow," Caffery said.

"What?"

"I can smell it."

"Oh." She looked at her feet, embarrassed.

"We're not after that. You have my word."

"Um." She tucked her bottom lip under very white teeth. "Okay, okay." She turned. "You'd better come in."

They followed her into the cool depths of the house, past a mountain bike propped up against the banister, Essex glazed over by the swinging hair and long tanned legs on the stairs in front of him.

Inside the flat, she led them through a small hallway—in a bedroom to the right Jack glimpsed a discarded pair of cotton knickers in a pool of sunlight before Rebecca pulled the door closed—and showed them into a large room.

"My studio," she said.

Light streamed through two tall sash windows, casting twin white rectangles on the bare floorboards. The walls were hung with five oversize watercolors in brilliant, splashy pigments. In the center of the room a girl wearing a lime-green halterneck and black bell-bottoms was hurriedly spraying puffs of deodorant into the air, wafting it around, her bracelets jingling. When she heard them she dropped the deodorant, grabbed a small cling-film packet from the table and turned to them, hands behind her back like a guilty child. Her hair was dyed Viking blond, her face like a painted china doll, comically wide blue eyes, a button nose. Caffery could see she was stoned.

"Joni?" He flipped open his warrant card. "Joni Marsh?"

"Um—yeah." She peered at the card. "Who're you, then?"

"Police."

Her eyes widened. "*Police?* Becky, what the f—?"

"It's okay. They're not interested in the gear."

"Yeah?" She was dubious, twitchy, moving from foot to foot.

"Yeah," Caffery said.

Joni pushed hair behind her ears and inspected him—weak blue eyes flittering suspiciously, her mouth closed—taking in the shirtsleeves, the dark uncombed hair, the hard stomach. Suddenly she giggled loudly. "No, hang on." She put a hand to her mouth. "*Rilly* the Bill? You *sure?*"

"Tell you what, Joni." Caffery put his warrant card in his shirt pocket. "Do you want to get rid of that stuff? So we can move on?"

She blinked uncomprehendingly at him, at Rebecca and back to Caffery. Her makeup reminded him of the autopsy photographs, bright sea-color eye shadow and lips painted in a high Cupid's bow. "You *sure* you're the Bill?"

"Joni?" he repeated. "The blow. Do you want to go and dump it somewhere?"

"Joni." Rebecca took her arm. "Come here." She led her into the kitchen and the two men heard Rebecca talking in a low patient voice. Through the door crack Caffery could see a large oak table, Matisse prints on the walls and a chest freezer in an alcove. Presently he heard Joni's footsteps on the stairs, a door slamming, her feet clattering back down and then the two women talking in the kitchen—giggling and clunking around in the fridge.

Caffery put his hands in his pockets and wandered around the room, looking at the sketches dotted on trestle tables. Many were smudged charcoal nudes, an arm decipherable here, a tossed head there. One—a large watercolor—showed a woman three-quarters to the artist, rolling a stocking down her calf.

"Hey." Essex was looking at a half-finished painting propped on a wooden easel. "Jack. Check this out."

A woman stood in front of a tasseled burgundy curtain, her arms raised with studied insouciance. The watchers—her audience of three men—had been sketched over the background wash in broad, flat sweeps of charcoal.

"Thought you'd find that," Joni murmured from the doorway. "It's me."

The men turned.

"She's a stripper, you know." Rebecca stood beside her holding an ice bucket filled with beers.

"We know," Essex said.

"Yeah." Joni pushed one hip out, hands in pockets. "Thought you might."

Rebecca came to stand behind them at the easel.

"Did you do this here?" Caffery asked. "In the studio?"

"No, no. I started it in the pub. I was just doing some finishing touches."

"You do a lot of work with the girls? You know a lot of them?"

"They're not monsters, you know." She smiled at him with her head on one side, as if he made her want to laugh. "I did it myself for a while. It put me through art school. Goldsmiths."

"Maybe we should . . . uh." He looked around the room. "Look, why don't we all sit down? Have a talk."

"Ah." Rebecca put the ice bucket down and wiped her hands. The bucket had left a little darkened patch on the corduroy dress. "Now, *that* sounds sinister."

"De-*eeep*," Joni agreed.

"Maybe it is. Maybe it is."

"Well, if it's going to be heavy," Rebecca announced, pulling beers from the bucket, "I, for one, need a drink." She held a bottle out to Essex. "Can I tempt you and then sell the story to the newspapers?"

Essex didn't hesitate. "Yeah, ta."

She handed one to Caffery—who accepted it without a word—crossed to the window and sat on the sill, her bare knees raised, her own bottle clutched against her narrow ankles. Essex stood near the kitchen doorway, shifting from foot to foot, fiddling with the beer cap and stealing looks at Joni's breasts.

"Right." Jack cleared his throat. He stood in the center of the room. "Business."

He told them quickly, presenting the facts in neat, unadorned packages: the five women lying in a morgue only streets away, the connection with the pub. When he'd finished Joni shook her head in disbelief. She wasn't smirking now. The fun was over.

"Oh man. This is bad."

Rebecca sat motionless, staring up at him with dismay in her clear, feline eyes.

"Do you need some time?"

"No, no." She curled up tighter, hugging herself, her arms shaking, her knees drawn up to her chin. "No, go on."

Caffery and Essex waited patiently for the two women to work through their shock. They spoke for almost an hour, at first in disbelief—"Tell me again—Shellene, Michelle *and* Petra?"—then later constructively, turning the dry facts over in their own hands, becoming sleuths. The Dog and Bell emerged quickly as a touchstone for the local drug and prostitution community. Anything, it seemed, that was going to happen in east Greenwich was likely to have a connection with the beat-up little pub on Trafalgar Road. It was there that Rebecca and Joni had met Petra Spacek, Shellene Craw and Michelle Wilcox. They also believed they knew victim four.

"Very bleached, white-blond hair, yeah?" Joni held up a chunk of her own hair. She was sober now, clearheaded. "Like mine. And a Bugs Bunny tattoo, here?"

"That's right."

"That's Kayleigh."

"Kayleigh?"

"Yeah, Kayleigh Hatch. She's a, you know—" She mimed an injection to the inner elbow. "A *serious* user."

"Address?"

"Dunno. She lives with her mom, I think. West London."

Caffery noted the name. He was seated now, against the wall on a small wooden bench near the easel. After Rebecca had brought more beers from the kitchen she had pulled a chair up and sat less than two feet away from him—bent forward, her slim arms folded loosely on her knees. Innocent: but Jack found her closeness unnerving.

He looked across at Joni.

"Something else."

"Yeah?"

"You worked with Shellene Craw last week."

"Uh-huh. I did."

"Think back—did she leave with anyone on that day? Did anyone come to collect her?"

"Uh—" Joni licked her lips and stared at her tangerine-painted toenails peeping out from her cork-heeled sandals.

"Hello?"

"Yes, I'm thinking." She looked up. "Becks?"

Rebecca shrugged but he caught the ghost of the look Joni had given her. It was gone in a second, like a burst soap bubble, leaving him to wonder if he'd imagined it.

"No," Rebecca said. "She didn't leave with anyone."

"You were there?"

"I was painting." She indicated the sketches on the trestle table.

"Okay. I want—"

He stopped. Off guard for a moment, he had noticed how goose bumps had raised on Rebecca's legs. This sudden, close, microscopic sense of her skin put him off track and she caught the change. She dropped her eyes to where he was looking, understood, and raised her eyes to his.

"Yes?" she said slowly. "What else do you want from us? What else can we do?"

Caffery straightened his tie—*she's a witness, for Christ's sake*.

"I need someone to identify Petra Spacek."

"*I* can't do it," Joni said simply. "I'd puke."

"Rebecca?" His will stretched out to her. "Will you do it?"

After a moment she closed her mouth and nodded silently.

"Thank you." He swallowed the remainder of his beer. "And you're absolutely certain you didn't see Shellene Craw leave the pub with anyone?"

"No. We'd tell you if we had."

* * *

They walked back to the car. Essex looked drained.

"You okay?"

"Yes," he croaked, clutching his chest and grinning. "I'll get over it. I'll get over it. Do you think they're gay?"

"You'd love that, wouldn't you?"

"No, seriously, do you reckon?"

"They had separate bedrooms." He looked at Essex's face and wanted to laugh. "They weren't real, you know."

Essex stopped with his hand on the car door. "What you talking about?"

"Joni. Silicone. They weren't real."

Essex put his elbows on the car roof and stared at him. "And what makes you such an expert?"

He smiled. "Experience? Three decades of changing shapes in *Men Only*? I can just tell. Can't you?"

"No." Essex was openmouthed. "No. Since you ask. No, I couldn't tell." He climbed huffily into the car and put his seat belt on. They'd driven a short way when he turned to Caffery again. "You sure?"

"Sure I'm sure."

Essex sighed wearily and looked out of the window. "What is the world coming to?"

It was still light when Caffery got home, and he found Veronica on a recliner on the patio, sullen and silent, watching the shadows lengthen in the garden. She wore an apricot mohair cardigan draped around her shoulders and there was a half-empty bottle of muscadet next to the recliner.

"Evening," he said lightly. He wanted to ask her what she was doing in his house again, but the stiff angle of her head warned him she'd like to draw him into an argument. He passed and went to the end of the garden, linking his hands into the wire fence, facing away from her.

From across the railway cutting a thin plume of smoke rose into the pink sky. Caffery pressed his face against the wire. Penderecki.

Sometimes, in the evenings, Caffery would watch Penderecki in his garden, moving around, smoking and absently scratching between his buttocks like an old gorilla preparing for sleep. The garden was little more than a patch of gray earth between the house and the railway cutting, scattered with old engines, a fridge and a rusting axle from a trailer. The land on that side of the cutting had once been a brick field and gardeners in the row of fifties houses still turned up half London Stocks on their hoes.

Hard soil to dig. Caffery didn't think Ewan was buried there.

Penderecki, his back to Caffery, wore his customary nicotine-brown vest. One hand rested on a rake—next to him the battered incinerator coughed smoke into the air. Seventeen years ago Penderecki had discovered Caffery's habit of collecting things, going through his rubbish, taking everything that might provide clues about Ewan. And this had become ritual: burning his household refuse and, to ensure that Caffery knew about it, doing it in plain view, in the back garden.

As Caffery watched, Penderecki cleared his throat, hawked out phlegm onto the earth and became perfectly still, one hand on the incinerator lid, responding with his acute sensitivity to Jack's presence. The knowing pose, the womanly hips, the gray hair slicked down over a bright pink scalp; Caffery felt the stirrings of ancient anger unraveling from him, as if Penderecki could reel it in across the hundred yards of evening air which separated them.

Penderecki turned slowly to face him and smiled.

Blood rushed to Caffery's face. He pushed himself away from the fence, angry at being caught, and strode back down the garden.

From the patio Veronica regarded him steadily.

"What?" He stopped. "What are you staring at?"

In reply she breathed out loudly through her nose and half closed her eyes.

"What? What is it?"

She sighed heavily.

Caffery opened his hands. "*What?*"

And then he remembered. The tests.

"Jesus." He shook his head, deflated. "I'm sorry. You've heard?"

"Yes."

"And?"

"Oh, I'm afraid it's back. The Hodgkin's is back." The eyes narrowed, her face twisted, but no tears came.

Caffery stood quite still, staring at her. This was it, then.

"Dr. Cavendish called. The fact is I have to start the chemo again." She tightened the cardigan around her shoulders. "But, look, we're not going to make a fuss about it. Okay?"

Caffery dropped his head and stared blindly at the concrete. "I'm sorry."

"Don't be sorry." She reached over and patted him on the hand. "It's not your fault."

"We'll cancel the party," he said.

"No! No, I won't have anyone feeling sorry for me. We're not canceling the party."

Nine

BY THE TIME the morning meeting started Caffery had spoken to Virgo, an East London agency who represented twenty-two-year-old Kayleigh Hatch, stripper, sometime prostitute, full-time drug user. They remembered the Bugs Bunny tattoo, and when Caffery heard that the last gig Kayleigh had done was at the Dog and Bell, he asked Virgo to courier over a photograph.

He taped it to the whiteboard next to the shots of Petra Spacek, Shellene Craw and Michelle Wilcox.

"This pub's our starting point." He rested his elbows on the desk and looked at the assembled investigating teams. "We've got surveillance on it as of this A.M. but the DCS has made it clear that before we go in mob-handed he wants IDs on the victims. So today we're working on that." He nodded at the new photo. "Now—Hatch. At last a name. I think this is victim number four we're looking at. And the only one, if you think back to the PM protocol, who didn't have the wounds to the head. Other than that she fits the pattern: drug use, prostitution. And, like the others, she *wasn't* raped. If she had intercourse it was consensual and a condom was used." He paused, allowing that to sink in. "Hatch's mother put her on the missing persons two weeks ago. She's over in Brentford, so, Essex, you might like to make that an action for this morning. But notice that the only other person reported missing was Wilcox. All the others were suspiciously easy to spirit away, weren't they? Think about that when you're on the knock. Now, Logan." He addressed the exhibits officer. "How's that DNA coming along?"

"Almost worthless for much more than blood group, sir. Too degraded even for a polymerase chain."

"The blood group?"

"AB neg. Not Harrison's."

"Anything from toxicology?"

"Nothing at present."

"So we still don't know how he's sedating them?"

"Still no guesses."

"Okay." He took his glasses off and rubbed his eyes. He was tired. Last night Veronica had slid effortlessly into sleep beside him, while he, restless and wide-eyed, lay far into the night, staring at her back, as if he might see the specter of the cancer creeping through the soft muscles and veins. "Okay, Logan, let us know when you hear anything." He put his pen down and nodded at Maddox. "Yes. That's all."

"Right." Maddox leaned forward in his seat. "Now—I know I'm pissing in the wind here but I'm going to ask you nicely, very nicely, to make sure none of the team attach a moniker to this case. We refer to him as the 'target' or the 'offender.' None of this 'Birdman' shit I've been hearing. And I never want to come in here and find the blinds up, I don't care how hot it gets. The press are holding fire, but for how long is anybody's guess. So, just to reiterate, I can't say it enough times: *be circumspect.*"

He looked around at the faces with his intense gray eyes, trying to spot a weak link. Everyone met his gaze. He nodded, satisfied.

"Right. Bollocking over." He put his fountain pen in his pocket. "That's all for now, gentlemen. Get those actions knocked out today, phone-ins every two hours and see you back here at seven. Be careful out there, and all that shit." He had risen from his seat and was gathering his papers when someone spoke from the back of the room.

"Yes, sorry, sir, there's something else."

All heads turned. DI Diamond, neatly shaved and dressed in a dark gray Pierre Cardin suit, sat tapping his fingers on his knee. Everyone in the room leaned forward a fraction.

"Inspector Diamond." Maddox sat down.

"A result from the door-to-door. A sighting."

The room became very quiet. Caffery reopened his file and put his glasses back on. This should have come up at the beginning of the meeting.

"A *sighting*?" Maddox frowned. "Why didn't you—?"

"It's a sensitive one. Sir."

"Meaning?"

"It's an IC3, sir. A black male. Sits in a red car outside the crusher's yard. Hangs around for hours, doing nothing, parked up, just his side lights on."

"Okay." Maddox opened his file and uncapped his fountain pen. "Any follow-ups? Plates?"

"No. Possibly might be talking a D reg. I thought, you know, being an IC3, might be a sensitive subject. Then there's this." He bent over and pulled a bag from under his seat. It was a plastic exhibits bag, tagged and double-labeled. He held it up; a few earth-caked bottles rolled against each other.

"You've lost me," Maddox said.

"Wray & Nephew rum." Diamond's face was pale, controlled, as if there was a smirk waiting in the cheek muscles. "These were found within five feet of the first body. More were found near the others." Maddox looked blank. "Wray & Nephew, sir. It's as Jamaican as signing on."

Caffery and Kryotos exchanged a look. Maddox put his pen down.

"Not necessary or constructive, Mr. Diamond." His face was tight. "And you need my permission to remove anything from the exhibits room."

"It's a lead."

"A *lead,* for fuck's sake?" Caffery muttered.

Diamond stared at him, suddenly cold. "And you've got a better idea?"

"Several."

"Okay," Maddox interjected, tapping his pen impatiently. "We'll add this as a slant to all interviews. If a name comes up find out *subtly* what color they are. And I do mean subtly." He capped his pen. "We'll apply for a second surveillance on the yard. Even if this *isn't* the target we still need to speak to him. And Diamond—"

"Yeah?"

"Cut the racist crap." He stood up. "Okay?"

Ten

CAFFERY LEFT THE MEETING without speaking to Maddox. He didn't like the change in the air. He didn't believe that the killer was black: he believed, just from Krishnamurthi's findings, that Birdman's trail would be picked up somewhere between the Trafalgar Road pub and a local hospital. Not a doctor and probably not an unskilled ancillary worker—but someone connected to the medical profession, possibly from the skilled or professional ranks. Maybe a technician or administrator. Even a nurse.

He parked outside the junk shop and was about to put money in the Pay and Display when a door slammed and Rebecca trotted out to the car. She was wearing a short cotton shift dress in pale pink and her long cinnamon hair fell in a straight line to her waist. She jumped into the backseat and the battered old Jaguar was suddenly filled with her perfume.

He swiveled around. "You okay about this?"

"Why wouldn't I be?"

"I don't know," he said truthfully, and put the car into gear. "I don't know."

They drove the two short blocks to the mortuary in silence, Caffery watching her in the rearview mirror. She stared out of the window, her shoulders relaxed, one hand in her lap, her long glossy legs pushed negligently out, as the shadows of lampposts and houses flickered across her face. Rebecca's cooperation was a fragile oddity, and he wasn't sure he knew how to preserve it.

"Do you mind if I ask you a personal question?" he said as they walked through the memorial garden toward reception.

"About what Joni does? What I *did*?" She didn't turn to him. She held her head erect with an odd, First Lady solemnity. "Are you going to ask me how I ended up doing that?"

"No." He patted his pockets, feeling for his tobacco. "I was going to ask you why you share with Joni."

"Shouldn't I?"

"You're very different people."

"Because she's from a lower class, you mean?"

"No. I—" He stopped. Maybe that *was* what he meant. "She seems much younger than you."

"We're in love. Isn't that clear?"

Caffery smiled and shook his head. "I don't think so."

"But that's what you wanted to hear, isn't it? It's the first thing most men want to know: are we screwing each other?"

"Yes," he nodded. "I'm human, it was the first thing I asked myself. But I'm thinking of something else. You've got your painting; you've got a purpose. Joni's just—"

"Drifting?"

"Yes."

"And because she takes drugs?"

"I don't think *you* do."

"I do if I feel like it." She flashed him a smile. "I'm an artist, Mr. Caffery, I'm expected to be dissolute. And Joni will find her purpose soon. It took me long enough."

"You're going to hang around and wait?"

She thought about this for a moment, her head tilted on one side. "Well, yes," she said slowly, pushing her hair back. "I owe her, I guess . . ." She paused, thinking how to phrase it.

"It sounds dumb, thinking about it, a dumb reason for sticking by someone, but Joni—" She caught his look and broke off, smiling. "No. I'm making this too easy for you."

"Oh, come on."

"I've just told you, I'm making it too easy." She paused outside reception and turned to him. "Anyway, now you have to tell me something."

"Go on, then."

"Am I ever going to be able to forget what I see today?"

"It gets different people different ways."

"How does it get you?"

"You want to know?"

"That's why I asked."

Caffery glanced through the smoked-glass doors into the air-conditioned reception area. "I think that ending up here, accounted for, is one step better than disappearing forever. They might never have been found."

At that Rebecca looked at him thoughtfully for a long time, her mouth in a soft, straight line, until he could stand the scrutiny no longer.

"Enough," he said, holding the door open for her. "Shall we go in?"

In the viewing booth the purple curtains rustled, proof of the presence of a mortician busying himself over Spacek's body. Rebecca stood with her head twisted away, her fingers lightly resting on the glass.

"It smells like a hospital," Rebecca said. "Is *she* going to smell?"

"You won't get that close."

"Okay," she said tightly. "I'm ready."

The electric curtains slowly peeled back. Petra Spacek's eyes and mouth were closed. The stitching, where Krishnamurthi had pulled her scalp back over her skull and sewn it closed, was muffled in purple satin. The body had been prepared for this viewing—small cotton pads lay under the eyelids to plump out the flat eyeballs—but Caffery realized too late how bruised and distorted Spacek's face was. He had forgotten in the carnage of the first postmortem how it had been eroded away during the months in the crusher's yard. Now he was embarrassed.

"Rebecca, look, maybe this is a bad idea—"

But she had turned to see. Her eyes scanned the face for less than five seconds. She made a small noise in the back of her throat and turned away.

"Are you all right?"

"Yes." She said it to the wall.

"I shouldn't have brought you here. She's not recognizable."

"She is."

"You think it's her?"

"Yes. I mean, maybe. I don't know. Give me a moment."

"Take your time."

She drew in a deep breath and straightened her shoulders. "Okay," she muttered. She caught her hair up into a bunch and held it against her neck, using the other hand to cover her mouth. Slowly she turned back to the body. Her eyes moved over the face, taking her time now, daring herself not to look away.

"What are those marks on her forehead?"

"We don't know."

She dropped her hair and turned to him. It was intended to seem casual but Caffery sensed it was to prevent her having to look at Spacek any more. "I think it's her." She spoke in a whisper, her eyes flicking sideways, as if she were afraid Spacek might be listening.

"You think?"

"No. I'm sure it's her."

"Her face has lost a lot of definition."

Rebecca closed her eyes and shook her head. "She was thin anyway. You could always see her—her bones." She opened her eyes slowly and looked at him. For the first time he realized she was shivering. "Can we go now?"

"Come on." He put a hand on her arm, conscious of the sudden coolness of her skin. "We'll do the paperwork in reception."

He brought her water in a waxed paper cone.

"Thanks."

"I want you to sign this." He sat next to her and opened his briefcase, searching for the forms. Rebecca put a cool hand on his wrist and pointed into the Samsonite.

"What's that?"

Spacek's postmortem photographs were visible in a clear plastic envelope. Caffery closed the briefcase.

"I'm sorry you saw that."

"Was that when they brought her in? Was that what she looked like?"

"I shouldn't have allowed you to see that."

"Oh God." She crushed the paper cup. "It wasn't any worse than the nightmares I've had since you two came knocking at my door."

"We're trying to keep it brief."

"If that's an apology it's accepted."

He put the briefcase on his lap and spread the forms out on it. "Here." He uncapped a pen with his teeth and placed crosses on the forms. "I need you to sign here and here. This tells me you've viewed the body and—" He broke off. Someone had cleared their throat forcibly. A distinct *shut up for a moment* warning.

They both looked up.

DS Essex stood at the reception entrance, the door held open, one hand extended to usher in two women dressed almost identically in jeans and blouson leather jackets. They filed in meekly and took the seats Essex indicated without a word.

"I'm just going to make sure that everything's ready." Essex touched the hand of the older woman. "Tell your sister if you need anything. Okay?"

She nodded dully and pressed a tissue to her mouth. Her face was expressionless, blank. Her jeans were skintight, and there were little scabs on her ankles where her sandals had rubbed.

Rebecca stared stupidly at the two women, knowing, without knowing how she knew, that these were the relatives of another victim. Caffery was silent. He knew more. He knew the details. He knew that this was Kayleigh Hatch's mother and aunt.

The aunt, who had been staring out past the potted palm to the sun-filled memorial garden, shifted in her seat, sighed and placed her arm around the other woman. Soft leather creaked.

"It mightn't be her. That's what you got to tell yourself, Dor."

"But it might, mightn't it? Oh, Jesus." She turned dull eyes to the window. "You'd think they'd let you smoke in here, wouldn't you?"

The glass doors opened and one of F team stepped into the cool, a half-smile on his face. DI Diamond followed, removing sunglasses, laughing. He glanced at Rebecca and let the laugh fade to a small, knowing smile as the two men crossed reception on the way to the coroner's office. When they had rounded the corner the laughter continued.

"How about this one, then, eh?" Diamond said. "Listen, yeah?"

"Yeah."

"Okay. What's the difference between a hooker and an onion?"

"Go on, then. What?"

"C'mon, a hooker and an onion."

"Yeah, *what*? I give up."

"Okay." He paused, and from the squeak of shoe leather on lino Caffery knew Diamond had stopped and turned to the other officer. "You can cut up a hooker without crying."

In reception four people stared at the floor. Caffery sprang to his feet and rounded the corner.

"Hey."

Diamond turned mildly surprised eyes to him. "All right?"

"Use a bit of fucking decorum," he hissed. "You know where you are."

"Sorry, mate." Diamond raised a hand. "Won't happen again." He turned and the two men continued in the direction of the coroner's property office, softly snickering, their shoulders dipping into each other as if Caffery's intervention made the joke even sweeter. Caffery breathed out slowly and returned to reception. The damage was done. Kayleigh's mother's face was wet with new tears.

"Oh, Doreen, oh, Dor." The aunt buried her face in her sister's collar. "Don't cry, Doreen."

"But what if it's my baby in there, my baby, my little, little girl? What if it's her?"

Eleven

KAYLEIGH HATCH was identified by her aunt.
"She's cut her hair, but it's her. I'm sure of it."
And AMIP had four positive IDs out of five. The chief superintendent had decided to lift the press moratorium that evening, so Maddox agreed they could risk a visit to the pub.

The rain had settled with depressing familiarity on London. It was a fresh, acidic rain, spring-bright compared to the usual greasy drizzle, but it was still rain. Seven of them, carrying raincoats, set out in two cars. Diamond drove two of F team in the Sierra. Caffery took his Jaguar, with Maddox, Essex and Logan for passengers.

The Dog and Bell, flaking paint and grime, occupied a plot on the suffocating Trafalgar Road between a dilapidated travel agent and a Kleenezie launderette. Inside, it smelled of stale tobacco and disinfectant. All conversation stopped and in the blue-smoke pall the punters, nursing their precious pints, turned expressionless faces to the seven detectives. DI Diamond moved to the far exit, DC Logan stood guarding the big, curved stairway with its polished Victorian banister. Maddox closed the door behind him with his foot. The barmaid, a woman in her sixties, as wiry as a leather strap, with high blue eye shadow and dyed-black hair, stood smoking behind the bar, unsurprised, watching them with bright thyroidal eyes.

"Okay, gents." Maddox held up his warrant card. "It's all completely routine. No need for panic."

Caffery slipped away from the bar and within ten minutes had accounted for two of the names in Harrison's list. The barmaid was named Betty and the dancer that day, a tall, irritable blonde from somewhere in the North, with closely spaced blue eyes and feet and hands like a teenage boy's, was named Lacey.

She was wearing stockings under a baggy hip-length red jumper and was in the upstairs toilet brushing silver glitter on her cheekbones when Caffery knocked on the door, carrying a double vodka and orange. The fundamental rules of trade.

"Shut the door," she muttered, taking the drink. "It's that fucking freezing in here. Supposed to be summer."

He closed the door and sat on a small stool in the corner. Lacey pecked at a cigarette, drawing smoke into her nostrils, leaning against the sink and watching him as he broke the news.

She was philosophical.

"That's the way with those types," she shrugged, turning to the mirror. "You won't catch me worrying about it. I'm too careful."

"We know you knew Shellene."

"Knew them all. Doesn't mean to say I trusted them. Or even liked them." She placed the cigarette on the edge of the sink, where it smoldered, adding its mark to the countless orange nicotine trails. "Couldn't leave your clobber in the dressing room with her around. That's the problem with scag. If you ask me, they've got that desperate for a hit they've gone and done a trick for some fucking lunatic."

"And Petra?"

"She wasn't a user, so she'd never do it for drugs. But it don't mean she never turned a trick. Does it?"

"Do you know the punters here?"

"I'm not here that often." She took another drag of the cigarette and threw the butt under the tap. "Ask Pussy Willow—she does nearly every show. It's empty today but when she's here the place gets rammed. All in love with her and her blow-up tits."

"Any of the punters hospital workers?"

"Solicitors, civil servants, students. This place isn't exclusively for the scum of the earth, you know." She sipped the vodka. "And there's a couple of types come in suited and booted, I think they're doctors or something like it."

Caffery took tobacco from his pocket and crumbled it into a Rizla. "Where do they come from? The doctors?"

"From over St. Dunstan's."

"Do you recall any names?"

"No."

"Any of them downstairs now?"

She thought for a moment. "No. Not when I last looked."

He bent his head to light the roll-up. "Thanks for the help, Lacey, thank you very much."

At the foot of the carved Victorian stairway Caffery stopped, his arm resting lightly on the worn banister.

Maddox was a foot or so in front of him, watching the room, arms folded. The officers were dotted around, their raincoats crumpled on stools next to them. On each table the four photos of the girls battled for a place amongst the glasses and ashtrays, circular beer stains seeping through the paper. Diamond sat with his jacket unbuttoned, his trousers riding up to reveal a small expanse of novelty Warner Bros. sock, the Tasmanian devil. Opposite him a pair of laborers frowned into their beers.

The door opened and a young black man in his twenties ducked in out of the rain. He wore a gray Tommy Hilfiger baseball cap, high-top Nikes, and was slight but muscled. His left canine was capped in gold. He was almost at the bar before he realized everyone was staring at him.

DI Diamond was on him in seconds, haunches twitching with the thrill of the hunt. He placed a hand lightly but pointedly on his shoulder and steered him toward a table.

"You can't let him interview him," Caffery muttered in Maddox's ear. "Not as a witness. He'll turn it to a suspect interview."

"Don't interfere," Maddox said.

"He's already made up his mind who he's looking for."

"That," Maddox said, "was an order."

Jerry Henry, known on the streets around Deptford as Gemini, had never been busted. He put it down to the fact that he was small-time. That was his strength. For the Bill he simply wasn't worth the effort. He saw himself like a basking shark, just trailing around the hems of Deptford, picking off whatever drifted out from the two big outfits that had the area sewn up. He didn't do any harm.

But the flip side of this coin was that small meant defenseless. The Bill weren't stupid; they knew that the goods had to come from somewhere. Sometimes they'd go for someone like him, just to push it back further and further until it splashed up against one of the *ranks*. The Bill wouldn't think twice about sacrificing him if it meant opening up one of the big South London outfits.

Whatever it is they want, he told himself as he followed the cop over to a table, *keep cool, deny it, let them prove it.* He ran through what he had in his inventory today. It could just about pass as personal use, but Dog from New Cross had sneaked some crack out of one of the Peckham labs for him, just a little, cookies Gemini had broken down. "*Keep it in your mouth, man. Swallow it if you get any shit.*" But Gemini hadn't wanted to, it was tucked in his high-tops, and now he was going to pay the price.

"Deny it. Style it out."

"What's that you said?" the cop asked.

"Not'ing," Gemini mumbled. He sank into the seat.

"All right, now it's just a routine inquiry." The cop pulled the sides of his jacket back, straddled the stool and sat facing him, his small, round belly settling on his thighs, his elbows on the circular table. Gemini slouched back, one hand shoved into the waist of his Calvins, his head tilted, mouth deep and sullen.

"Keep cool. Deny it. Let them prove it. Style it out," he muttered.

That infuriated the cop. He shot his face forward until it was inches from Gemini's. "What? Are you trying to *co-mmun-icate* with me?"

"Don't get vex." Gemini didn't flinch at the bitter breath. Casually he opened his hand where it rested on the seat. "An' who you, man?"

The cop swallowed hard and pulled back. He tapped his ballpoint on the table. "Detective Inspector Diamond." He enunciated the "Detective Inspector" with care. "Are you a regular here?"

"What it to you, man?"

"Do you know any of the girls who work down here?"

"No." Gemini clicked his tongue against the back of his teeth dismissively. "I don't know dem girls."

"You've never met any of them? I find that surprising." The cop held his gaze with his arrogant, washed-out eyes and pushed a photograph across the table. "Does this help?"

Gemini recognized them immediately. Especially the blonde. Shellene. He'd been retailing to her for months and cabbying for her. A couple of weeks back she'd given him a little blow job in the backseat of his GTI, in return for some rock. He wondered what the girls had been telling the Bill about his operation.

"I ain't seen dem. Maybe this one, a dancer here, ain't it? But it's all."

"You know she's a dancer here."

"I seen her."

"When did you *last* see her?"

Gemini shrugged. "Long time now, innit."

"Have you ever seen anyone leaving with any of these girls?"

Gemini gave a derisory laugh. He knew how the question was angled. "Now, why you arxing me this dibby-dibby question, boy? And dem say English police is clever!"

"Are you going to answer me?"

"I know what yous is like."

The cop became very still. He was staring at his hands. Gemini could see his anger spreading out under the smooth white skin. When he looked up, his pupils had narrowed to pinpoints. "Mr., uh?"

"Mr. No One to you."

"Ah, yes, of course. Mr. No One." He lifted his hands; they'd left sweat prints on the table. "Well, Mr. No One, Mr. *Fuck-All,* I didn't understand your last comment. Was it, by any chance"—he leaned in, his lips peeled away from his teeth, his voice low—"a *slur* on the law-keeping force in this country, the country which has generously supported you, and will support any number of *pickaninnies* that you spawn, house you, feed you and pick up the pieces after you mug some poor little old lady of her pension? Is that what it was?"

"You's a racist man," Gemini said, smiling lazily. "I might be stupid nigger boy to you, but me know me rights. I know what de PCA is. I read de Macpherson report."

The cop didn't flinch. "If you *really* read the Macpherson report you'd know you haven't got a leg to stand on. No one can hear what I'm saying. I can spade, darkie, nigger, sooty you all I like." He smiled. He was enjoying this. "I can throw it all at you. And you know what? At the end of the day it's your word against mine. With every little jungle bunny in the system jumping up and down and shouting 'racist,' you think anyone is going to listen to you, you low-life little shit?"

Gemini's composure drained out of him. "I ain't have to listen to this." He stood up. "You want me to help you, *Raas,* you come get me."

The cop was on his feet in a second, blocking the door. "Where the fuck do you think you're going?" he said pleasantly. The words slipped out like honey. "Nigger cunt."

And Gemini snapped. Grabbing a pint from the nearest table, he threw it in the cop's face. The cop wasn't quick enough to close his eyes. The beer made contact, and he spun away, his hands flying up to his face.

"*You little shit!*"

But Gemini was out of the door before anyone could react.

To Caffery, standing at the bottom of the stairs, the whole encounter seemed to have the slow-motion surrealism of a silent film. The two men had been smiling, talking almost casually, then in the next second Diamond was doubled over, clutching his face as if he'd been slashed. Caffery expected blood, but Diamond quickly wiped his eyes and ran out the door, jacket flapping. Two of F team leaped up, interviews forgotten, to stand in the doorway, letting the rain splatter their shirts as they stared off down the street at their DI.

They didn't have to wait long. Mel Diamond reappeared in the doorway, breathing hard, his jacket dark with rain and beer.

"It's okay." He leaned over and spat on the pavement. "Got his plates. The little shit."

On the way back to Shrivemoor, Caffery drove. Maddox sat next to him, his wet raincoat folded inside out on his lap, Essex and Logan slouched in the back, smelling vaguely of beer. Caffery was silent. In the wing mirror he could see the Sierra following at a short distance. Diamond drove. Caffery caught glimpses of him talking and laughing each time the wipers cleared the windscreen: the Sierra was misty with condensation, the Jaguar's windows remained cold and clear.

"They've all agreed to come in for a mouth swab." Maddox sighed and looked out as they passed the twin eggshell-blue cupolas of the Naval College. "Every last one except Diamond's newfound chum. He drives a red GTI, two witness statements put Craw leaving with him—"

"White," Jack murmured. "White through and through."

"Sorry?"

"Series killers hardly ever fish in other racial pools. They just don't. It's such a basic principle it's almost laughable."

For a moment no one spoke. Maddox cleared his throat and said, "Jack, let me explain: there is nothing, *nothing,* on God's green earth guaranteed to get the chief's hackles up like profiling. I think we discussed this when you transferred."

"Yes." He nodded. "And I think it's time you and I talked about it."

"Go on then, talk."

Caffery glanced in the mirror at Essex and Logan. "In private."

"Really? Good. Let's do it. Now. Come on. Stop the car."

"Now? Fine." He took a left into the park, stopped the car at the edge of the road, put the hazard warnings on. The two of them jumped out.

"Right." Rain from an ancient oak overhead hissed and bounced off the pavement against their ankles. Maddox held his coat over his head like a monk's cowl. "What's going on with you?"

"Okay." Caffery hiked his jacket over his head and the two men stood closer. In the car Essex and Logan tactfully found something else to stare at. "It feels, Steve, it feels as if you and me are walking in different directions."

"Keep going. Get it off your chest."

"I meant what I said. This is not a black crime."

Maddox rolled his eyes. "How many times do I have to—" He stopped. Shook his head. "We've gone through this already—I told you the chief's position."

"And if he knew we'd taken one look at a couple of poxy *rum bottles,* for Christ's sake—rum bottles brought in by the team's resident Nazi—and decided we had a black target, what would his position be then? Think about it." He held his hand up, his fingertips pressed together, white with pressure. "Think about the bird. Can you really picture that useless bit of shit in the pub having the savvy—or even the *imagination,* for Christ's sake—to do something like that?"

"Jack, Jack, Jack. Maybe you're right. But look at it from my point of view. I don't want this to be an IC3 any more than you do, and nor does the governor, which is exactly why we have to eliminate hard evidence."

"*Hard evidence?*" Jack sucked in a breath. "You call that hard evidence?"

"There was an Afro-Caribbean hair pulled from Craw's scalp and a sighting near North's construction yard—plus all the shit we've collected in the last hour. Plenty enough to worry me. Don't take offense now, Jack, but remember, in B team the buck stops with me, not you. And if I have to choose between listening to a new DI who I've known five minutes and brown-nosing the CS, well, Jack, with all respect . . ." He paused, took a breath. "Well, what would *you* do?"

Caffery looked at him for a long time. "Then I want this on the record."

"Go ahead."

"We're steering in the wrong direction. Someone out there thinks he's a doctor. We should be looking for a hospital worker. A *white* hospital worker."

Maddox raised his eyebrows. "Based on?"

"Based on what Krishnamurthi said, the target's got rudimentary medical knowledge. Steve, today wasn't an average
day in the pub—we got it wrong. On your average day the
place is full, and some of the punters are hospital workers."

"Okay, okay, calm down. Hold fire until tomorrow's
meeting, yeah? Then we can look at this in the cold light of
day."

"I want to start now."

"What do you think you're going to do? Stake out every
hospital in area four—RG, PD and PL?"

"I'll start with RG. Right here. St. Dunstan's. It's the nearest to the pub. Approach personnel. Narrow it down through
them, then do a blanket interview. If that draws a blank, *then*
I'll have a look at Lewisham, maybe Catford."

Maddox shook his head. "They won't have it. These personnel people are tight as arseholes."

"Let me try."

Maddox lowered the raincoat and turned his face to the
sky, his eyes screwed up against the rain. When he looked
down, his face was composed. "Okay. You win. You can have
Essex, if you want him, and you've got four days from Monday to come up with something."

"*Four days?*"

"Four days."

"But—"

"But what? You'll find the time. And you don't skip a
single team meeting and if I need to pull you off I'll do it at a
moment's notice. Anything else?"

"Yes."

"What?"

"You still coming to our party, sir?"

"Ask me when I'm not pissed off with you."

Twelve

THE GIRL IN THE BACK of his GTI was wearing a lime-green spandex miniskirt and platform sandals. Her hair, cut bluntly at jaw level, had one gold-sprayed chunk in it. She was dark-eyed, coffee-skinned, and Gemini knew Africa was somewhere in her bloodline.

She'd approached him in the Dog and Bell last night, before the trouble, before the police, and asked him to meet her tonight at the north side of the Blackwall Tunnel to drive her to Croom's Hill. She had some business there. At the time he'd thought nothing of it, but since the pub raid this afternoon he'd been nervous.

Gemini was no more than a wannabe Yardie gang-banger born in Deptford. In spite of his walk and talk the closest he'd ever been to Spanish Town Road was the Bounty rum his aunts brought to London each visit. Dog—his main contact—knew this and played on it, using Gemini to shift stuff that was too white for his own tastes: Es, microdots, scag. Last week it was sixty grams of "Special K": Ketalar, horse anesthetic. Gemini, disgusted and shamed, had no choice but to move it for him, and now it looked like one of those girls the cops were asking about had blabbed. Or—the thought made his blood run cold—what if one of them had gotten ill on something he'd sold them? The crack should have been as pure as morning. But as for the scag—everyone in Deptford expected local scag to be a cut deck. But cut with what? Baby laxative? Dried milk? *Ammonia?* Or something even deadlier. If that had happened it wouldn't be just the police Gemini had to worry about—the public would turn it into a witch-hunt and then the ranks would want to know who had put them in the spotlight.

And now it crossed his mind that the girl in his car might be a setup. He kept her in his rearview mirror as he drove. They'd passed St. Dunstan's when she leaned forward and tapped him on the shoulder.

"I heard in the pub maybe you could help me."

"Yeah?"

"Like rock or H or something."

He studied her in the mirror. Whatever the police were onto, he couldn't afford to shy away from a deal. It was lifeblood.

"There's somewhere here," he said eventually, and flicked the indicator, turning the red GTI into a cul-de-sac. It had stopped raining midafternoon. Ahead he could see the four towers of the London Transport power station against the orange sky, and a column of smoke rising from the damp allotments next to the railway. He cut the engine. The girl smoked silently, gazing out of the window with cool disinterest. He was sure—had to be sure—she wasn't a cop. He swung around in his seat, hugging the head rest with his right arm. "So what can I help you wid?"

She didn't look at him, just went on staring out of the window. "What you got?"

"I ain't stupid, know what I'm saying? From where the Bill are crawling around me, you know, I decide I ain't going to put my feet straight in no trap."

"I want H. Heroin, horse, smack . . . whatever the fuck you call it. Drugs, okay? I ain't no cop."

Gemini relaxed a little. "Okay, okay. I got a bit. Me mostly into rocks, draw, know what I'm saying?"

"One wrap."

"One?"

"Yeah. More's waiting for me."

He'd been hoping for something higher, but his grin didn't falter. "Okay, sweet, sweet. That's a tenner."

"And then let's go."

"Okay, okay." From the pocket of his blue Helly Hensen sou'wester he flipped a little folded envelope into his palm. Holding the wad between his middle and forefingers, he extended his hand between the seats. She better not drop anything, he thought. At the end of the night he was going straight down to Creek Road and get his car cleaned inside and out. He'd heard that the Bill had techniques that could vacuum the car out and detect the smallest grain of gear.

The girl checked it, rewrapped the package and paid him. "Let's go."

Gemini jammed the car into reverse. "Croom's Hill?"

"Yeah. Blackheath end."

On the heath they stopped for pedestrian lights.

"Do a right here, and then you can drop me."

"You live up here?"

"My friend does."

"Is it?" He tapped his fingers on the steering wheel and stared at her in the mirror. He'd dropped a couple of the girls up here in the last few months and they'd all said the same thing. Maybe there was a punter up here. "Who your friend, then, girl?"

"Just a friend." She looked out of the window and went on smoking. She had a little mole above the top left-hand corner of her mouth.

"I drop some of dem girls up here before."

"Did you?" She wasn't interested.

"Coupla white girls."

"Is it?"

The lights changed. Gemini pulled off to the right, liking the way the car felt. "She went in one o'dem big houses. Know what I'm saying?" He grinned at her in the mirror but she ignored him.

"You can stop here."

Gemini pulled the car into the curb and put it into neutral. "Four quid."

She got out of the car, slamming the door. Dropping a five through the two-inch gap of opened window.

"And hey—"

"Yeah?" He looked up, grinning.

"You should stop with the Yardie shit." She held a delicately extended finger in the air, her eyebrows arched sarcastically. "'Cause, y'know, you sound a real prick, yeah?"

She turned away. Gemini picked up the note from his lap and watched her legs flash away from him in the twilight. He wasn't offended.

"You got a *sweet* nigger's arse under that skirt, girl," he whispered, still grinning. "Someone's going to get a piece tonight."

She turned down the twist in Croom's Hill and Gemini let the car drift forward a few feet. But she had disappeared. He waited a few moments, to see if she'd appear from behind the curve in the road, but she didn't. Mosquitoes circled lazily under the security lights of a brick-walled house—the road remained empty. Clicking his tongue against the roof of his mouth and shaking his head, Gemini cranked up Shabba Ranks and headed back down to east Greenwich.

It wasn't till he got back to the pub that he remembered the last time he'd seen that Shellene girl the cops had been asking about. Last week. Last Monday. After the blow job, he'd dropped her in exactly the same place.

Thirteen

THE HOUSE:

A rambling Regency villa, set back from the road within a walled garden, overlooked by a stooping crowd of cedars. Once it had been owned by a wealthy patron of the Bloomsbury group, who had commissioned trompe l'oeils, grisaille murals. There was even a two-hundred-square-foot orangery rumored to be a Lutyens. The last visitors to this place, if asked to recall, would have remembered gardens on a far grander scale than was usual for most town homes. One could disappear in one of the many hived-off areas and lose track amongst the topiary and espaliered plums. White Pascali roses bloomed over trellised arbors, bees flew in straight lines down corridors of yew, searching out pyracantha and fuchsia.

But now there were blankets of rotting leaves piling up against the walls, and partially hidden near the garage entrance lay the skeletonized remains of a dog, trapped there since last summer. The curtains remained closed during the daytime. The cleaner, because of the trouble, had been sacked months ago, and gradually areas of the house had become unfit to live in. Harteveld moved through those parts at night only, shuffling along through the mess. But during the day the heavy oak door which led to that part of the house was locked. He couldn't risk unexpected visitors accidentally seeing his things. His *belongings*—

Tonight he had locked the door and was in the "public zone": the area he could afford to show outsiders, comprising the hallway, the kitchen, the cloakroom, the small study and the living room, where he stood now, by the fireplace in front of the portrait of his parents.

He's spent the afternoon cleaning—making it *safe* for tonight, hooking a hose to the sink in the main kitchen and sluicing disinfectant through the waste disposal. The smell, though, had defeated him. It was coming from—but at that point he had hesitated, his hand on the old door. For a long time he stared at the marquetry panels; the bamboo and spindly bridges supporting parasoled geishas. No. He turned away. Nothing he could do about the mess in there.

Now he swallowed two buprenorphine, washing them down with pastis and water. Then he opened a lapis lazuli snuffbox and, with the long, sharpened nail of his little finger, scooped a pile of cocaine into his left nostril. He rubbed the residue on his gum and closed his eyes for a moment.

If she didn't come soon he believed he would explode.

He bit his lip and stared up at the portrait of his parents: Lucilla and Henrick.

No, he realized, no, he wouldn't *explode*. What he would do was to haul himself up onto the mantelpiece, wait until he was sure he had his balance, then carefully lean forward and very precisely, with a minimum of fuss, bite Lucilla's face out of the canvas.

Fourteen

"THE KILLING FIELDS."

The words jumped out at Caffery from billboards outside newsagents as he drove to St. Dunstan's. Last night the news had been confirmed through the bureau, and now the press were crawling over Greenwich, clogging the streets, harassing the residents, setting up camp outside North's construction yard. The *Sun*'s banner was "Millennium Terror" with color shots of Shellene, Petra, Wilcox and Kayleigh above a black-and-white shot of the yard. The *Mirror* had a single photo of Kayleigh: she wore a cherry-pink satin off-the-shoulder dress and was holding a drink up to the camera. There were the predictable comparisons with the Wests, photos of number 25 Cromwell Street—"How could it happen again?" asked the *Sun*. The *Mirror* dubbed the killer, predictably, "the Millennium Ripper." Caffery had bet Essex that, of all the sobriquets, this would be the favorite.

The rest of AMIP were liaising with intelligence at Dulwich—putting a spotlight on Gemini, running checks to see if he was already "flagged," wanted by another Met unit. So Caffery, conscious that the stopwatch was running now, drove to St. Dunstan's Hospital alone. He parked at the foot

of Maze Hill where the lime trees and red walls of Greenwich
Park ended.

They're as tight as arseholes, these personnel people, Jack.
No magistrate in the country is going to grant a warrant to
open up the personnel files of an entire hospital because a
wet-behind-the-ears DI has a "feeling."

More than a feeling now, more than just a sense—now he
believed that the man he wanted knew this building. Whatever shape the road took he was certain that it would end
here. He stood for a moment, outside the hospital, imagining he saw something off center about the gray buildings,
the Portakabins in the brilliant yellow sunshine. The sky over
the incinerator chimney was the same saturated, surreal blue
as Joni's eye shadow, flattening perspective into Mondrian
blocks. But then he realized he was resketching the sky, the
world, to suit his picture of this place, and that the lines of
the buildings were straight, the windows unremarkable. He
straightened his tie and pushed through the plastic fire doors,
glad to rest his eyes.

Inside, the hospital was shabby; the corridors were hot
with the steam from unseen kitchens and sterilizing units,
a faulty fluorescent strip flickered. He was alone—his only
company footsteps echoing briefly from beyond a bend in the
passage, and a starling, flapping amongst the pipes in the ceiling. It dropped a tin-white pellet inches from Caffery's feet as
he pushed open the door marked "Personnel."

Take it slow. Take it too fast and they'll see you're
desperate.

The office was large, divided by portable screens, the
only sound the halting *tap . . . tap . . . tap tap tap . . . tap* of a
keyboard.

Caffery peered around a screen. A small, round-backed
clerk with a receding hairline, wearing a graying nylon shirt.
Tapping at a keyboard.

Not promising.

Caffery cleared his throat.

The clerk looked up. "Morning, sir. For the committee, is it?"

"No—not for the committee, Mr. . . . uh." He checked the nameplate on the desk. "Mr. Bliss. Detective Inspector Caffery. The head personnel officer, is he . . . ?"

"*She.*" He half stood. "*She's* sitting on the committee. They won't be out till eleven." He held his hand out to Caffery, who shook it. "Maybe I can help, Detective . . . sorry."

"Caffery."

"Detective Inspector Caffery."

"I'd like access to your personnel files."

"Oh." The clerk sat back and peered myopically up at him. "If I said no would you get a search warrant?"

"That's right." He wiped his hand discreetly on his trousers. Like the hospital itself, the clerk's hand was damp. "That's right, a search warrant."

"And then you'd get all the information you'd need anyway?"

"That's correct."

"Can I be rude enough to see your badge?"

"Of course."

Caffery stood in front of his desk, hands in his pockets, watching the clerk fastidiously jot down the details from his warrant card.

"Thank you, Detective Inspector Caffery." He placed the warrant card on the edge of the desk and leaned forward. "I'll okay it with my boss when she comes back from her meeting, but who do you want to know about? Anyone special?"

"No one special. Doctors, morticians, nurses. Anyone with surgical experience."

"Mmmm." The clerk scratched his pink ear. "What did you want? Home addresses?"

"Age, home address, contact numbers."

"It's going to take some time. Can I fax it to you? I think our fax machine is still working."

Caffery scribbled a number on the back of his card. He had, by fluke, hit this at the right angle.

"And is there a staff room? Somewhere quiet I could do interviews when I've sifted?"

"Mmm. Let's see . . . Wendy, one of our officers, is covering in the library. Maybe she'd open the back reference room for you. Let's go and have a look." He came out from behind the desk, pausing to lock the office as they left. "I hope you parked somewhere sensible. It's a funny old area."

"Up the hill, next to the park."

"You have to fight for a place these days—what with all the committee members and their big cars and their parking permits. I haven't got a choice. I'm not leaving the car at home, too much building construction—just trust some workman to accidentally chuck a spanner through the windscreen—so I come in and battle it out with the bigwigs. They're here all this week, you know, can't get away from them." He stopped. "Here we are. The library." He opened the door. "Wendy?"

They were looking at a small paneled entrance hall. Behind a sliding pane of glass a woman in a pearl-gray cardigan and batwing glasses looked up from her *Reader's Digest*. When she saw Caffery she blushed and shoveled the balled tissue she was clutching into her sleeve. "Hello."

"This is Wendy. She's usually with me in personnel."

Wendy gave Caffery a damp smile and extended her hand.

"Hello, Wendy." She blushed deeper as he took her hand. It had the same limp humidity as her colleague's.

"We're wondering if we could help Inspector Caffery here. He wants somewhere discreet to do some interviewing. Is that little back room of yours available?"

Wendy stood up and pulled the cardigan tightly around her breasts. Caffery saw she was younger than he'd thought; it was the clothes that belonged to an older woman. "I don't see why not. We're very old-fashioned about the police here. We like to give you all the support we can."

"I'll be on my way, then." The clerk held his hand out again and Caffery shook it.

"Grateful for your help. I'll wait for the fax."

Left alone, Wendy stared at Caffery in shy awe, waiting for him to speak, until he became irritated by her silence.

"The room?"

The spell broke. "Sorry!" She blushed and dabbed her nose. "Silly me. We don't get many policemen in here. We do admire you, admire the work you do—actually, we think you're wonderful. My brother wanted to join the force but he wasn't tall enough. Now, come through, come through." She unplugged an orange card from the computer and clipped it on a chain around her neck. "It's the little glass room at the back. I'll open it for you—see if it's appropriate."

The library was very quiet. Sunlight came through unwashed windows and lay in dusty slabs on the floor. A few doctors sat in little booths, absorbed in study. A pretty Indian woman in a white coat looked up at him and smiled. In front of her a periodical was open at a page headed "Amnion Rupture Sequence" and beneath it a large color photograph of a red accident of birth, a baby, headless, spread out next to a tape measure like a deboned chicken. Caffery didn't smile back.

Wendy stopped at a small glass-walled room. Blinds were drawn in the windows, isolating it from the library. "This is the quiet room." She opened the door. "Oh, Mr. Cook."

In the shadows at the back of the room a figure was rising from behind a desk. He wore a green overall, open to reveal a tie-dye T-shirt. His eyes were bloodshot, strangely colorless, and his pale red hair was long enough to fasten in a net at the nape of his neck. As Caffery's eyes got used to the dark, he saw that some of the hair sticking out of the neck of the T-shirt was gray.

Cook caught him looking. "Is it that bad?" He cast a sorrowful look over the shirt, his face deep in shadow. "I'm color-blind. Helpless as an infant when it comes to choosing clothes."

"It's very—young."

Cook raised his eyes to the ceiling. "I thought as much. They lie to you, these shop assistants. It's like a game to them." He shuffled around to the edge of the desk and for the first time Caffery noticed a book on the table. He just had time to register a black-and-white photo of a Stryker bone saw when Cook snapped the book shut, tucked it under his arm and shuffled to the door. "I'll be getting out of your way, then." He drew a pair of sunglasses from his overalls and rubbed his eyes. "All yours." He slipped outside and closed the door quietly.

Caffery and Wendy stood in silence for a moment until Wendy shook her head and made a disapproving clicking sound in her throat.

"Some of the people we employ. Really, it's a shame." She mopped her nose with the tissue from her sleeve and straightened her glasses. "Now, Inspector Caffery, can I get you a nice cup of tea? It's machine, I'm afraid, but I've got a little Nestle's evaporated under my desk I'd be happy to let you have . . ."

In Caffery and Maddox's office the blinds were up and the afternoon sun coming through the dusty window had grilled everything on the desk. Caffery could smell the hot plastic of the phone as he opened a window, pulled the blinds, leaned on his elbow and picked out Penderecki's number on the keypad. He let it ring and watched the hands on the clock turn. He knew it wouldn't be answered.

One day last year he had tried calling Penderecki midafternoon. He knew Penderecki's movements so intimately that he was puzzled when the phone wasn't answered. He let it ring, watching out of the French windows, wondering if the unthinkable had happened and Penderecki was lying dead on the floor of the house.

But then Penderecki's stout figure appeared in the back door, braces worn over a dirty vest. The trees were in full foliage, but Caffery could make out his face and the glutinous white arc of his arm waving amongst the leaves. It took him a moment to realize Penderecki was waving at him, putting his thumbs up, grinning his toothless smile. He was telling Caffery that he knew who was phoning.

From that day on, whether Caffery called him from the office or the house, Penderecki let it ring. On the rare occasions he did answer, it was with a dry accentless "Hello, Jack." Caffery assumed he'd bought a digital readout for the phone. Now the only pleasure was knowing that the sound of the phone ringing was filling the house for as long as he chose to let it. *Small childish pleasure, Jack. Maybe Veronica's right about you.* Sometimes he called several times a day.

He let it ring for ten minutes, then replaced the receiver and wandered into the incident room to see if a fax had come from the clerk at St. Dunstan's.

Fifteen

LUCILLA WAS half Italian, half German, the most volcanic presence in the Harteveld house. Dense-boned and walnut-skinned, as tall and wide as the door frames, at parties she couldn't be dissuaded from singing, propped against the Steinway, mascara running down her face, moved to tears by some aria. Toby Harteveld, remote behind his beautiful-English-boy hauteur, found it impossible to believe that this woman, with her black flaring hair and jealous rages, was really his mother. He learned early to hate her.

It was the summer between prep school and Sherborne when he walked into an unlocked bathroom to find her naked, one leg up on the commode as she shaved the thick black hairs trailing from the pubis down the inside of the thighs.

She smiled. "Hello, puppy. Here—" She held the razor out to him. "You can help."

"No, Mother." He was calm. As if he had always known this would happen.

"No?" She laughed. "No, Mother?" Her head lowered. "Are you a little poofter, T? Tell me? Are you a little buggerer? Mmm?"

"No, Mother."

"I'll tell your father you tried to touch me."

"No, Mother."

"No, Mother? You think I won't?" She inspected him with her shining black eyes, head on one side as if she were deciding which end to devour first, then with an impatient toss of the dark head she flung open the window and leaned out over the gravel court below, soft breasts spilling across the ledge. "Henrick! Henrick! Please come for your son."

Toby took the opportunity to slip out of the door. He raced down the stairs, ignoring the indignant shouts from the bathroom, past vibrating chandeliers and shocked staff, through paneled passageways and out into the grounds. He found an elm bole at the lakeside, curled up beside it and hid until the evening.

When he returned, the house was quiet, as if nothing much had happened. His father ladled lobster bisque at dinner, his thin lips slightly paler than usual, and the incident was never mentioned again.

Over the following months Toby became withdrawn. He demanded a lock on his bedroom and in the afternoon lay with his pale hands folded lightly over his stomach listening to Lucilla's explosive passions in the passages outside. Her mere existence made his internal organs contract; sometimes he fancied she had slyly removed his pillowcases from the laundry and rubbed herself, her juices, into them; he seemed to be able to smell her wherever he went. He learned to sleep facedown, his stomach pressed securely into the mattress in case she found a way to let herself into his room. He never, *ever* fell asleep until he was sure, absolutely sure, that his mother was safe in bed on the other side of the house.

Two years later in the family library after his first hunt, Toby met Sophie, the daughter of a local barrister. Long, thin and aloof as marble, she stood erect and white against the rich paneling. Everything Lucilla wasn't. Toby, fourteen, handed her a glass of champagne and was surprised and thrilled to notice that the fingers which took it were colder than the chilled glass stem.

Lucilla instantly sensed the attachment and chose that summer for his rite of passage. She sent father and son abroad. They washed up in Southeast Asia, Luzon to be precise, and Henrick, full of his own notions about how to rear his young, took Toby to a Makati whorehouse where he was presented with fifteen girls slouched on their *salung-puwets* behind a floor-to-ceiling pane of glass.

Toby chose the thinnest, palest of the girls. In bed he ordered her not to speak, not to move, no thrashing or wailing. Sipping coffee and eating fried *sinangag* on the balcony the next morning, overlooking sun-filled Pasay, he was overwhelmed with the sense that something abnormal was being born in him.

A month later his mother caught him in the yew topiary with Sophie, he with his jodhpurs around his knees, she closed eyes, long calm face, holding still as if for an X ray. By the time Toby had dressed and got back to the house Lucilla had already created pandemonium. The staff were milling about in the sun and Toby narrowly avoided being mowed down by the grim-faced Henrick reversing the Land Rover in a spray of gravel across the forecourt and down the driveway.

The message was clear—Toby was to deal with Lucilla alone.

Watched by the staff, Toby climbed the steps and placed his white hand on the heavy oak door, his eyes half closed as he waited for the subtle trembles which would map for him where in the house his mother was waiting.

She was in the formal dining room, pacing the length of the wall under the Antwerp tapestries, breathing loudly through her nose. The blue light from the window illuminated the fine tracery of tears on her jowls. It was the first time they had been alone together since the incident in the bathroom.

"Mother."

"Sit."

He sat at the head of the table, his father's place. To his left the blue window held the hazy sweep of the lawns and shadowy cypresses, but the paneled dining room was dark, as if the years of tension had collected there. Lucilla dropped into her usual mahogany chair, closed her eyes, placed both hands on her hot neck and shook her head. "That anemic creature. Her father is a damn pederast, she is a mistake of nature."

Toby was calm. "I don't have time for a display, Lucilla. Just tell me what I do now."

She opened her eyes at that, her hands trembling at her neck. "What did I do to deserve you for a son?"

"Tell me what I do now."

"You'll board at Sherborne until it is time to go to university."

"Is that it?"

"And in the holidays, since you hold me in such contempt, you will stay with the Chase-Greys in Connecticut. We'll make you an allowance."

"You don't want to see me again?"

Lucilla crossed herself, an ancient gesture he remembered her doing only once before. "I don't want to see you again."

Toby went back to Sherborne and he and Sophie didn't see each other again. Three years later she married a defense budget coordinator and went to live in Walton-on-Thames. Toby adapted well. Sophie, he had come to see, was not the cause but a symptom of something bigger. He had a sense of it gathering inside, dark and malformed, as charged as a storm.

In his last year at Sherborne he focused on getting into medical school. He was bright and the newly formed United Medical and Dental Schools of Guy's and St. Thomas's— UMDS—accepted him.

It was at UMDS that Birdman first began to unfurl and examine his wings.

Sixteen

NINE P.M. and in Shrivemoor Street the lights came on, yellow sodium streaked the hot night. The building was silent, dark save for a single strip of fluorescent light peeping through the blinds of a first-floor room where Caffery and Essex, ties off, collars loosened, sat facing each other over an indexer's desk, working their way through two four-packs of Speckled Hen real ale and a family drum of Kentucky Fried Chicken.

On his return to the incident room that afternoon Caffery had chosen not to tell Maddox of his progress. When the fax arrived at 4:00 P.M. just as DI Diamond was leaving to get a warrant for Gemini's red GTI, Jack had beckoned Essex into the SIO's room.

"Got plans tonight?" He showed him the long roll of paper. "It puts me a jump ahead, but it's just the beginning."

Now the fax was unfurled over the desk, drooping over the edge and settling in ripples on the floor.

"One hundred and sixty-eight women," Essex said, mouth full of chicken. "Take away from three hundred and twenty makes, um—"

"One hundred and fifty-two."

"Thank you." He scribbled the numbers at the bottom of the list, leaving silvery grease spots with his fingers. "Eliminate anyone over, say, fifty?"

"Which won't be many."

"At a guess, what, twenty more? And we're left with one hundred and—"

"Thirty-two." Caffery pulled a beer tab. "Run it through HOLMES and if nothing comes up we interview. We can't do a thing over the weekend, but starting on Monday, average interview twenty minutes, we could probably knock out fifty a day between the two of us and be narrowing it down by the Wednesday—that keeps us inside our timetable. Just."

"Piece of piss," Essex said, picking up his beer.

"You lie." Caffery raised his drink. "And for that I will be eternally grateful."

They touched cans and drank. "Funny." Essex wiped his mouth and leaned back in his seat. "Funny how you can't see it."

"See what?"

"Maddox's confidence in you."

"*Confidence?*" He shook his head, smiling at the irony. "This is confidence? He's given me *four days*."

"That's four days more than he's given any other DI. The man's a play-by-the-book merchant, Jack. A plodder. And you . . ." Across the room the MSS printer sprang to life. "Well, look at it through his eyes." Essex stood, wandered over to the printer and lifted the Perspex cover. "Scared as he is that you'll capsize the case, he's giving you rein. Think about it." He peered inside as the printhead ping-ponged across the paper. "Ah, from our specialist adviser at Lambeth."

"The lab?" Caffery was pleased to change the subject.

"Yup." Essex smiled. "It's Jane Amedure. Jane Amedure— the little Bootie genius. She showed me the ropes when I did exhibits on Operation Ambleside."

"Ambleside?"

"Last year." Essex didn't look up. "Algerian did his old lady and left her in a freezer in a council flat Old Kent Road way. Six months before they found her." He took a swig of beer. "The power had been off for three."

"Unshockable. Aren't you?"

"Yup. Then there was our chum Colin Ireland. Killed his victim's cat and put its mouth around the victim's—"

"Yes. I heard. Thank you." Caffery was suddenly tired. He rubbed his eyes. "Go on, then, what's she giving us?"

"Um." Essex skimmed through the report. "Let's see: toxicology and histology, hair analysis. Okay, here goes. Toxicology: now, our unidentified victim—the one that died first—well, she was a user. There was benzoylecgonine and diamorphine in deep tissues."

"Benzoylecgonine and diamorphine—that means coke and heroin?"

"Ten out of ten. On Shellene Craw—well, we didn't really need confirmation, but the SA's giving us it anyway, positive for smack, crack, Es, the works. And Wilcox's confirmed, also smack. Hatch, as we thought, positive, and, surprise, surprise"— he looked up—"a negative on Spacek. Not even crack. Clean."

"Cause of death?"

"Uh, yes." He scanned the report and gave a low whistle. "Krishnamurthi, the man's an Einstein! Balls-on accurate." He looked at Caffery, excited. "Heroin. Injected straight into the brain stem. Everything would've shut down instantly, heart, lungs, the lot. They wouldn't have known a thing."

"See?" Jack said. "Do you see what I'm getting at?"

"Yeah—the hospital thing."

"The *brain stem,* for Christ's sake. Can you see some low-end dealer knowing where to find a brain stem? I mean, Jesus—"

"You're preaching to the converted," Essex murmured, reading the report. "You know that." He held up the paper. "You'll like this too, Jack. Birdman—can I call him that?"

"If you keep it in this room."

"Birdman's a clean freak. That or he knows enough about forensics to get rid of his evidence." He carried the report to the desk, folding it carefully along the perforated page dividers. "Looks like they did have consensual sex, but Birdman uses a condom *and* Amedure says he makes the girl wash afterwards. That or he washes them postmortem. They've all got traces of soap in the vagina. Look, each sample's got the same concentration sodium stearate to fat. Manufacturer: good old Wright's coal tar soap."

"So if he's so careful how do you explain the semen on the abdomen?"

"He spills a little when he takes the condom off?" Essex shrugged. "Or he withdraws, takes the condom off and finishes wanking—sorry, let's be technical—*masturbating* on her stomach. Gets her to clean herself, or he cleans it off himself later, after he's done her. But"—he held his hand up—"he's not quite as careful as he thinks, because he leaves a trace." He finished his beer and crumpled the can. "Now then— here's hematology, mass spectrometer analysis of the dustbin liner, hairs. There wasn't a follicle on that black hair so no DNA, but it *is* head hair, it *is* Afro-Caribbean. And, hey, check this out." He looked up. "The target wears a wig."

"A *wig*?"

"Yeah, look—the blond hairs Krishnamurthi took from the victims?"

"Yes?"

"Amedure says, 'The hairs were dyed, of Asian origin, none of them had roots and both ends were bluntly cut. Not ripped or torn. I'd expect to see this in hairs taken from a wig.'"

"They were long hairs," Caffery said. "A woman's wig."

Essex raised his eyebrows. "Michael Caine."

"What?"

"*Dressed to Kill*. You never seen that?"

"Paul—" Caffery sighed.

"Okay, okay." He held up his hand. "I keep forgetting: I'm the comedian in this partnership and you're the humorless git."

"And proud of it."

"Yeah, and sad." He went back to the report, chewing his thumbnail. "And friendless, don't forget that." He paused. "Uh, look, the precipitin test."

"Precipitin test? That's to, what? Check for human blood?"

"Yup. Distinguish it from animal."

"We're talking about the birds?"

"We are." Essex scanned the sheet, his mouth working noiselessly. "It says that tissue in the birds' air sacs was human."

"*What?*" Caffery looked up.

"That's what I said. Human."

"You know what that means?"

"No?"

"Well, how do you think it got into the lungs?"

"They *breathed* it in?"

"Yes. Meaning—"

"Meaning . . . oh—" Essex suddenly understood. "*Shit*, yes." He sat down on Kryotos's desk, his levity gone. "You mean the birds were still *alive*? They died in there?"

Caffery nodded. "Surprised?"

"Well, kind of. Yeah."

They were silent for a moment, pondering this. The air in the room had shifted subtly, as if the temperature had dropped a degree or two. Caffery stood up, finished his beer and pointed to the report. "Go on. Go on."

"Yeah, right." Essex cleared his throat, picked up the report. "Okay. What d'you want?"

"How does he sedate them?"

"Uh—" He ran his fingers down the paper. "Hematology says uh—oh—"

"What?"

"Says he didn't."

"What?"

"He didn't sedate them."

"Impossible."

"That's what it says here. Nothing except for, except for alcohol, some cocaine but not enough to do any damage, no phenols, no benzos, no barbs except Wilcox and young Kayleigh. Um . . ." His eyes raced over the page. "Nothing. Except for maybe our anonymous lady number one who is chockfull of scag. But heroin's always awkward; everyone's tolerance is different."

"He must have used *something*."

"No, Jack. He didn't. Bits and pieces of junk in all of them, but nothing that would have done the trick."

"You sure?"

"Sure I'm sure. Jane Amedure says so. Must be true."

Caffery was exasperated. "So how did he keep them still enough to stick a sodding great needle in their necks?"

"They're not magicians, you know," Essex said solemnly, looking up from the report. "These guys who spirit our loved ones away from under our noses, they're not specially clever. Most cases I look back on and realize how very *un*clever they were."

"Unclever?" Caffery echoed, absently looking at his black thumbnail. He wondered how *unclever* Birdman was. How *unclever* Penderecki was. How *unclever* you had to be.

"Accidentally lucky," Essex said.

"No. Birdman's not lucky. He *knows*." He stood and wandered over to the photos. "Doesn't he?" He appealed to the dead women staring blankly from the walls. "Well? How did he do it?"

"Jack," Essex said from behind. "Look at this."

The women stared back at Caffery: Petra, thin arms, sparkling smile and leotard; poor, dull Michelle Wilcox clutching her wild-haired daughter—

"Jack."

Big, toothy Shellene. Kayleigh in the pink party dress, holding up a glass to the camera. "*What if it's my baby in there, my baby, my little, little girl? What if it's her?*"

"How's he doing it?"

"*Jack!*"

"What?" He turned. "What is it?"

"Entomology." Essex was shaking his head. "I know why it looks like he's not raping them. Disgusting bastard."

"Why?"

"You know what we've got on our hands, Jack?"

"No, what've we got on our hands?"

"We've got a necrophiliac. A full-blown necrophiliac." He tapped the report and held it out to Caffery. "It's all there. In black and white."

Seventeen

ARLY 1980S. UMDS. Gross Anatomy 1.1 B stream lab rotation.

Standing in a class of ten, dotted amongst the green-shrouded shapes on stainless-steel gurneys, the sweet tang of formaldehyde deep in his nostrils, nineteen years old and Harteveld knew that something life-changing was happening.

He was paired with a young female student and assigned to the corpse of a middle-aged woman. For the next year she would be stored at night, in a stainless-steel cadaver tank, and wheeled out in the daylight hours under her green cotton sheet, to be dissected, mulled over and rearranged by his trembling gloved fingers.

She was sharp-featured with small yellow pouches for breasts, thin pubic hair, razor-sharp hipbones jutting up under papery skin. Her dark blond hair was smoothed back over the scalp.

"Doris awake and ready?" the girl student would call cheerily to the technicians as she entered the lab, pulling on her gloves.

"She's overslept this morning. Look at her, can't get a thing out of her." They'd wheel her out. "Hey, Doris, wake up. You're on."

And she'd be delivered to Harteveld, who stood trembling and silent, not joining the joke, sweating at the thought of the inspired frigid stillness which waited under the green sheet. Sometimes he found himself shaking so much next to her supine body that the scalpel fell from his fingers.

"You haven't the stomach for it," his costudent murmured, nudging him in the ribs during peritoneal and upper GI topology. "Get it? You haven't the—oh, forget it."

He'd saved the allowance made to him by his parents and bought a flat in Lewisham—a ground-floor flat with a square garden and brick wall in the front. After class he lay in the bedroom, curtains closed, and fantasized about the corpse so often that it seemed to have rubbed part of his brain raw. She took on the proportions of a goddess in his mind: waxen, motionless white face; serene and cool, a marble Muse, blue veins showing in her lips, her blond hair fanned out on the pillow for him. Waiting in infinite stillness. It was the stillness and pallor which attracted him: so unlike the plump, wriggling Lucilla.

Panic-stricken, he made clumsy attempts at self-administered aversion therapy. He wrote to researchers in the States asking for supplies of Depo-Provera. When they refused he tried injecting himself with diamorphine before anatomy class. But it made him too nauseous to get to his feet. Worse, it offered no relief from the fantasies.

It was only six weeks later, almost at the end of his first term, just before Christmas, when disaster truly struck.

The lab technicians had overstayed their welcome in the Standard and hadn't returned the anatomy specimens to the cadaver tanks in the anteroom. Harteveld, sick and shaking with the possibility this opened to him, loitered behind after the last anatomy class of that term, crouched in the comer, at eye level with the polished pneumatic valves used to raise and lower the dissecting tables.

It was 2:00 P.M., and already the flinty northern light was fading from the sky. The old heating system creaked and shuddered in the belly of the building, but in the lab the air was chill and stale. Harteveld wrapped his arms around his knees and rocked himself gently. The bodies lay silent in the weak hibernal light, skin stripped in neat sections from the arms, clamps, hemostats, retractors sprouting like small spines from their gelid gray stomach meat. *She* was in the center of the room. From here he could see the dun fall of her hair.

And then the big door at the far end of the lab opened.

Security.

Harteveld's heart stilled. He musm't be found here. He should stand up and pretend casually to be collecting something. Quickly now. But his legs were trembling, useless. A cold sweat broke out across his scalp. He was trapped.

And then something happened which changed everything.

The security guard locked the door, from the inside, and pulled the blinds.

Eighteen

AT 10:30 P.M., when Caffery left Shrivemoor, the night was still warm. He left the radio off and drove in silence, promising himself a bath and a healthy shot of malt whisky when he got home. Under the moment-to-moment preoccupations—his tiredness, traffic lights, the too-bright headlights on the South Circular—he was aware of a new inhabitant in his thoughts, like a scrawled image at the bottom of a shifting lake, the beginnings of a picture, a real picture, of Birdman.

A necrophile. How could they have missed it?

He turned left at Honor Oak, right across Peckham Rye. The ghostly white dabs of gravestones in Nunhead Cemetery floated beyond the trees. The bloody arc of Birdman's career fleshed itself out in his head. A man—*tall? short?*—squatting like an incubus, a carrion crow, eyes running with excitement, moving his hands over a corpse. The dead and the undead. An unholy alliance.

And the backbeat of unanswered questions continued: a live bird sewn inside a body cavity, long after death. Why? *And why can't you forget that image?* The strange, ordered cuts to the scalps—*except Kayleigh,* his subconscious prompted. *Why not Kayleigh?* And how did Birdman keep his victims still for the injection? This problem breathed its own peculiar brand of unease. It whispered mind control—worse, it whispered a toxin that modern forensics couldn't identify.

He parked the car under his neighbor's flaking plane tree and wearily climbed out, his head thudding. All he wanted now was quiet. He slung his jacket over his shoulder. A Glenmorangie and a bath.

But something unnaturally pale waited for him in the shadows on the doorstep.

He stopped, hand on the gate, as his eyes adjusted to the night. When he realized what was gleaming gently in the half-light he knew it was Penderecki's work.

Two dolls, naked, the color of lifeless babies, plastic limbs linked, face to genitals, face to genitals. Splayed out on the step in front of them a note on a pink Ladbroke's chit: "*Ringing me is like wringing your neck.*"

Caffery unbuttoned his shirt cuff, pulled it down over his hand and carefully turned the bundle. A girl's doll, blond nylon hair, lolled outward, blank eyes turned upward, arms held up and out as if ready to catch a beach ball. Barbie or Sindy. Smooth nippleless breasts, finger's-width waist and, scribbled obscenely on the slope of plastic between its legs, overlarge as if infected, a raw, red ink vulva.

Very Penderecki.

He prodded the other doll and rolled it onto its back. Action Man or G.I. Joe, the same blind stare and scratched-in genitalia, the same rigid beseeching hands, HASBRO stamped in the small of the back.

And this Caffery recognized. This had once been Ewan's toy.

He clearly remembered the mystery of its disappearance. One sunny afternoon in the early seventies. Before lunch it had been lying facedown in the grass in the back garden, pinned by the lead weight of miniature grenades and water canteens. After lunch it was gone. Spirited away. "*Well now, Ewan,*" their mother, as mystified as they were, giving the sky a suspicious look, "*maybe it was stolen by a crow.*" The next day she bought the all-new Action Man from Woolworth's in Lewisham. "*Look at his hands, Ewan. They can grip. Isn't that better?*"

This was not new from Penderecki, this subtle torture. Caffery gathered the dolls up, found his keys and wearily pressed inside his front door.

The kitchen light was on and he could see a pile of his shirts freshly folded on the ironing board.

Veronica.

In his tiredness he hadn't noticed her car outside.

Be good to her, Jack. She's ill. Don't forget, be good.

In the kitchen he threw his jacket on the chair, took a roll of cling film and carefully wrapped the dolls individually, ready to be filed away in Ewan's room. The Le Creuset was on the hob and from the living room Gershwin's *Rhapsody in Blue* came twining around the good cooking smells of ginger and coriander. From the shelf he took a glass and the Glenmorangie and poured himself a large shot. His body ached with fatigue. He wanted silence, his whisky, a bath and then bed. Nothing more. He certainly didn't want Veronica.

"Jack?"

"Yeah, hi," he called dully into the hall.

"I let myself in. I hope you didn't mind."

Well, Veronica, if I do mind, what good will it do me?

"Come up."

In Ewan's room. Why did she always gravitate to that room? Taking the dolls and the whisky, he slowly climbed the stairs.

She was sitting in the middle of the floor, wearing a carefully tailored navy skirt suit with white starched cuffs secured by gold pins. She had kicked her shoes off so he could see the pale moons of her toenails through the flesh-colored tights.

Scattered around her were the contents of all his Penderecki files.

"*Veronica?*"

"What?"

"*What* are you doing?"

"I'm tidying up your files. I thought people might want to look round the house at the party so I'm tidying your files for you."

"Well, don't." He put down the whisky and the wrapped dolls on the desk and started to pick things up. "Just don't."

Veronica stared at him. "I was only trying to help—"

"I asked you not to come in here." He turned. "I'll say it again: don't come in here. And don't go into the files."

Her forehead furrowed, her mouth pushed out a fraction. "I'm sorry. Here, let me put them back—"

"No." He brushed her away. "*Just—leave—them!*"

Veronica flinched and he stopped. *You're shouting, Jack. Don't shout at her.*

"Look." He took a deep breath. "I'm sorry. I'm really —Veronica—"

Too late. Her face was already undoing itself, the forehead twisting, the mouth moving from side to side. She stood up and tears sprang to her eyes.

"Oh Jesus." He closed his eyes and forced himself to lean into her, to run his hands across her shaking shoulders. "Veronica, I'm sorry, I'm sorry—it's been a bad day."

"It's the cancer, isn't it? You want to leave me because of the cancer."

"Of course I don't want to leave you. I'm not going anywhere." He pulled her against him and rested his chin on top of her head. "Look, I've been stockpiling my shifts. If you want I can take time out—come to chemo with you."

"You've taken the time off?" She stopped sniffling and looked up at him.

"I want to be with you."

"Really?"

"Yes, really. Now, come on, sit down." He pressed his hand on her shoulder and together they sat on the floor, backs against the wall. "I don't want to hear any more of this, okay?" He twisted his fingers around hers. "I am not afraid of the Hodgkin's."

"I'm sorry, Jack." She wiped her eyes with the back of her hand. "I'm sorry this has happened to me. I wish I could change it, I really do."

"It's not your fault." He buried his head in her hair. "Now, don't forget—" He cleared his throat. "Don't forget we're in this together."

"I won't."

They sat in silence watching the mushroom-brown moths softly bounce out of the dark night against the window. He held her hand up to his mouth, kissed it lightly and turned it over to look at the palm.

"You all right?"

"Yes," she murmured.

He kissed her hair and looked at her hand, half smiling. "How come you didn't have the dye test this time?"

"Mmm?"

"The one you told me about. The one you had last time."

"I did," she said dreamily.

He held her hand close to his face. The skin was pale, faintly spotted, like a fish. But there was no tracery of lines, no subcutaneous network sunk deep in the cool flesh. "I thought you could see the dye afterwards."

"Not really. It fades pretty quickly." She pushed her hair behind her ears and looked at him. Semicircles of mascara underlined her eyes. "Jack?"

"Mmmmm?"

"Maybe I should go on my own. I'd like to show Dr. Cavendish I don't need my hand held."

"You sure?"

"Yes, really."

"Okay, okay." He drew the hem of her skirt lightly down her thigh and studied the curved surface of her knee. He had never seen Veronica cry before. Strangely it made him horny. "Are you allowed a drink, then?" He drifted his hand down onto her inner thigh. "There's some Gordons in the fridge if you fancy it."

Nineteen

IN 1984 LUCILLA HARTEVELD—age fifty-five, weight eighteen stone—was admitted to King Edward VII Hospital in New Cavendish Street with chest pains. In the coronary care unit an ECG showed she had suffered a mild myocardial infarct. She was pumped with anistreplase and disopyramide. Henrick Harteveld immediately contacted his son.

After a cautious mother-son reunion—Lucilla smelled in her hospital bed, as if she'd done something secret under the covers and was enjoying the discomfort it gave her visitors —Toby and Henrick walked solemnly through Mayfair for dinner in the Oxford and Cambridge Club. Left together, unshepherded by Lucilla for the first time in years, the two men talked until midnight. Henrick, who expected to lose his wife, sat upright in his chair and ordered Perrier-Jouët. Toby confessed he had dropped out of medical school and was spending his days sitting uselessly in the small southeast London flat.

The next day Henrick set to work.

Without consulting Lucilla he floated his pharmaceutical company—Harteveld Chemicals—on the stock market, retaining a majority interest and passing £1.5 million of the profits to his son. He was going over Lucilla's head and it made him tremble—alone in the paneled library, he actually *shook* with fear and excitement—to think how she would respond to this act of psychosis. To lend the event some respectability, he appointed Toby assistant director of marketing, a job so pantomimic that it required him only to put on a suit every few days and show his face at the chrome and smoked-glass company headquarters outside Sevenoaks.

And so Toby Harteveld became wealthy.

He temporarily abandoned the tiny flat in Lewisham—with its elderly neighbors and sleepy cats on the walls outside—and acquired the house on Croom's Hill, hiring landscapers and builders, cleaners and gardeners. Using the Harteveld name's high profile in the pharmaceutical industry, he got himself appointed to the private sector steering committee on St. Dunstan's Hospital Trust. He threw parties, the villa filled with lofty creatures: heart surgeons and heiresses, shipping magnates and actresses, women who knew how to wear raw silk and men who knew how to summon a wine waiter with a glance. The conversation danced over futures dealings, fringe theater, dinghy sailing in Kennebunkport. He tried to build form and significance into his life and briefly he was able to maintain the illusion of sanity.

But, as outward he struggled toward perfection, as his life acquired the hue of success, inwardly his despair and alienation increased. His secret sickness grew.

None of his acquaintances knew about the girls he paid for, about meeting them in the street and bringing them to Croom's Hill, about sending them naked into the garden to stand until they were blue with cold, so they could come glazed and shivering into his double bed. Or him demanding they lie still and unresponsive, eyes rolled back in their heads—

"*I can't, it gives me a headache.*"

"*Shut up, can't you, just shut up and keep still*"—while he mounted them, still able to reach climax only with his eyes locked tight, turned ferociously inward on fantasy.

One day, as he sat in his temperature-controlled, double-glazed office in Sevenoaks, lunchtime aperitif at his elbow, watching Canadian geese landing on the artificial ponds, he suddenly saw the weight of the burden in a new light. Maybe, he thought, maybe he was incurable. The idea brought him up short. Was it possible, he wondered, that every human is sentenced to a particular lifelong exercise of will, with a duty to accept it with grace and strength? And was it possible that here, in his obsession, he had encountered his own life struggle?

He took a deep breath and straightened in his chair. Very well. He would carry it. He would exist side by side with perpetual restraint and compromise.

But he needed help.

He ran a finger down the tall milky glass of pastis. He needed an end to awareness, and it would have to be better than drink.

Two weeks later he found the safety valve he wanted: dining one night with an ex-Sherborne friend fresh from Ph.D. field research in the rain forests of Tanjung Puting. After dinner the friend collected a small Gladstone bag and put it on the table in front of Harteveld.

"Cocaine, Toby? Or something more escapist? There's opium. Sweet, velvety opium, just mmm." He rubbed his fingers together. "Just *caressed* out of the land by the Malaysians."

Harteveld hesitated a moment, then let his eyelids droop down. He opened his hands on the table, palms up in a gesture of relief and gratitude. Here it was, then, what he had been searching for. The good, welcoming shore of escape.

Twenty

M R. HENRY, DI Diamond here. We met at the Dog and Bell the other day." A scrabbling noise and the letter box lifted, a warrant card appeared briefly, the small tanned nose familiar. "I'm putting some photographs through the letter box. I think you've seen them before." A shower of eight-by-tens landed on the floor. Gemini, back against the wall, stared mutely down at the faces in his hall. "We've got corroborative statements putting at least three of these girls in your company. Anything you'd like to say?"

Gemini was silent. On the other side of the door Diamond coughed.

"Maybe you'd consider coming down to the station for a chat?" He waited a moment. Gemini remained silent, staring at the letter box, listening to the sound of thin paper being folded. His mother was still sleeping in the bedroom at the bottom of the hallway; he didn't want her awake, didn't want her being troubled.

"I'm also putting a copy of our search warrant through. Under the provisions of the Police and Criminal Evidence Act I'm obliged to ask you if you will consent to the search of your car, registration C966HCY, and give you this opportunity to pass the keys to me."

Gemini slid down the wall to his haunches.

"I'll take that as a 'no.'" A carbon copy fluttered to the floor. "The warrant, Mr. Henry. We'll be back with a record of everything seized, which for the purposes of this investigation will mean the car and its contents."

"You ain't takin' no car."

"Hello?" A pallid blue eye appeared at the letter box, blinking. "Hello?"

"You takin' my car, is it?"

"That is correct."

"Because you think them girls was in my car?"

"You know why we're interested in them, don't you?" Even from here Gemini could smell Diamond's sour breath. "Don't you?"

"Maybe," Gemini whispered. "Maybe."

"It's not Gemini," Caffery said. "It can't be."

Maddox turned up his raincoat collar against the dying shreds of a storm and looked at him with red-rimmed eyes. They stood at the foot of a high-rise housing project, part of the Pepys Estate, Deptford, as FSS technicians in green overalls secured Gemini's red GTI to the lab's low-loader. High above them the clouds were tugged by invisible winds away from Deptford, off over to the Thames. It was a Saturday, the interviews at St. Dunstan's were scheduled for Monday and Caffery was in downtime. He'd elected to spend his time sitting on the team's heels.

"Have you heard of serotonin? Free histamines? First and second instars?"

"I'm not a scientist."

"The wounds were postmortem," Caffery said. "I mean *very* post."

Maddox put his hands in his pockets. "We knew that from the autopsy."

"No. We thought they were inflicted in the heat of the moment, as soon as they were dead, as part of the killing act." He glanced at the lab technician tying a white Seized Property tag on the GTI's windscreen wiper. "Steve, look. The women *were* raped. He used a condom because he's a clean freak, or phobic about AIDS, and did it postmortem."

"Postmortem?"

"That's why there was no sign of force, no bruising to the genitals. Dead tissue doesn't really react to noninvasive violence."

"How did you dream this up?"

"Forensics say the wounding was up to *three* days after death."

"*Three* days?"

"It's been bugging us why they weren't raped. And here's the explanation. He's been hanging on to the bodies. The rape probably happened at the same time as the mutilation, probably repeatedly, and probably after the rigor had worn off." Caffery saw Maddox's face tighten a fraction. "He's a necrophiliac, Steve. It doesn't explain the ease with which he killed them, but it *does* explain why he wants the killing so unfrenzied, why there was no knock about bruising, no black eyes."

"I don't think I want to hear this."

"The death has to be quick, unfussy. He isn't interested in killing. That's not the fun. The fun is the corpse. He only disposes of them when they become too putrid." Maddox shuddered as if the sun had gone behind a mountain. The last weak spatters of rain subsided. Caffery put his hands in his pockets and took a step closer, dipping his head into Maddox. "Birdm—*the offender* keeps the bodies for three days and then, when the murder itself is just a memory, *then* he mutilates them. You know what it means?"

"Apart from he's even more of a weirdo than we thought?"

"It tells us more than that."

Maddox bit his lip. New, washed sunshine flickered against the concrete buildings and he looked suddenly old. He glanced up the edge of the nearest high-rise to Gemini's flat. "He's got privacy?"

"Yes, and he lives alone." Caffery followed Maddox's gaze to the flat. The curtains were drawn. "Most likely he's got a freezer."

Maddox cleared his throat. "We can't get a warrant for the flat: the friendly magistrates've gone PC on us."

"Okay." Caffery started walking to the entrance of the project.

"Where d'you think you're going?"

"I've got something to show you."

"Hey." Maddox caught up. "I don't want you rattling him, Jack."

"I won't."

In the hallway a young girl of about ten, with long dirty blond hair and a crusty-nosed baby on her hip, stared out through the glass at them. She wore a filthy pink T-shirt and had scuffed bare feet. Caffery tapped on the glass. She opened the door, stood back and looked at them in silence.

"Thanks." He slammed his hand on the lift button and the doors opened. He stepped inside and turned to look at Maddox. "What floor's he on?"

"Seventeen. We're not speaking to him, mate. Not yet."

"No." Caffery hit the button for the seventeenth floor." Get in and let's see, shall we, how many times the doors open between here and the seventeenth. Let's just see how feasible Mel Diamond's idea really is."

The two men stood, hands in pockets, faces turned up to the red light traveling across the panel above the door. "Imagine you're him, Steve. You've got a body in a bin-liner right here on the floor. That's a woman's body we're talking about. Cut and curled up. Stinking."

The lift climbed: nine, ten, eleven. Maddox was silent, watching the red light crawling. Twelve, thirteen, fourteen. It stopped and the doors opened. An old woman with a waterproof shopping case and a tiny shivering Jack Russell on a lead looked at them.

"Going down?"

"Up."

"I'll come with you anyway." She stepped inside smiling, tying a plastic hood over her perm. "You never know if it'll stop on the way back down."

Caffery looked at Maddox and whispered, "Remember now. On the floor."

A mother with two toddlers got in on the fifteenth floor, and after stopping on the seventeenth the lift continued to the twentieth, the top floor. Now there were six people and a dog in the lift. Maddox shifted uncomfortably from foot to foot. On the way back down they stopped a further three times. The lift was full by the time they reached the lobby.

"It's daytime," Maddox said as they stepped outside into the daylight, rubbing his face wearily. The girl with the baby pressed her nose against the window as they walked away. "He moved them in the night."

"Yes, but can you imagine going down all those flights day *or* night? Looking at the numbers like we've just done, and then, after all that, pulling it out of the lift." He started to pace toward the car park. Beyond him the lowloader's hydraulic ramp jerked closed, the GTI shuddered in its moorings. "All this way across the forecourt." He stopped, his hands open. "Look up. How many windows can you see?"

"Jack, this is the Pepys Estate. It wouldn't be the first time a dodgy-looking package was dragged across this forecourt in the middle of the night, be assured of that."

"You saw those PMs." He lowered his voice. "Don't pretend you didn't notice the smell. Even three days into death they smell, Steve, they *stink*. You know. It's a smell you never forget, a smell you can't wash out."

"He might've got another place."

"Sure." Jack nodded, sucking breath in through his nostrils. "Mmm, sure. And you just hang on to that, okay. Just hang on to that hope."

At that Maddox's face changed. The blue of a vein pulsed in his temple and when he spoke his voice was low, almost inaudible. "I had the governor on this morning: he's heard we've got a profiling buff on the team. So now I'm in the business of covering up for you."

"The DCS prefers fluke sighting and circumstantial evidence?" He shook his head. "Steve, face it, F team have probably knocked on the door of every racist in east Greenwich, and everyone is going to be ecstatic at the chance to shop some miserable local drug dealer. Get him hauled in, out of their hair for a few days. DI Diamond just *loves* it, it's in his veins, and I'm wondering, Steve, if he's doing it because he knows he can, because—" He shoved his hands in his pockets and met Maddox's gray eyes with his dark blue: full on, defiant. "Because *you're letting him.*"

"You're still on three-month trial with us, Jack. Don't forget that."

"I haven't forgotten."

"I'll see you back at Shrivemoor. Wish Veronica luck for the chemo."

"Steve, wait—"

But he was walking away and Caffery had to shout above the roar of the low-loader.

"*Superintendent Maddox!*" His voice bounced between the high-rise flats. The children in the doorway poked their heads out, startled by the noise. "*I'm going to prove you've got the wrong person in the frame, Superintendent Maddox— I'm going to prove he isn't even black!*"

But Maddox continued to walk. The low-loader changed gear and Gemini's GTI, covered in a white tarpaulin, set out to be paraded like an Indian wedding barat through the streets of Deptford.

The pub was empty. An Alsatian, asleep next to a gas heater fire, head on its paws, opened one eye to watch Caffery walk to the bar. Betty, the barmaid, dressed in a low-necked nylon lace blouse, a pair of large framed glasses on a chain around her neck, didn't bother greeting him. She put her cigarette out and simply stood there, varnished nails resting lightly on the beer taps, waiting for him to speak.

Caffery held his card up. "Old Bill."

"Yeah, I remember. You want a drink or not?"

"Go on, then. A—" No single malt in this pub. "A Bells." He felt in his pockets for change. "How's business?"

"Look at the place. The reporters have come out of the woodwork, scared half the punters away."

"Have you talked to them?"

Betty snorted and her dangly turquoise earrings shivered. "I wouldn't take their dirty money. I'm telling you, I wish none of this had ever happened."

"We all wish that." Caffery peeled his feet from the sticky carpet and sat on the stool. "Betty, do you remember the young man we interviewed in here?"

"The colored lad? The one who scarpered?"

"Yes."

"That's Gemini. They give their kids such funny names them lot, don't they? 'Ere." She beckoned him with her veiny hand. There was no one else in the pub, but it seemed to satisfy her when Caffery bent in dose enough for her to whisper. "That Gemini." She closed her hand around his wrist. "The papers are saying them girls were users. You know—drugs."

"Yes."

"Well, they have to get it somewhere, don't they?" She tapped her nose conspiratorially. "And that's *all* I'm saying." She wiped a tumbler with a J Cloth, pushed it under the optic and set it in front of him. "He pretends he's just cabbying for them, but I'm not blind. I know it gives them a chance to do their little, you know, *transactions.*"

"Does Joni know him?"

"Of course." Betty squinted at him, and Caffery got the full treat of her eyelids, flashing like the underside of a king-fisher. "She always gets a lift from Gemini. Her and Pinky, if she don't bring her bike."

"Her and *who*?"

"They called her Pinky when she was working."

"Rebecca," he murmured, oddly embarrassed on her behalf.

"That's her. She's an artist now. She'll sit in that corner in the saloon bar, with her paints, serious as anything, and not say a word all afternoon."

Suddenly the Alsatian sat up and growled. Caffery looked around in time to see the door close and the shadow of a man retreat beyond the frosted glass.

"Come in, love, it's open," Betty called, throwing the cloth over her shoulder and coming out from behind the bar. She opened the door and stood for a moment, chewing her nails, gazing into the street, before giving up and letting it swing closed. "One of the regulars. Must of saw you and thought you was the newspapers." She picked up his glass, wiped the bar and replaced it on a clean mat. "That or he knew you were the Bill."

The dog sat down next to the heater and scratched its ear with a grizzled hind paw, eyes squinty with pleasure.

When Caffery left, the streets were empty. The pavements had dried but the trees were still dripping and earthworms slid from between the gaps in the flagging. Suddenly he was aware of a shadow on the paving slabs keeping pace with his, and the soft squeak of bike gears. He turned.

"Afternoon, Detective."

Rebecca stopped the bike and put one long leg on the curb to balance herself. She wore brown shorts, a loose oatmeal sweater, and her long hair was caught in a ponytail. A leather portfolio was secured over the back wheel by worn canvas straps.

Jack put his hands in his pockets. "Is this a coincidence?"

"Not really." The lilac tree above them dripped onto her sweater, leaving small dark spots. "I keep coming back to the pub, you know, wondering—I saw you leaving."

"I see." He saw she had something to tell him. "You've remembered something?"

"Well, yes." Her mouth twisted apologetically. "But it's probably nothing. Probably a waste of your time." Strong white nails worked at the tiny stitches of the canvas straps. He'd forgotten how pretty she was.

"Nothing's nothing."

"Okay." She spoke warily, ready to be laughed at. "I remembered something about Petra."

"What?"

"Sometimes when I fall asleep, you know that bit just before you go under completely, the part where all your dreams from the night before come back?"

"Yes." Caffery knew too well. It was the place he often met Ewan and Penderecki.

"I'm sure it's not important, but last night I was half dreaming and I remembered Petra telling me she was allergic to makeup. She never wore it. You can see it in my paintings. She was always pale." The sun broke through the cloud cover and cast the sharp shadow of Rebecca's eyelids over green-gold irises. "That photo in your briefcase, she looked like—like a doll. I've seen dead things before, and they look realer than she did."

"I'm sorry you saw that."

"Don't be."

"Rebecca."

"Yes?" She tilted her head and looked at him. A drop of rain fell out of the tree onto her cheek. "What is it?"

"Why didn't you tell me about Gemini?"

"What about him?"

"He left with Shellene that day. Why didn't you say?"

She folded her arms under her small breasts and looked at her toes. "Why do you *think* I didn't say?"

"I have no idea."

"Don't be naive. He deals drugs, deals to Joni, that's why."

"Oh Jesus." Caffery shook his head, frustrated. "You know, don't you—Rebecca, you do *know* how serious this is."

"Of course I know. Don't you think I've thought of nothing else?" She bit her lip. "Gemini's got nothing to do with it."

"Okay, okay." He rubbed his forehead. "I think you're right. But the problem is I'm alone with that. Everyone who matters thinks Gemini looks pretty bloody choice right now. He's in trouble, Rebecca, genuine, no-fucking-around trouble."

"It's *not* him. I don't know how you can even think—"

"*I don't!* I just told you—*I don't think it's him!*"

"Jesus." She turned the handlebars away from him, suddenly subdued. "There's no need to be shitty about it."

"Rebecca—look." He subsided, suddenly feeling foolish. "I'm sorry. I just—I need some help here. I need someone to be straight with me, give me a break for a change."

"Oh, for God's sake," she murmured. "We all need a break. And *you're* being paid to figure it out."

"Rebecca—"

But she didn't look back. She pedaled away, the sweater slipping off one brown shoulder, leaving Caffery to stand in the middle of the pavement for several minutes, angry and confused, watching the exact point where she was swallowed by the city.

Twenty-one

LUCILLA HARTEVELD, having failed to shift the medically recommended six stone, suffered a second MI in 1985. This one produced uncontrollable arrhythmias and was fatal within thirty minutes. After the funeral Henrick came back to Greenwich with Toby and they walked together in the park.

In the shadow of Henry Moore's *Standing Figure,* Henrick paused. He turned, unprompted, to his son and, quietly, in his rich, Gelderland accent, began to tell the story he'd kept to himself for nearly sixty years. She had been a Dutch nurse, he explained, he'd last seen her on Ginkel Heath, September 20, 1944. Later he was told she'd perished in the chaos of the Arnhem battle, along with the members of the South Stafford Brigade she was tending. He had continued to believe this until thirty-five years later, when she resurfaced—freshly widowed by a wealthy Belgian surgeon and working in an orphanage in Sulawesi.

Toby stared past Henrick as he spoke, down into the valley, where the pale pink colonnades of the Queen's house glowed like the inside of a shell. Slowly it was dawning on him that for most of his parents' marriage his father had been marking time.

A month after the conversation Henrick sold the Surrey estate, passed another £2 million to his son and moved to Indonesia.

With his father abroad and the new money, Toby slipped further out of the mainstream: he rarely went into the Sevenoaks office. Now the only time he put on a business suit was for committee meetings at St. Dunstan's. The rest of the time he stopped shaving and dressed as if on permanent vacation in linen suits, expensive shirts—sleeves rolled up—espadrilles or calfskin shoes on bare feet. The opium, and later the cocaine and heroin, were doing their job; they blotted up his worst impulses, they tamped and quietened, leaving no evidence that they had harmed him physically. He was careful not to keep a large supply in Croom's Hill, using the lonely little Lewisham flat as a safe house. None of his contacts knew the address and he could replenish his stocks incrementally.

For over a decade he maintained a shaky control of his life.

By the late nineties, however, the parties had taken on a different hue, a new casualness. Now, along with the chilled glasses of Cristal and Stolichnaya, came cocaine served in willow-pattern Japanese *miso* bowls. Girls he had met in Mayfair clubs slouched against the walls, smoking St. Moritz cigarettes and tugging at the hems of their miniskirts. He shopped closer to home too, using a discreet network of contacts to guide him to resource pools. Some of his acquaintances lingered on, but they were soon hopelessly outnumbered by the new breed of guest: the girls and their tagalongs.

"This is wild, isn't it?" one said to Harteveld, who—seconds-fresh from a heroin hit—was lowering himself into the walnut highback in the library.

"I'm sorry?" He looked up, hazy. "I beg your pardon."

"I said it's wild, isn't it?" She was a tall, calm girl in her mid-twenties, fine-boned, with swinging chestnut hair and long supple legs. He had never seen her before. She was oddly out of place in her pared-down makeup, buttoned gray wool dress and low pumps.

Is she really one of the girls? Really?

"Yes," he managed. "Yes, I suppose, I suppose it is."

"I've never seen anything like it. Apparently the guy who's throwing it shoots up for people if they want. Just go into the bathroom and he's there—oh—handing it out like candy. Even shoots it for you if you're going to be a baby about it."

Harteveld stared at her in disbelief. "Do you know who I am?"

"No. Should I?"

"My name is Toby Harteveld. This is my house."

"Ah." She smiled, unrattled. "So *you're* Toby. Well, Toby, it's nice to meet you at last. You've got a lovely house. And that Patrick Heron on the landing—an original?"

"Indeed."

"It's exquisite."

"Thank you. Now—" With an effort he pushed himself out of the chair and held out a shaky hand. "Regarding the heroin. I take it an invitation to partake would not be rejected?"

"No." She shook her head, still smiling. "Thanks but I'm crap with drugs. I'd only throw up or something pathetic."

"Very well. A schnapps perhaps? In the orangery. There's a, let me see, a Frida Kahlo in there. I believe you'd be interested."

"A Frida Kahlo? You're joking, aren't you? Of *course* I'm interested."

The orangery, piggybacked onto the house, was chilly. Mango loops of light from the party fell on the potted trees, casting plush gray shadows on the stone floor. In here it smelled of plant food and cold earth, the voices of the guests were muffled. Harteveld scratched his arms, his thoughts meandering. Now, why were they here? What was it he wanted?

The living blue of her veins, Toby, raised and frozen. Her hair soaked and smoothed away from her forehead.

The girl turned and looked up at him. "Well?"

"I'm sorry?"

"The painting? Where is it?"

"The painting," he echoed.

"Yes. The Kahlo?"

"Oh that—" Harteveld scratched his stomach, looking down at her soft-edged face. "No, I've got it wrong. It's not in the *orangery*. It's in the study."

"Oh, for Christ's sake." She turned to go but he gripped her arm.

"Look, there's something I need you to do. Usually—" His head was swarming. "Usually I give two hundred, but with you I'd make it three."

She gave him an incredulous look. "I'm not on the *game,* you know. I came with my flatmate. That's all."

"Come on!" he said, suddenly alarmed by her rejection. "Four hundred, make it four. And I'm not hard work—all you have to do is keep still, that's all. I don't—"

"I said, I'm not working."

"I don't take long." He tightened his grip. "If you keep very still I'm over in a few minutes. Come on—"

"I said no." She shook her arm to loosen his fingers. "Now, let go or I'll scream."

"Please—"

"*No!*"

Harteveld, shocked by the new imperative in her voice, dropped her arm and took a step back. But the girl had been ignited, wasn't dropping it. She matched his movement, advancing on him, furious.

"I don't care—" She lashed out, catching him under the chin with clean, pink nails. Drawing blood. "—who the fuck you are."

"Shit." He grabbed his neck, stunned by her sudden viciousness. "Shit, what did you—*what did you do that for?*"

"You learn to take no for an answer." She turned on her heel. "Get it?"

"*You!*" he called after her, clutching his neck. "*You. Listen, little bitch.* You're not welcome in this house. Understand?" But her soft black pumps retreated across the stone floor. Smug, self-fulfilled. "You come here and take my hospitality, my wine, my drugs—and do this, you little cow. You are *no longer welcome!*"

But she was gone, and he knew, as he pulled his hands away and examined the dark streaks, that his control was slipping, that trouble was near the surface.

He didn't return to the party. The cleaner found him the next day, coiled on a sofa where he had dragged himself in the small hours, his hands folded crablike over his head, tears on his face, blood crusted into his collar. She said nothing, flinging open the windows and noisily tidying away ashtrays.

Later she brought him coffee, sliced fruit and a glass of Perrier, setting the tray on the Carrara marble table and giving him a pitying look. Harteveld rolled away and sniffed the bright air coming in through the windows. There was a promise of winter in it, of cloud and snow. And something else. Something bad in the distance was coming to town. It smelled to him like crisis.

December the fourth, his thirty-seventh birthday. And it arrived.

He found the girl under the piano just before 3:00 A.M. when the party was beginning to break up. Her eyes were rolled back in her head, her arms hugging her shoulders.

From time to time she moaned and wriggled gently like a fat cocoon. She was very plump and wore a short baby-blue dress. There was a tattoo on her biceps which looked as if it had leaked through her skin, and whitish strands of matter webbed her mouth.

Amused by her, he rested his elbow on the piano and leaned in to look at her. "Hey you. What's your name?"

Her eyes rolled back, trying to focus on the noise. Her mouth opened and closed twice before sound came out. "Sharon Dawn McCabe." In the three words she had identified herself as a child of the Gorbals.

"You know you're out of your head, don't you?"

She hiccuped once and nodded, her eyes closed. "Ah know ah am."

So he carried poor, fat Sharon into his bedroom, undressed her in the dark and put her to bed. He fucked her very quickly and silently, dry-eyed, holding onto her cold breasts from behind. She didn't move or make a sound. Downstairs the party ended, he could hear the caterers clearing glasses. Outside, snowflakes hurried past the dark window.

Next to him Sharon Dawn McCabe started to snore very loudly; he fucked her again—she was too drunk to know it had happened, he reasoned—and fell asleep.

He dreamed he was back in the anatomy lab at Guy's that winter afternoon, crouched on the floor, watching in horrified excitement as the fat security guard improved the thin stump of his erection with a soft white hand and, standing on tiptoe against a dissecting table, a look of intense concentration on his face, slid the hips of the lifeless woman to meet his.

Harteveld could bear it no longer. He let his breath out in a thin sigh.

The security guard stopped, frozen in the fading light, his eyes rolling as he tried to spy out who was watching him. He wasn't a tall man, but to Harteveld crouched on the floor, he seemed to block the horizon. His eyes were wet and cold.

There should have been a chance to stand up, protest, disassociate himself from this tableau, but Harteveld was deadlocked with fear. And in the second he chose not to move, the security guard, sweat streaking his forehead, recognized that the thin med student in his scrubs had been waiting in here in the darkness for the privacy to do exactly what he was doing.

The moment shimmered a little. Then the guard smiled.

Harteveld woke, years later, in the Greenwich house, mewling like an animal, the image of the smile hot in his mind. It was still dark in the room, a thin crack of moonlight coming from the curtains. He lay in a deep sweat, staring at the ceiling, listening to the juices of his heart slowing, waiting for his thoughts to settle.

I understand, the smile had said. *I am like you, the inhuman and sick cannot stay apart for long. They will collide.*

Harteveld ran his hands through his hair and groaned. He rolled onto his side, saw what lay next to him on the pillow and had to stuff fingers into his mouth to stop a cry coming out.

Twenty-two

SHARON DAWN McCABE was less than ten inches away, on her back, her eyes open. A blood-tinted froth foamed out of the nose and mouth and trickled in mucusy tracks down her chin and neck.

"Oh—my—God," Harteveld whispered in awe. "Oh sweet Jesus Christ, what the fuck have you done to yourself?" He shoved a hand under the sheets and felt for a pulse.

The clock on the bed table said 4:46 A.M.

Heart thumping, he hurried into the bathroom and filled the sink with cold water. He plunged his face in until the water lapped around his neck.

He counted to twenty.

Restraint, the long pull of desire, days becoming weeks becoming years, and now, after it all, *this,* this trip wire of fate lying still and white in his bed. Exactly what he had been wanting all these years, the one thing he couldn't get from the girls, no matter what he paid.

He straightened, gasping, dripping.

His face blinked out at him from the mirror. Haggard in the oblique light, his thirty-seven years showed; as if he had been *sucked at* from the inside, juiced dry by the strain. He pinched his cheeks hard, hoping pain would bring him clarity. But all he got back was the dull, familiar tug in his belly.

"Help me, help me, please."

His voice was shallow, little more than a whisper. Nothing was going to help him. He knew that. He dried his face and went back into the bedroom.

The room was heaped with predawn purples. She lay staring blankly at the ceiling, her mouth open, the sheets demurely pulled up to her collarbone as if she had wanted to die neatly. Shakily Harteveld crossed the room and opened the window. The night air was cold and sweet, stained with snow. The cedar of Lebanon brittle against the star-freckled sky.

If you wanted to, if you really wanted to—she couldn't tell you to stop. No one would know. No one has to know.

Trembling, he crossed to the bed and slowly unpeeled the sheet, stripping it from her torso, bunching it at her feet. Her arms were splayed wide. He rearranged them, resting them neatly beside her hips, her still-pink palms curling inward. The snail's trail of mucus on her chin winked in the dull light. Edema. From the lungs. He brought a damp towel from the bathroom and gently wiped the mess. Then he cleaned between her legs where her bowels had opened, changed the soiled sheets. Rigor hadn't started and she was easy to move, a calm mound of pliable white circles in the cyan light, round breasts, round stomach, thick, lapped knees, long oval thighs: all lines sliding gently to meet at the dark bruise of the pubis.

The inside of the right arm was traced with scabs. She'd probably taken some of the good-quality heroin that he supplied his guests, he told himself. She must have been used to Gorbals street scag; her body couldn't tolerate the pure stuff he served. Toppled by purity. Harteveld wasn't blind to the irony.

He squatted level with the small white feet. The skin, folded over the tendons of the instep, looked like salted fish. Her sightless eyes gleamed in the purple light. Carefully he ran fingers up over the ankles, the stubble of shaved hair abrading his fingertips, the coolness of the skin making his heart quicken. She was soft. Soft and cool. And *still.*

The house was quiet and dark as he unclenched his fists and unfolded himself onto the bed.

Afterward he was so filled with self-disgust that he drank a bottle of pastis straight. He vomited most of it back up, and was furious to find himself still alive in the morning. And the gray, used corpse at his side.

He locked the big oak door at the bottom of the stairs and went back to bed, lying there all day next to her, his hands rigid at his sides, staring out of the window at the spire of the neighboring church, as it absorbed the color of the winter air: from cold, bone gray, warming up through coral, to blue and white, then dipping back into gray again. The cleaner arrived, knocked on the oak door. When he didn't answer she gave up and before long the sounds of the day started as usual: the hoover moved up and down the corridor, ice dripped from the cedar, glasses clinked as they were packed into their rightful places.

Harteveld continued staring at the church.

He was strangely calm. The bridge was crossed, a deep lever had been nudged and would never be returned. He knew that his world was folding in on itself.

He rolled over and gently stroked the rigid nipples.

When the cleaner came back later that week Harteveld met her at the front door with a white vellum envelope containing £250 and a note dismissing her. He was resigned to it—he knew exactly what was going to happen in the coming weeks. He couldn't afford witnesses.

The mechanics of death were simple for someone with his training. He slipped easily into killing. Over the next six months others came. One every five weeks or so. Harteveld believed he was dying, being consumed from the inside out. The only relief came in the hours he spent with the women.

By late May, there were five bodies, his responsibility each one.

Peace Nbidi Jackson, twenty years old and the second lovely daughter of Clover Jackson, had appeared at the house on the Thursday night, just as the Detective Chief Inspector in Eltham was issuing a statement to the press—so that when the doorbell had rung, Harteveld still knew nothing of the police's discovery: those five grim worm-casts uncovered on a wasteland in east Greenwich.

He placed his glass on the mantelpiece, lightly touched Lucilla's varnished face and went to the door.

"You came. How nice."

She stood on his threshold, bare arms glazed copper in the twilight. He stared at her for a long time, knowing he would be the last person in the world to see this girl alive.

"Can I come in or what?"

"Yes, yes, of course. I'm sorry." He stood back and let the girl wander in, eyes wide at the cathedral-like spaces of the house. If she noticed the smell he was worried about, it didn't seem to bother her. "Go through, I'll get you a drink." He followed her into the living room, switched the lights on and opened the drink cabinet. "Would you like something from here? Or wine?"

Peace sat straight and neat against the Braquenie silk cushions. "Have you got Baileys?"

"Yes. Of course." Harteveld reached into the depths of the cabinet. He should have guessed. The girls always wanted something sweet. He poured the Baileys into a heavy crystal tumbler. "I suppose you've got a name." He held the tumbler up to the light in his long fingers. "Haven't you?"

"Peace."

"That's nice." He didn't smile.

Peace looked at him sideways. "Why'm I supposed not to say nothing about this?"

Harteveld placed the glass of Baileys on the table and returned to the cabinet to pour himself a pastis. "Peace, I am in the fortunate position of caring less about money than about discretion. Here." He opened the calfskin wallet and pulled out ten twenty-pound notes, creasing and folding them expertly, a little effeminate flick of the fingers as he held them out to her. "I'll keep *my* end of the bargain. And believe me, I'll know if you haven't kept yours."

Peace looked around, at the grand piano, the portrait of Lucilla and Henrick over the fireplace, the crystal decanters, and seemed satisfied. She picked up the Baileys and leaned back against the cushion. "I didn't tell anyone."

"Good. Now . . ." He sat on the arm of the sofa. "If you look on that end table, you'll see a little ivory box. Can you see it?"

On the Chinese lacquered table lay an exquisite Ju wood and ivory box. Peace leaned over and inspected it. "Yeah."

"Open it."

She lifted the lid. A silver coke spoon lay in a bed of white powder.

"It's the best. The purest. Or maybe—" He sipped his drink. "Maybe you'd prefer some heroin."

"Heroin?"

"Yes."

She looked up and flashed a white smile. "If it's good, of *course* I do."

"The best, the best." Harteveld stood, his shirt a dull radium glow reflected in the darkened window. He held out his hand. "Come with me, then. We'll go and find it."

Peace wanted to know what lay beyond the oak door. "Smells bad," she said. "Don't you ever clean up in here?"

"Don't worry about that." Harteveld steered her away from the door, down the main hallway.

"What's in there, then? Is that the rest of the house?"

"I'll take you in there later," he promised, pressing her shoulder. "Nothing to worry about now."

In the kitchen he quickly heated some smack in an eggcup-sized pan. Peace smiled as she watched the bubbles rise, the sides of the pan clear silver.

"Good gear," she said.

"Pure. I'll shoot it for you. I can do it painlessly."

"Yeah?"

"I was a doctor."

"But not in my arm, okay? My mom checks my arms."

"Okay."

He sat her on a stool and tied a tea towel just under the bulge in her calf, and when the vein showed blue trapped between the soft coffee skin and the white of her anklebone, he popped the skin and the vein lining with the needle and squeezed the syringe contents out.

"Ow," she yelped lightly, grinning, clasping her hands over her ankle. "Ow. You *butcher.*" She smiled as the rush took her and dropped her into the red leather booth. "You're not a doctor, you're a butcher," she mumbled, smiling distantly. Her head lolled, the black window reflected her saucer eyes. "Oh God—'s good, though, 's good."

Harteveld took his pastis and stood by the fridge watching her. He thought of what he could do with her that night, what *she* could do for *him,* and a deep, hard strength filled his abdomen. She could help him to forget in a way even heroin couldn't. A precious, sweet amnesiac, this girl.

"If you want an even better rush I've got another way." He sipped his drink. "Want it?"

"Yeah, want it." She laughed lazily and swung herself out of the booth, hanging her head. "First I'm gonna puke like, if that's cool."

"There's the sink."

"Ta." She smiled as she pushed her hair from her eyes and vomited over the pile of dishes and glasses. "*Euch*." She smiled up at him and wiped her wet nose. "*Euch*. I *hate* that. Don't you?"

"You want the quick rush?"

"Yeah, yeah yeah." She turned on the tap. Her head was wobbling very gently. "Wan' it, wan' it, I *want* it." She started to laugh at her own singsong voice. "Peace wants it, give it to Peace."

As he filled a second syringe, she slumped in the booth again and dropped her head back, staring at the ceiling, her foot jerking. "Give it to Peace." She bounced her shoulders, opened her mouth, jerked on the seat, dancing on the spot to an internal tune, drop ping her hands heavily on the bench and laughing herself weak as if there had never in the world been anything quite this funny.

Harteveld watched as he worked. Even in his panicky excitement he was cold-minded enough to stop and see this moment for what it was. The last minutes of her life, the breath of death enhanced life: she had looked this beautiful—crumpled in his kitchen, singing softly to herself—only once before, at her birth. This moment, lit by the soft kitchen lamp, was her essence caught in amber.

"Lift your hair up, Peace." He had to bite hard on the words to stop his voice from trembling. "Lift it up and let me get round the back here. You won't feel anything."

She obeyed, glazed eyes swiveling to the window to watch her reflection. "Wha' is it?"

"It's H. Just a little. But take it like this and the rush is like *nothing* you ever felt before."

"Sweee-eeet," she purred, and curled her neck down.

A drop of sweat fell from Harteveld's cold face onto the leather seat, but he didn't tremble. Once, only once, it had gone wrong. The girl hadn't wanted it and he'd had to tie her, gag her with a bath towel and bind her hands and feet with two of his shirts. She had struggled like an animal, but she was very small and Harteveld had been able to get her onto the floor—ignoring her hot urine squirting on his calves—and push the needle through the cervical bones . . .

In the booth Peace's bowels opened, and her head jerked once. It was the only movement.

Harteveld sank back against the wall and started to shake.

That had been two nights ago. Now he was sitting here in the dark with Peace wrapped in cling film on his floor. She had been with him long enough now. It was time for him to do what he had to do: say good-bye to her, do the necessary.

He found the keys to the Cobra and opened the orangery door.

Twenty-three

HE DREAMED about Rebecca, standing in the street with rain dripping on her hair from the lilac tree, and woke with a start at 6:15 A.M. Downstairs Veronica was already in the kitchen, cutting bread and opening blinds to let the sun in. She wore a sleeveless Thai silk dress in aquamarine. Two dark crescents were visible on the cloth under each armpit as she lifted the skillet from the hob and slid a curl of Normandy butter onto saffron-bright kippers. She snipped parsley from a terra-cotta grower in the window and Jack, standing sleepily in the doorway, realized he had no idea when the pot arrived or how it had got there.

"Morning."

She cocked her head and eyed him, taking in the tousled hair, the T-shirt and boxers he'd started wearing in bed. She hadn't commented on them before and clearly she wasn't going to now. Instead she used a teaspoon to fish a vanilla pod out of the coffee pot, poured a mug and handed it to him.

"Morning."

"How you feeling?"

"I'm not to go into the office today, put it that way." She shook the skillet and threw in a handful of chopped herbs. "This isn't for me. I couldn't touch a thing."

"After last night?"

"I feel awful. I peed red this morning and these kippers smell like petrol."

"I didn't want to wake you." He put a hand on her shoulder. A flat, neutral hand. "How did it go?"

"As expected, I suppose." She pushed her hair out of her eyes. "What's that all about?"

"Hm?"

"That *thing* in the hallway."

"Oh, I, uh . . ." Penderecki's Barbie doll, still wrapped in cling film, lay on top of his Samsonite by the door. All night its image had chased him. He had woken at 2:00 A.M. certain that it was significant to Birdman, had got out of bed, retrieved the doll from Ewan's room and left it in the hallway to remind him. "Nothing," he murmured. "Just an idea." Idly he picked up a twist of vegetable from the cutting board. "What's this? Ginseng?"

"*Ginger,* you moron. I'm doing my *dal kofta* for the party."

"Are you sure about this party thing?"

"Of course I'm sure. I want to know if they all look like David Caruso."

"Do *not* get your hopes up." Caffery ducked his head out of the window, checking Penderecki's back garden. "He's been quiet since the doll thing."

"Now, don't be so nosy." She twisted a lemon onto the kippers and shoveled them onto a plate. "Here. Sit down and eat."

By 7:00 he had eaten, shaved and dressed—"*Veronica, I can do my own ironing. In fact, I'd rather do my own ironing*"— and was at the office. Essex had news.

He'd finally tracked down Petra Spacek's family and Rebecca had been right. Petra *had* been allergic to makeup, never worn it. No signs of an allergic reaction meant it had been applied either very soon before the slaughter or postmortem. From what Caffery now knew about Birdman, he doubted it had been antemortem.

He retreated into the office to sneak a cigarette before he and Essex headed on to St. Dunstan's. The doll, mummified in its plastic shroud, lay like a silver chrysalis on the desk. Next to it a blue loose-leaf folder, a CC letter to the Commissioner from Spanner, the SM rights group, sellotaped to the front as a comment from an anonymous exhibits officer. Inside, mounted and laminated, photographs of every example of SM paraphernalia hauled in by vice in the last ten years. Caffery had learned more than he wanted to about spreader and suspension bars, penis-gag masks, anchor pads, D-rings, 0-rings, sport sheets, curb-tip surgeon's scissors and rubber-gag masks with their twin nasal tubes to allow the "bottamer" to breathe.

He was still thinking about the marks on the victims' foreheads. He had searched the file in vain for anything commonly used to puncture the skin. But the cuts on the victims were too small, too clean to be caused by anything in these photos. If Birdman had placed a spiked or barbed mask on the victims, the flesh would have been ragged, chafed, the diameters erratic. In fact the wounds were as precise and even as the punch holes on a doll's head.

A doll.

He unwrapped the Barbie doll and held the head between his white thumb and black thumb.

'*Just like the Black and White whisky Scottie dogs,*" his mother used to say.

He thought of Rebecca propped up against the bike saddle, tanned fingers picking at the stitching on the canvas straps, pretty dark eyes splintered by the sun, telling him about Petra.

"*She looked like a doll with all that makeup on.*"

There! His palms tingled. *There was the link.* Makeup. Punctures. Makeup. Punch holes. Follow it. *Come on, Jack, think!*

Why didn't he do it to Kayleigh? Why was she different?

She was the only one without the marks. Someone, around the time of her death, had cut her long hair to shoulder length. Her hair was blond, the same almost white blond as the samples of wig hair. Wig. Makeup, punctures. *Rebecca's tanned fingers. White nails playing with the stitching.* "*Like a doll with all that makeup on.*" The trim had left Kayleigh's hair at almost exactly the same length as the wig.

He flipped the doll onto its front, ran his nails down the rows of perforations in the scalp, each sprouting a pinch of nylon hair, and the answer lifted, leaped at him.

Stitching.

"Marilyn." He threw open the door of the incident room. "Marilyn."

She looked up, startled. "What is it?"

"Where's Essex?"

"In exhibits."

"Good." Caffery could feel the sinews in his hands twitch. "I need a look at the PM photos. I think I know what those marks are."

In the tiny exhibits room there was only space enough on the Flex-Stax shelving for evidence from the current operation. Evidence from all past cases had overflowed and was kept in lockers in the tearoom.

"Essex. I need—" He stopped. He'd walked in in mid-conversation. Essex sat at the tiny desk, his face tired and motionless. Behind him Diamond leaned casually on one of the shelves, sleeves rolled up, the faintest of smiles on his face.

Logan, the exhibits officer, sat with the yellow grab box at his feet, a computer printout in one hand, a buff docket in the other. When he saw it was Caffery he stood up so hurriedly that the paper air-drying evidence bags on his lap slid to the floor.

"Ah!" He snatched clumsily at the bags. "Morning, Boss."

"The PM photos, Logan."

"Of course, of course, no probs, sir." Moving a trifle too quickly, he stacked all the bags back on the desk and busied himself with a blue box file in the corner. Essex met Caffery's eyes for a moment, then looked away. It was enough. Caffery closed the door behind him and leaned against it with his arms folded.

"Well?" he said. "What's up?"

"The SA at Lambeth's been on regarding Gemini's car," DI Diamond said calmly.

"I see. What's she got for us?"

"Four hairs found." His washed-out blue eyes had centers of hard indigo. "Didn't match any of the victims."

"Yes?"

"But that doesn't matter." In the corner Logan gave a short discomfited cough and Essex stared at his hands. Diamond took the time to run his hand over the hard, gelled helmet of hair. He sniffed, straightened and plucked the report from the desk with an ornate flick of the wrist. "Numerous smudged partial prints, and someone had had Kodian-C out to the interior."

"An industrial-grade cleaning fluid," Logan explained.

"Which seems dodgy to me." Diamond blinked slowly like a lizard in the sun. "Then the lads at Lambeth found three prints with enough points to make a match."

"I see."

"One with Craw and one with Wilcox."

"He cabbied for them."

"He says he doesn't even *know* them."

"Okay." Caffery pushed himself away from the door. "Does the super know?"

"Oh yes. We caught him on the way to the CS's." Diamond smiled and rolled his sleeves down, buttoning them carefully. "He's clearing it with Greenwich. We're going to give that shitty little scrote a chance to come in and answer some questions voluntarily. And if he doesn't want to play, we're arresting him. Don't want him heading back home and losing himself in the Blue Mountains."

"You can see his point, I suppose," Essex said, and Caffery could feel his empathy straining out.

"I suppose," he said coldly. He turned to go, stopping briefly, his hand on the door. "Essex."

"Sir?"

"I still want those PM photos on my desk."

Twenty-four

MRS. FROBISHER took her coat off and hung it carefully on the rack in DI Basset's Greenwich office. She kept her hat and gloves on.

"A cup of tea, Mrs. Frobisher?"

She smiled. "That *would* be nice."

Basset kept a discreet eye on her as he opened the blinds and flicked the switch on the kettle. A little worm of unease was crawling across his stomach. Mrs. Frobisher was well known to the staff at Greenwich police station: in the last six months she had been a methodical visitor, complaining about anything from the fights in the council block opposite, the dirt and noise of local construction work, to the antisocial behavior of the tenant in the flat below. She had refused to be foisted off onto the environmental health department, and was considered by the duty team to be part of the Monday morning drudgery.

Until this Monday, when, at 10:00 A.M., she ambled in as customary, wearing her best hat and coat on a hot summer's day, and gave a statement to the desk sergeant which made him reach for the phone. DI Basset, who had been one of the first attending CID officers at the construction yard last weekend, canceled his morning meeting with the community liaison officer and invited Mrs. Frobisher into his office.

She sat, sparrowlike, on the edge of the chair, staring out of the window at the sun on the striped awning of Mullins dairy on Royal Hill. "It's lovely here, isn't it?" she sighed. "Absolutely lovely."

"Thank you," Basset said. "I think so too. Now—" He lifted the tea bags on a spoon and dropped them in the wastepaper basket. "Now, Mrs. Frobisher, our desk sergeant tells me you've been having some bother. Shall we have a little chat about it?"

"Oh, that? It's been going on months, not that any of them would take a blind bit of notice." She took her gloves off, put them in the matching fawn mock-leather shopping bag and zipped it up. The hat remained in place. "I've been in here like clockwork every week, and no joy until now. Wouldn't listen to me. I might be old, but I'm not stupid. I know what they're saying—crazy old witch—I've heard them."

"Yes, yes." He held a mug out to her. "I'm sorry about that, Mrs. Frobisher. Sincerely sorry. It's just you've had one or two of our lads out to you in the past, and I think they feel—"

"Only for the foxes! At this time of year they will insist on having their little romances and whatnot. The noise they make! It sounds like a woman screaming, and you can't be too careful, not in this day and age." She took the tea, resting it on her knee. "When my George was alive he used to throw bricks at them. Now, *he'd* know the difference between a fox and a woman screaming." She leaned forward, glad of the audience. "I was born in Lewisham, you know, Officer, and I've been in Brazil Street fifty years now. Got a special fondness for this area in spite of every thing. I've seen the Jerrys bomb the place, the council get their hands on it, the foreigners and now the developers. They've pulled everything down I cared about and there's new buildings going up. Hyper this and Hyper that, loft conversions and I don't know what."

"Mrs. Frobisher." Basset placed his tea next to his notepad and sat down opposite. "In the statement you gave our desk sergeant you talked about a neighbor of yours, is that right?"

"Him!" She cocked her head back and pursed her lips. "Yes. *And* there's him. As if I haven't got enough worries."

"Tell me about him. He owns the flat downstairs?"

"Owns it. Don't mean he gives a tinkers for it, does it? Never bloody home."

"Been there long, has he?"

"Years. Ever since my George died. No sooner had I got him in the ground than my son decides the old place is too big for me—has the council in, the planners, the gas board and I don't know who else, and even more dust if you please. They bricked off the staircase, put a door round the side and one of those carport affairs, horrible American-looking thing, I can't be doing with it myself. Next I know they've sold that floor off to *him,* and me and the cat are marched off upstairs like a pair of lepers in our own home."

"His entrance is at the side?"

"At the back, under the carport—so he's got the garden, you see. Not that he looks after it. Oooh no." She sucked in a breath and shook her head. "No, no no. Not with him never being there. Covered in bindweed it will be by July the rate he's going. But even if he did get it nice, what then? Who'd want to sit out there with the noise and dust and hammering every minute of the day? And if it's not that, it's them over the road screaming and shouting—you can't win, Officer, you can't win."

"I'm sure." Basset nodded. "I'm sure you can't. Now, shall we concentrate on what you were telling the desk sergeant about your neighbor?"

"I was telling your sergeant that I think he's left that freezer of his unplugged again. The smell! Well, you've never known the like of the smell, Officer. It's not healthy whatever it is. He was all right when he first moved in—kept the place reasonable from what I could tell. But, see, now he's got to the point where he'll leave the place for days on end, never check on it. And this—"She tapped an arthritic finger on the desk to punctuate each word. "*This* is the *sort* of *thing* that is *bound* to happen. You'd think, wouldn't you, him being a professional, you'd think he'd show a bit of respect." She put the mug on Basset's desk and started to unpin her hat as if she was finally comfortable. "It's his patients I feel sorry for."

"He's a doctor?"

"Maybe not exactly a doctor, but he's something to do with the medical profession, that's what my son says. Must be something important with him and his nice car and his two properties. But it don't stop him being an odd one. The way he neglects the place—"

"But there was something particular that bothered you," Basset prompted. "Wasn't there something, Mrs. Frobisher? Didn't you say something to the desk sergeant about—about some *animals*?" He paused. Mrs. Frobisher was blinking at him. For a moment he wondered if the PC had misheard. That this was all a mistake. "Didn't you mention there were some animals involved? Something about them being mistreated?"

"Oh that." The light dawned. "Yes. That as well. He doesn't look after them proper. I found two dead ones in the bin outside. Looked like they starved to death." She sipped her tea and sighed. "Now, that's a nice cup of tea. They say you don't get a nice cup from a bag, but I can't agree in this case."

"Mrs. Frobisher." Basset took a calming breath. "Mrs. Frobisher, are we talking about *birds*? Were they *birds* you saw in the dustbin?"

"That's what I said." She looked at him as if he was slow. "That's what I said. Birds."

"And what sort of birds? Big ones? Pigeons? Crows?"

"Oh no, no. No no. Little ones." She showed a span of two inches between her arthritic fingers. "Little tiny ones a person might keep in a cage if they didn't have a cat to think of. With red feathers. Reddish sort of feathers."

"Could they have been finches?"

She paused, egg white cataracts wandering across her eyes. "Yes, that's it. That's it. Finches. I'd bet any money."

"Good." Basset wiped his forehead. "Good." He leaned forward and put his hands on the table. "Now. I'm wondering if you'd like to tell one of my colleagues the story?"

"Will he do something about it?"

"He'll certainly be very interested."

Mrs. Frobisher settled back, pleased by the attention. "I'd feel better." She folded her hands on her lap. "Is he coming to speak to me?"

"I'm going to call him this very moment."

Basset sat on the edge of the desk and dialed the Croydon switchboard to put him through to Shrivemoor. He watched Mrs. Frobisher sipping her tea as the line clicked and connected. He was feeling faintly sick.

Essex shuddered when he saw the doll's unblinking, forget-me-not blue eyes gazing at him. "Don't leave the windows closed or that thing'll come to life. Haven't you ever seen *Doctor Who*?"

Caffery put his head in his hands. The tiredness was deep in his muscles. "Gemini lied."

"Yeah. Bad news, that." He looked around the office. "Where d'you want these photos?"

"He could have turned the whole thing on a word. *Yes.* Yes, I knew Shellene. Yes, she was in my car. Yes, I supplied her, had sex with her or any of the other things he did. We know he cabbied for the girls, he should've just said." Caffery sat back in his chair and opened his hands. "All we've got going for us is the blood group on that sample; knowing our luck, it'll match." The phone on his desk rang. He stared at it blankly. "Have we got a warrant for his flat?"

"Diamond is just leaving for the warrant office. Then they'll take him in for questioning."

"Jesus." Caffery tapped the desk impatiently. "Our options are closing down here. Something had better come out of these St. Dunstan's interviews." He reached for the phone but it stopped ringing. "Shit." He sank back in his chair, rubbing his face.

"Do you want these or not?"

Caffery nodded and held his hand out. "I think I know what the wounds on the head are." He slid the photos out of the envelope and spread them on the desk. "There. Do you see? These slits, very clean. Krishnamurthi still isn't certain of a weapon."

"But you are?"

"Yes."

"Well?"

"The holes are stitching."

"*Stitching?*" He picked up the photo of Shellene, held it close to the window and squinted. "Okay. I'm with you. What's he stitching?"

"Remember what Kayleigh's aunt said?"

"What?"

"She said Kayleigh had changed her hairstyle."

"Yes."

"Kayleigh didn't have those puncture wounds. Her hair was almost the same color as the wig. Shellene's blond was darker. Gold, not ash."

"And?"

"He didn't stitch anything to Kayleigh's head because he didn't need to. He cut her hair the way he wanted it. That wig we thought the offender was wearing? Your *Dressed to Kill* wig?"

"Yeah?"

"It wasn't him wearing it. It was the girls. He stitched it on to stop it falling off when he played with the bodies. When he pulled the wig off, the skin tore, split between the stitching. He's trying to make the girls look identical." Caffery shoveled the photographs back into the envelope. "That's what the makeup and the mutilation to the breasts are all about. He's making clones. Probably keeping them in his bed for days." He stood and pulled his jacket on. "Now if we could find *who* he wanted the victims to look like we'd be halfway to the Old Bailey." He took his keys out. "Shall we?"

"Shall we what?"

"St. Dunstan's, I think."

The incident room was busy. Officers wearing short-sleeved shirts in deference to the early arrival of summer carried dockets to and fro. The blinds were down, the lights on. Kryotos had her shoes off under the table and was slowly eating a piece of fudge cake as she prepared HOLMES for Jack's St. Dunstan's Hospital interviews. She would have to create up to 180 more nominals just to cover all the cross-references needed.

"Jack Jack Jack," she murmured. "What goes on in that head of yours?"

The effect Caffery had on women was not lost on Kryotos, earth mother, she of the matronly observant eye. She watched the indexer girls behind their monitors when he walked through the room, touching their hair, crossing and uncrossing their legs, distractedly reaching down to rub their calves and run fingers under ankle straps. And he would wander away, casually trailing his air of detachment, the occasional shaving nick—Kryotos was in no doubt about what the girls would like to do with those shaving nicks. But Caffery seemed somehow *removed* from it all; as if there were more worthwhile preoccupations in his world. Kryotos was curious to meet Veronica, famously brave Veronica, going ahead with a party this week, in spite of the fact that she was in chemotherapy.

When no one in the SIO's office had answered after five rings, DI Basset's call was automatically transferred to the incident room, to the phone on the desk next to Kryotos's. DI Diamond, pulling on his jacket and heading for the door on the way to pick up Gemini's warrant, stopped and answered it.

"Incident room." A pause and then: "DI Caffery's not here, mate. Who wants him?"

Kryotos looked up. "*He's in his office,*" she mouthed.

"He's tied up just now. Anything I can do?" Diamond listened for a moment, picking at a green Met-Call sticker on the phone. "If you've got a lead, then hows about you take a statement yourself, MSS it to us, and if we like it we'll pick it up?" He broke off. "All right, mate, whatever you say." He pulled out a pen, uncapped it and positioned himself to write. "What have you got for me, then?"

He jotted down a few notes, glanced hungrily at Kryotos's fudge cake, listened, recapped the pen, tucked the phone under his chin, looked at the cake again and idly scratched his ankle just above his sock. More theme socks, Kryotos noticed. Wallace and Gromit this time. Just about what she'd expect. She turned back to the monitor.

"Look, Mr. Basset—*Basset*! If I can *just* get a word in edgeways. Thank you. Now, tell me—are we talking an IC1 here—a white male? We are? Good. And this woman—a habitual caller, is she?" He listened and smiled. "I see. No no no. We treat all tip-offs as serious. Thanks for the pointer. I'll get it circulated to the crew. Okay?"

Replacing the handset, he tore the page out of the book, stood, stretched, and scratched his belly. "Jesus." He yawned. "Some of the shit you get thrown at you as soon as the public get a whiff of anything." He licked his lips. "Where's your file thirteen, dolly?"

Kryotos looked up. "Sorry?"

"Where's the trash?"

She nudged the tagged confidential wastepaper bag out from under the desk with her bare foot. "The shredder's on the blink. You'll have to use this."

"You're a good girl. You know that?" He scrunched the paper into a ball, took a few steps back and zinged it into the bag. "Fucking foxes."

"Fucking detectives," Kryotos said under her breath. She delicately removed a gobbet of fudge from her fingers, used a tissue to wipe her hands and went back to her work.

Twenty-five

WHILE DIAMOND, swollen with confidence, the self-appointed conductor of the mission to pull Gemini in, drove victoriously to Deptford, Caffery and Essex's route split off to St. Dunstan's in Greenwich. It was a good bright day, and on the streets where chestnut trees hung over the park wall, women in floral prints walked with prams, occasionally stopping to wait patiently, hand out, for a fat-legged toddler to catch up. Cars lined the streets—they found a parking space almost half a mile away.

"I wonder what he's doing on a day like today," Essex said, looking at the sky as they parked. "Birdman. I wonder if he's thinking about the next one."

"Thinking about a woman with blond hair."

"The clone. Someone he knows?"

"Or someone he thinks he knows." Caffery opened the windows a crack, locked the car and pulled on his jacket.

"So we're looking for someone who drives, knows their way round anatomy and has the hots for a blonde with small tits."

"Poetic."

"Ta." They separated to allow a female jogger in a black and white Nike sweatshirt past. Essex turned and watched her, the zinc-blond ponytail bobbing in the sun. "Maybe he's already got the next one." He looked at Caffery. "Maybe's he's doing it with her now."

Caffery pictured this possibility as they walked in silence toward the hospital. Neither spoke for a while. It was Essex who broke the mood, stopping suddenly, to rock back on his heels and give a long low wolf whistle.

"Whoo-eee. Chickidout."

Near the hospital gates, in a residents' parking bay, glinting in the sun, sat a green Cobra convertible, wire wheels, cream upholstery, walnut steering wheel. Essex approached it reverently, the same glazed expression he'd worn at Joni and Rebecca's on his face. "Oh baby, mamma mia, excuse me while I ejaculate."

Caffery rolled his eyes to the sky and sighed. "For God's sake—if you must, then make it discreet. And quick, Detective Sergeant Essex. This fair city is counting on you."

Wendy, the librarian, in her customary cardigan buttoned to the top and ankle-length skirt, blushed when she saw Caffery. She had the room ready.

"You nearly lost it, though. One of the committees sit today. I thought for a moment they were going to want this room. I expect you had trouble parking, didn't you?"

The blinds were drawn, and placed thoughtfully on the desk, a writing pad which he wouldn't use and two polystyrene cups of steaming tea with evaporated milk. Essex discreetly smuggled the tea out, tipped it in the urinals and got coffee and Twix bars from the canteen. Then he wandered away with the list to herd some interviewees in.

It was 12:30 P.M., and Caffery had interviewed three occupational therapists and an ophthalmology department technician, when the door opened and Cook came in. His shaggy coppery hair was curled up in a hairnet, and he had removed his scrubs to reveal a rainbow-striped nylon tank top, a canvas marijuana leaf appliquéd on the chest. He wore overlarge dark glasses which he only removed when the door was closed. Caffery was once again struck by the sore, wet eyes.

"We've met." Caffery extended his hand.

"Thomas Cook."

"Easy name to remember."

"This is about those girls, isn't it?" He ignored Caffery's hand and pulled a chair back without waiting to be asked. "Since I saw you here last time I've been expecting a visit."

Caffery steepled his fingers. "You know about it?"

"It's been all over the papers and Krishnamurthi was on the shout. They're saying it was a Jack the Ripper copycat." He had a soft, nasal, womanly voice. "From that I guess this guy *cut* them. Am I right?"

"Do you know Krishnamurthi?"

"I'm a techie. I helped him on a few PMs before he went bigtime with the Home Office."

"You're a mortuary assistant?"

"I wanted to be a doctor." His face was expressionless. "This job was bottom of the spectrum, but it pays the bills."

"Mr. Cook. I'm clearing up routine inquiries. As I hope my DS explained, you are under no obligation. You *are* talking to me of your own free will, I take it?"

"That's why I'm here."

"You live—" Caffery put his glasses on and checked the address on the list. "Where? Lewisham?"

"The Greenwich side. Near the Ravensbourne."

"Do you know a pub on the Trafalgar Road? The Dog and Bell."

"I don't drink."

"You don't know it?"

He crossed his pale, hairless hands on the table in front of him. "I don't drink."

Caffery took his glasses off. "Do you know it?"

"Yes, I know it. No, I don't go in it."

"Thank you." He put his glasses back on. "Have you ever seen this woman?" He pushed the shot of Shellene over the table.

"Is this the one whose face was crushed by a bulldozer?"

"You've heard a lot."

"People whisper." He tilted his head and peered at the photo. "No, I don't recognize her."

Caffery slid the photos of Petra, Kayleigh and Michelle across. Cook put a finger on Kayleigh's smiling face and dragged it closer.

"Know her?"

He pushed the photograph back and looked at Caffery with his raw, colorless eyes. "No. I'd remember her."

"If it helped in our investigations, would you consider giving us a swab, a saliva sample, for DNA analysis?"

"No problem."

Caffery looked at him carefully. "No objections to that?"

"You think because I look like a hippie I live by the civil liberties bible? Well, I don't: I trust science; I *am* a scientist. Of sorts."

"Could you tell me what you were doing on the night of the sixteenth of April? And the night of the nineteenth of May, that's two weeks ago?"

"I wouldn't have a clue. I'll ask when I get home. She'll remember. My north, my south, my east, my west." His expression didn't change. "My social secretary, my memory."

Caffery fished inside his suit for a card. "When you remember give me a call."

"Is that it?"

"Unless you've got something to tell me."

"You obviously haven't got a lot to go on."

"We've got DNA evidence."

"Course you have." Cook stood. He wasn't tall. His limbs were rounded and his hands were big. "I'll be in touch." He reached in his back pocket for his sunglasses and, pulling them on, went out into the light-filled library.

In the darkened room Caffery sniffed. Cook had left a slight, sour smell. Something like a mixture of old milk and patchouli oil. He tapped the pen on the desk thoughtfully.

After a while he wrote: *Cook: says he is married/lives with someone. Believe him???????* He pondered this for a moment, then scribbled underneath: *No.*

For lunch he and Essex had *pasta funghi* and Spitfire beer in the Ashburnham Arms. Back at the hospital for the afternoon session, the library was quieter. Essex wandered off to round up staff from radiology and Caffery took a seat near the window to check through the morning's notes. Slowly he became aware of a gray-haired figure in a white coat sitting in a booth on the far side of the periodical stacks, his head bent intently in study. There was something familiar about him.

Caffery approached.

"Afternoon."

The man took his steel-rim glasses off and looked up mildly. "Good afternoon."

"I'm sorry to interrupt."

"Not at all. Can I help?"

"Yes." Caffery sat down and put his elbows on the desk. "You're Dr. Cavendish."

"This is true."

"You've moved from Guy's?"

"No, no." He closed the book and put the glasses in his pocket. "I'm here for a satellite clinic. Sickle cell. Unusually high incidence in southeast London."

"We've met."

Cavendish looked embarrassed. "Forgive me. If there's one lacuna in my character it is the ability to recall faces. I am not an individual primarily steered by visual stimuli, a quirk that Mrs. Cavendish has found to be of great benefit over the years."

Caffery smiled. "We met about four months ago. You were treating a friend in a follow-up Hodgkin's clinic. Gave her an ultrasound."

"Plausible, plausible. To check the spleen."

"We're very grateful."

"Thank you. How is she progressing?"

"Not good. She's had a relapse. You treated her yesterday afternoon at Guy's."

Cavendish's eyes narrowed. "Ah yes, I see. I believe you are confusing me with Dr. Bostall?"

"No. Veronica Marks. You saw her yesterday."

"Well, yes. I know the name, but I didn't—" He broke off and crossed and uncrossed his legs under the table. "You'll appreciate that I am bound by the ethics of my profession. At the risk of appearing offensive I will refrain from discussing individual cases."

"But you *did* see her last night?"

"Hmmm." He opened the book and put his glasses on." I think we'd be best advised to truncate this conversation now, Mr.—?"

"Caffery." Caffery sat down opposite him, his heart thumping. "Dr. Cavendish. I need to ask you something."

"I think not. I find myself rather embarrassed."

"Not linked to any particular case. It's just, I—I'm intrigued by some of the new diagnostic tests for Hodgkin's."

Cavendish looked up. "Intrigue is healthy and devoutly to be desired. Especially in the young."

"The dye test."

"Not related to a specific case?"

"No."

"Gallium or lymphangio?"

"The one that goes in through the feet. The one you can see."

"The lymphangiogram. Indicates if the cancer has spread to the lower body. My patients lead me to believe it is an uncomfortable procedure."

"You haven't changed the test recently? You don't put a different dye in? One that fades more quickly?"

"No, no. Still linseed oil. It takes several days, sometimes weeks to leave the system." He ran a finger across dry lips. "Mr. Caffery, if you find you have a true interest in this I'd draw your attention to an article on vinblastine in the *British Medical Journal* this month. Very interesting, written by a colleague coincidentally, but I recommend it in the true spirit of impartiality."

"Thank you." Caffery offered his hand. "I think you've told me everything I need to know."

Twenty-six

BY 7:00 P.M. the day had become windy, the breeze yanked low, brown clouds across the sky, drivers pulled visors down against the on-off flashing of the late sun.

Caffery didn't want to go home. Veronica would be there, faux pallor and weariness, and he was afraid of what he might say—or do—to her. Nor did he want to go to the office and have conversations die around him, the knowledge that he was backing a loser against all the odds, holding out for Gemini, who even now was on his way to Greenwich police station. What Caffery wanted was to see Rebecca. The excuse, when it came, was reassuringly legitimate.

He dropped Essex at the station, in the heart of a sudden shower, did a U-turn and retraced his steps through rush-hour traffic on Trafalgar Road. At Bugsby Way the rain stopped as suddenly as it had started and the evening sun came back for one last try at drying the world, glinting on the silt-heavy Thames, casting the long shadows of peeling billboards across the road. The only things that moved were stray plastic bags rolling along the empty service routes, and Caffery was struck once more by the strange end-of-the-world loneliness of this landscape.

The construction yard had changed dramatically. The scene hadn't yet been released, but the forensics team had finally completed their fingertip search; the GPR equipment had gone, the conveyor belt and the sieves lay unattended and the alloy crush barriers intended to restrain the press stood redundant, a length of police tape fluttering lazily from one.

DC Betts sat, unobtrusively, in the team car parked at the end of the service road, quietly warming his face in the evening sun. Caffery acknowledged him and ducked under the perimeter tape. Since he was last here the ground had sprouted a fine summer cover of new vegetation, wet from the rain. He headed back toward Bugsby Way, retracing the steps he'd taken with Fiona Quinn that first night. It was hard going; strange long grasses, the color of mud, clung to his ankles, and by the time he'd reached the far perimeter fence the shadows were longer, his socks sodden, studded with seed heads.

He stood still and lifted his face into the air, eyes half closed, smelling the bad, bitter perfume of wild poppy mingling with the river smells. The search had revealed only one sizable gap on this side of the fence. On the service road the holes were numerous. The accepted theory was that Birdman had parked in the service road and carried the bodies almost a quarter of a mile across this difficult terrain, going back to the car to retrieve the gardening spade which they thought he'd used to make the graves. Caffery believed that Birdman had had reason to come here before the killings, or to pass it on his way somewhere. For a St. Dunstan's worker this could be part of the homeward journey to any number of places: Kent or Essex, even parts of Blackheath.

A snarl of DS Quinn's fluorescent tape, peeled and discarded in the fingertip search, lay at Caffery's feet. He picked it up and studied it thoughtfully, turning it in his hands. All the bottles and cans recovered from here were now speckled in fingerprint dust and bagged in the evidence room at Shrivemoor: Heineken, Tennent's, Red Stripe, Wray & Nephew.

Wray & Nephew—Gemini—drugs. Something about that connection glittered with significance. Drugs and the ligature marks on Spacek's wrists and ankles.

Only Spacek had struggled. A connection buried in there somewhere. Two seagulls swooped over the yard, eyeing him. Caffery's thoughts rolled slow as clouds.

Four of the girls were users. Only Spacek wasn't. There *was* a continuity. He dropped the tape and turned it over with his toe.

Something—*tape?*—to bind Spacek. Drugs.

And then, abruptly, he knew. He put his head back and breathed deeply, surprised to find his heart was thudding.

The offender had to tie Spacek up because she was the only one who wouldn't stay still. She wasn't a user, he couldn't *talk* her into taking a needle in the back of the neck. The target wasn't drugging the girls to keep them still, nor was he threatening them. The truth was far simpler, far more tragic.

The victims were doing it voluntarily; rolling over, maybe even holding their hair up, looped over a wrist, to give him access to that vulnerable knot of bone, ligament and fluid which is the body's second-to-second, day-to-day neural switching center. The brain stem. He'd convinced them this was what they wanted, a fast way to get high—"*quickest way into the bloodstream*"—and they were *just* desperate enough to try it. He had enough rudimentary medical knowledge, confidence, a little jargon. It was a real possibility, especially if the girls, with wills eroded by years of heroin use, already knew and trusted their killer.

"Oi. You!"

Caffery turned. The man coming toward him was tall and barrel-chested, dressed in a pinstripe suit, the jacket flying open to reveal braces over a dark blue shirt and blue tie. His thinning hair was greased back like Diamond's. Gold glinted at his neck and wrists. "The Bill should've stopped you. I've had enough of your sort clambering around."

Caffery showed his card, and the man stopped a few feet away. "No, mate. I'm sorry. A little flash like that. It ain't good enough. Hand it over here." He tapped his palm. "Poxy press card, is it?"

Caffery leaned forward and held the card up. "Okay?"

The man rubbed his nose and shoved both hands hard in the pockets of his trousers. "Yeah, yeah. You can't blame me. I had the place crawling all yesterday."

"You're North. The owner."

"I am."

"We weren't introduced, but I saw you. The first night we were here." He returned the card to his pocket. "I'm having a look around."

"Think he'll come nosing back here, do you? They say a dog returns to its vomit." He tipped back on his heels and looked at the sky. "Well? When can I expect to see you off my land, then?"

"As soon as we've charged someone."

"I was onto your super this afternoon. I hear they've got someone up at the station. Is it true?"

"I can't discuss that."

"Black lad, is it?"

"Who told you that?"

North shifted his weight and rubbed his nose. "Heard this morning the whole area is under compulsory purchase orders. It don't rain but it pours, doesn't it?" He jingled change in his pockets and looked up at the sky where new clouds were gathering. "Maybe I should be approaching you for compensation. Eh?"

"I can't stop you trying." Caffery turned. "Now, if you'll excuse me."

"Yeah yeah." He stood motionless watching Caffery make his tortuous way back to the road. Only when he had completely disappeared did North move. He dropped his head and sank to his haunches, his face in his hands.

Over the Thames Barrier it had started to rain again.

* * *

After he'd done what he had to do with Peace's body, he continued driving. There was only one thing left to do: keep going.

Better not look down, Toby.

He spent the whole day driving, as if he could blow the taste away by perpetual travel, through the storms and the sun, through the dripping, leafy Nash terraces of Camden, the green sweeps of Hampstead, the sticky red roads of Hyde Park, until the Cobra's engine grew hot and hoarse and the sun dropped behind Westminster.

Just after dusk Harteveld found himself on London Bridge. His breath caught in his throat. London laid itself out to him, from the diamond point of Canary Wharf, west through a million lights reflected in the Thames, to the Houses of Parliament.

He stopped the Cobra, found his coke kit in his pocket and unwrapped it. Using his nail, he scooped a small pile of coke into his left nostril. To his right, behind Guy's tower, where it had all started, the moon hung low and smooth. Harteveld leaned back in the seat and stared at it.

Beneath the bridge the water lapped against the pilings. He rubbed his temples and hurriedly started the Cobra.

Better not look down.

Twenty-seven

A SHORT MARIGOLD DRESS, bare arms and a heavy copper Kara bracelet on her wrist: Rebecca was getting ready to go out when Jack called. A private view at the Barbican, ordinarily she'd have avoided it, but it got her out of Greenwich for the evening. She needed the diversion. Since the day DI Caffery and DS Essex had come to the flat, Rebecca had thought of little else—she spent her days in front of the easel, not working, absently stroking a sable brush between thumb and forefinger, reconjuring the faces—Kayleigh, Shellene, Petra—while Joni hummed to herself and rolled cones of Acapulco Gold with her tea and toast, staying stoned until bedtime. Joni had made it clear that she didn't want to discuss what was happening—rarely came home and when she did a strange, pseudo-quiet descended on the pair.

In the quiet Rebecca heard the first faint knockings of a change.

Well, Jesus, it's been long enough coming.

Worlds apart—everyone said it—the two of them were worlds apart. And their only link, which once had glittered with significance, was now fading.

Rebecca was a Home Counties girl. Her father—a tall, solemn man with a classic, philosopher's face—only truly touched happiness alone in the study amongst his gold-tooled editions of Elizabethan love sonnets. Meanwhile his wife stumbled around upstairs pressing handfuls of prescription trazodone into her mouth. The professionals muttered about bipolar disorders. Sometimes she lay in bed for days, forgetting to wash or eat. Forgetting she had a daughter to care for.

So this was what Rebecca had to build an identity on: Spenser's *Amoretti* and amitriptyline. And bedtime beatings. If little Becky was noisy, Mummy's tranquilizers found their way into her orange juice.

She grew into a thin, solemn teenager, believing herself quite alone, quite unique.

It's fathers who abuse—not mothers—nothing in the papers or on TV about mothers.

She escaped from Surrey, setting out for university but landing instead in London. And suddenly there was Joni— sashaying toward her along the streets of Greenwich in shorts and heart-shaped sunglasses, a spliff between her teeth, raging like an evangelist about her shitty childhood. For her it had been high-rise projects, welfare lines, vomit in the stairwells and pigeons coupling on her windowsill. But the theme was so familiar it stopped Rebecca in her tracks.

"Mum. It was Mum who got me onto drugs. If it'd been a bad day she'd make me take her trannies just to keep me quiet—shove them in my mouth and scream the place down if I didn't swallow. She should've been committed before I was born, the mad fucking cow."

Then Rebecca:

"Once she made me wash her in the bath. She was crying. I was eight and I started crying too. She gave me sweeties to calm me down."

"Don't tell me—Tofranil."

"Yes, or something like it. And if she wasn't eating properly, then neither did I—once I lived on banana Nesquik for a week.My father said I was getting thin and that scared her. She drove straight to Bejam's in Guildford, came back with five tubs of Neapolitan ice cream and force-fed me until! threw it all up."

"And then beat the crap out of you, I s'pose."

They knew they were different but they swore that inside they were sisters. Together they lived out their happy, slap-dash early twenties, sharing boyfriends and lipstick—neither caring to stop and note that while Joni spent her days sleeping off the night before, Rebecca was getting up early and taking a bus to Goldsmiths College. Slowly their intimacy was fracturing and now Rebecca confessed as little to Joni as she might to a child.

Especially the things she'd thought about Detective Inspector Jack Caffery.

A cop? A cop, for Chrissakes, are you mad?

But the other day, outside the pub, she'd become momentarily transfixed by his neck—such a stupid thing, but she'd been obsessed—by the junction of tanned skin and white collar, the hair cropped close around his ears. And she'd caught herself several times wondering how he'd look as he climaxed. . . .

Now—sitting in the studio in her party dress—she put the image away carefully.

Really, Becky, just get some nice, clean, middle-class thoughts into that diseased little head of yours.

Waited for the blood to go from her face and arms, and buzzed him into the building. Soon he was standing outside her door, tired and faintly unshaven.

"Come in." She opened the door wide and hooked her leg up to slip on a leather pump. "I can't be long." She pressed her other foot in its shoe and followed him into the kitchen, switching on the wall lights as she went. "Glass of Pouilly?"

"Is it open?"

"Wine *flows* when I'm nervous."

"About what?"

"Apart from the obvious? The Millennium Ripper?"

"There's more?"

"Fear of arty gatherings, if you must know, terror of the black turtleneck, goatees, endless arguments, Fluxus versus

German expressionism, blah blah blah. You know the routine. Coxcombs paying two hundred guineas to have paint flung in their faces or whatever the saying is. So if I've *got* to come out of my atelier and make intelligent noises, I'm bloody well going to fortify myself with an intelligent little Fuissé."

Seeing he wasn't smiling, she closed her lips and took the wine from the fridge, placing it on the wooden table, where condensation pooled around it. "You said you wanted to tell me something." She stood on tiptoe to search the cupboards for glasses.

"Gemini's been taken in for questioning."

Rebecca stopped, two long-stemmed glasses poised mid-air. "I see."

"I thought you'd want to know."

She dropped to her heels and stood very still, staring at the fridge. "We talked about this."

"I know."

"What went wrong?"

"We talked too late. If you'd told me about Gemini and Shellene when I first asked—"

"Are you blaming me?"

"Or when we were at the morgue."

"So you *are* blaming me."

"Wasn't what you saw in that body bag more important than your friend's drug supply? Maybe I should have shown you more of Petra. He *cut* them, you know. Cut their breasts, opened them—"

At that she turned to him. Caffery stopped, a blank look on his face as if he couldn't quite believe what he had just said. "Shit. I'm sorry."

Rebecca shivered. "It's okay." She put the glasses on the table, poured the wine and handed him a glass. Her fingers were trembling. "I used to work in that pub. It could have been me. Or Joni." She looked at him. "That *is* where he finds them, isn't it?"

"It's something we need to talk about. You and I."

"So that *is* where he finds them."

"Probably."

"He follows them when they leave?"

"That's been the assumption." He lifted the wine and looked at it thoughtfully, rotating it to catch the last splinters of sunlight from the window. "But you need to know what *I* think."

"Go on. What do you think?"

"I think they've *arranged* to meet him. To do a trick, or to score. I think they knew him, even trusted him to some degree, certainly enough to be somewhere private with him: his car, probably even his house. I think he seems very well adjusted; maybe he's a doctor, a lab assistant, a hospital worker." He paused, choosing his words carefully. "He's certainly someone they trusted enough to let him inject something into their bloodstream."

Rebecca stopped, the glass halfway to her mouth. "*What?*"

"He told them it was a fast way to get high. Maybe he was someone they had dealt with before. Someone they had scored from before."

"Why are you telling me this?"

"Because I think you've met him. Met him, maybe even know him. And I think Joni has too, although she doesn't realize it. So I'm asking you now—if you're protecting anyone else for any reason, no matter how insignificant it seems—"

"You can stop there." She held her hand up. "I'm not protecting anyone. I swear."

"I believe you." He sipped his wine thoughtfully, watching her over the rim. "Do you remember meeting anyone in the pub who worked at St. Dunstan's? The hospital?"

She frowned. "I don't know. Well, Malcolm, I suppose. He's something to do with a hospital. Someone Joni's known from years back."

"Second name?"

"Don't know. She hangs out with him if she's got nothing better to do—lets him buy her drinks, that sort of thing."

"Is he sort of hippie-looking?"

"Nope."

"You don't know a Thomas? Thomas Cook."

"Like the travel agent? I think I'd remember, don't you?"

"Long red hair. Weird eyes. Distinctive."

She shook her head.

Caffery sighed. "Well, my P45'll be in the pipeline for everything I've told you tonight." He put the empty glass on the table and smiled at her. "Maybe I'll become an art critic."

"I won't gab."

"Thank you." He meant it. "Thank you."

She stood at the front door and watched him disappear down the stairs. He was almost out of the building when she called after him.

"Inspector Caffery?"

His dark head appeared beneath her in the stairwell. "What is it?"

It was out of her mouth before she knew she'd formed the thought. "He scares me, you know. The killer."

Caffery didn't answer. Suddenly he looked immensely tired. "I'm sorry," he said, wearily rubbing his forehead. "I've got to go. Call me if you think of anything."

The streetlights had come on in central Greenwich and the buildings were lit white and gold, festive as ocean liners in port. A thin pink rind behind the roofs on the western horizon was all that was left of the day. Taxis stopped, people queued outside the cinema. Rebecca stood next to the Hotel Ibis, trying to get a cab, clutching a cardigan around her shoulders.

She was jumpier than usual. Since leaving the High Road she'd had the unnerving sensation that she was being watched from somewhere high up amongst the gargoyles in

St. Alfege's. The back of her shoulders tingled and her sweat
grew cold. She couldn't wait to get out of Greenwich for the
night.

From the Spread Eagle restaurant terrace came the discreet clink of expensive glass and silver. Orange and bay trees
in pots dropped leaves into the street below, sunken lighting
cast their magnified shadows on the whitewashed wall above.

Something about those shivering leaves made Rebecca
pause.

*What had Jack said? That they trusted their killer enough
to let him inject them.*

The answer reached her—its breath cold and clear. The
orangery in Croom's Hill. *Toby Harteveld.*

Of course. She dropped her head back and stared up into
space. *Harteveld.* She'd never even thought about it before.
Of the endless possibilities that had traipsed through her
mind, this one had never presented itself. Now it seemed as
obvious as the sky.

She shivered in spite of the warm night and, buttoning
her cardigan tight, turned for home. Forget the Barbican. She
wanted to speak to Jack Caffery.

Twenty-eight

VERONICA WAS SITIING at the kitchen table preparing for the party—a glass of wine at her elbow as she shredded and cut, adding to a pile of mint and tomato on the marble chopping block. She wore a silk blouse pinned at the neck with a gold brooch and had draped a Heals tea towel over her navy pinstriped trousers. The couscousier hissed softly on the hob, steaming up the darkened window.

"I was just about to arrange a search party," she said, smiling. "I expected you back by seven."

Caffery reached to the shelf above the door for the bottle of Glenmorangie. He filled a tumbler, dipped his finger in and sucked on it.

"There's a couple of Oddbins boxes on the terrace need unpacking." She wiped the knife on a tea towel. "You could make some garam masala for the spinach if you feel like it and the pestle needs washing."

After putting the glass on the top of the fridge, he found tobacco and papers in his suit pocket.

"I couldn't find any decent glasses so Mum's lending us her Florentine goblets. They'll need taking care of. Okay?"

She halved two lemons, jammed one onto a squeezer and looked over her shoulder at him. "Jack, I said okay?"

Caffery dropped a plug of tobacco into the paper, rolled it, sealed the cigarette and felt in his pocket for a lighter.

"Jack. Did you hear me?"

"I did."

She put the lemon down and hooked her arm over the back of the chair. "Well?"

"Well what?"

"Mum's lending us her lickle babies. Her favorite glasses. Imagine that. She's trusting our evil friends not to smash them. We're supposed to flop around on the floor in gratitude."

"Not me."

Her face changed. "No—seriously. We should be grateful, you know."

He removed a piece of tobacco from his tongue. "I am serious."

She regarded him carefully and then gave a short laugh. "Okay, Jack." She turned back to her work. "I've got a million things to do for tomorrow. I really haven't got the energy for—"

"You lied to me."

"What?" She turned slowly back." *What* did you say?"

"I thought you might die."

"What?"

"I *believed* you. I believed the Hodgkin's was back."

She wrinkled her mouth, shaking her head in disbelief. "You're sick, you know. You really are. You think I'd make up a thing like that?"

"I saw Dr. Cavendish."

Veronica became still. He could almost see the ticker tape of possible lies, possible excuses, rolling out behind her eyes. After a moment she pressed her lips together so tightly he saw the muscles in her neck flex. She turned and started furiously halving the lemons, squeezing them, tipping the juice into a jug with jerky movements.

"I said I saw Dr. Cavendish."

"Yes—so?" She threw the lemon rinds into a pile. "I *thought* it *was* coming back. You can't blame me. You're difficult, Jack. It's been very difficult for me to be with you."

"Well, thank you. It's been very fucking difficult to be with you too."

"I don't think you realize what a mess you were when I met you, Jack. A *mess*. You'd only get out of bed for work or to spy on that fat fuck over the railway, moping over your idiot brother. I've pulled you out of that." She used the heel of her hand to drive the knife into the lemons. "Me, it's me has pulled you out of it, made you forget your wallowing. Everyone—Mummy, Daddy—they all said I was wasting my time, but I didn't listen. God what an idiot I was."

"I don't love you, Veronica. I don't want you in my house anymore. You can leave the key."

She dropped the knife and turned to him in amazement, staring at him for a long time, until he was uncertain whether she was formulating a reply or trying not to cry. Eventually she forced out a high brittle laugh.

"Well that's *fine*, Jack, that's *fine*." She leaned forward in the chair, her shoulders trembling. "Because I've been thinking." She pointed a shaky finger at him. "I don't love you either. I don't think I ever loved you."

"Then we're quits."

"Yes, quits." She was shaking now. "I'll—I'll stay for the party and then I'll get out of your life. And don't think I won't, because I will."

"We're canceling the party."

"No we're not. You can't. Not now. If you cancel it I swear . . ." She paused a moment, tears in her eyes. "I swear . . . Oh please, Jack, I swear you'll finish me if you do this."

"For God's sake."

"Please, Jack! It's my party too. My friends are coming. Please don't ruin it for me!"

Caffery picked up his glass.

"Where are you going?"

"To have a bath."

"Look." She jumped up and placed a shaking hand on his chest. "I'm sorry, Jack, I'm sorry. I am. It's because I love you so much—"

But he gave her a look of such distaste that her eyes filled again with tears. He lifted her fingers carefully away from his chest and pushed her back into the chair. She sank down, sobbing uncontrollably. "You bastard—you bastard! You *made* me do it, you made me lie. You and that fucking obsession of yours."

Caffery took the bottle from the top of the fridge, closed the door and went upstairs.

Later, when his pulse had returned to normal, he took the bottle of Glenmorangie into the bathroom and slid into the water, his eyes closed, his fingers curled around the steamy tumbler on the bath edge. A body-length wave of tiredness engulfed him. He lay motionless, breathing through his nose, thinking, absurdly and self-pityingly, that this was all Penderecki's fault. That Penderecki had set a small stone in his heart which had stopped him growing well and healthily, excluded him from a universal birthright, the right to love.

He thought he could hear Veronica downstairs, moving something heavy, the front door clicking softly closed. He drank more whisky and slid under the water. His mother's St. Christopher on its chain around his neck floated up to the surface and bobbed gently under his chin, soft as a nibbling fish.

He thought about Rebecca. About her face at the top of the stairs. "*He scares me, you know. The killer.*"

A stair creaked. For a moment he was sure the mobile was ringing. He lifted his head, straining to listen.

Silence. He let himself slide back under the water. *Rebecca.* He could feel the familiar longing deep in his stomach.

Would he do to her what he had done to the others, force
her to unmask herself, skin away the fragile dignity and then
lose interest, abandon her because he had something so much
more important to think about?

He sat up and finished the whisky, got out of the bath
and dried himself. In the bedroom Veronica was lying on her
back, quite still.

"Veronica?"

She was silent, her eyes blank.

"Veronica? I'm sorry."

She was silent.

"I've been thinking."

"What?" she said dully. "What've you been thinking?"

"The party. I'll do it."

She sighed and rolled away from him. "Thank you."

"I'll sleep on the sofa tonight."

"Yeah," she said, her arms limp on the bed. "You do that."

Twenty-nine

THE POLICE SURGEON'S ROOM at Greenwich police station had no windows. The only decorations were a yellowing heroin poster and a laminated copy of a detainee's right to legal advice. Scattered on a low Formica table, leaflets that no one would ever read: *HIV—Are You at Risk?*, *Crack/Cocaine—A Legal Guide* and *Victim Support Group—Help for the Victims of Crime.*

"Roll your sleeve up." The forensic medical examiner, scrubbed skin, clean white hands swaddled in latex gloves, tore open a sample kit: syringe, kidney bowl, vials, labels, swabs. Gemini fixed his eyes on a single loose thread on the third buttonhole down on the white coat. Things, he had to admit, had gone bad.

When DI Diamond put his nose through the letter box two days ago and said "You know why we're interested, don't you?" Gemini hadn't seen the news. He was impressed enough by the police activity to guess that the girls were dead, and that the gear he'd off-loaded for Dog was responsible. But by the time DI Diamond came knocking on his door a second time, things were worse. Gemini had read the papers and knew the truth. He knew that this wasn't a drug thing.

Knew that he'd got a little too close to the wrong people. And
now he was scared enough to start praying.

But they didn't want to arrest him, DI Diamond reassured
him, no obligations, just a few questions, just to eliminate
him, and had he ever heard of civic duty? And so he'd pulled
on his YSL sweatshirt and gone, cool as ice.

Style it out, style it out.

In the station everyone seemed relaxed. They'd given him
coffee, cigarettes, promised he'd be reunited with the GTI
soon. Someone showed him the four photos again and, although now he was terrified, he shrugged.

"No. Ain't never seen them."

And they'd smiled "okay" and asked if he felt like giving
a sample.

"Just a formality to eliminate you, Mr. Henry, then you're
free to go."

Head hair, pulled from the root with tweezers. Pubic
hair (same routine). Urine: the doctor stood next to him
in the toilet watching his pee splashing into a white plastic
cup. And then, in the corridor coming back from the toilet,
Diamond's hand placed lightly on his arm, sour breath on
his face, the pallid eyes twitching as if he couldn't contain
his excitement.

"Don't get comfortable, you fucking little phony." A whisper so the doctor couldn't hear. "We all know you're lying."

"Roll your sleeve up, please."

"Wha'?" Gemini looked up.

"Your sleeve." The doctor snapped open a blood-pressure
cuff, cracked it like a whip and leaned over to fasten it around
Gemini's biceps.

"Wha' you want now?"

"Don't worry." The doctor flicked a vein in the bend of
his arm, drew an antiseptic wipe over the skin and the can-
nula went in. Gemini flinched.

"Rahtid, man. How that gonna prove I did them girls? Eh?"

The surgeon looked at him steadily. "You can refuse but technically the law allows for refusal to supply an intimate sample to be regarded as affirmative evidence."

"Wha'?"

"And if you don't let me take this blood we can compel you to give a saliva swab, consent or no consent." He slowly drew back the plunger and the vacutainer started to fill. "Hold still, please, Mr. Henry."

But Gemini snapped his arm away.

"No, man. You tell me wha' you got on me and how my pee in a cup goin' to prove I done dem t'ings yous is chattin' I done."

The FME eyed the needle dangling from the vein. "You've consented, and you'd make life a lot easier if you'd keep still."

"Well, hear me now." He slammed his hands on the desk, the inside of his elbow popping forward. The FME backed his chair up a fraction. The needle wobbled but remained visibly folded inside the big medial basilic vein. "I *unconsent*. I done *tell* the man already, you know, I tell him I don't know them ladies. I ain't done *not'ing*!"

The FME pressed his lips together.

"Very well, Mr. Henry." Eyes on the needle, he rose and left the room, to reappear in seconds accompanied by DI Diamond, who stood in the open doorway smiling expansively.

"Mr. Henry!"

"You." Gemini sucked his teeth in disgust. "Why you go running at the mouth and come tell me I is lying to you?"

"You *are* lying to us. Those girls were in your car. There's forensic evidence."

"*Sssssttt!* Suck your mother."

Diamond's eyes narrowed a fraction. He turned to a PC in the corridor. "Get the custody officer."

"Last time I seen that girl she was fine and well, man. You want look at one of dem fat punters in dem fancy houses in Croom's Hill. Now get this *t'ing* outta my arm."

Mel Diamond folded his arms. "Jerry Henry—"

"I ain't done not'ing—"

"*Jerry Henry*—I am arresting you on reasonable suspicion of the rape and murder of Shellene Craw of Stepney Green, London, on the night of May the nineteenth."

"I ain't done *rape* no girl."

"You do not have to say anything. But it may harm your defense if you do not mention when questioned something which you later rely on in court. And under section 54e I'll ask you now to remove your clothing." He looked at the doctor, who had retreated behind the desk. "Get one of those Andy Pandy things for him to wear."

"I ain't done no rape! Nor murder no girl either!" The needle broke from his skin, ripping an arch of blood from the vein as it cartwheeled to the floor. Diamond skipped neatly back into the corridor away from the blood. Two PCs appeared behind him.

"Does he want cuffing, sir?"

"Watch the blood. He's a smackhead."

"Is right, I'm a smackhead nigger an' I feel for give you all dem AIDS." Gemini shoved his arm in their direction, baring his teeth. "Pigs!" Behind the desk the FME calmly ripped open a box of latex gloves. Gemini rounded on him. "Wha' you doing?"

The doctor didn't blink. "Protecting my colleagues, Mr. Henry." He tossed gloves to Diamond and the two PCs.

"You want vex me or wha'?" Gemini curled his lips and closed on him, his arm raised, blood sliding to the floor. "You want dem AIDS, is it?"

"Calm down."

"Yup." Diamond, more confident now, pulled gloves on. "I think he wants cuffing."

"*I ain't done nothing!*" He snapped around to face him. "*I gave them some crack is all! I ain't done no murder!*"

"Okay, son." The older PC expertly moved Gemini's hands behind his back and snapped the cuffs tight. "Let's get it over with."

"*I ain't no killer! I ain't no raasclaat killer!*" He coiled up and spat at Diamond, his feet dancing crazily, his head snapping backward. "*You want find a murderer you find their punter in Croom's Hill!*"

Diamond sighed and held up his hand. "You have the right to legal advice. We'll contact the duty solicitor if you choose. If you waive your right I want to know why. For the purposes of the code of detention the rest breaks will be measured from now and not from the time you walked in. Now, will *somebody* get the fucking custody officer in here."

A bent old Jamaican appeared with a mop and bucket to clean Gemini's blood from the medical room floor. Superintendent Maddox arrived from Shrivemoor with a bundle of dockets and a headache to find the custody room in chaos.

"You did *what*?"

"He was getting violent."

"Well now, I see we are nostril-deep in the shi-*it*." Maddox put a cool hand to his head. From the holding cell he could hear Gemini's wails of protest. "Twenty-four hours puts us ten o'clock tomorrow morning. Tell you what, Diamond, *you* can be the bright spark who interrupts the JP's breakfast for an extension."

The doctor leaned out of the medical room and waved a sheaf of forms at Maddox. "FSS ones. Who wants them?"

"Yeah yeah, I'll get our exhibits officer down."

"The samples've been divvied. When the brief gets here they're ready."

"Let our DI here give them a lucky kiss before they go. They're all he's got."

DI Diamond sighed at that and rolled his eyes to the ceiling.

Six miles across town in the Shrivemoor incident room Caffery took advantage of the nearly deserted offices, cupping his hands around a cigarette to light it.

"Tut tut." Kryotos looked up from her terminal.

"Believe me I need it."

"I believe you." She took a sip from a Dr Pepper can, leaned back in the chair and folded her arms. "Well? What's your latest theory?"

"Something crazy."

"Crazy?"

"Yes." He put his glasses on and stood behind her, looking over her shoulder at the VDU screen, at HOLMES flexing its mighty brain. "I think I've met him. I think he's already in here somewhere. Can you just—" He gestured at the nominals and actions columns crawling up the screen like green fireflies. "Just let it go on scrolling."

"Sure." They watched in silence as the names slipped past, their digital pulse replaying the last few days of the investigation: names that had come out of interviews, faceless people who had never been traced, false leads, blind alleys, pubs in Archway, red sports cars, Lacey, North, Julie Darling, Thomas Cook, Wendy—

"Stop!"

Kryotos dropped her finger onto the keyboard with a slight intake of breath. "What? What can you see?"

"Here." Caffery leaned in and tapped the screen. "What's this next to Cook's name? This figure two here?"

"Just means he's come up twice on the database."

"And this entry?"

"That's out of your St. Dunstan's interviews."

"So why's he come up again?"

"Because—" She scrolled through the names, tongue between her teeth. "There." She pointed at the screen. "See. He came up this morning. That letter 'T'?"

"Yes?"

"Means he left a telephone message. As it happens he left it with me; see my nominal there? Number twenty-two?"

"You spoke to him?"

"He said he'd checked and he was home both of the nights you were asking about."

"Ah, yes. The supposed girlfriend. I'm bothered by that." Jack tapped his teeth with his black thumbnail. "He said he was color-blind. Said he had no one to help him choose clothes."

"Ergo no girlfriend?"

"Strange, eh?" Caffery stubbed out the cigarette, lifted one of the blinds a fraction and peered out. The day was bright, hot. "Yes. I think I'll go and see him."

"Better make it quick; he's leaving for Thailand tomorrow." Caffery dropped the blind. "*You're kidding.*"

"Nope. Says he's got a taste for Golden Triangle mountain air."

"I'll bet he has." He retrieved his jacket and car keys from the SIO's room and was almost out of the offices when Kryotos called after him.

"Jack!" She was tipped back in the chair, the phone receiver held to her chest. "It's Paul. You'd better divert to Greenwich. Someone's waiting to speak to you. He says you'll know who it is—says she's, and I quote, *babe-a-licious.*"

"Oh Jesus." He pulled on his jacket. "Rebecca."

"He says the locals are dragging their tongues on the ground and it's making her jumpy."

"Okay. I'm on my way." He fished in his pocket for his keys. "While I'm gone get on to Cook, will you? Don't rattle him, but find out where he'll be today."

"Will do."

"And I'll see you tonight."

"Are you sure about the kids?"

"Course I'm sure. I'm looking forward to it." He blew her a kiss and closed the door, leaving Kryotos to wonder why it mattered to her—married with children as she was—that Caffery was interested in someone called Rebecca.

Thirty

MADDOX WAS ON the steps of Greenwich police station when Caffery arrived. He was standing in the sunlight, eating a samosa from a greasy bag and staring vacantly at students drinking bottled beer outside the Funnel and Firkin. The pronged worry lines between his eyebrows were deeper today. When Caffery asked, he frowned, jerked his head toward the station and said:

"Just the little shit-for-brains in there. He arrested Gemini. Never even consulted me. That's all."

You surprised, Steve? Are you honestly surprised?

"I suppose the party's off, then."

"Oh Jesus." Maddox pressed his forehead. "No." He shook his head, dropped his hand, exasperated. "Fuck it. There's no overtime left in the pot anyway. No—we'll put Diamond at the incident room, let him make amends. Betts can kick off the interview with someone and I'll look in on them later."

"You only have to say the word, Steve—I'll drop it. I'm only doing it for—"

"I know. We're *all* only doing it for them. That's the point. This is the guv's latest initiative: happy home lives makes happy cops. No wife-beaters, no alcoholics, no suicides."

"Very nineties." Jack opened the door. "Eight o'clock, then?"

Maddox finished the samosa, rolled up the bag and shot it into a council bin at the foot of the steps. "Eight o'clock it is."

Caffery avoided the custody room. Instead he went up to the second floor, to the cluster of rooms reserved at this, and every other, Met police station, for AMIP's exclusive use. Inside, Rebecca was sitting alone, staring out of the window, twirling one elegant foot in a distracted gesture of impatience, sucking the Mexican silver pendant on the chain around her neck. She wore olive-green slacks, a pale poplin shirt, and when she saw Caffery she dropped the pendant and smiled tightly. "Hello."

"It's nice to see you."

"Is it?"

He paused. "You're upset?"

"Yes."

He sat down opposite her and thoughtfully steepled his fingers. "Tell me."

"Am I hassling you? I don't want to appear hassley, but I was deadly serious. I think he's important."

"Ah. You've got me there. I'm lost."

"I told your answer service."

"My *answer service*?" Caffery tilted his head back. "And this was—?"

"Yesterday evening."

"On my mobile?"

"Yes."

Veronica. Caffery shook his head. "Rebecca, I didn't get the message. I'm sorry."

At that her eyes softened. "I don't mean to push, but I've been awake all night. It's what you said about it being someone very organized, someone they might trust. Someone they might trust to—" She shuddered and he could see goose bumps on her wrists. "Someone they might trust to *inject* them with something."

"I shouldn't have told you that. I hope you—"

"I haven't told anyone." She leaned forward and her long clean hair swung across her shoulders. "Last year Joni took me to a party. The host made no secret of the fact that he had heroin in the place and would inject it for anyone who wanted it. He'd been a doctor and he knew how to do it without hurting, exactly how much to give, that sort of stuff." She leaned back. "There was no shortage of takers."

"He was a doctor?"

"Had been, or had trained to be, years ago. Now he's something high-powered in a pharmaceutical company and I think he's something to do with St. Dunstan's." She lifted her fringe from her forehead to cool herself. "A lot of the girls in the area used to end up at his place. All the freebies they wanted, the *best,* set out in little bowls. Usually at the end of the night he'd turn punter if any of the girls wanted to do a trick. A good one too. It's been going on for years."

"It hasn't come up in interviews."

"He's very secretive; if you want to get invited back you don't gab. He's well off, intelligent, sort of good-looking in a weird way. Oh and he's got a Patrick Heron to die for." She shook her head in mild disbelief. "Just up there on the wall, and all these hookers standing around next to it snorting coke, giggling—none of them knowing what the hell they were looking at." She paused for a moment, looking at her hands. When she looked up her face had changed. "He went for me that night. It was no big deal. He thought I was a hooker, asked me to stay, I said no and—well, we scrapped. Nothing dramatic. I scratched him pretty badly across his neck."

"He stopped?"

"Eventually. But if you asked me is he capable of cruelty, rape, maybe murder . . ."

"You'd say?"

"I don't know why, but I'd say yes. Absolutely yes. There's something *desperate* about him."

"Where does he live?"

Rebecca swiveled around on the chair and nodded out of the window. "Over on the heath. One of those big houses off the Croom's Hill side."

Thirty-one

"A NOTHER PLATE GONE." Veronica closed the kitchen door on the voices of the guests and shoveled the broken pieces into the pedal bin. "I'm thinking of hiding Mum's glasses before one of those goes too."

Caffery pulled the cork on a bottle of Sancerre, sniffed it and turned the cork over in his hands to check it hadn't crumbled. He had retreated here for a moment of peace and wasn't surprised when Veronica chose the same moment to come into the kitchen. She pulled a Tupperware container from the fridge, and when she saw he wasn't going to answer her, slammed the door loudly. "You know who's funny?"

"No. Who?"

"I'm not being rude, Jack, but Marilyn. What a cow. I was having a really nice conversation with her husband, he's *really* lovely, and then for no reason at all she comes up and starts being really snotty, really iffy with me."

Jack didn't answer. He knew exactly where Veronica was heading with this. She'd been in full-on martyr mode all night—gallantly traipsing through the house, carrying plates brimming with *crostini,* grilled peppers and *tapenade,* a sad, brave smile on her face. But what she really wanted was some attention, wanted a splash of trouble to make the evening complete.

"You're not listening to me, are you?" She began spooning out hummus, tapping the spoon loudly on the edge of the bowl. "I thought at least we were still friends, but now it seems we can't even have a conversation."

"I'm not rising to this, Veronica." He threw the cork into the bin and retrieved a bottle of Médoc from the cupboard. He had no more energy for her tonight. The party itself was a sacrifice—his time precious. Maddox couldn't know that here was one relationship which was beyond the good intentions of the DCS. "I won't fight with you so don't bother."

"God." She shook her head resignedly. "You're so screwed up, Jack. You are *so* screwed up. I think you should see someone about it, I really do."

"You're drunk."

"Of course I'm not. Honestly, what a thing to say!" She slammed the bowl down onto a tray and suddenly her face was calm, as if absolutely nothing had happened. "Now then." She picked up a tea towel. "How are we doing with the Piper-Heidsieck? Did you take those bottles out of the freezer? They'll explode if you leave them in a second too long." Casually she leaned over to the window, lifted the curtains on one finger, looking out as if searching for something beyond her reflection and tutted. "Those kids." She let the curtain fall. "It's too late for children to be up. They'll come to no good out there, mark my words."

The night was warm and the French windows were open but perhaps the guests, like the storm flies gathering above the halogen lights on the patio, sensed the weight of rain in the sky: only the children were using the garden. The adults stood inside, grouped in polite little clumps, balancing plates and glasses, occasionally looking up to check their reflections in the windows. No one breathed a word about the case, even when the children were out of earshot, as if a mere whisper might bring poison through the doors. Caffery, Sancerre in one hand, Médoc in the other, orbited the room filling glasses, stopping to allow Kryotos to feed him a triangle of nan.

"Jack—" She checked quickly over her shoulder and lowered her voice to a whisper. "Jack, your chum Cook? Is he still in the frame? It's just you didn't come back to me and—"

"Oh shit." He tried to wipe his mouth on the back of his hand without spilling the wine. "Shit, I'm sorry, Marilyn, I'm sorry—I got started on something else. I completely forgot."

"He's booked on an Air India flight out of Heathrow at fourteen hundred hours tomorrow. I could get onto ID division for you."

"No. Let him go. He was just, I dunno, me clutching at straws, I s'pose."

She put her plate down and held her glass out for a refill. "Okay, but if you change your mind—"

She broke off. Her small daughter, Jenna, had hurtled into the room from the garden and crunched herself up against her mother's legs, squealing and shaking her head. "*Mummy! Mummy!*"

"What is it?" Marilyn bent down. "Tell Mummy."

"Summonindagardin."

"Someone what?"

"Monsty."

"Jenna." Kryotos took her daughter's tiny, balled-up hand and shook it lightly. "Speak properly, please."

"Monsty in—in—" She stopped for a breath, staring back over her shoulder into the garden. "*In the garden.*"

Kryotos looked up at the others and rolled her eyes. "Wouldn't you know it, we're just getting comfortable and now there's only a monster in the garden."

"'S true, Mum." Dean, Jenna's older brother, appeared in the French windows, his face as white as the moon. "We heard it."

Kryotos colored. "Dean, now, don't mess around. I've warned you."

"Honest."

"Dean!" She held a finger up. "That's enough."

"Tell you what, Jenna sweetheart." Maddox rolled up his sleeves with the soft gravitas of someone who remembered vividly being the father of small children. "How about me and my men go outside and arrest the monster? You'll have to tell us exactly what *sort* of monster it is, of course. So we know how to handcuff him."

"Don't know what sort it is," Dean said solemnly. "We didn't *see* it, we *heard* it. Walking about in the leaves."

"Oh, that's all right, then." Essex heaved himself out of his chair. "It's probably just one of them invisible compost heap monsters."

"Maybe," Dean agreed seriously.

"We deal with stacks of them every day in the police. Even your old mom could take one of those out with her hands tied behind her back."

"*Noooooo!*" Jenna wailed, gripping her mother's skirt, small feet tattooing on the floor. "Mummeeee stay!!"

Kryotos stroked Jenna's head. "Mummy'll stay. Look. The police are going to make sure monsty's gone."

"*Monster busters!*" Essex sprang from the patio, dropped onto the lawn in a warrior crouch, hands tensed like blades, eyes narrowed, a thin keening coming from the back of his throat. "Mon*star* meet Suzie Wong, flower of the Orient and great Doshu of the Way of the Lotus, mistress of the secret dislocation technique *kan*"—punch—"*set*"—punch—"*su*"—punch—"*waza!*"

On the patio a ghost of a smile flickered over Dean's face.

"I strike without conscience. *Ki-ai!*"

Caffery, grateful for the distraction, put the bottles down on the windowsill and wandered into the center of the garden as Essex corkscrewed his arms at the shrubs, throwing

Kali-esque shadows on the lawn. Maddox followed, making a great show of beating the shrubs, checking under a clutch of Russell lupins, carefully brushing aside the weeping willow. "Nope. No one here!" he called. "No monsters here."

"No one there!" Caffery relayed back to Jenna, who risked peeling her tearstained face away from Kryotos to plug her knuckles in her mouth and stare tentatively out into the garden.

Essex executed a few step-punches, surprisingly agile for his size. "Suzie Wong say, 'Lun for your rife, monster.'"

Jenna smiled shyly around her finger and dropped her forehead back against Kryotos, not fear this time but little-girl coyness, the smile twitching the edges of her cheeks. "Suzie's a girl's name," she snuffled. "Not a boy's. He's silly."

"Isn't he," Marilyn agreed.

"*Munen mushin! Ki-ai, ki-ai!*"

"Yeah, *ki-ai, ki-ai,*" Caffery echoed patiently, and climbed the steps back into the house, smiling up at the faces grouped in the lit window. "Don't you feel so much safer knowing we have men like Essex to protect society?"

Kryotos seesawed her head to get a view of the garden. "Now, how on earth has the old sod done that?"

"What?"

"He's gone."

Caffery turned. The garden had fallen silent.

She giggled nervously. "Must've been eaten."

"Mmm. There'll be a terrible mess."

"I don't know, Jack." Maddox came to stand next to him, flushed and grinning, holding out his glass for a refill. "I think even a monster would pass on Essex."

"Not to worry," Caffery sighed. "I'll clear up what's left in the morning."

"Nah, you don't want to do that." Maddox shook his head. "Leave it. Raw pig is good for the roses."

"That's disgusting," Kryotos said.

They all stared into the silent garden, hearing only the soft hiss of the weeping willow in the prestorm breeze. Essex, indeed, seemed to have vanished into thin air. Caffery scanned the dark corners, trying to see the trick, straining to see how he had hidden himself so quickly.

"Where is he?"

"The monsty got him." Jenna started to cry softly.

"Don't be silly."

Maddox shot Caffery a look, eyebrows raised. Caffery shrugged. "Don't look at me."

"Monsty's ate-n him."

"Ridiculous," Veronica said softly, coming out onto the patio to look wonderingly into the garden. "There are no monsters in your garden. Are there, Jack?"

Caffery put the bottles down on the patio and walked slowly down the steps onto the lawn. "Paul?" The flower beds were silent, the small ghostly spots of clematis stellata blooms floating in the darkness. He lifted the weeping willow and looked underneath. Over the railway cutting the darkness was thicker. Penderecki's lights were off.

"I'll kill him for this." Maddox came up behind Jack. "I'll kill you for this, Essex. Joke's over. You're upsetting the kids—" He stopped.

"What is it?"

"Did you hear that?"

"What?"

"That?"

Something dark hurtled at them out of the shadows. Maddox ducked instinctively and on the patio Dean cried out. Caffery jumped back, breathing hard—"*Jesus!*"—and then, in the shock, he saw it was Essex loping toward them across the lawn, an ape hip-hopping out of the jungle, arms swinging.

"*Ki-ai, ki-ai.*"

"Idiot." Caffery shook his head, laughing. "You. You're dead meat."

On the patio the guests dissolved into giggles.

"Bloody deranged lunatic." Maddox held his finger up. "You'll pay for this."

Essex was wounded. "*Ki-ai, ki-ai? Munen mushin?*"

"Where'd you hide?"

He ran his hands over his hair and shook his head. "Oh, they just, y'know, took me away in a spacecraft."

"Did sexual experiments on you, I suppose?"

"Wow, it happened to you *too*? Spooky." He put his arms around Maddox and Caffery, propelling them toward the house. "What year is this? Is that lovely Mrs. Thatcher still on the throne?"

In the living room Jenna stared at Essex, not knowing whether to cry or laugh. Kryotos, flushed, thumped him on the biceps. "Don't do that again, you big—you big *walrus*." She smiled, put protective hands over Jenna's ears and dipped her head to Veronica. "God didn't give them enough blood to service their brains *and* their winkies. And if they try and use *both* at the same time—oh!" She shook her head sorrowfully. "Calamity is not the word for it."

"You don't have to tell me," Veronica said tonelessly.

The rooms grew hotter and closer with the threat of rain. More people arrived, and in the living room the pile of *ficelle* baguettes was reduced to a scattering of crumbs, the ice in the stainless-steel buckets melted, the platters of cheeses and chorizos lay plundered and abandoned. Someone had found a CD of Strauss waltzes and Marilyn was dancing with Essex, bumping into people and giggling. The room blazed intermittently with the metallic blue of heat lightning.

Caffery nursed his wine in the corner, watching Dean. He was about the same age Ewan had been. To Dean the room had the same dimensions, the same fears, the garden the same dark excitements. Standing upright, he was eye level with the dado rail, just as Ewan had been.

"Nice house." Maddox came up behind him. "You didn't get this on a DI's salary."

Caffery turned, reverie broken. "No, no." He looked into his wineglass. "Parents. Left me with it."

"They left it to you?"

"No. Left me with it." He smiled and swirled the wine. "They sold it to me cheap, very cheap. They were glad to see the back of it. Of me too."

"Still alive?"

"Sure. Somewhere."

"Interesting." Maddox nodded thoughtfully. "It's interesting you've never mentioned it before."

"Yeah, well—" He shifted his feet, cleared his throat. "Wine?"

"Go on, then. One more won't hurt." Maddox held the glass up. "Romaine's given Veronica's cooking the official thumbs-up. She's done well tonight." He half emptied his glass. "But I'll have to be making tracks, mate. I want to stop in at Greenwich to see how Betts is doing."

"How was it going?"

"At time of going to press? Pretty shit."

"It's not going to work, is it?"

Maddox considered Caffery's face for a moment, then took his arm and led him to one side. "Between you and me?"

"Yes."

"We'll never make it stick. Not in forty-eight hours."

"I won't say I told you so."

"Thanks." Maddox sighed. "Tomorrow morning nine o'clock our first extension starts, and when that's up we'll have to charge him, sufficient evidence or not: serology are dragging and the search on the flat turned up zilch, the clerks in the warrant office reckon we're pretty fucking funny, laughing into their spritzers all over Greenwich. And—"

"And?"

Maddox drained the glass and swilled the wine around his mouth as if he didn't like what he was about to say. He straightened up. "He's given us a lead. Says the girls had a punter in Croom's Hill. Dropped the last one of them off there ten days before we brought him in. Thinks it was Shellene Craw. Says he had sex with her. Accounts for the hair."

"*Croom's Hill?*"

"Yeah. Know it?"

"Steve." Caffery leaned in and spoke excitedly. "It's come up, this afternoon. Essex and I were working on it."

"Ah." He nodded. "Go on."

"He's affluent. I mean really up there in the top one hundred. But he's got a little problem: hot and cold running category As. Does a nice Colombian, and the opium is Golden Triangle. A regular little Khun Sa; he's also the majority shareholder of HC Plc."

"Who are?"

"Pharmaceutical company. Heard of Snap-Haler?"

"Somewhere."

"For asthmatics. HC've just won the worldwide license, stocks are soaring, life is sweet. He's also—"

Thunder cracked over the garden, vibrating a tray of fine stemmed glasses so polished that their trembling scattered the light. Some of the women jumped and Marilyn giggled at her own nervousness. Essex unwrapped himself from her and moved to shut the French windows, but Veronica put a cool hand on his arm.

"No, leave it. I like the rain." She gazed off into the garden as if she was waiting for something to happen. The drops began splattering on the patio, the smell of wet earth drifted into the room. Jack turned back to Maddox and murmured in a low voice:

"He's also on a steering committee at St. Dunstan's."

Maddox was silent, staring out at the rain. He closed his eyes briefly, then straightened his tie and nodded. "Go on."

"He trained to be a doctor. Shoots up for his party guests. I was ready to put someone else in the frame—a technician from St. D's—though it was shaky, then bingo, this one comes up and the pennies drop—everything just slots in—and now *you* come along and chuck Croom's Hill into the pot." He lifted his glass, drained it in one. "Give me surveillance. A week. I'm so confident I'd go out there now and do it myself."

"Jack, I can't just snap my fingers and—" He looked at Caffery's face and shook his head. "All right, all right. I'll get the governor to okay forty-eight hours. Then we review."

"Now, Jack, I feel I already know you well enough to give you a good telling off." Romaine gently inserted herself under Maddox's arm and smiled up at Caffery. "You have to learn the golden rule. No talking shop."

"We weren't," Maddox said.

"You're lying. I can see it in your face."

"Ignore her, Jack. She wants me to take early retirement."

"You have to understand my husband." She patted his chest. "He tries to keep everyone happy. It weighs on him."

Maddox took the hand and kissed the inside of her wrist. "We've stopped now, I promise. I was just looking at Marilyn's lot. You know—thinking about Steph and Lauré at that age."

"Oh yuck. Sentimentality." She kissed him and drew back, wrinkling her nose. "Poo! I see I'll be driving." She fumbled in her handbag. "I thought you were working tonight."

"I am." He opened his mouth and allowed his wife to squirt a tiny green dose of breath freshener in. "I've only had a couple."

"My fault," Caffery said. "I'm head wine waiter—"

He stopped. Romaine's face had changed. She put a finger up to her mouth.

"Look," she mouthed, her eyes locked beyond him, on the French windows. "Look behind you."

And as she spoke Caffery became aware of other conversations dying—guests pausing in midsentence and turning to look at the door. Odd, frozen expressions. His earlier excitement drained away.

"Look," Romaine repeated, jabbing a finger toward the garden.

Slowly, half dreading, half knowing what he would see, he turned.

Dean was sitting on the sill, his face pale and pinched, shocked into stillness by the apparition only inches from his face. Beyond him Veronica was smiling faintly—almost fascinated. The French windows were open to the night and in the pale glow of the electric light, streaming with rain, his arms holding an odd, jumbled assortment of ochers, stood Penderecki, his thin hair wild and fluorescing in the sheet lightning.

The room dropped into absolute silence. Caffery stared stupidly into the heavy-lidded eyes, unable to decipher exactly what Penderecki was holding in his arms.

Then Penderecki licked his thick lips and smiled, taking one simple step forward. The crowd parted, he blinked slowly and with something that sounded like a sigh let the armful of bones fall into a splintering mass amongst the feet of the guests.

Thirty-two

ONLY LOGAN AND ESSEX stayed until 1:00 A.M. Maddox had to be at Greenwich and the other guests departed hurriedly, throwing Caffery embarrassed glances where he sat, on the stairs, gazing at his hands, breathing deeply, willing his heart to keep beating.

Veronica, surreally calm, tried to stop them from leaving. "*It's nothing to get excited about. Don't go. We can always sit in the dining room.*"

When she realized she was fighting a losing battle she slammed the front door closed and moodily retired to the kitchen to load the dishwasher. Logan drove to Shrivemoor for his grab bag, and Essex spent the thirty minutes administering to Caffery, doling out the remainder of the Glenmorangie in a series of short, digestible shots.

"Like a baby," Caffery muttered, staring into the tumbler.

"Like a big, snotty, nappy-wearing baby," Essex agreed. "Well? Are you going to tell me?"

Caffery looked at the living room door, pulled closed so that he couldn't see the nightmarish splatter of bones on the floor. "I think that might be my brother."

Essex's face dropped. "Your *brother*?"

"He walked down the railway track at the back of the house. September the fourteenth, 1974. Never been seen again."

And there, in the weak electric light, Caffery unburdened himself of the story, told Essex of the argument in the tree house that had given him the permanently blackened thumb, of Ewan slipping out of his reach, down onto the banks of the railway cutting—*"We called it the death trail. What an irony"*—of the way his mother sobbed and shouted in the back garden, biting her own arms as the police searched Penderecki's home only to emerge after ten hours with nothing, not one scrap of evidence that Ewan had ever set foot in there. Then the finger of suspicion turning to his own father, his being led away, detained for two days—*"My God, it nearly finished their marriage."*

The Glenmorangie dwindled in its bottle.

"Eventually everyone gave up, dropped it, I suppose they had to. But I couldn't. You see, I know he hid Ewan's body—just for the time they searched the house. Maybe he took it out to the countryside. There's some bits and pieces, bills, letters"—he jerked his head upstairs—"clues I've salvaged over the years, keep trying to sort them out, sit down and get a lead from them. But I'm certain of one thing." He swilled his drink and swallowed it whole. "He's hung on to him. Penderecki's still got Ewan."

"So you're waiting here. For him to return your brother?"

Caffery stared at his thumbnail, blinking painfully. "Is that what he's done tonight? Do you think that's Ewan lying in there?"

Essex got slowly to his feet, wincing as the blood returned to his legs. "I don't know, Jack. But we're going to find out."

The summer storm moved southwest across Greenwich, the silver wand of the Crystal Palace transmitter trembling in the moonlight. Even the houses studding the edge of Blackheath seemed to crouch a little closer—as if they could stop the old heath rearing off in the wind.

Harteveld was silent—sitting at the mahogany table in the living room, a copy of the *Times* spread out in front of him, a bottle of pastis at his elbow. The pressure in the air made his temples ache—no matter how many painkillers he swallowed, how much coke he did, he couldn't get rid of the pain. And his hands. His hands were cold. Like ice. He was reading about the bodies they had found at the Millennium site. Kayleigh Hatch, Petra Spacek, Shellene Craw, Michelle Wilcox—and a girl they couldn't identify because she was so badly decomposed. He knew exactly who she was—the Glasgow street child whose death he had slept through. No one had reported her missing.

Suddenly he swept the paper from the table, dropping his face into his hands. For several seconds he sat like this, rocking his head from side to side, raking his fingers into his scalp, as if he might be able to dislodge his thoughts with his nails. Then, trembling violently, he jerked to his feet. He grabbed the pastis and stumbled into the orangery, throwing the doors open. The wind boomed across the garden, hitting him in the face, rattling the windowpanes.

Toby Harteveld stood quite still, his face turned into the gale, listening to the long grasses in the parterre bowing and hissing like rain. The storm was coming. It was rushing out of the night sky toward him, moving faster than a comet, its target the very center of his chest.

Thirty-three

WHERE CROOM'S HILL twists down past the site of the old Ursuline convent, Greenwich Council Environmental Service's refuse lorry was halted in the center of the road by an unmarked white van. Minutes later the lorry continued on its way up the hill, stopping outside the Harteveld house as usual. The van turned away and made a wide, looping swing through Blackheath, arriving at the top curve of Croom's Hill—similarly concealed from the house—just in time to meet the truck a second time. The driver took two full refuse sacks from the workers, passed them carefully to a colleague in the back of the van and slammed the doors closed. Back in the driver's seat he adjusted the wing mirror until he could see, down in the elbow of the hill, a gray Sierra parked almost out of sight under a dripping oak. The van driver didn't turn. With a minutely subtle movement he extended his thumb a small degree, holding it against the mirror.

He waited until the two men in the Sierra nodded in response, then started the van and headed up the hill.

In his walled garden Harteveld saw none of these exchanges. He was propped against a stone bench, blinking at the morning with bloodshot eyes. Next to him, in a bed of violets and moon daisies, lay an empty pastis bottle and a small pile of cigarette ends. He had been there all night, listening to the storms and sirens chase each other up and down Greenwich, not taking shelter, but waiting motionless as the clouds swelled and broke, dropping their rain on his face, turning the maze of paths into rushing gullies. The sheet lightning had turned the bone-white church spire blue, and by morning fruit trees had lost branches, the lawns were boggy and the lovely irises along the west wall lay exhausted and flat. The orangery doors stood open to the morning and the copy of the *Times*, which had been lifted from the living room floor by the winds, was distributed around the orangery and patio. Kayleigh Hatch's face hung in the branches of the cedar of Lebanon.

Now, as the shadows in the gardens faded and the new sun dried out the rain-drenched cobwebs in the copper beeches, Harteveld began to stir.

In the Sierra, Betts turned and looked at Logan. Somewhere in the alley next to Harteveld's house a car had started. Presently garage doors opened, and a green car, a beautiful, high-reared classic car, swung out into the alley. It turned left onto Croom's Hill and headed off into the bright morning.

Betts's mouth twitched slightly as he reached for the ignition.

Five miles away, in Shrivemoor HQ, Caffery's phone rang.

"DI Caffery? Jane Amedure speaking. Your SA at the Forensic Science Services. I'm in receipt of two black plastic dustbin liners and contents. I can run a GC/MS on those compared to the ones submitted from the autopsies and have the results later today." She cleared her throat. "And, uh, something else came my way from DS Essex this morning."

"Yes," Caffery said dully. He was exhausted. "That was personal. From me. We're not reviewing yet. Not officially."

"I know, DS Essex filled me in. If it doesn't go any further I might be able to sneak it in under Operation Walworth."

"Good of you."

"Yeah, well, I heard the story."

"Anything you can tell me?"

"Not much visually, they're old and very fragmented. In the event they prove to be human I'll run a mitochondrial DNA test, so I need to know if your mother is still alive. Hello?"

"Yes, hello."

"I said is your mother still alive, or one of her relatives?"

"Yes, she's—you think they're human?"

"I can let you know for sure later today, maybe tomorrow."

"Thank you, Dr. Amedure. Thank you very much."

He replaced the handset, leaned back in his chair and stared out of the window for several minutes. He had a blunt, toxic pain between his eyes. He'd got to bed at 4:00 A.M. On Betts's return they had worked for an hour: while Veronica wrapped her mother's goblets and placed them in a tea crate, Essex shut himself in the living room, tagging and bagging the bones, carefully, as if he were turning Caffery's emotions in his hands. By 10:00 the next morning, just as Gemini's extended period of detention was starting, everyone at Shrivemoor knew the story, knew about Ewan and Penderecki, understood Caffery a little better. The women in the incident room looked at him with something new, something, he imagined, curiously like fear. If he let it, he could be undone in the time it took Amedure to make a report on the bones.

"Got a minute?" Maddox was standing in the doorway. "Someone to see you."

"Yeah. Go on, then."

"Do you want to be alone?" Maddox asked the figure in the corridor. "I can butt out if you want."

"You might as well hear." North, the owner of the construction yard, stepped into the room. He wore a white polo neck under a suit, polished shoes, a heavy gold chain over the neck of the sweater, and was sweating profusely in the heat. He sat in the chair Maddox offered, his gaze unsettled.

"I feel a right cunt being here, if you'll excuse my French."

Jack and Maddox sat, placed their elbows on the facing desks and folded hands a few inches apart. Maddox tilted his head. "Sounds like you want to talk."

"I suppose I've got to." He pinched the crease in his trouser knee and shook it lightly, watching it settle. "It's been dragging me down the last few days, and the wife—well, she's got the right hump, won't let me through the door till I've done the proper thing and come down here."

"What's on your mind?"

"That lad down at Greenwich—"

"How do you know about him?"

"The truth?"

"Yes. If you feel like it."

"I've got a mate in this department."

Caffery and Maddox exchanged a brief look.

"It's a black lad, isn't it?"

"Is that important?"

"In a way." North stared at the trouser crease and Caffery sensed he was trying hard not to squirm. "I might have told someone something—well, wrong like."

"When you were questioned?"

"No. Later. In the pub." His face slackened. "Mel Diamond, Inspector Diamond—"

Maddox sighed. "Yeah. What about him?"

"He's an old mate. Old Charlton supporters we are." North bit his lip. "Look, my daughter lives in east Greenwich, near the yard. She's got problems with her neighbors. Nigerians. Noise, smells, ignorant animals they are, got rats living in which come through the holes in the wall, under the floorboards and up into the baby's room." He paused. "Not that I've got anything against them, but they drive around in their flash cars, God only knows how 'cause not one of them's in work, and there's my daughter scratching a living and can't get herself a job round her way 'cause every post goes to a black with the world being what it is."

"What are you getting at, Mr. North?"

"I lied."

"Lied?"

"Can't you see my position? You'd have done it too if your daughter was living where my girl is. I can promise you that."

"When you say you lied—?"

"All right, all right: I told Mel Diamond I'd seen a Nigerian in a red sports car hanging around outside the yard. I thought if I could shake those boys up a bit—but you went and took someone else in."

"We had a lot of witnesses came up with the same sighting."

North twisted his wedding ring on his fat livid finger. "Well, I don't know about them but the honest truth is that I ain't never seen no one sitting outside. There. I've made a right prat of myself. Hope you're happy."

"Mr. North." Maddox stood, extending his hand. The phone was ringing on his desk. "We appreciate your honesty. Now, if you'll excuse us."

As North left he picked up the phone.

It was Betts, calling to let Jack know that Harteveld had left Croom's Hill.

The inside of the Cobra smelled of leather and, faintly, of hot tarmac as the air conditioner sucked in some of the outside world. He stopped at the traffic lights where Tooley Street sloped up to meet London Bridge. It was a bright blue day; the sun pulled out the sparkles in the new buildings along the Thames so they looked as if they were built from packed sugar.

He stared blankly out at it all from his hermetic bubble. He hadn't noticed the sleek gray Sierra five cars behind or the two men unmoving behind their sunglasses. He was very thin—he must have lost two stone since Christmas—but now he was sweating like a fat man, in spite of the air-conditioning, and yellow sweat wet the front of his shirt.

The traffic lights changed, but the car in front didn't move. Harteveld hardly noticed. His long hands resting on the wheel looked as if they were trying to curl in on themselves. Maybe, he thought—hoped—his body was giving up.

The usual babble of people crossed the road, dark suits, women in heels and light-colored tights, the occasional white jacket of an intern hurrying out of Guy's to catch the post. On Harteveld's left, Guy's hospital tower, studded with satellite dishes, seemed to spy him out amongst the other cars. He shuddered. He should find somewhere to park, but to stop, get out and walk the few yards to the York clinic: it seemed easier to tow the earth across the galaxy on his shoulders.

His plan was vague and desperate. After days of wishing that his heart would spontaneously burst, stop him from having to make the decision, now he knew he needed to throw himself at the feet of the psychiatric community. To do this in the York clinic, in the grounds of his alma mater where the seed had been sown, seemed symbolic and right. Cathartic, if there was a catharsis available for this.

But as he imagined it, as he imagined unbuckling the load and passing it across a discreetly decorated room, tears sprang to his eyes. Even a professional couldn't forgive him what he'd done. Even a professional recoils at the stink of shit. He was trapped. Nowhere to turn.

He sat there, hands clamped on the wheel. The lights changed once. Twice. The traffic didn't move. Harteveld leaned slightly to his side and from the white flash of sun on a metallic badge realized that he was two car lengths away from a police roadblock.

Very quietly, very discreetly, he started to cry.

*   *   *

Diamond caught up with North outside the building. "What the fuck do you think you're doing here?"

North folded his hands over his abdomen and continued walking.

"I said what the fuck are you doing here?"

"I had to tell the truth."

"What did you tell them?"

"That I never saw no one outside the yard."

"Shit."

"I'm sorry, mate."

"Sorry ain't fucking good enough. I took that and ran with it. Made a good case on the basis of what you told me."

North stopped, sun glinting on the gold around his neck, and looked at Diamond. "Now, you *knew* I was lying."

"Bullshit."

"Course you knew. You couldn'ta been happier when I said I'd seen a spade hanging around."

Diamond put his hands in his pockets and shook his head. "That's not how I remember it, my friend. That's not how I remember it."

PC Smallbright of Vine Street station was in a great mood. He was good-looking and in love. It was a pretty, blue day, and the sergeant had let them wear short sleeves under the fluorescent traffic police vests. The ten of them stood at the top of London Bridge with their white shirts flapping in the warm breeze. It was good to be alive, he thought, as he bent over to look through the driver's window of the green Cobra.

"Morning, sir." The cadaverous expression on the driver's face didn't stop Smallbright's smile. He tapped politely on the window. "Could you—" The window rolled down and the rush of stale cold air and the yellow face made him pause. He bit his lip. "Sorry to stop you, sir, but we're doing a vehicle check. Completely routine, just having a little look around at things, okay?"

Taking the silence as assent, he went to the back of the Cobra, glancing back, a new unease clouding his thoughts. The driver, oddly, looked exactly as if he was crying.

Maddox leaned his forehead against the windowpane and sighed.

"I'm asking myself what I've done to deserve this. It's my balls are going to be on the butcher's block for this. Not Diamond's."

"You think he invented the door to door interviews?"

"What do you think?"

"I think we should have a look. If Gemini's been rotting in that cell all this time on the strength of a false statement—"

"Don't say it, Jack. Just don't say it."

Harteveld sat cold as rock as the PC checked the rear of the Cobra, ran his fingers along the bumper, around the taillights. The sweating had stopped now. The hard glitter of sunlight on water reflected in the glass buildings. On the north of the river he could see a tiny wisp of cloud spiraling up into the sky over the bluish dome of St. Paul's Cathedral, as if a spirit were leaving a body. Vapor which would re-form in a different strata of the atmosphere, commingle with other vapor, crystallize, liquefy, and one day drop again onto the earth. Purer. Diamond clean.

"Who's one hundred and sixty?" Caffery shouted over the heads of the receivers and officers milling around the room. He was in shirtsleeves, one hand on the desk, looking at an indexer's monitor. A flashing cursor at the top of the screen highlighted the message.

Record locked port 160.

Someone else in the room had opened the house to house file, denying him access.

"I said who is one hundred and sixty?"

Over the piles of blue duty sheets and the buff-colored actions dockets a dozen sets of unblinking eyes stared at him. In the corner, by the exhibits room, only one person wasn't looking up. Diamond's head gleamed, bent under the gray ellipse of a VDU. The strip of blue Dynotape stuck on the monitor read 160.

Caffery and Maddox crossed the room.

"What the fuck are you doing?"

Diamond looked up with mild blue eyes. "Just entering some actions."

"That's Marilyn's job."

"Oooops," he said simply, pushing the keyboard away. "Sorry. Hope I haven't cocked anything up."

"I don't feel like spending the day reading up on false-hood and prevarication discipline," Maddox said.

"Of course you don't. Sir."

But later, when Kryotos checked HOLMES, she found that the street numbers in the house-to-house entries had been deleted or never entered in the first place.

"Inspector Diamond?" Maddox found him with his feet up on the desk in the exhibits room.

"Sir?"

"A word."

Caffery stood in the corridor watching as Maddox opened the door of F team's office and placed his hand on DI Diamond's back, gently propelling him inside, closing the door behind them with a soft click.

When PC Smallbright came back he was shocked at the change in the driver's expression. It was as if a hand had been there and smoothed all the lines down, like sand raked free of prints. Peaceful. The eyes were fixed on a point on the other side of the river.

"Did you know you've got a smashed brake light, sir?"

"Is that so?" Harteveld opened the car door and stepped outside, unraveling his long, cadaverous body into the sun. He stood quite still, his eyes closed, his face turned skyward, as if he had never before felt the sun on his skin. His suit hung on him, and his hands dangled out of the sleeves like the clappers of ancient bells.

"Sir?"

"Yes."

"It's just a smashed brake light. Nothing serious. You've got a smashed brake light."

"Of course. And please take into account the dead girls."

"Sir?"

"Tell them what I've done, if you'd be so kind."

PC Smallbright glanced nervously at his sergeant, who was leaning into the driver's window of a Mazda. He turned back to Harteveld. "Do you want to talk about something, sir?"

"No, kind of you, but I think I'll be off now."

PC Smallbright had never seen anything like what happened next. "The river had never looked better, never bluer or more sparkly," he told people later. "But the guy, he looked like a corpse, looked just like a dead thing, gray yellow, like milk gone off."

And in that sphere of humans, as Harteveld pinpointed the coordinates of his place of death, five cars back, two men, not much younger than he was, sensed simultaneously what only Harteveld knew. It was outside their remit, but DC Betts understood the emergency.

"*Go go go!*"

They hurled themselves out of the car, scattering city workers, who shrank back, awed by the two men in suits and sunglasses, faces straining, ties streaming behind them. They covered the hundred yards to the bridge in less than twenty seconds, but even moving slowly Harteveld was ahead of them. If he was aware of their presence he only indicated it with a slight inclination of the head, as if he'd heard something of vague, momentary interest. He took the low parapet of the bridge almost without breaking stride, and, as if the next step were no different from any of the others, stepped simply out into the blue air.

PC Smallbright shouted. The two men rounded the head of the traffic and flung themselves at the parapet. Smallbright ran toward them, reaching them seconds later. The three men stood, panting, as fifty feet below, Toby Harteveld's calm face broke the surface like the underbelly of a yellow fish. He twisted, moved his arms twice, jerkily, like a puppet, and rolled onto his front, disappearing from view under the green water.

Thirty-four

"Y OU FEELING ALL RIGHT mate?" Maddox asked Caffery later in the office.

"Just tired."

"About what happened, your brother . . . We can review and I can clear you for compassionate. Up to two weeks if you want it."

Caffery nodded. "Thank you."

"When do you want—?"

"No. I won't take it."

"Okay." He fiddled with a paper clip. "I wish you'd told me. We could have done something."

"I'd see you do something with Mel Diamond first."

"I've cautioned him. One more mistake and we skip reprimand and go straight to a hearing."

"Gets off easily. Doesn't he?"

"A verbal warning's all I can do at this stage. I've got to let it slide."

"Jesus." Caffery slung his pen down with a clatter. Maddox looked up, startled.

"What?"

"I don't know—all I see, Steve, is this. The man is shit. He screws up just about everything, and *you*—" He paused, took a breath. "And you just seem to bottle it. You and the Met Boat Club and the frostbite run and your old-boys network—"

"Hang on, hang on." Maddox held up a hand. "I'm not stupid, Jack. We all know Diamond gets by on flattery. And this old-boys network thing? Doesn't exist. Maybe other places but not in AMIP." He paused and his voice dropped a tone. "Look, Jack—"

"What?"

"I shouldn't need to say it, but I will. You *are* a better cop than him. He *will* trip. Sooner rather than later. You?" He broke the paper clip in two and threw it in the wastepaper basket. "You, Jack, you won't. You . . ." He sat back in his seat, folded his arms and looked at his DI with an expression of something like satisfaction. "Well, just don't worry, okay?"

"Sir." Kryotos appeared at the doorway sucking the chocolate off a Twix bar. "The courier's here from FSS."

"Thank you." Maddox got wearily to his feet. "This should make our decision whether to charge or not a little clearer."

He left the room, leaving Kryotos and Caffery to stare at each other.

"Yes? What?"

"Oh, nothing. Just hope you're okay. That's all. We're worried about you."

Caffery subsided in his chair, embarrassed by his anger. "That's—that's good of you."

"Not good. Human." She turned to go and stopped in the doorway, one chocolatey finger in her mouth. "I take it you don't want to interview Cook now?"

"No."

"Good, because that Air India flight is leaving in an hour. Are you sure?"

"Yes—let him go."

"Oh, and there was a message for you on last night's crop. Call Julie Da-a-a-rling. You know, Little Darlings." She curled a smile at him. "Darling."

He could tell from Julie's voice that he'd woken her.

"I'm sorry."

"That's okay." She stifled a yawn. "I'm a late riser. Goes with the territory."

"I got your message." He tucked the phone under his chin. "Is there something you remembered?"

"Not remembered. Something's happened."

"I'm listening."

"You told me to call if anyone skipped out on me."

"Yes."

"Someone has."

Caffery paused. "Okay. Who?"

"Her name's Peace. Peace Nbidi Jackson. She's, I don't know, half Ghanaian or something. She didn't turn up to a gig in Earl's Court, and I haven't heard hide nor hair since."

"Where did she last show?"

"She was booked in east Greenwich. The Dog and Bell. Last Wednesday."

The day before we were there. He got in before us—

"Julie." He reached in his drawer for a ballpoint and un-capped it with his teeth. "Have you got an address for her? Let's set our minds at rest, shall we?"

In the incident room Kryotos already knew all about Peace Nbidi Jackson.

"She's one of the lot the Yard's been onto us about. One of thirty." She scrolled down the screen. "Here we are. Clover Jackson, that's Peace's mother, reported her missing yester-day. Peace has got a little drug problem. Heroin. She took a bus from East Ham to somewhere near the Blackwall Tunnel.

Mum thinks she'd been in Greenwich recently, and when she didn't come home Mum called the cops, half out of her mind with worry."

"Okay. Let's get someone over to her house. Start a file. Maybe he's slipped up for the first time. Taken someone who's been missed." He looked up. Maddox stood in the doorway, a paper in his hand. Caffery recognized the blue and red FSS diamond in the right-hand corner. It could only mean one thing.

Maddox waited until the incident room was quiet.

"Right. The good news is we can give up knocking down the magistrate's door." No one spoke. "That poor bugger in Greenwich is going home. Even if they had a better sample they wouldn't have needed it. It's not even the same blood group."

In his chair against the far wall Diamond's jaw muscles worked under the tanned skin, the pinched nostrils pulsing gently as if they wanted to flare. Kryotos's phone jolted to life, making everyone jump. She stared at it for a moment, red-faced at having been singled out like this. It was Betts calling from London Bridge. Kryotos listened, looked at Maddox then at Diamond and handed the phone silently to Caffery.

Gemini stared at a textured black streak on the cell wall wondering if it was what he thought it was. *Don't they clean these rahtid places?* The door opened and the custody sergeant came in, holding Gemini's clothes in a plastic cover. The Nikes were perched on the top like twin loaves clean, fresh and new from the oven.

"Mr. Henry."

"Whassup?"

"You're going home."

Gemini rolled his eyes suspiciously. "Is it?"

"Yes." The officer placed the clothes on the bunk beside him, straightened up and gave him a bored look. "It is."

* * *

Caffery was on the phone to Fiona Quinn when Essex and DC Logan knocked on the door. Essex had a grim look on his face.

"On our way to Harteveld's." He held up the familiar yellow grab box.

"I'm a step behind you. Quinn's meeting us there."

"Jack."

"What is it?"

Essex leaned in so Logan couldn't hear. "Dr. Amedure's been trying to reach you from the lab."

"Yes?" Caffery straightened up and covered the mouthpiece. "Did she have something?"

Essex paused. "She's got something."

"Well?"

"She says they're animal. Pig bones. She's sorry."

Caffery sank back in his seat.

"You all right?"

"Yeah. It's not a surprise."

"They could probably do Penderecki for breach of the peace. Get him bound over. You've got witnesses coming out of your ears."

"No." Caffery was tired. Tired of what Ewan was costing. "Thanks. But I'll let it go. It won't be the last time."

Thirty-five

THE DOORS to the orangery stood open. Caffery taped the warrant and schedules to a windowpane and stood back to allow DS Quinn and DC Logan, like a brace of thoughtful ghosts in their white Tyvek suits, to enter. Essex and he remained outside, shuffling through the gravel, examining a soggy pile of cigarette ends in the bed of moon daisies.

On this—a day belonging not to early summer but to later in the season, where autumn begins—the wind was bright, the sun fluttered strobelike in the overgrown trees, Japanese maples, a towering ginkgo, filling the garden with sparkling green and yellow light. Similar to the September day that Ewan had wandered off down the humming rail tracks. Bones on an anonymous bench in the forensic science lab. Pigs' bones. Penderecki still stirring the pot.

"Sir?"

DS Quinn was standing at the head of the black-and-white-tiled hallway, gloved hand resting on a heavy oak door.

"Locked," she said when he approached. "Can't find the keys anywhere."

"Well? What do you think?"

"I can't say I'm looking forward to it." She put her head back and sniffed the air. "I mean, can you—?"

"Yes." Caffery nodded. "Yes. I could smell it from the garden."

Essex found a chisel in the garage, and after Quinn had dusted a small downstairs window for prints, he carefully pried away the molding, letting the pane swing out on its sash. The smell released made them all take an involuntary step backward.

Quinn quickly pulled a face mask out of her grab bag and smiled. "You stay here and put baggies over your shoes."

She and Logan took it slowly, stopping on the ledge to shine a torch up the curtains and below the window. "Strong smell in here, Jack," Logan confirmed.

"You don't say."

"Give me some of those stepping plates out of my grab bag." Caffery passed them a stack of yellow, lightweight plastic blocks and Quinn and Logan disappeared behind the curtains, leaving Essex and Caffery with nothing better to do than pull bags over their shoes and stand there in the shade of the cedar of Lebanon, whistling to themselves and jangling change in their pockets.

"So," Essex said after a long silence. "What do you think the smell is?"

Caffery was surprised to notice a faint sheen on his face. Essex was *nervous*. In spite of his bravado, he was actually afraid of what they might find inside.

"What do *you* think it is?"

"Birds?"

"Maybe."

"Peace Nbidi Jackson?"

"I hope so."

"God." Essex loosened his collar and rubbed his face. "You're a better man than I am, Jack. I mean that."

Quinn reappeared at the window. A light had been switched on in the room behind her.

"Well?"

"Well what?"

Caffery sighed. "Where's the smell coming from?"

"Oh, *that*. There's some food left lying around. But—" She looked over her shoulder.

"But?"

"But mostly it's coming from the bathroom on the second floor. Put your hands in your pockets and I'll show you."

They moved carefully through the ground floor, Quinn allowing them glimpses into rooms, but not entry. "Not for now. I want the camera crew to go through here first." She had switched on all the lights and taped off a path on the floor in fluorescent tape. They looked into the first room. Harteveld's Bang and Olufsen sound system sat in one corner, an empty bottle of pastis and two milk-crusted glasses on top of the amplifier. The floors were deep in newspapers and fast-food boxes, chairs upended, a table covered in clothing. In a small utility room at the front of the house they disturbed a swarm of flies, which rose to reveal piles of dirty plates, topped by two chicken carcasses. Everywhere the curtains were closed.

"Okay, upstairs now." Quinn led them up the staircase. In the corridor Logan was waiting outside the bathroom, his expression neutral.

"This is where the smell is coming from." Quinn smiled at them. "You can see why."

Logan opened the door.

"Shit," Essex said simply.

The bathroom was small and high-ceilinged, a brightly striped blind pulled tight across a large, oblong window. Across the marble-topped vanity unit someone had abandoned empty toothpaste tubes, yards of gray dental floss, used razors, two or three condom packets, a grimy bar of soap. All were covered in dust.

"That's the problem." Logan pointed to the toilet. "That's the smell."

The seat was up. In the porcelain bowl swam a mess of feces and toilet paper. At some point the toilet had flooded onto the floor, and the stew of excreta and tissue had washed up against the tiled walls, the edge of the bath, the shower stall. Later the water had evaporated, leaving a stinking black sediment, pocked with pink tissue.

"No Peace?" Essex asked.

"No human remains. A few pubic hairs, that's all. And we'll take samples of *that*." He indicated the brown swamp in the toilet bowl. "We've found some fingerprints too." He lowered the toilet seat to show where he had dusted it, and pointed out two thumbprints on the rear. He lifted the seat and showed four inverted fingerprints, small, like a woman's, on the underside. "Look at how they're spaced. What do you suppose she was doing?"

Caffery held his own hands in the same formation. "Holding the seat? To vomit. Heroin maybe."

"I wouldn't need heroin to puke at this mess."

"*Before* it was blocked. One assumes."

"What's blocking it?" Caffery peered tentatively into the bowl.

"Okay." Quinn pulled up the mask and rolled the cuffs of her latex gloves up to seal her white paper suit. "Let's have a look." She crouched on the floor and thrust her hand deep into the U-bend. *Like a vet feeling for a breach birth,* Caffery thought. Logan unraveled a plastic sheet onto the floor as Quinn's arm disappeared. "Yup, there's something here, all right." Essex paled and rolled eyes at Caffery as Quinn squinted, laying her face against the rim to get a better grip. "Here we go."

The accumulated mess of hairs, condoms, toilet paper and feces was dumped, dripping and stinking, on a plastic sheet in the center of the bathroom floor. Essex covered his mouth and took a step back, shaking his head, his Adam's apple dancing in his throat. Quinn sniffed and straightened up, poking at the mess with a finger. "These—" She pulled out two tangled objects and dropped them into the bag Logan held open for her. "These're the problem."

"A skirt. A pair of tights." Caffery was disappointed.

"They'll have to be dried out at the lab."

"It's still just clothing."

"Not what you were expecting?"

"Not really. No."

Essex, hand still over his mouth, watched Logan tag and label the bag. "Know something?" he said later, patting him on the back. "You've got a gift for this exhibits thing. Tell you what, if I get exhibits officer next case, I'll trade you."

Thirty-six

BY THE END of the day they had found Shellene's prints on a tumbler, a bone-handled fork and a bottle of Malibu pulled from the back of the drinks cabinet in the living room. Two aubergine-colored hairs were caught in the drain trap of the ground-floor cloakroom and Logan found syringes in a lacquer box and small amounts of heroin and cocaine in two antique blue-glass and silver ink bottles. Everything was painstakingly sealed in evidence bags.

"But I'm still worried," Fiona Quinn admitted at the evening's meeting. "I was expecting organic evidence of the mutilations. I don't think I've got it from today's search."

Nor had she found suture material, the surgeon's scalpel that Krishnamurthi believed had been used in the mutilations or the Wright's coal tar soap.

"He should have made more mess. There would have been leakage when he opened them: blood, putrid matter. We should have *some* trace evidence, at least in the drain traps. FSS have pulled plenty from his car, from the boot, and I think that's our key—I think he took them somewhere else. Maybe to kill them, but possibly *after* he killed them. It'll be where he's keeping the cage birds."

"Schloss-Lawson and Walker," Caffery said. "Family solicitors. They're drawing up a list of his other properties and I'm with Quinn: we find anything else, we search it."

"Yes," Quinn murmured. "And when we find it, I think we'll find Jackson."

No one spoke for a moment. Essex's first task tomorrow was to call Clover Jackson—ask her to come in and look at Polaroids of the articles recovered from Harteveld's bathroom. See if the lime green skirt was the same one her daughter had been wearing the night she disappeared.

"Okay," Maddox sighed. "Marilyn, actions to be generated in the morning re Harteveld's other residences. I want Jackson before this weather gets working on her."

After the meeting Caffery, exhausted, took his tie off and called Rebecca.

"I was on my way to the park," she said. "I want to paint the naval college."

"Can I meet you there?"

"Oh sure. Half an hour? Hey—are you okay?"

"Yes. Why?"

"Oh." She was quiet for a moment. "You don't sound okay."

"Well, I am. I'm fine. Honestly."

When Essex heard this he started jumping. "You randy little fucker you. You kept that quiet. Get her to put a word in with Joni for us, eh? Tell her how sensitive I am or some shit."

Caffery locked his tie in the desk drawer, splashed water on his face in the washroom, put the mobile in his pocket and drove to Greenwich. The late sun was turning the Royal Observatory's ancient windows gold when he arrived at the park. With Harteveld dead he should feel relief. Instead he was uneasy, his nerves pared and ready as if his body was preparing itself for more hurdles. *You're just tired, Jack,* he told himself. *Get a night's sleep, the world'll look better tomorrow.*

She was sitting on the grass in front of Flamsteed's onion
dome, a block of watercolor paper on her raised knees, one
paint-brush between her teeth as she mixed paint with another. Caffery stopped, enjoying the luxury of watching her
unseen. The sun lit the curve of her cheek; he almost believed
he could see each fine hair gold on her skin. In the short tartan skirt she seemed shockingly vulnerable. Like an encour-
agement on this spread of emerald grass.

She put the brush down, wiped her hands on a small piece
of rag and, as if she had known he was there all along, looked
up, squinting slightly, a slim brown hand shading her eyes
from the low sun.

"Hello." She had no makeup on, and he could see the
beginnings of a laugh line on the right of her mouth. "Hello,
Jack."

"You know my name."

"Yes." She looked down, hair dropping to hide her expression. "Look, I've got burgundy." She opened a rucksack
and held a bottle and a corkscrew out to him. "And this. A
whole bag of fresh nectarines. I hope you weren't looking
forward to a McDonald's."

"This means we're having a drink together."

"So?"

He shrugged, pulled his jacket off, sat on the grass and
took the bottle from her. "I'm not the one who's worried."

"Anyway, it was *you* who wanted to see *me*."

"True."

"Why, then? What do you want?"

The truth? I'd like to—

He stopped himself. Began pulling the foil from the bottle. "We've got him. It was Toby Harteveld. We released it to
the press an hour ago."

"Oh." Rebecca dropped the rucksack and looked at him.
"Toby."

"Something else."

"What?"

"He's dead. You'll see it on the TV, but I wanted you to know now. He jumped from London Bridge this morning at ten."

"I see." She let her breath out slowly and stared out at the ocean floor of London spread out below them: upstream, London Bridge put its shipwrecked elbows up out of the blue mist, and downstream, shimmering near the smog-streaked horizon, the Millennium Dome, like a cleaned bone against the blue. Beyond that the construction yard . . . "It's over, then."

"I suppose so."

Rebecca was silent for a long time. Eventually, as if she had decided to shake it off, she took two glasses from the rucksack and placed them next to him on the grass. She looked at him and smiled. "We've got something in common. You and me."

"Good." Caffery lifted the arms on the corkscrew. "What?"

"Fingernails." She looked at her hands. "Ever since this thing began I haven't been able to touch anything without my nails crumbling. It's as if that's where the stress comes out." She paused. "What's your excuse?"

He smiled, holding up his bruised thumb. "This?"

"Yes?"

"Oh—you really want to know?"

"Of course."

"Well, let's see. We had a tree house. That's the first thing."

"A tree house?"

"Almost all gone now. Maybe one day I'll show you where it was."

"I'd like that."

"My brother, Ewan, pushed me. I was eight. The black should have grown out, but it hasn't. Doctors are baffled. I'm a medical marvel."

"I hope you killed him for it."

"Who?"

"Your brother."

"No—I—" He paused. "No. I forgave him. I suppose."
He fell silent and Rebecca frowned. "What've I said?"

"Nothing, nothing." He uncorked the bottle and poured
wine into her glass.

"I'm sorry, I didn't mean—I'm sort of tactless sometimes."

"Don't!" He held his hand up. "Really, don't, Rebecca.
Just—don't—worry."

They stared at each other, Rebecca puzzled, Caffery stuck
with a confident, lying smile stitched on his face. In his jacket
pocket the mobile found the embarrassed gap in their conversation and rang loudly, making them both jump.

"God." He put the bottle down, reached over, caught the
sleeve between his middle and forefinger and dragged the jacket,
bumping, across the grass. "Talk about timing. I'm sorry."

"Don't be." She sank back on her haunches, half grateful
to be off the hook. He answered the phone.

"I've done it." She sounded very faint.

"Veronica?"

"I've done it."

Caffery glanced at Rebecca and turned away, cupping his
hand around the mouthpiece. "Veronica, where are you?"

"I've done it. I've finally done it."

"Don't talk in riddles."

Silence.

"Veronica?"

"You bastard." She caught her breath as if she was crying.
"You deserved it."

"Look—"

But she had hung up.

Caffery sighed, placed the phone between his feet and
looked up at Rebecca. She was drawing lines in the grass with
the butt of a brush, not looking at him.

"Who was that?" she asked eventually.

"A woman."

"Oh. Veronica? Is that her name?"

"Yes."

"What did she want?"

"Attention."

"Well"—she dropped her chin into her hand and looked up at him—"are you going to give it to her?"

"No."

Rebecca nodded. "I see."

She doesn't believe you, Jack.

He fumbled for a cigarette, and suddenly, from behind the red roofs of the observatory, a flock of squabbling starlings rose into the air. Caffery paused and stared at them, inexplicably shocked.

"Birds."

Rebecca tipped her head back to look and the late sunlight slipped across her face. "Ah." She smiled. " 'Thou wast not born for death, immortal Bird! No hungry generations tread thee down.' " The starlings pivoted on the air, paused for a shivering moment, then plunged toward the ground, filling the air with wings. Rebecca drew her shoulders up. "Oh."

The birds swiveled again and were gone as suddenly as they had appeared, deep into the air over the hill. A feather seesawed through the air and landed at Jack's feet.

"I thought they were going to attack us!" Rebecca laughed, straightening her hair, giggling at her nervousness. Then she saw his face and stopped. "What is it?"

"I don't know." He shook his head. He'd seen the birds close, seen mottled irises, and it had made his innards twitch. He thought about Veronica, about the pile of bones, her tight, unhealthy smile when Penderecki stepped into the room, almost as if she'd planned it.Suddenly he tamped out the cigarette and stood. "I'd better go."

"So you *are* going to give her attention."
"Yes." He rolled his sleeves down. "I suppose I am."

Veronica's red Tigra was parked outside the house. Smug. As if it had a right to be there. It was dark now, and over the roofs, on Penderecki's side of the railway cutting, a thin column of smoke rose. The house was in darkness. Caffery let himself in, cautious, prepared for the worst.

"Veronica?" He stood on the doormat, nervous in his own home. "*Veronica?*"

Silence. He switched the hall light on and stood blinking. Everything was as he had left it, the hall carpet slightly rucked, the bag of dry cleaning he'd forgotten that morning still slouched against the skirting.Through the open door of the kitchen he could make out the outline of his morning coffee cup on the table. He closed the door, hung his jacket on the banister and went into the kitchen.

"Veronica?" It was airless in here. On the windowsill one of her plants, a bougainvillea, had flowered an obscene red during the day, and now it seemed to him that it was leaching the very oxygen from the house with its fat fleshy leaves. Hastily he opened the window, let the smoky tang of night air into the kitchen and took a quick welcome swig of Glenmorangie straight from the bottle.

The living room was undisturbed, Veronica's precious glasses in their tea chests still waiting to be collected. He opened the French windows and went back into the hall. It was in the dining room that he found the first evidence of her presence. The room had been cleaned thoroughly, obsessively, the scent of lavender furniture polish was heavy in the air.

He stood in the doorway for a long time before he noticed, propped on the mantelpiece, a black edged card, the type used for funeral services. The message was simple.

Fuck you, Jack.
Love, Veronica

"Thank you, Veronica." He put the card in his pocket, opened the bay windows and went back into the hallway. The only noise was the grandfather dock ticking and the lazy mechanic buzz of a dying fly. Upstairs, then. She must be upstairs.

"I'm here, Veronica." He stopped halfway to the landing, looking up at the closed bedroom doors. "Veronica." Silence. He mounted the last few steps and paused, his hand on the bedroom door.

He was suddenly overwhelmingly tired. If she had over-dosed and was lying on his bed he would spend another sleep-less night. Casualty. Stomach pumps. Psychiatric evaluation. Her granite-gray family sitting silently, letting him know he was responsible without saying a word.

Or he could, he *could*—the thought made him shiver—simply turn around and walk out of the door. Call Rebecca, apologize for leaving, meet her for a drink, spend the night trying to coax her into bed while Veronica silently slipped over the edge, alone.

He stood, pulse racing, while the possibility exhausted it-self. Then took a long, deep breath and slowly, very slowly, opened the bedroom door.

"Shit."

She'd made the bed and dusted in here too. But there were no startling death images, no arterial spray on the wall, no empty pill bottles. No Veronica.

He quickly checked the cupboards. Everything was as it should be, towels folded neatly in candy striped piles, bedside clock ticking quietly. Ewan's bedroom, then. He went back onto the landing and found the door to Ewan's room open. Veronica stood a pace inside, staring at him.

"Veronica."

They regarded each other for a moment, pulses pounding. She was wearing a white silk blouse and white linen slacks. A scarf printed with tiny gold buckles was secured at the neck by a diamond pin. Her face was white and controlled. There was nothing about her to suggest she had tried to harm herself.

"Why are you in my house?"

"I came to collect Mummy's glasses. Is that allowed?"

"Take them and get out."

"Civility." She sucked in a breath through her teeth and arched her eyebrows. "Know that word, Jack? *Civility*."

"I'm not here to argue—" He stopped. He had focused farther into the room, the empty shelves, the box files on the floor—open, every one cracked wide, emptied.

For a moment he stood, taking this in, silent and unmoving, only the congested thudding of his heart for company —*Shit, she knows exactly where to push me*—then stepped forward, ignoring her standing calmly next to him, and crouched amongst the debris, his hands shaking. As he picked through the files—lifting them, upturning and shaking, running trembling fingers through their white spaces—he knew he would find little. He knew how thoroughly a coiled heart like Veronica's does its work.

"Well?" he said eventually, sitting back on his heels, breathing hard. "Well? What've you done? Where've you put it all?"

She shrugged as if his interest surprised her and turned casually to look at the window. Reluctantly he followed her eyes. Beyond the pale, lifting curtains, phlegmy tendrils of smoke drifted across the moon.

"Shit," he sighed. "Shit, yes, of course, I should have guessed." He got wearily to his feet and crossed the room, placing cold fingers lightly on the window frame. And there, just as he had expected, on the other side of the cutting, lit black and red by drifting embers, stood Penderecki, holding up the incinerator hood to throw in another handful, whistling to himself and smiling as if he'd been waiting and watching for Jack to come.

"Oh, Veronica." He rested his hot forehead against the pane and expelled a long breath. "You should have ripped my heart out instead."

"Oh, come on, Jack, don't overreact."

"You bitch," he murmured. "You little bitch."

"What? *What* did you call me?"

"Bitch." Caffery turned calmly to her. "I called you a fucking bitch."

"You're crazy." She looked at him in disbelief. "You know, sometimes you make me hope that pervert *did* kill your brother. And slowly too." Her face twisted. "Because you *deserve* it, Jack. You deserve it for the way you're killing me. You're *killing* me—" But Caffery had grabbed her roughly by the arm. Her cuff buttons exploded across the room. "*Jack!*"

He dragged her to the door, crunching and scattering the empty files undedoot. "*Jack!*" She kicked at him. "*Let go of me, Jack!*"

"Shut up." Anger made him strong and composed. He wrenched her down the stairs, enjoying her powerlessness, enjoying the futile spitting and struggling, the manicured nails ripping on the banisters. At the foot of the stairs he stopped and held her at arm's length, regarding her calmly.

"*Christ.*" She wrenched her arm from him and took a step back, massaging her elbow, her eyes wide, hair disheveled. A vein had burst in the white of her left eye but her face was dry. He saw he had scared her. "Don't touch me again, okay? Don't—"

"Just shut up and listen."

"*Please.* Daddy'll take it very seriously if you come near me."

"*I said shut the fuck up and listen!*" He pushed his face close to hers. "Now, I'm telling you once: if you *ever* come near me again I will kill you. I mean it. I will fucking *kill* you. Is that clear?"

"Jack—please—"

He shook her violently. "I said *is that clear?*"

"*Yes, yes!*" Suddenly she started sobbing. "Now g-get your hands off me, okay? Just get your fucking hands off me."

"Out of my house." He released her, his mouth curled in disgust, wrenching the front door open. "Go on. Get out of my house *now*."

"Okay, okay." She hurried down the steps muttering under her breath, glancing over her shoulder to make sure he wasn't following. "I'm going, okay?"

Caffery went into the living room, picked up the tea chest and carried it back to the front door. Veronica stood on the garden path shakily stabbing out a number on her mobile phone. When the door opened she stepped back in momentary fear. Then she saw what he was holding and her face changed.

"Oh *no*," she wailed. "They cost a fortune."

But he passed her—out into the street, launching the tea chest into the air. It pinwheeled gracefully, spurting lead crystal glasses and green tissue, bounced once on the bonnet of the Tigra, splintered the windscreen and came to a shattering halt in the center of the road.

"I mean it, Veronica," he murmured in her ear as he passed her on his way back up the path. "I will kill you." He slammed the front door, bolted it and went into the kitchen to find the Glenmorangie.

Thirty-seven

THE ALARM went off at 7:00 A.M. and he lay there on his side, looking at the shadows of leaves on the walls. After an eternity he rolled onto his back, covered his eyes and started to breathe.

Too far. This time it had gone too far.

Over the years there had been others like Veronica; other relationships come unstuck within months. But, even where there had been bitterness, the revenge had never whipped back so violently. Never wounded him before.

Are you supposed to be learning something from this? Is this a "life lesson"?

He pressed his temples and thought of Rebecca, pushing her chestnut hair out of her eyes. He wondered if he would get that wrong too—wondered how long it would take for him to junk it. Six months maybe. Or a year if he worked at it. And then he'd be back here again. Alone. Childless. He thought of his parents, optimistic, hopeful: starting the lives of their two sons—right here in this bright summer bedroom.

"Jack, Jack," he muttered. "Get a grip." He hauled himself up onto his elbows, blinking in the new light, and pulled the phone onto the bed. Rebecca answered quickly, sleepily.

"Did I wake you?"

"Yes."

"It's Detect—Rebecca, it's me, Jack."

"I know." A dull tone.

"I'm sorry about last night."

"That's okay."

"I was wondering—"

"Yes."

"Maybe tonight. A drink. Or a meal?"

"No." A pause. "No. I don't think so." She hung up.

That'll teach you, Jack, he thought, and rolled out of bed.

Maddox, fresh-faced in a short-sleeved shirt, met him in the hallway at Shrivemoor, a cup of coffee in his hand.

"Jack. What's up? Not that wee pervert again?"

"It's nothing."

"You look like shit."

"Thanks."

"How was the traffic?"

"Not bad. Why?"

From his pocket he produced the keys to the team car and jingled them. "'Cause you're going to turn right around and head back."

"What's happened?"

"We think we've got Peace Jackson. Woman found her in a wheelie bin fifteen minutes ago."

Royal Hill, connecting Greenwich to Lewisham, winds upward as if it had fully intended mounting as high as Blackheath but had at some time lost heart; after a quarter of a mile it turns left and sinks back down to meet South Street. By the time they arrived and parked the car a crowd had already gathered. From the top windows neighbors peered out with arms folded, net curtains hooked up out of the way. The coroner's appointed undertakers, two boxy men in dark

embroidered waistcoats and black ties, stood waiting next
to their black Ford Transit. A PC was taping off the small
front garden, and on the tiny concrete path, unmarked except by the wide berth it was given by the officers, stood the
wheelie bin, the lid gaping open. DI Basset stood at the gate,
his head down, in deep conversation with Quinn. When he
noticed Maddox signing in with the PC, he came forward,
hand extended.

"DI Basset." Maddox shook his hand. "What've we got?"

"Looks like one of your Harteveld's, sir. Female, naked,
partially wrapped in three plastic bin-liners. Quinn's had a
peer in there and I can assure you we've got good reason for
calling you. She's got some nice little telltale stitches on her
breasts, her sternum's been opened. We can't see her head,
she's nose-down, but she's Afro-Caribbean if that's any help."

"Yup. We've got someone in mind."

"Her legs are curled into her chest so it means she's lost
her rigor."

"Ah, charming." Maddox wrinkled his nose and looked
at the sky. "When are we going to deal with some nice fresh
corpses?" He accepted the face mask and latex gloves Logan
was holding out and turned. "Jack. Why don't you have a
word with the woman who found her? Logan and I'll deal
with things out here."

Inside the two-bedroom terraced house Caffery found the
woman in the kitchen with the woman police constable, the
WPC. They were staring at the electric kettle in silence. When
he came in they jumped, startled.

"I'm sorry, the door was open."

The WPC frowned. "Who are you?"

Caffery fumbled for his warrant card. "AMIP. DI Caffery."

She reddened. "Sorry, sir." She nodded at the kettle. "Ms.
Velinor and I were making some tea. Would you like some?"

"Thank you."

The woman smiled wanly at him. She was attractive, a stern, carved, Egyptian face, dark hair pulled back in a band. She wore an expensive tailored business suit. Her briefcase stood on the table, next to it a scatter of magazines: three *Management Todays*, a stack of Saville & Holdsworth psychometric tests and a *Guardian,* folded over, Harteveld's photograph staring at the ceiling. Filling the window beyond, four marigold-yellow bath towels hung on the washing line. "You want to ask me some questions," she said. "Just let me drink some tea. I've been sick, I'm afraid."

"Take your time." He helped them collect milk and sugar and take everything to the small table. They settled next to the window. Ms. Velinor sipped her tea and slowly her color returned, the edges of her face softened.

"That's better."

Caffery pulled his notebook out. "Take me through it, slowly, at your own pace. You were on your way to work and putting the rubbish out?"

She nodded and put her cup in the saucer. "I thought someone had dumped something awful there as a prank. My partner's white, I'm—well, you can see I'm mixed race, and people are still funny about it, you know. Two weeks ago the front door was graffitied. I thought it was the beginning of a campaign. You hear about all sorts of awful things they put through letter boxes, don't you? I thought it was something like that."

"So you opened it."

"I had to see what it was. It—*she*—smelled so awful. I was prepared for something—" She pressed the bridge of her nose and screwed her face up. "But not that. I hadn't expected that."

"How long do you think it's been there?"

"I don't know. I've no idea."

"How long do you imagine?"

"I *imagined* since last night. But that can't be right, can it, because Harteveld's been dead, what? Since yesterday morning?" She stared at the *Guardian* with serious brown eyes. "That—that *girl* outside, she *is* something to do with him, isn't she?"

"What made you think it was last night?"

"Well . . ." she said slowly, puzzled. "I don't know. Maybe I just assumed I'd've *known* if a body was lying in my wheelie bin." She laughed at this small piece of absurdity. "But I suppose that's not necessarily true. I mean, the lid was down tight, and if I hadn't put the rubbish out this morning I'd've walked straight past it and never known."

"When was the last time you put rubbish out?"

"I've been trying to think. The dustmen came on Monday. My partner was over on Tuesday night and we had a few drinks. It was his birthday. So there was a bag full of gift wrapping and bottles, that sort of thing. Now, I *thought* I put that out last night. But I must have been mistaken, I must've put it out yesterday morning."

"Where do you work, Ms. Velinor?"

"St. Dunstan's Hospital."

Caffery raised his eyebrows. "St. Dunstan's?"

"Yes. Why?"

"Can you think of any reason why Mr. Harteveld would have chosen you to do this to?"

"*Chosen me?*" She shook her head. "No. I mean I knew him vaguely—we'd been on the same hospital committee once or twice, he knew one of my colleagues—but I can't imagine I stood out to him more than anyone else. He hardly knew I existed."

When Caffery had finished and came to the front door, the bin, covered in silver fingerprint dust, had been tipped over onto its side and laid on a large plastic body sheet across the path. At its opening squatted Logan, dressed now in a white suit and bootees. Next to him Quinn was on her hands and knees, her upper body almost entirely inside the bin. Maddox stood outside the roped-off area blinking seriously over the white mask.

Quinn shuffled out a little and looked up at Maddox. "Bingo!" she said, her voice muffled behind her mask. She waved her hand around her head. "She's got the marks on her head. Let's get her out."

Caffery stood on the doorstep, hands in his pockets. They were only about a third of a mile from Rebecca's flat. She probably walked past the end of this road on her way into the town center. Strange, life's invisible undertangle, he thought.

Quinn and Logan looped their hands under the corpse's pelvis. As she came out of the bin Caffery was reminded of a birth: the skin was mottled and moist, the hair slimed in the mucusy cowl of decay, the limbs helpless next to the two professionals in white. She slithered out and landed in a wet heap on the sheet, her head lolling. The PC at the gate put his hand over his face and turned away. The features had been loosened by putrefaction, but from the doorstep the two men could see the familiar makeup on the eyes and mouth, the cobalt-blue stitching on the breasts. The ragged thoracic incision.

Quinn bent close to the face. Her eyes narrowed, she looked up at Maddox and pulled the mask down.

"I think there's a mole above the upper lip."

Maddox nodded, his face tightening minutely. "Jackson. That's Jackson."

Thirty-eight

MALPENS STREET, just a hundred yards from Lola Velinor's front garden, is quiet and treelined. The haughty Edwardian houses sit back from the road hidden beyond opulent gardens crammed with lime trees, jasmine, hibiscus.

Shortly before 9:00 that night, in a basement kitchen, the window open to let a breath of honeysuckle into the room, Susan Lister was preparing a red-wine marinade for the evening meal. She'd been jogging, her usual route, along Trafalgar Road, up past St. Dunstan's, over the park, and was still dressed in gray jogging pants, a black and white Nike sweatshirt over a sports bra: her blond hair, slightly damp, was up in a ponytail. She wouldn't have time to take her bath before she collected Michael from the station. He was working late, taking the 8:55 from London Bridge. On the scrubbed pine table behind her, the portable TV was switched to BBC1 for the headlines.

She pinched the end of a clove of garlic and peeled away the loose skin. Behind her a strike of the clock and the first headline. "Another body found in southeast London. Scotland Yard have not ruled out a link to the Harteveld killings."

Susan quickly put down the garlic clove, turned up the volume and rested against the counter with her glass of wine. "As more details emerge MPs call for a swift evaluation of the PRCU's proposed Serious Crime Research Project." The home secretary stood on the green outside the Houses of Parliament, the breeze lifting strands of thin hair off his head. He confirmed his sympathy for the relatives of the victims and trotted out the drop in crime figures this year. Then the commissioner, spruce at a press conference table, told the cameras that Greenwich CID and AMIP were perfectly competent thank you very much, and no, they weren't ready to confirm or deny that this was a Harteveld victim.

Susan sipped her wine thoughtfully. Harteveld had lived only half a mile away; God, she'd discovered that the distinctive green car she'd got used to seeing parked outside St. Dunstan's on her morning runs had belonged to him. And now this. Another body.

The scene cut to show a London street, instantly recognizable as Royal Hill. Three gray-suited detectives arrived carrying a yellow crate. Then a helicopter shot, a fleeting glimpse of the roofs of Malpens Street, and then a cut-back to ghostly figures in white suits meandering among police tape.

"This brings the unofficial death toll to six, only four of whom have been identified. Tonight Chief Superintendent Days of the southeast London Area Major Incident Pool refused to confirm they were investigating a link to Toby Harteveld."

In her kitchen Susan, suddenly seized by an irrational fear, reached over and closed the window. A body in Royal Hill. How close had she come? Subdued, she finished chopping the garlic, uncomfortably conscious of her reflection slipping silently across the ghostly honeysuckle in the window. Chinese five-spice, a dash of soy, and drop the pork in. Quickly she rinsed her hands and took the car keys from the top of the fridge. Michael would be waiting.

Outside, it was warm and soft, the evening filled with jasmine from the flowering bush in the neighbor's garden. She paused for a moment. It was all over. Harteveld was dead, lying in a morgue somewhere, and she could give up this buzzing anxiety. The road looked as it usually did at night, insects swarming under the yellow streetlights, the palms in the neighbor's garden lending the air a swampy scent, as if you should expect the sound of cicadas. There was nothing unusual. A car she didn't recognize, something French, a Peugeot maybe, empty.

Maybe tonight she'd suggest to Michael that they fitted an alarm system on the house. With him working these late nights she'd feel safer. Or a dog. She walked the few yards to her Fiesta. That was an idea. A dog.

The car was still hot inside from a day in the sun and filled with a sharp smell. Her husband had a habit of leaving his used cricket kit in the boot for days on end. "I'll kill you, Michael," she murmured, fumbling with the keys. She'd make him take the kit out and wash it before he went to bed tonight, remind him that they both had jobs and that he had to pull his weight around the house.

She chewed the inside of her mouth and fastened her seat belt. A dog was a good idea. A boxer or a Doberman. Something big. Something muscular. She could take it jogging with her too. Maybe that would make the truck drivers on Trafalgar Road think twice before they yelled at her on the street. By the light from the streetlamp she found the ignition key, started the engine and checked the mirror. On the backseat a man sat up and smiled at her.

Thirty-nine

THE NEXT MORNING Harteveld's body was hauled from the river at Wapping and taken to Greenwich for an autopsy. At the same time his solicitors, Schloss-Lawson and Walker, came back to AMIP with their client's property portfolio. Maddox and Caffery took one look and saw immediately what they wanted.

"A warrant for Halesowen Road, then?"

Maddox nodded. "And when's the Jackson autopsy?"

"This afternoon—after Harteveld's."

"Okay—you attend Jackson's. We'll give Logan Halesowen —get someone from the crime unit to go with him, Quinn if she's free."

When Caffery arrived at the Devonshire Street morgue, Peace had already come out of X ray and the external examination was complete—she had been photographed, taped for hair and fibers and given anal, oral, vaginal swabs. One of the morticians handed Caffery a mask and oil of camphor.

"Your mobile," she murmured, "if it's not already—"

"Of course. Of course." He switched off his phone, took a place on the loading bay ramp, leaned against the railings and looked down into the dissecting room.

"Good afternoon, Mr. Caffery." Krishnamurthi, in his green wipe-clean apron, didn't look up. He was making the coronal mastoid incision, slicing over Peace's head from ear to ear. "I see you've drawn the short straw."

"That's right."

"I am told that the Mr. Harteveld I encountered on my table this morning is the very selfsame Mr. Harteveld responsible for keeping me in work these last few weeks." He gripped Peace's scalp between thumb and forefinger and slowly peeled it down, drawing away her face, exposing the blood-clotted cranium. "Am I right?"

"You are. Have we got a time of death on Jackson?"

"I'm not an entomologist, but you're welcome to look." He gestured to a row of stoppered phials on the side bench. "I think you'll find your usual suspects—Diptera and Calliphoridae, first or second instar, on the mouth, the nose, the vagina; and then on the wounds, flesh flies still larval. There's a PMI chart in the scrub room if you're really interested."

"No, it's okay. It sounds just like the others."

"That's right, Mr. Caffery. *Identical* to the others."

Less than half a mile away, Susan Lister woke. A bird was singing and a warm light played across the network of veins in her eyelids. Canned laughter from a TV somewhere. She thought she was in bed at home until she smelled urine and realized the insides of her thighs were wet. Then she remembered.

A drill howling at her temple—a drill or was it an electric saw?

She opened her eyes and tried to sit up—for a moment jolting around uselessly on the floor, banging her head. Something had her restrained. She subsided and lay still, her heart thudding.

Don't draw attention, Susan. Wait a moment. First think through it.

She licked her sore lips and looked around herself. Assessing.

She was lying on cord carpet in a room lit by a fluorescent strip. About a yard away, under a brown velour sofa, she could see curls of hair and chocolate wrappers. A fine gray dust covered everything—now she could feel it gritty in her mouth, in her eyelashes. He'd arranged her on her side, her hands and feet trussed up behind her, laced together beneath her buttocks by something stout—it felt like nylon rope. But worse, much worse—her heart sank because this detail told her more than she wanted to know about this assault—she was naked.

He was going to rape her.

Oh Jesus! She took a deep breath and tried not to cry out. *Come on, Susan,* she urged herself, *keep calm—think sensibly; Harteveld is dead. This is a rape and you've always said you could live through rape if you had to—you've read about it—you'll survive if you don't fight, comply with everything he tells you and make mental notes of everything you see and hear. Vigorous notes. Everything. Okay? Now . . . ready?*

She took four deep breaths and twisted her eyes upward.

The room was high-ceilinged. Artexed. There were two doors into the room. Paneled doors. Coves on three sides—it must be a conversion. A boarded-up fireplace was flanked in each alcove by wood-effect shelving units displaying hard-spined books, something technical. The distant laughter came from an episode of *Bewitched* playing quietly on a small TV: that might mean cable, which would limit the number of streets she could be in. Her confidence rose momentarily. But then she saw what was pinned to the walls and a small cry escaped her.

Photographs, tom from pornographic magazines; acts she could never have constructed, even in her darkest imagination. One showed a child being sodomized.

She started to shake.

Susan! Susan. No—don't panic. Panic and you could die.
Remove yourself. Be impartial—an observer. Be an observer.
But her confident survivor's mind was weakening. By
twisting her head up and back she could see, scattered on the
floor about two feet away, seven or eight books. Some were
open, some closed, their titles embossed in dull gold.

Appleton and Lange's—she narrowed her eyes—*Appleton*
and Lange's Review for the Surgical Technology Examina-
tion. Next to that: *The Atlas of Craniofacial Plastic Surgery;*
Surgical Palliation of Unresectable Carcinoma; Stereostatic
Core Breast Biopsy.
Fear put down new long roots in her chest.
She dropped her head and started to sob.

Krishnamurthi was three-quarters of the way through the
PM. He carefully ladled fluids from Peace's body cavity into
a measuring jug perched on a dissecting table over her legs.
"Right, team." He straightened up and looked around
the room. "What say we give Virchow a whirl today—just
to keep our hands in. Pickups, Paula." The mortician placed
forceps on his palm. He carefully lifted the soaking little form
out of Jackson's body cavity and dropped it onto the scales.
Paula chalked up the weight on the board. No one appeared
surprised by the bird. Harteveld's case was notorious—they
all knew what to expect.
"Good. Now . . ." Krishnamurthi peered into the chest
cavity. "Yes, extensive avulsion under the breastplate just as
we saw with the others. Someone look up the *Read* code for
avulsion, for heaven's sake—keep the researchers from snapping at my heels."
"Avulsion," Jack asked from the ramp. "What's avulsion?"
"Tissue ripped from the bone, or from its natural con-
nective tissue." Krishnamurthi pushed his face shield up and
looked at him. "And, Mr. Caffery."
"Yes?"

"Your SA, Jane Amedure, tells me this victim was recovered at a different site from the others."

"That's right."

"And was never taken to the wasteland?"

"No. Surveillance has been sitting on it for the last two weeks. Why?"

"There's cement dust in the decedent's hair—on her face, just like the others. I think with the others we assumed it had come from the wasteland."

Caffery frowned. "Okay." He pressed his fingers lightly to his temples.

The flat in Halesowen Road.

He looked up. "The CSC's got another residence to search this afternoon. I'll tell her to look out for it."

Dear God, what are they going to find there?

Susan heard him come into the room and immediately quietened. She lay quite still. Preparing. She heard him cross to the opposite side of the room and tap, tap, tap on the wall. Agitated.

Reason with him. You can talk your way out of this. Talk —make him think of you as an individual. He wants to objectify you. Don't let him.

Slowly, every muscle on alert, ready to start talking, ready to fight for her life, she dared to lift her eyes.

He wasn't even looking at her.

He stood about three feet away, side on. He wore bird-egg-blue hospital scrubs and a surgical mask and his hair was hidden in a checked cap, the type worn in operating theaters. At his feet was a red plastic toolbox. He was short, chubby. But he was agile, she knew, from the way he'd almost vaulted over the car seats last night. And he was strong. He was stronger than she would have believed.

He was staring intently at a photograph of a woman's face, tapping it with his finger. She had the small, smooth face of a doll. White-blond hair. Overly made-up. Blue eye shadow and plum-shined lips. He pressed his hands on the photo, covering her features, his two big thumbs neatly over the mouth as if he'd like to get them past her teeth, her tongue, her tonsils.

Then suddenly he turned. "Well?"

Susan flinched. *He'd known she was watching. Without even looking at her he could tell she was watching.*

"Well?" He stepped toward her. Above the mask his eyes were round, restless.

"My name's Susan." She spoke quickly, not a stammer. *Don't show you're scared.* "My father is a magistrate. He's very powerful."

"A magistrate!" The voice was light, amused. "Is that meant to *worry* me?"

"No—I—*oh God, what do you want from me?*"

"What do you think? What do you *think* I want?"

Pray that he only rapes you, Susan, pray it won't be more.

"Please don't hurt me." She curled up, sobbing, trying in vain to fold her tethered arms around her breasts, like a trussed, delimbed turkey. "Please don't."

"Isn't it uncomfortable with *paps* that big?" Damp hands reached over and gripped her breasts, trying to contain the struggling. "How do you sit at a table with those in front of you? Don't they get in the way?"

Susan recoiled. She had felt the touch reach down into her stomach. Her groin. A betrayal. "*Please no, please—*"

He stood and a gobbet of granular brown phlegm landed inches from her face. "You know what I have to do. Don't you?"

She shook her head, tears falling into her hair.

"Answer me."

"Don't hurt me."

"*I said you know what I have to do, don't you, with your big fucking tits!*" He kicked her in the side and suddenly his voice became calm. "And shut up that crying. You'll upset Mrs. Frobisher."

Susan gasped and rolled onto her front, still sobbing. He straddled her, her shoulders gripped tightly between his fat knees, and yanked her head back by the hair. "Now look."

He leaned over and opened the toolbox.

She could see Wilkinson's scissors, tweezers, a tapering sable-tipped brush, curved palettes of iridescent makeup, turquoise, peach, fuchsia, red.

"This one, I think." The click of metal, the snap of latex gloves being pulled on, something being removed from the toolbox—*my God, what's that, a scalpel?* He reached down and held her right breast. "Now." A drop of sweat fell from his forehead into her hair. "Are we ready?"

At 3:00 P.M. DS Logan and DS Fiona Quinn arrived at the small flat on the Lewisham-Greenwich border. Accompanied by a uniformed officer, they approached with serious expressions and warrant cards at the ready. They didn't expect an answer. Quinn spoke into her Sony Professional:

"It is three-fourteen P.M., 7 Halesowen Road. Note for the search register that the flat is unoccupied, no one here to allow us entry, no neighbors, so under the Premises Code"— she held the pause button down and stepped back to allow the officer to step forward—"we are using force to enter in pursuance of a section 8 search warrant—*bugger*. Hold it." In her pocket her mobile was ringing. She switched off the Professional, dug inside her overalls for the phone. It was Caffery, asking her to landline him. She did, from a phone box.

"How does it look?"

"If you'd let me get in I could tell you."

"Look out for cement dust—maybe an outbuilding, a garage. That's where he's kept the bodies."

"Will do. Now, can I get on with it?"

"Of course, of course. I'm sorry."

Forty

A T SHRIVEMOOR the investigating teams didn't care that the search—the last formality—wasn't complete. They sensed they were near the end. Maddox gave them a speech warning them not to relax, reminding them they still needed airtight matching of samples, but he had to raise his voice to be heard. Kryotos had opened the blinds and the afternoon sun streamed into the room for the first time in days. The photos of the dead girls were turned to face the whiteboards and Betts and Essex slipped out to pick up beers while seats were pulled up to the windows, shoes kicked off, corkscrews retrieved from the bottom of desk drawers. Maddox shook his head, bemused. "All right, but don't forget we're back to normal tomorrow."

F team rinsed coffee cups, bringing them in for the beer. The indexers, seeing there was to be no more work today, pushed their chairs back from the desks and allowed Betts to slosh wine into paper cups. Caffery, just back from the mortuary, loosened his tie and opened a Pils beer while Essex, happy as a puppy, stripped off his shirt, knotted his tie around his naked neck and found a spot where the late sun came into the room to recline with his feet on the desk. He swiveled around to look at F team, who had gathered at the top of the T-shaped desk, a beer can in front of each man. "We'll get shot of you lot; on the road back to Eltham."

"At least you can go back to reading *Woman's Realm* without shame," one said. "Away from our 'orrible judgmental little eyes."

"And back to wearing my favorite frock again," Essex said wistfully. "The peach one."

"You'll be among people who understand you."

"You'll feel more comfortable."

"More confident."

"Nicer to be with."

"Nicer to look at."

Caffery leaned back in his chair, staring off down the corridor. The door next to his office was open: F team's office, Diamond's headquarters. The corridor was dark. From the opened door a striped oblong of sun lay across the floor. From time to time a shadow muddied it. DI Diamond was in there, moving back and forward—packing his belongings to go back to Eltham.

The laughter continued. Essex had Kryotos on his lap. "With the help of the lovely Marilyn I'm going to show you how to accessorize in this difficult day and age when we all understand the importance of thrift . . ."

Caffery stood, unnoticed. Unsnapping another can of Pils, he quietly left the incident room.

DI Diamond was packing things into a yellow crate, occasionally brushing his hair back from his forehead where it flopped down, free of the usual hair gel. From the little pots of cacti, the family photograph on the desk, Caffery realized that Diamond had expected to be here longer than two weeks. He stood silently in the doorway and watched as the DI blew the dust off the plants and unhooked the Michelin calendar from the wall. It was five minutes before he finished.

He gave the desk a last wipe, emptied a pot of paper clips into the bin and straightened up.

"Yes?"

Caffery stepped inside. "I brought you a beer." He placed it on the desk and gestured at a photograph lying on the top of the folders in the crate, two small boys, smart in their blue school ties. "They look like you. You must be proud."

"Thanks." Diamond gave him a long look with his powder-blue eyes. A faint sweat had broken out around his mouth and he wiped his forehead with his sleeve. He placed the photo facedown, carefully pushed the beer back across the desk, turned away from Caffery and pulled Sellotape over the crate. "But I don't drink on duty."

When Susan woke he was gone. She was in a bedroom—he had tied her to the bed—groggy and disorientated, red and black, the pulse hard in her face and breasts. Her eyes had swollen so that the upper lids chafed against the lower lids, as if her eyelashes had been turned inside out.

He had gagged her with packing tape and taken Polaroids as he tortured her, showing them to her afterward. Susan had cried when she saw the first one. She didn't recognize her poor swollen face, the bulging eyes. But after the first she remembered little. She began to slip in and out of unconsciousness.

Now the clock on the wall said 5:30, she'd been asleep—*unconscious?*—for eight hours. She knew she had the beginnings of a fever and knew it meant the wounds were infected. She could smell them, and the top of her right nipple was yolky and swollen around the crusted black incision.

She lay still, listening carefully. The noise of a bird somewhere in the flat, not singing, but chirruping sickly. And outside the creak and whir of—*what was that? a crane?*—the occasional thundering shudder of a dump truck's load. Construction work. She wasn't near Malpens Street, then. There was no construction work in her area, *so where? Where are you, Susan?*

Something answered that she wasn't far from home. She was still in Greenwich or Lewisham.

She closed her eyes and tried to force her memory. Where was the nearest building construction site to Malpens Street? *Where?* But the effort exhausted her. She'd rest for a while. Then she was going to try to get to the window.

The party started to break up. Essex, wearing his shirt again, combed the desks for empty cans, and Kryotos, who had picked up as many mugs as she could in both hands, hooking her fingers through the handles, was standing next to the printer watching a SPECRIM report arrive. Betts was taking the photos down from the walls.

Caffery had had trouble relaxing as instinctively as the others: his eyes were sore from the morgue formaldehyde, and he wanted the search complete, wanted the cement dust matched. He had spent most of the evening sitting at an opened window smoking thoughtfully, blowing the smoke upward into the evening air. It was a few minutes past seven when Fiona Quinn's car pulled up in the street below.

Jack sat forward, pinching out the cigarette. Something was wrong. He could sense it in DS Quinn's tempo as she climbed out of the driver's seat.

He met them in the corridor. "What's up?"

Logan dropped the yellow exhibits crate on the floor and ran a weary hand through his hair. "Don't ask."

In the incident room everyone looked up expectantly. When Maddox saw Quinn's and Logan's expressions his face fell. "Oh, for God's sake—don't tell me."

"Sorry, sir. Some drug paraphernalia—almost a third of a K of heroin—but for what we want the place was kosher."

"Nothing organic," Quinn said.

"Shit." He put his fingers to his forehead. "Back to the drawing board, then. Are we ever going to get shot of this?"

"Sir?" Everyone turned. Kryotos was standing next to the printer with a puzzled expression on her face. A baroque wave of feed paper—a SPECRIM—rose and curled into her hand.

"What?"

"We've got a casualty in Greenwich. Victim dumped in a wheelie bin. She's alive but—" She looked up. "But the offender did a little amateur surgery on her."

Forty-one

SUSAN LISTER was unconscious and still in intensive care when they arrived. The paramedic who brought her in, Andrew Benton, a fresh-faced young black man with a buzz cut so short it looked like only a day's growth, was shaken by the experience. They talked in a small room next to the nurse's station.

"Fucking hell, you know, I've got to tell you. I've seen some things in my time, but this—" He shook his head. "This has really done my head. And as for him, her husband—"

"He found her?" Maddox said.

"Can you imagine? Finding your lady in that state. She was in the dustbin in the front of their house. That's the value this wanker put on her. A human life, no better than rubbish."

"What time did you respond?"

"Eleven. I was told it was a purple plus." He looked from face to face. "You know, Mr. Lister thought she was a goner when he called the services. The guy, the *animal*, had dumped the lady head-down in the wheelie bin, left her for dead." His face creased. "God. If *I* won't sleep tonight, just think how *he* feels."

"Tell me about her. Was she dressed?"

"Not dressed. She was wrapped up in a bin-liner. I think some of your lot took it in for evidence or whatever. They were trawling the whole place. BeforeI even got her out of there they were taping it off."

"We like to protect a crime scene." Maddox was embarrassed. "Prevents contamination."

"Yeah, I know. I didn't mean no offense."

"None taken. Her injuries?"

"Bad. She's so cut up she'll probably die from blood loss, if not septicemia. Consultant says she's got bronchial pneumococcal and renal failure; they've hooked her up to the ECMO. She was in and out when I got to her."

"Where are the cuts?"

"On her breasts." He rubbed his face. "She'd been stitched up. First thing I thought was she might have been in for surgery, I don't know, some cowboy thing. But then her husband's wailing about how she'd disappeared and then I got her on the gurney and—"

"And?"

"I'm no genius, you know, but even I could see there was something wrong."

"Something wrong?"

"It was so infected it was difficult to see, but the sutures were all, you know, crazy."

Caffery looked at his hands. He remembered similar words coming from a CID officer's mouth at North's yard that first Saturday night. "How about her head?"

"She's been smacked a couple of times, on the side of the head, and she was covered in makeup, like a tart. Hubby reckons she had a haircut too. He kept saying it over and over again. 'Why'd he cut her hair? Why'd he cut her hair?' like that was the most important thing in the world."

"No wig. He chose this one," Caffery muttered.

Benton shot him a look. "What was that?"

Caffery stood up and pulled on his jacket. "Nothing." He looked at Maddox. "I'm going to have a look at Mrs. Lister. Meet you at the scene in, what? Two hours?"

"Where you going?"

"I won't be long. I've got an idea. Just let me speak to someone at Lambeth first—see if I'm on the right road."

She lay on a blue pillowcase, on her back with her arms opened outward, her face turned to the door just as if she'd been expecting a visitor but had got tired waiting and had dropped off to sleep. The hair fringing her bruised eyes was almost white, the color of sun-bleached sand. Someone had made a rudimentary attempt to clean her, but the mouth was still stained red with lipstick and her hands and nails were grimy with, Caffery realized, dust.

His breath fogged up the window. He pulled his shirt cuff over his fist and rubbed a hole. A nurse had appeared in his eye line and stood checking the drip lines, obscuring his view. Jack stepped back from the door. He'd seen all he needed to see.

"*It sounds just like the others?*"

"*That's right, Mr. Caffery.*" *Krishnamurthi at Jackson's autopsy.* "Identical *to the others.*"

Now he thought he understood what was happening.

It was getting dark by the time he parked outside the Forensic Science Laboratories in Lambeth Road—the windscreen of the Jaguar was speckled with midges. The foyer lights cast long shadows of potted yuccas across the mosaic in the corridor: Catherine Howard, patiently clutching her rosary in the shadows.

The security guard roused himself from the desk and handed Caffery a pass. "I'll tell her you're on your way up but we're closing in ten minutes, sir—you'll need to be out in ten minutes."

She met him at the lift. She was wearing marl-gray jogging pants, a green sweatshirt and Reeboks and was carrying an opened Coke can. With her gray hair in a neat bob, her long body almost shoulder-to-shoulder with his, Jack found Dr. Jane Amedure oddly beautiful.

"I'm sorry, Inspector Caffery." She led him through hushed corridors lined with neat rows of Audubon prints, past security guards making last-minute checks, technicians pulling off disposable lab coats. "I'm sorry about the news, and I'm sorry I had to pass it on through a third party. I tried to call you but—"

"No—don't worry. Thanks for your help but it's not why I'm here."

She looked sideways at him. "Well, sadly, I don't believe you're here to ask me for a date. So my astute scientist's mind concludes that you're here about Operation Walworth?"

He smiled. "Brilliant."

"Come on, then." She held her office door for him. "We've had everything from you lot today—Harteveld's samples, a hair that interested me—"

"Maggots."

"Oh yes. Those too, horrible little buggers. They've already been forwarded to the Natural History Museum, thank God. Dr. Jameson'll run a test batch—match the environment they were in and see them through to pupation." She pushed a chair in his direction and squeezed behind a desk dotted with piles of paperwork, Coke cans, ashtrays. A desk light was pulled low over the working surface and, propped in the window behind Dr. Amedure, a Nigerian shrine mask stared shark-eyed down into the office. "From a glance everything looks okay, you know, a couple of anomalies but otherwise it looks exactly the same as the others."

"I know. That's what Krishnamurthi said. It's what's worrying me."

"Worrying you?"

He pulled his chair closer to the desk. "Just explain to me the flesh flies, the ones that laid eggs on the wounds."

"No, no. Not eggs. Our little friend the sarcophagid doesn't bother laying eggs. She lays larvae."

"Always on a wound?"

"Yes." She lifted a Coke can and shook it. Empty. She moved to the next, trying to identify the one she had just abandoned. "Now, from the little I understand of entomology, it goes like this: the blowflies lay their eggs on the mucous membranes—that's the mouth, the anus, the vagina, eyes and nostrils, et cetera. With your common or garden violent deaths there are wounds, blood—so at the same time as Diptera are doing their work, the flesh fly homes in on the wounds."

"But this didn't happen with Jackson?"

"Nor with any of your victims. Although sarcophagidae is larval, like Diptera, the flesh fly doesn't go through instars: so we knew they were a much more recent arrival. That was the flashing light for us: we figured then that the wounds were postmortem. The serotonin levels in the wounds helped us narrow it down." She had located the full Coke can. She took a swig and looked up at him. "You're probably looking at a sixty-to-seventy-two-hour gap."

"*Sixty?* That's the minimum?"

"I'm only estimating."

"Okay, but what's the earliest they could have laid?"

"Ballpark? With the widest cover-my-arse margin in history? I'd say—oooh—Wednesday morning? Like the others— about a three-day gap." Dr. Amedure paused and lowered the can. "Inspector Caffery? Something interesting to you?"

"Yes." He put fingers to his temples.

Surveillance was watching Harteveld since Tuesday afternoon. By 10:00 A.M. on Wednesday he was dead.

"Dr. Amedure." He dropped his hand. Looked up. "There was cement dust recovered on all the victims."

"I know. I think with the others we all assumed, didn't we, that it was picked up in the construction yard. Some red faces, I suppose—but we're onto it. We've started an X-ray diffraction. When that's complete we'll get the CCRL database in Gaithersburg to trace the source."

"There isn't a database in the U.K.?"

"Maryland's got the best one. They can work with a diffractogram or a phase analysis printout and compare chlorates, metakaolinite, sulfates with their samples."

"How long would it take?"

"Our end? Less than twenty-four hours. But Maryland— I don't know. They're usually pretty quick."

"Can you start it tonight?"

"Ahem, Inspector Caffery." She smiled at him over the top of the can. "I don't think we need to be reminded how much AMIP'd be charged for an overnighter."

"You don't know, do you?" He shifted, uncomfortable. "Something happened in PL tonight that's chucked all the cards back in the air. We don't know for sure but we might've got someone else out there."

Dr. Amedure's face changed. She put the Coke can down, picked up the phone and dialed. "I'll speak to the duty manager. If we've got the staff we might be able to fit you in." Waiting for the line to connect, she fumbled under the papers and pulled out a spectrograph. "The hair I was telling you about. Same color and length as the wig hairs but a nice round cross section—Caucasian, bleached. And it fell out naturally."

"From one of the other victims?" Caffery leaned over and took the paper. "Transferred from his furniture maybe?"

She shook her head. "It doesn't match any of them—not even superficially. And all we can get from it is mitochondrial DNA and some pointers on the owner's lifestyle. You see that handsome peak in the middle? It's the metabolite of marijuana."

"And this one?"

"Aluminum."

"Aluminum?"

"Well, that—" She shifted the phone to the other ear. "That could mean almost anything. One I saw went off the page almost, turned out to be an OCD patient—obsessive-compulsive. Their compulsion was antiperspirant."

"Which might mean another victim we don't know about yet?"

"Exactly."

Caffery put the paper on her desk and got to his feet. "Dr. Amedure, this trade examination. Whatever it costs, okay?"

"If you say so." She put her hand over the receiver. "If AMIP's got the money there's nothing we can't do."

One A.M. and the summer night had turned chilly. Greenwich had supplied a floodlighting unit and cordoned off the road; the press, who earlier had swarmed the area, had headed off to the hospital hoping to smell Susan Lister's blood more closely. Caffery and Maddox sat in the Jaguar, under a street-light just inside the road-block.

"Dust," Jack told his superintendent. "Cement dust." He twisted around on creaky leather, draped his arm over the back of the seat and looked at Maddox. "Let me explain."

Carefully he laid out his ideas—his bare suspicions—the first sketchy pegging-out of what he believed was happening. Raw and half formed—but he thought he had the right germ. He explained each link, justified each small jump of his imagination.

"I dunno, Jack," Maddox said after a long silence. "I'm not convinced . . ." He tapped his fingers on the dashboard and stared off into the street. DI Basset stood outside the cordoned-off area, under a floodlight, drinking coffee and watching as Quinn, unmissable in her luminous white suit, mixed dental stone in a small plastic container. After a long time Maddox straightened and began buttoning his jacket.

"I need to think about it. Let's catch a few z's. Get back to Shrivemoor for what? Six? You can run it by Essex and Kryotos before the meeting—see how it hits them."

After Maddox had gone Jack rolled one last cigarette and wandered a few yards back down the road. The gardens smelled strongly of jasmine. He stopped and stared up at a yellow rectangle of light over the roof of a low garage. It was then that he realized where he was.

Malpens Street was a sharp right off South Street. They'd come at it from a different direction, but now he saw he was only four or five doors down from the junk shop. A low wall bordered the gardens in the main street, and the angle allowed him to see the rear bays, sliced diagonally by a garage roof. One lit window was opened a crack to the night air.

Rebecca's kitchen.

He backed up and leaned against the car, away from the streetlights, pulling his mobile from inside his jacket. He could hear Rebecca's phone ringing from over the roofs.

"Hello?" But the line clicked for a beat and he realized he was talking to an answerphone.

Joni's voice: "*Sorry you've gone to all the trouble and expense of calling, when we haven't the decency to be in for your call.*"

Caffery swore under his breath. "Look, I know someone's there. This is Jack, DI Caffery. Answer the phone." He waited. Nothing. He sighed. "Look, Rebecca, Joni, if you're listening I want you to be careful. This thing isn't over yet. Just—just keep your windows and door locked, okay? And, Rebecca—" He paused. "Give me a ring. When you have the time."

He hung up and stood in the dark looking at the window. A few moments later the light in the kitchen went off and a figure came to the window and closed it. Caffery couldn't see who it was. He put his mobile in his pocket and got back inside the Jaguar.

Forty-two

WITH THE HELP of half a bottle of Glenmorangie he managed three hours of intense sleep before he was jolted awake by a thought:

Susan Lister hadn't been opened.

He sighed and rolled onto his back, his hands over his eyes. No bird sewn deep inside. No bird.

Why? Why didn't you give us the symbol this time?

It's not meant as a symbol.

Jack flinched. He hiked himself up on his elbows and blinked, his heart thumping. The answer could have been spoken by someone in the room.

Not a symbol? Then what?

Susan Lister was living. No bird. And for the six sad pieces of carrion in the morgue? A live, struggling bird. Struggling so hard that it ripped tissue from the bone beneath. Harteveld's work seeming to stretch out from beyond death.

The moonlight shifted, cold on his skin, and Caffery lay back, breathing carefully, listening to his heart. He thought he knew what the bird meant. And he thought he knew exactly how it fit into the puzzle. Now he knew where he was going.

* * *

F team—some of whom had already moved their belongings —had been contacted and were due back at Shrivemoor in time for the morning's meeting. Caffery met Maddox, Essex and Kryotos an hour in advance. They were all tired, dispirited. Caffery stood for a few minutes in the center of the incident room holding his glasses—thinking, locking his ideas into place—while Maddox sat in the corner, head propped in his hands, staring across at him. Kryotos was in the kitchen, making coffee. They could hear the sound of spoons rattling in the cups all the way down the corridor. She hummed as she brought the coffee into the incident room—as if she thought noise might alleviate the depression in the air.

Maddox sighed. "Right." He ran his hands down his face and looked up at Essex and Kryotos." You both know what happened last night."

"Yeah."

"And a hair turned up on Jackson that we can't file. We have to read that as another victim, so I don't care how tired everyone is, think 'shit' and 'shovel' on this." He looked up. "Jack? You ready?"

"Yeah."

"Go on." He waved his hand in the air. "Go on. Tell them what you told me."

"Yeah, okay." He hesitated a moment more, still staring at the floor. Then his face cleared. He put his glasses on and turned to them.

"It's Birdman," he said simply.

Essex and Marilyn exchanged glances.

"A copycat?" Essex said.

"No. I mean *this* is Birdman. The press never got enough for a copycat. Harteveld was the killer. Birdman is the mutilator. Harteveld is dead, Birdman's still working."

Marilyn stopped spooning sugar into her coffee and stared at him. Essex was frowning: twisting his coffee cup into a circular groove on the blue and silver Met mouse mat.

Maddox propped his chin in his hand and studied their reactions. Then he swiveled his eyes to Caffery. "You're going to have to convince them."

"I can." He opened his briefcase and handed Kryotos the notes he'd made at the FSS. "Jane Amedure says the PM woundings on Peace Nbidi Jackson were consistent with the others—three days after death."

"Meaning?"

"Meaning Harteveld was either under surveillance when they were done or already dead. Quinn and Logan couldn't find any evidence in the Halesowen Road flat because *Harteveld didn't do the mutilations.* It was someone else."

"Like a little club." Kryotos handed the notes to Essex and resumed stirring the coffee. "A necrophiliac's club. Usual rules: no blacks, no Jews, no spikes in the clubhouse—"

"No, no." Maddox held his hand up. "Let him go on. We can have a snigger when he's given us a working scenario."

"Right." Caffery sat down opposite them. Opened his hands on the table. "I think it went like this: Harteveld's a necrophiliac, no doubt about that. But he's unusual for this kind of paraphiliac because he's educated: he *knows* the sort of shit it could land him in, so he keeps it under wraps, doesn't act on it; if he's your average perve it could've been brewing for years. Then, seven months or so ago, something sets him off—he gets hit with his key stressor, maybe a relationship goes sour, there's a professional upheaval, we might never know exactly what, but anyway his tendency kicks in. He acts without thinking, gets his jollies, and then, when it's over, he sees the trouble he's in."

"He's stuck with a body."

"And spooked about disposing of it. But that's okay, because he knows someone who can help. Not another necrophile. But an opportunist. A sexual inadequate, a sadist. Someone ill enough not to care if the victim is dead or alive. It's him, not Harteveld, who's cleaning the bodies."

"Cleaning secondhand goods," Essex murmured.

"Quinn never found any of that soap at Harteveld's." Maddox picked at the lid of a miniature UHT milk carton. "What was it?"

"Wright's coal tar."

"Hmmm." He was silent for a few moments. He tipped the milk in his coffee, tapping out the last drops, and looked thoughtfully at his DI. "Come on, then, Jack. I'm halfway there." He threw the little carton in the bin and settled back in the chair. "Talk us into it."

"Okay. Remember we couldn't understand how Harteveld was so balls-on accurate about picking on victims who wouldn't be missed? Now, Logan showed Gemini a photo of Harteveld and he blanked. The barmaid did too. Like he's never been in the pub. Gemini was cabbying the girls up to Croom's Hill for a meeting that had already been made. So here's what I'm thinking: what if this second offender was doing the preplanning? Getting to know the girls, finding out who's not going to be missed, making the arrangements. That way Harteveld is never seen in the pub—he already knows who he's after because someone's marked her for him."

"And the same offender comes in again later?"

"And *he's* the one, not Harteveld, who's doing the decoration—the wigs, the makeup."

"This is the Lister offender we're discussing?" Kryotos was less dubious now. "Striking out on his own?"

"Exactly. He's got a taste for it now."

"It would answer a lot of questions," Essex said. "Like why that bird in Royal Hill never knew there was a body in her wheelie for two days. Maybe it *had* only been there overnight like she said. Maybe the other guy dumped it *after* Harteveld did his swan song."

"Now." Caffery leaned forward. "Jackson had cement dust in her hair, the same dust that was on the others. At first we thought it came from the recovery site, the construction yard, but Jackson never went there. Lister too. The FME cleaned her up, swabbed off some gray dust. Maybe we've got another Fred West, maybe he's in the building trade or doing work on his house. But most importantly I think he's got links with St. Dunstan's."

"Marilyn." Maddox got to his feet and tapped a ballpoint against his teeth. "Marilyn, get me the CS. He's going to love this. And Jack—" He sat on the desk and looked at his DI. "I know what you're working up to."

"You do?"

"Oh yes. You've already got an idea. Haven't you?"

"Yes, I have. I shouldn't have let him go in the first place."

"Go on, then. Take Essex. You can have Logan too when he gets here."

"Hang on, hang on." Everyone paused. Kryotos was frowning. "I thought the FME told you there were no marks on Lister's head."

"Didn't need to be," Caffery said. "Same as with Hatch— her hair was the right color. He cut it to match. He picked her because she was nearer to what he wanted. She was a jogger—St. Dunstan's was on her route. I think that's when he targeted her. This is the first time he hasn't had to take what he was given: this one he chose. He's hunting for himself now."

"But she wasn't, uh, you know, cut open. The bird. No bird."

"Yes." He took his glasses off and rubbed his eyes. When he looked up again everyone could see how tired he was. "That's because she wasn't dead."

"What?"

Caffery placed his hands palm-down on the table and stared at the piebald thumbnails, pressed together. "He opened them to put the bird in. He's not like Harteveld, he doesn't *choose* to have his victims dead. He's a sadistic rapist, but death isn't the fun for him. He'd rather they were living so he can enjoy their fear." He looked directly at Marilyn, trusting her not to flinch. "Lister wasn't opened for the simple reason that she had her own, healthy heart pumping in her body. A heart he could hear reacting to the torture."

"*What* are you telling us?" she said faintly.

"I know what he's saying," Essex said. "The birds were alive when they went in. They'd have struggled. Like—" He began rolling his sleeves down, as if the room had become cold. "Like the sound of a heart."

"Exactly." Caffery stood up and pulled on his jacket. "Exactly."

With all last night's excitement he had made himself late. He had *so* much on his mind. His coming birthday, Joni and, of course, the person who had spent a day and a night in his flat, broken and folded up.

It made him tremble to think how easy the abduction had been, how easy and *symmetrical* the disposal—in her own front garden, for her husband to find—and what, of course, this success promised for the future.

At first, when he sat up on her backseat with the cordless power saw in his fist, she had simply lost all control of her body. He thought she was having an epileptic episode: her head thrashed, her feet drummed on the car floor, her mouth worked soundlessly, teeth *click-clicking* in the darkness. But once he'd made the decision to knock her out—with a punch of the saw's hand piece to the side of the head—it became easy.

There had been only one drawback. He had believed, after days of studying her as she jogged past St. Dunstan's in the mornings, that he'd chosen the right one, that there would be no need for surgery. So it was a bitter disappointment to him, when he'd undressed her in his flat, to see her breasts—to realize that some cutting would be necessary. Still, that had been a small detail compared to the overwhelming success of the event, and his confidence, already swollen in the last few months, took another lurch ahead. By his birthday he'd be ready for the real thing. He pondered this in his scruffy, hothouse kitchen as he opened a bag of M&M's and absent-mindedly wriggled his finger between the bars of a birdcage, where four abject, half-bald zebra finches shivered on the floor. He couldn't remember the last time he had fed them, but that didn't matter now.

One day left until his birthday. Just one day now. He took the chocolates and wandered into the bathroom. It was time to get ready.

At 9:00 A.M. on the dot, the phones in St. Dunstan's personnel office came off answerphone.

"Personnel. Wendy speaking."

"Wendy." Caffery tucked his tie in his shirt and leaned forward on his desk. "DI Caffery speaking. Area Major Investigation Pool. You helped us with that little room in the library."

"Oh yes, yes. Hello, Inspector, hello. I've been wondering when we'd hear from you. It's all been quite a shock. Did you know Mr. Harteveld was quite a familiar face here in personnel? I have to say I'm most terribly sorry, terribly sorry. I hope his behavior hasn't tarnished St. Dunstan's in your eyes. We'd all be very sad if . . . You see we're proud of our reputation and if I thought *for one moment* that that dreadful man had harmed it, I'd—"

"Wendy."

"Yes." She caught her breath with a little gulp. "Forgive me."

"Do you have records of who is currently taking leave?"

When he told her whom he was looking for she said, "Now, Inspector Caffery, I'm going to put you on hold while I get his file." She treated him to a few bars of Pachelbel's *Canon* and was back in less than a minute, breathless and fluttery.

"Hello? Inspector?"

"Yes."

"Mr. Thomas Cook's on leave, due back June the eighth."

"Or so he says."

"I'm sorry?"

"Nothing. Have you got his address?"

Cook lived on the bottom floor of a two-flat conversion in Lewisham. No construction work in the street or the front of the house. Leaving Logan in the Sierra, a plane tree dripping water steadily onto the bonnet, Caffery and Essex pulled their raincoats over their heads and crept across the tarmacked forecourt, through the wooden side door and into the garden. The garden was overgrown—again no evidence of cement or construction work—and the house silent: the windows blank, all the curtains on the bottom floor closed.

They stood in the wet grass and were looking up at rain dripping from the gabled roof when their radios came alive.

"Bravo six-oh-two from Bravo six-oh-six." Absurdly, Logan was whispering. "Sir?"

Caffery spun the radio out of the belt holster. "Bravo six-oh-two receiving."

"Some movement, sir. Inside the house."

"Got you. We're on our way. Out."

They trotted back around to the Sierra.

"Who is it?"

"Little old lady."

"Old lady?"

"You know, gray hair, bifocals."

"The upstairs neighbor?"

"Well, if she's the neighbor, then I'd like to know what she's doing in the target's flat."

"What?"

"Downstairs. I meant *down*stairs. Look."

They turned. In the front windows on the ground floor they got a glimpse of a large pair of hands as a curtain was opened.

"Okay." Caffery started to walk back to the house. "Maybe it's my mistake."

"Jack." Essex had to trot to keep up. "What do you think you're doing?"

"Maybe it's my mistake, maybe 27A is downstairs and 27B upstairs." He leaned on the doorbell and next to him Essex shivered.

"I don't like this, Jack."

"What're you talking about? It's just a little old lady."

"*Dressed to Kill,*" he hissed. "Dressed to fucking kill, that's what I'm talking about."

Footsteps sounded in the hallway, heavy footsteps, and as Caffery pulled his warrant card out of his pocket Essex took a step back from the front door.

"I mean it, Jack. I don't like this at all."

His face in the stained mirror above the sink, with his bad teeth and shiny red skin, reaffirmed his life belief that anger was his civil right, that he had a license to fury. He'd never had a day, an hour, of being unashamed of his appearance: he was inclined to fat and had never really lost the soft womanly hips and chubby legs of toddlerhood. The tops of his thighs rubbed together when he walked, and nightly he cleaned lines of waxy white deposit from the folds in his flesh. And he, with the lust of a bull. He was brutally oversexed and yet it was no surprise when he had reached the age of twenty a virgin.

His first paltry sexual conquest was in a sodden alley in Camden in exchange for a half-bottle of Pink Lady. Later a St. Lucian prostitute in Hackney for ten pounds and four Pernod and blackcurrants. It was at the age of twenty-two, while retaking biology, physics and chemistry A levels, that he got a job as a security officer in UMDS and his life changed.

His duties, in the shadow of London Bridge station, allowed him time to study; they included checking passes, directing visitors, shivering in the car park Portakabin outside the pathology department, and, every other week, alone, at night, doing the time-key patrol: through the polished corridors, the empty canteen smelling of mashed potato and sour milk, the lecture theaters, the path lab, the anatomy lab.

The anatomy lab, where, one winter sixteen years ago, his life had become inextricably bound to Harteveld's.

Theirs had been a peculiar meeting of disjointed minds. Looking at each other over the green-draped shapes and stainless-steel dissecting tables, they knew, with a conviction like that of lovers, that like had met like. Neither needed to vocalize the personal struggle they'd lived. Straight-backed, hard-boned aristocrat looked down across the classes and quite simply, quite poetically *knew*.

He didn't pass his A levels and soon afterward he gave up his dreams of being a doctor and left the security company. Harteveld, too, left UMDS, but the allegiance between the heir to a pharmaceuticals fortune and the ex-security guard weathered the years. Their particular, specialized interests remained the same.

There had been four or five rapes over the years; in car parks, forests, girls too drunk to remember the license plate of the small man who pulled over and offered them a lift. That was how he had first come south of the river. She was a stripper from Greenwich. It was 2:00 A.M. on his birthday, and he found her wandering the roads north of the Rotherhithe Tunnel, trying to hitch a ride. She was the most beautiful thing he had ever seen, in her PVC miniskirt and leather jacket, her Nordic blond hair cut in a neat fringe. Even now, in his dank bathroom in Lewisham, he groaned involuntarily when he thought of the love he'd spilled over Joni.

She had sat limply in the front seat of his car, noises coming from her throat, as he groped at her soft body pressed and folded under the seat belt. Inside the leather jacket, her heart fluttered like a weak bird. It was only when he tried to lift her skirt that she resisted. She stumbled drunkenly out of the car and sat woodenly on the pavement, her livid makeup smeared, pushing him away when he climbed out of the car and tried to touch her.

"Not now, yeah?" she muttered. "I feel sick."

He stood looking down at her ash-blond head, her knees in torn stockings, and suddenly chose not to rape her.

Just like that.

It was an unexpected deviation. He took her home and said good night. Just like that. As if it were *nothing*. As if this were normal for him.

Afterward he felt virtuous, elated, filled with light. He quickly decided his generosity to her was an expression of love. He wanted her so much that his head ached when he thought about her.

But Joni pushed his advances away, got angry when he appeared at her pub performances, angrier when she heard he'd got a new job in St. Dunstan's and had purchased the ground-floor flat of an old lady's converted house in Lewisham, less than a mile from her home in Greenwich.

He didn't flinch at her anger, she was his reason for living. His flat was a shrine to her, he photographed her in the street, bought her drinks in the pub. Sometimes Joni gave him moments of pleasure—sometimes she smoked or drank so much that she softened to him and he was able to take her home and let her sleep it off in the spare bed. He didn't touch her. Not once. That wasn't the point. The point was for *her* to come to *him*. That was crucial. He kept the flat clean in the pained hope that she would understand how he cared for her: hiding his treasured pictures when she stayed, taking every precaution, spraying the flat with air freshener—Joni loved things to smell sweet.

And eventually she did come to tolerate him in a resigned, tired way. In return he learned to tolerate her thoughtless, patternless acts of faithlessness, her flirting with other men, her refusal to touch him. Even when she had driven him to the brink of fury, arriving that day, four years ago, fresh from the surgeon's knife, her new, swollen breasts pouting on her rib cage, he had stayed calm, polite. It didn't matter what Joni did in the present tense, in the three-dimensional world, because she lived on in his internal fantasy theater as she had been that night, warm and pliable, with her small, soft-tipped breasts and drink on her breath.

Back in the kitchen one of the battered little zebra finches had found the strength to get up to the perch. It stared at him with its bright little eyes. He grunted and shook the cage, hard, until the exhausted bird was dislodged and fell to the floor, too stunned and starved to flap. It lay there on its side panting and blinking at him as he finished the M&M's, crumpled the bag and started to get dressed.

Forty-three

THE DOOR WAS OPENED by a woman who was indeed wearing bifocals. She had cropped gray hair and large hands and was sensibly dressed in a Fair Isle cardigan, tweed skirt over solid, English hips and brown leather walking shoes. When Caffery flashed his warrant card and explained they were interested in the upstairs neighbor she gave them a gentle, tilted smile and opened the door.

"A cup of tea, I think, gentlemen."

They went into the hallway, Essex hanging back, still not sure if he trusted this woman. Caffery stood for a moment, staring at the blank doorway at the top of the stairs. He ran a finger over the banister, pressed it to his white cuff. Nothing.

"I don't know their names," the woman said from inside her flat. "The couple up there."

"The *couple*?" Jack turned back. "Did you say the couple?"

So there is *a girlfriend.*

"That is who you're interested in, isn't it?"

She held open the door and led them into a small hallway which had been sectioned out of a high-ceilinged room using plasterboard. When he saw the airbrush fantasy posters on

the walls, a silver-breasted Geigeresque woman, maned biker
heroes, gleaming winged bikes and dragons, Essex caught
Caffery's sleeve.

"*Check this gaff out,*" he hissed as they followed the
woman into the front room. Here the ceiling was hung with
Indian shawls, mirrored and tasseled, a Lava lamp stood side
by side with a teak Afghan water pipe.

"I know them to speak to." She picked up an orange bur-
lap cushion from the sofa and slapped it. "My son would
know their names, but he's off on his holidays." She paused,
the cushion dangling in her hand, and the three of them regarded each other in puzzled silence. Suddenly she laughed.

"Oh, I'm so sorry, I haven't explained myself." She
dropped the cushion and wiped her hands on her skirt. "Do
forgive me." She offered her hand to Caffery. "The name's
Mimi Cook. I spend so much time shuffling around here trying to keep the place clean, sometimes I forget it isn't my flat."

"Cook?" Essex murmured, glancing over his shoulder as
if someone might walk in behind him.

"That's right. This is my boy's flat. I'm his personal
busybody."

"Mrs. Cook." Caffery stepped forward and shook her
hand. "Pleased to meet you."

"Likewise I'm sure. Now"—she put both hands on
Essex's shoulders and gently moved him from the doorway
so she could get past—"some tea and then we can get down
to business."

While she clanked around in the kitchen, Caffery and
Essex got to work, Essex skimming over the book titles, rais-
ing his eyebrows at a fifties edition of *One Hundred Days of
Sodom* and a slim volume of Klossowski's *Sade Mon Pro-
chain* tucked amongst the Kerouacs and Colin Wilsons, while
Caffery, conscious of his wornout reflection in the mirror
over the fireplace, ran his finger over the surfaces, searched
the assortment of pots and ashtrays on the mantelpiece. He

found a stack of outdated travel cards secured in a rubber band, Cook's freckled face staring up at him, and next to it a small framed black-and-white picture. It showed Mrs. Cook, decades younger, dressed in a seersucker bathing suit, dark hair backcombed. She was sitting on a tartan rug spread over a pebbled beach, squinting at the camera. On her knee sat a white-haired little boy in bathing trunks, his arms straight down at his sides. Incongruously the toddler was wearing dark glasses, the large frames sticking out on either side of his head, giving him the appearance of a small beetle. When Mrs. Cook came in with a tray piled with cups, Caffery picked up the frame and said, "Your son, Mrs. Cook?"

"Yes."

"There's something wrong with his vision?"

"Oh yes. Achromatopsia. You won't have heard of it and why should you?" She smoothed the heavy skirt over her hips and sat down on the sofa to pour the tea. "Put simply, he can't tolerate sunlight. You'd imagine Thailand would be the last place, wouldn't you? But that's my Thomas. He's got a sixth sense for anything that's bad for him."

"Achroma—?" Essex blushed charmingly. "I'm not hot with long words."

"Achromatopsia." Mrs. Cook smiled patiently. "Congenital. His eyes haven't got any cones. Or is it rods? I can never remember. Anyway, the world's in black and white for him, just like a cat. It's very unfair. It means he's registered disabled."

"Partially sighted?"

"Not that it means much, except he can't drive and . . ." She smiled apologetically. "And that I've cosseted him more than the other two. Now." She handed Caffery a teacup. "You wanted to talk about the people upstairs? Is it *him* you're interested in? Thomas's father always says that the normal-looking ones are the worst."

*   *   *

"I thought he meant his girlfriend." Caffery called Maddox from the car as soon as they left Cook's. "When he said 'social secretary' I thought he meant a girlfriend. But he meant his mother. She comes in and cleans for him three times a week. Not only that, he can't drive."

"Says who?"

"Mum. Says he's partially sighted."

"Do we believe her?"

"I'm on the way to St. Dunstan's now to back it up, but all the signs are there. This avenue is dry."

Everyone in personnel was at lunch apart from the trusty Mr. Bliss. He met Caffery at the door, hand extended, top lip pulled down over bad teeth, his smooth face pink and shiny as if he'd given it an extra buffing at his shaving mirror that morning.

"Don't you eat lunch, Mr. Bliss?"

Bliss wagged his finger at Caffery. "Lunch is for wimps, Mr. Caffery. Didn't you know that?" He gave an odd, hiccuping laugh at his own joke and swiped his hand across his head to smooth the thin strands. "Sorry I wasn't here this morning to take your call—I was still out there battling away to find a parking space again. I'm sorry to report that the situation is not improving."

"Yes," Caffery interjected. "Yes, I remember. I—" He placed his hands on the back of the chair. "Mr. Bliss, I wonder if you can help me. We're still tying up a few ends."

"Ah, the terrible business at the Dome." He seated himself and looked up at Jack. "Still beavering away, are you?"

"We are."

"And how can *we* help?"

"You've got medical records for your staff?"

"Medical records? No. If they've taken life insurance through the pension scheme we might retain a copy of a doctor's report, but that's all."

"But you'd know if they were disabled?"

"The hospital's equal opportunities policy means we're obliged to employ our quota. They all fill in a questionnaire when we take them on. It would be in that. But you won't find Mr. H-Harteveld in there—he's not on our payroll."

"No, I understand that. I'm thinking of Mr. Cook."

"This is the mortician you spoke to Wendy about?"

"The same."

"She pulled his records for you this morning. They're still—" Leaning back dangerously far in his chair, he turned to look at the filing cabinets in the corner. "No." He swiveled to look at the bank on the other wall. "Ah yes, over there."

Caffery watched him walk to the filing cabinet. There was something odd about Bliss today, something springy in his step suggesting a trampled-down excitement.

"There!" He returned to the desk with a folder and slapped it down triumphantly. "Lucky I didn't file it away again. Now then, let's have a look."

He flipped over a few pages and skimmed the paper with pale eyes, his mouth working noiselessly, occasionally wiping his hands on his jacket. His teeth, Caffery noticed, had a milky deposit at the roots.

"Ah yes—here." He pointed to the page. " 'Any disabilities?' Cook answers 'Yes.' The form says 'Please describe.' " He licked his lips. "And Cook answers 'Achromatopsia.' " Bliss looked up at Caffery and blinked. "That's when you're missing the cones in the retina. He won't be able to see in color."

"And he can't tolerate the sun."

Bliss looked at a point above Caffery's shoulder as if he was trying to recall something. "Are we talking about a man with rather long red hair?"

"That's the one."

"Yes. I've seen him around. I remember the sunglasses. So he's a mortician, is he?" He rubbed his chin thoughtfully and smiled at Caffery. "You deal with so many different people in this job, it's difficult to put a name to every face." From the back of the file he pulled two photocopied forms. "Here's a doctor's report which confirms it. Achromatopsia. Registered partially sighted." He looked up at Caffery. "Ah. That seems to have worried you."

Caffery rubbed his face wearily. "No, no. Not worried. Just made life a little harder." He offered Bliss his hand. "Thank you for your help, Mr. Bliss, we're sorry to put you to trouble."

"No trouble. No trouble." Bliss leaped up and placed his hand in Caffery's. It was warm, slightly moist to the touch. "Don't hesitate if you have more questions. Wendy'll help you if I'm not here. I've got annual leave from tomorrow."

"Thank you," Caffery said dully. "A special occasion?"

"Indeed it is." Bliss sat down behind his desk and stretched his arms, lacing his hands together and cracking the bones. "My birthday!"

Forty-four

WHEN DI CAFFERY had gone Malcolm Bliss leaned back in his chair and stared at the door for a long time. Though he was newly confident, elated, humming with excitement, sometimes an intermittent, idiopathic anxiety plagued him. DI Caffery's visits didn't improve things. In the grips of such anxiety he found himself furious with Harteveld for putting him here.

"*But then, Harteveld,*" he muttered to himself, "*who else would you have turned to when you found yourself with a well-fucked dead girl on your hands?*"

"You're the only person who can help. The unthinkable has happened."

It was December when Harteveld had come, in the early hours of the morning, backing the Cobra into the carport and showing Bliss the human-sized chrysalis in the boot. A fat girl.

"Scottish. She's from Glasgow, I believe."

Wrapped from head to foot in cling film.

"It was all I could find to put her in. I don't want traces in the car."

"Have you fucked her?"

Money changed hands, the woman-chrysalis was placed on his bed. Harteveld pressed Bliss's hands, he squirmed at the touch, *hideous*.

"You're the only one who would understand." Harteveld was twitching. "I know you can deal with it, because frankly, I'm afraid I can't."

After Harteveld had gone Bliss closed the door and paced the flat, chewing the inside of his mouth, drinking cherry brandy. He talked to himself for a while, in senseless, protracted sentences.

She was in the bedroom, facedown where Harteveld had thrown her, her hands folded against her belly, her face smeared and flattened under the cling film. He liked the cling film, liked the way it held her. Even alive she would have been unable to struggle. Licking his lips, a faint scum of perspiration on his forehead, Bliss crossed to the bed and started unwrapping her, unfolding her arms, turning her over, inspecting her.

She had a tattoo on her forearm. The lividity was faint on her front, the majority of the blood had sunk down to the backs of her thighs, her buttocks and shoulders. Harteveld must have kept her lying on her back for some time.

"That's right. You put your feet up." He jabbed a finger into the pitted thigh and smiled. "You big-titted sow."

A fountain of exhilaration lifted from the pit of his stomach. This reminded him of UMDS, the first delighted realization that the dead cannot object to being poked, prodded, insulted, spat on and fucked. He could jism on her face, in her mouth, in her hair. There was nothing she would say no to. A big juicy-mouthed doll for his use alone.

But then, with a shudder, it occurred to him that she had already been used—Harteveld would have done all of those things to her already. There might be traces of him left. He hurried into the bathroom for a bowl, a tablet of Wright's coal tar soap and a face flannel. Joni's photograph, photocopied a hundred times and pinned to the walls, smiled at him.

He ran water into the chipped enamel bowl and swilled the flannel around. The zebra finches in their cage skeetered across the perch, banging into each other, shaking their feathers. Joni gazed at him, making him shift uncomfortably, scratch his neck, all those little eyeballs staring—

And then the idea of what to do with the body slowly took shape.

Back in the bedroom he washed the girl, formulating his plan, carefully opening her legs and squeezing water into her, allowing it to trickle out onto a towel under her buttocks. He repeated it time after time until he could be quite certain that anything left of Harteveld was gone. He wanted her clean, new for him.

It was dawn when he finished, he was due at the hospital at 9:00 A.M. Lola Velinor, his boss, was a stickler for time-keeping. Somehow he'd reward Velinor for her rigidity. He didn't know how yet, but he would pay her back. Sweating, in spite of the December chill, he bundled the corpse headfirst into the chest freezer, folded her legs in after her and went to work.

Over the years in personnel he had made sure he had access to every cupboard, every office, every nurse's station. He knew St. Dunstan's inside out and soon found what he wanted: suture material, a pair of Halsted mosquito artery forceps, a surgical needle and a scalpel. In Lewisharn he bought a wig, makeup, a set of brushes and a finely balanced pair of Wilkinson's scissors.

Back at home he changed into surgical scrubs, took the girl from the freezer and placed her in the bath to defrost while he busied himself preparing. By 8:30 she was ready: on his bed, the wig in place, the makeup on, bloodied fat and tissue from the breasts removed in a Tupperware container and flushed down the drain with steaming water and a helping of dishwashing liquid. He'd seen the procedure in books in the library and thought he'd done it rather well. The blue stitches did nothing to improve the appearance of her breasts, but better that than the big, fleshy cow's tits: they reminded him of Joni's deliberate destruction of her body, the one he'd so nearly possessed, so honestly, in the car that night.

The last touch—truly inspired—was the bird. If one opened the thorax (the incision didn't need to be as long as a classic TA) and sliced through the fleshy fan-shaped pectoralis major muscle and gently lifted up the sternocostal flap underneath, the marbled bones in their filmy visceral pouch revealed themselves. Just like a side of beef. Just like the bodies at med school.

The bird struggled as he slipped it inside—for a moment he thought it might free itself, flap around the ceiling spraying foul matter on him—but he leaned in, pressed the skin closed and hurriedly sewed the wound closed.

He put his ear to the cold breast.

The bird fluttered weakly. Just like Joni's whispering heartbeat that night.

Then he fucked her, twice, holding on to her cold shoulders, breathing sour breath into her purple face. And in the end it was, if not perfect, at least better than his own soft hand.

"Bitch," he told her afterward, flinging the condom onto the carpet. "Bitch." She was cold, solid as a joint of pork on the bone. She couldn't talk back. He slapped her face, and the wig slid backward, revealing her thick tabby hairline. "Bitch."

In spite of his attempts to keep the body frozen when he wasn't using it, it soon became putrid. He bundled it into two dustbin liners, took a gardening spade from the carport and drove out to where the A2 started. He knew this route well, it was the route he took every weekend—to the Kent bungalow left to him in his mother's will. There was a patch of scrubby forgotten land there, in the shadow of the new Dome. It was lonely in the daytime, deserted at night. He found a place that was undisturbed and did what he had to do.

Weeks later Harteveld came to him again, with his tight upperclass expression and Gucci suit, another whitened creature wrapped in cling film in his car.

After the body was safe inside the flat—Frobisher's bedroom light had not come on—Harteveld sat on the edge of the sofa, his perfect hands folded on his knees.

"The pub you go to, Bliss."

"Yeah." He scratched a patch of flaky skin on his forehead. "The Dog. What about it?"

"Most of the girls in there wouldn't be missed. Not for a day or two." Harteveld's brow was slick with perspiration. "Would they? It would be a day or so before anyone noticed they were gone."

"What are you saying?"

"You're a familiar face. No one would be surprised if you asked a few questions, got to know some of the girls. Found out which ones were safe. You could—uh . . ." He shifted unhappily. There had always been something uncomfortable about Harteveld. "You could send them to me."

And so Malcolm Bliss and Toby Harteveld entered into a diabolical pact, an arrangement which suited them both; Harteveld was never seen in the pub and Bliss, who over the years had become as transparent and unremarkable as a shadow to the patrons of the Dog and Bell, was able to discover which women had the most fragile connections at home, which were least likely to be reported missing in the first few days. In return he received payment and the full use of the women's bodies later. Moreover he was in a position to prevent Joni from becoming embroiled.

Gradually he became bold. He tried to persuade Harteveld to deliver the bodies to him at Wildacre Cottage, his mother's bungalow. It was the ideal venue—quiet, isolated: tailor-made for his purposes. But Harteveld refused—wanting to minimize the time spent transporting his cargo—he made it clear who was the master and who the running dog. Nor did Bliss

want to risk the forty-minute journey, so he acquiesced—
taking his enjoyment as quietly as he could, in the shuttered,
overheated Brazil Street flat.

His time would come. His confidence was growing.

He started to take other risks. He had stood one of the
last bodies in the living room for a day. Rigor had frozen her
there, propped up next to the TV set, stark naked like a show-
room dummy, so he could masturbate looking at her. When
the rigor wore off she had collapsed violently on the floor,
waking him from his sleep in the other room. Her stomach
had split and he'd had to get rid of her. Experience was telling
him when the bodies would start to smell too strongly.

His most delicious pleasure was to leave someone propped
up in his bed while he popped out to the Dog for a leisurely
drink. Sometimes he saw Joni, and when he did he smiled
gracefully. The man, the pub. He was like the other punters
now: out being part of the game, watching strange women
open their legs, in the warm knowledge that his stiff little wife
was at home, waiting for him and his new wet lust.

He was happy. As powerful as an eagle. Nightly he was
possessing a simulacrum of Joni. And slowly he saw that possessing her was weakening her. Something in his sense of her
began to erode. It became less important for her to come to
him. There are, Malcolm, *hundreds* of ways to skin a cat. He
stopped bothering about cleaning the house.

With the police involvement he had to change venue: he
left the last of Harteveld's leftovers for Lola Velinor to find.
It seemed appropriate to give the mulatta to the mulatta, he
told himself, like to like, a people cares for its own. He was
proud of the neatness. And now that Harteveld was dead he
was in complete control.

He drove to a hardware hypermarket, his heart bound-
ing along with excitement. The cordless drills and saws were
displayed on hooks—shiny in their plastic casing. He spent
an hour wandering up and down the aisle, assessing each one

in detail, eventually choosing the Black & Decker Versapak, 7.2-volt, 2,700-no-load-strokes-per-minute cordless power saw. It was designed for excising small pieces of wood, used a rechargeable battery locked in the handle, weighed less than seven pounds, measured only twelve inches from the handle piece to the tip of the blade and fit perfectly into the glove compartment of the Peugeot. At home he put a ham hock in the kitchen sink and practiced on it, slicing it neatly with a squeeze of the trigger.

Armed with his new friend he promoted himself to a live hunt. He had been watching her for a few days and she proved to be far better than the others. She was warm. She bled and thrashed—particularly when he'd used the clumsy aneurysm needle to sew her up. Her heart shunted along in her chest when he put his ear to her breastbone and Bliss wondered why he had waited so long to start hunting for himself.

Now he knew he was ready. Joni. *Joni.*

Only one day to go . . .

Malcolm Bliss stood, smoothing thinning hair over his scalp. It had been a stressful morning; he deserved a drink. He returned Cook's file to the cabinet, found his jacket and left the office.

Forty-five

THE WOMAN behind the bar always nodded, said hello to him. She was a dried-up old object, her face wasn't worth putting makeup on, but she always speckled it with carnival colors. Sometimes he forced himself to respond, but one day last week he'd been here early and spotted her talking to Detective Inspector Caffery. Bliss, standing at the bar, warm and agitated, decided that for her lapse of judgment the barmaid deserved to be ignored today. He took his drink into the lounge.

Joni would be here soon, and in spite of his excitement he was determined to remain dignified. With all the time he had spent here, tense and aching because Joni was rubbing her raw artificial teats in someone else's face, he had come to understand and master the behavior required of a pub drinker. So Harteveld's request for information about the women was an easy one. Bliss never made a move, just bought drinks and listened. So innocuous he was, the girls looked straight through him as if he were a ghost, and prattled out all their precious secrets, until he knew everything from how bad PMS was to how soon they'd be missed.

They'd have laughed if he'd made a pass at them or tried to squeeze their little thighs. So he kept still, waiting for the day when the girls would come to him, far sweeter in death than they had ever been in life.

Light streamed into the pub from an opened door. *Joni.* Aroused, Bliss raised slightly off his hindquarters, tasting the back of his teeth with his tongue. Then he saw, a footstep behind, the friend. He subsided, anger rising. He didn't like Joni's friend. She was a high-minded bitch, loftily referring to herself as "an artist," swanning around painting the girls in the pubs as if she could elevate them through art. And the punters too; he himself had been painted by her several times. But *he* remembered back to when she'd been one of the girls. Then her name was Pinky. *"Probably because of the way your clitoris pokes out from your hairy patch,"* he had whispered to himself. Pinky the Clitoris. He picked at a piece of dried skin on his nose and watched her thoughtfully. She headed straight to the bar, nose in the air, not bothering to acknowledge him.

Joni approached—bored-looking. He smiled, folded his hands sweetly in his lap. "Hello, Joni."

She sighed resignedly. "Hello, Malcolm. Thought you'd be here. Nothing changes, does it?" She dropped her belongings on the floor and slumped down on the padded bench a couple of feet from him, her bottom pushed to the edge of the seat, feet stuck straight out in front of her. She was wearing knee-high leather boots and a suede skirt which stopped midthigh. Her blond hair, pinned with two sweetheart clips above her brow, was cut in the way that all the girls on the streets seemed to be wearing it. Bliss didn't like it. It irritated him that Joni had a mania for fixing what wasn't broken, such an impulse for change.

He forced himself to smile. "A drink, Joni?"

"S'pose." She looked at her fingernails, her bottom lip sticking out. Joni had a fine way of behaving like a child. She hadn't grown out of it in all the years he'd known her. It wasn't cute anymore—he should tell her that. Tell her it wasn't cute—tell her it pissed him off more than he could contain. "Wine, I s'pose."

At the bar the artist waited to be served with her head held back, like a horse on a tight rein. Too good for this place. He approached, smiling politely, thinking of her clitoris. "Good afternoon."

She gave him a funny look—"Good afternoon"—and picking up the two glasses, turned away. Bliss smiled to himself. Bitch. He took the drink from the creature behind the bar and carefully wiped the sides of Joni's glass where it had been touched.

Joni didn't acknowledge him when he put her drink down, but he didn't mind. He'd become used to this.

"Are you both well, girls?" he asked politely. In his excitement his mouth had filled with saliva and he had to talk carefully to stop it from spilling out. "The world treating you well, is it?"

"No, it is *not*." Joni pressed her lips into a pout. "Some woman got pulled off the street just round the corner from us."

"Oh dear." Bliss sipped his lager. "Do they know who it was?"

"No." Giving him a dirty look, she jerked to her feet, impatiently threw her belongings over her shoulder, downed both drinks and headed up the stairs with a toss of her blond head.

Bliss and the Clitoris sat in silence. She sipped her beer quietly, a red flush creeping up her face. He let the silence settle around them before he spoke.

"Well, I must say I've never seen Joni quite so upset."

The Clitoris nodded. "She's worried." She spoke to her drink, not to him, the way most people did. "Says she's thinking of getting out of Greenwich. She wants to leave."

Bliss felt the skin on every inch of his body prickle. He let the tightness in his stomach and cock slacken before he spoke. "Does she, now?" he said, letting his gaze wander up the stairs. "I wonder where she'll go."

Forty-six

BACK AT SHRIVEMOOR Caffery couldn't relax. He wandered around the incident room turning over scraps of paper, stared at the whiteboards, stood behind the indexer girls and watched the screens over their shoulders, until Marilyn complained that he was making her jumpy. He went into the SIO's room and called Jane Amedure.

"Did you get anywhere with that cement?"

"The diffractogram's gone off to Maryland. We could know by the morning."

Then he pulled out the personnel fax that Bliss had sent from St. Dunstan's last week, scanned it, hoping something would catch the light, glint at him—and when nothing did he sat with his head in his hands until it grew dark outside, the offices were almost empty and Maddox looked in on him, jacket on, briefcase in his hand.

"This is all very noble but, a bit of realism, eh? I know I cracked the whip this morning but I didn't mean kill yourself."

"Yeah, okay, okay."

"You get some sleep, you hear?"

"I will."

He called Dr. Amedure again.

"Give them some breathing space, Inspector Caffery. I promise I'll call you first thing in the morning. We're closing shop now."

So he sat in the deserted offices, the building hollow and quiet around him, smoking out of the window and watching the world come home at the end of a long day. The watery sun dropped behind neat houses, a new poster was going up on the billboard opposite. He had been so swift to put Cook in the frame—so confident of his instincts—finding he had been wrong pressed hard on his nerves. Maddox was right—he should go home—but he was too conscious of Birdman's presence: powerful and almost close enough to touch; a big game fish weaving around his legs.

Over the road the Maiden Signs worker unrolled and pasted, unrolled and pasted, moved the rigging a few feet along and started the process again. The words *Estée Lauder* appeared at the foot of the billboard; above them the gleaming camber of the model's neck. He watched absently, thinking of the hair that had been tangled up in Jackson's. They were assuming it had belonged to another victim—to someone Birdman had not yet finished with, or someone not yet found. Caffery pressed the bridge of his nose lightly, trying to think.

Another explanation?

The color and cut matched the wig hairs so exactly that even Krishnamurthi hadn't noticed the difference. Maybe the hair belonged not to another victim but to the person Birdman was recreating. Maybe that person had been in Birdman's house. Or been close enough for him to take a trophy from her.

You were so focused on Cook that you didn't even stop to consider it.

And something—something . . .

Caffery looked up at the high-gloss face opposite and suddenly he knew.

The metabolite of marijuana in the single blond hair. The aluminum spike on the FSS spectrograph. Joni spraying the room with deodorant, the smell of it always in the flat.

It wasn't seamless. Joni didn't wholly fit the picture: fleshy and tall. That wasn't how he'd pictured Birdman's Galatea. Even so, as he switched off the lamp and found his keys, leaving the fax and papers scattered over the desk, excitement was balling like a fist under his solar plexus.

At 2:00 P.M. the Clitoris had drifted off: taking with her the paints, the drawing board, her snotty attitude—leaving Joni alone to do her second spot in the pub. Bliss knew this girl's mind so well. He knew that once Joni was hooked up to a free drink supply she didn't shake free that easily. The other punters drifted away, headachy into the afternoon, leaving him alone with her, to plug her up with Liebfraumilch.

At 3:30 she was sick on the stairs up to the ladies', and when he brought her back to his flat she was sick again, twice, in the bath.

He pretended he wasn't angry. He cleaned it up, rinsed it away and let her sleep off the lunchtime binge curled up like a big baby—blond and pink, wearing just knickers and a T-shirt—in the spare bedroom so she didn't wake up, see his collection of pictures and make a fuss. Even the construction work on the old schoolhouse failed to disturb her.

How many times had he patiently let Joni do this? he wondered as he sat in the living room picking at a spot on his chin—let her use him as a casual detox base. And never had the sense to do anything about it. How many times had he scrubbed and tidied—cleared the corridor and the bathroom and the living room of his pictures while she slept, and put them safely in a cardboard box, spraying sweet scent around the rooms? Only to have her wake up, pull the Walkman over her ears and stumble off on her way. Ignoring him. Treating him like shit.

And how things had changed now. His life had been re-written. As if he'd looked up one day to find the sun was a different color.

He got up from the sofa and made a pot of tea in the kitchen, piling a plate high with Bakewell tarts. In the bed-room he placed the tray gently on the pillow next to Joni's head. She stirred and put a hand to her face.

"Wake up. There's some tea for you."

She pinched her head forward on her neck and peered out with bloodshot eyes. When she saw him she groaned and dropped her head back on the pillow. "Oh no."

"Have some tea."

"No. I've got to go home." She propped herself up on her elbows and looked blearily around her. "God, Malcolm, I'm sorry but I never meant to end up here."

"Have a Bakewell tart first." His tongue was thick, the t's were muffled.

"No, that's okay."

"I insist."

"No really."

"*I insist!*"

Joni's eyes widened.

"I'm sorry," he mumbled, wiping a dash of saliva from his lips. "I want you to have something to eat. You need the strength. Look at you." Tongue between his teeth, he reached out and palpated her stomach. "All skin and bones."

It was meant to be a tender gesture, but Joni reacted badly, shooting back against the wall. "Get off!"

"But, Joni."

"Leave me alone, Malcolm."

"Just let me touch—"

"How many times do I have to tell you? *No!*" She scram-bled backward and dropped off the edge of the bed, landing on her feet, but Bliss lunged forward and caught her by the

T-shirt. She swung around and grabbed his hands, trying to pry his fingers away with her sharp little nails.

"Get off me."

"Joni."

"Get the fuck—" She pulled his hands up to her mouth and bit, scraping a tear in his thumb knuckle. "Get the fuck away from me."

"Don't do this, Joni." His fingers were covered with a mixture of saliva and blood. He bent at the waist, screwed his eyes up and held tight: Joni lost her balance and fell, smashing her shoulder hard against the skirting board.

He let go and stood back, gaping.

They stared at each other, speechless, shocked that it had crossed into violence. Joni was on her back, the T-shirt riding up over her stomach, the shape of her pubis clearly outlined in the pale pink knickers. She looked like a doll, stunned that she'd been broken so easily. For a moment she seemed to be struggling to breathe.

Bliss stepped forward, his hand out to her. "Joni."

"Get—away—from me. Get the fuck—away from me."

"But I love you."

"Bullshit." She clamped a hand over the injured shoulder and winced.

"Just spend my birthday with me. Tomorrow. That's all I ask. You owe me that, for leaving like you did."

"I didn't leave you. We didn't have anything, you fucking *lunatic*. You weren't my boyfriend."

Bliss gaped at her. "I was *in love* with you."

"In love? We *almost* had sex one night, *almost*, years and years ago, and that was only because I was too frigging drunk to stand up. If I'd been sober I wouldn't have come near you."

"Don't say that."

"You're *rilly* pathetic."

"I gave up everything for you." He stood with his head down, his arms limp at his sides. "I gave up my dream of being a doctor."

"Oh purr-*lease*. You were never going to be a doctor." She started to sit up, grimacing at the pain. "Face it, Malcolm, you're a fucking civil servant and you'll always be one."

"Don't," he whined. "Don't leave me. Please don't."

But she let him stand there and shiver while she got painfully to her feet and limped around the room, finding her boots, zipping them up, wriggling into the suede skirt. "This place is disgusting too." She found an aerosol in her bag and squirted it into the air. "It stinks—it absofuckinglutely *stinks* in here."

With a sob Malcolm fell against the wall and shrank into a ball in the corner, his head in his hands, his body shuddering. "*Please don't leave me.*"

"Come on." Joni's voice was softer now. He heard her come to stand next to him, and saw her foot close to his. "Don't be a baby."

"Don't leave me!" He stroked her suede-covered foot. "Don't go."

"I've got to go. Look, chill, yeah? We can be friends."

"No."

"Malcolm. Come on. I'm going now, yeah, Malcolm?"

But he was faster this time.

In one movement he grabbed her foot and drove it up high, above his head. Joni scrabbled for a hold, her hands slipping off the smooth walls. She slammed into the floor, arms flailing. Quickly Bliss rolled up onto his knees and rammed his elbow into her stomach. A second blow caught her on the side of the face, drawing a fine spurt of blood from her nose. Her face crumpled into unconsciousness.

Caffery paused outside Susan Lister's house. The curtains were drawn and, stapled to the gate, a typed note enclosed in plastic, the ink smudged where dew had crept in.

Members of the press:
My brother and his wife are going through a very difficult
period. Please respect our family's privacy and do not make
this time worse for all of us by pestering us with inquiries. We
have said all we want to say.
Thank you.
T. Lister

He pocketed his car keys, rounded the corner and stood
in the doorway of the junk shop, one hand on the door frame,
the other on the buzzer.

"Yes?" she called into the intercom. "Who is it?"

"DI Caffery. Wonder if you've got a few minutes." He
waited a moment. She didn't reply so he leaned back in. "I
said it's Jack Caffery—"

"Yes, I heard. Wait there. I'll be down in a minute."

It took a long time for her to come to the door. He grew
agitated standing on the doorstep and was about to buzz
again when he heard footsteps on the stairs and the bolts
being pulled back. She was barefoot, wearing a small fluid
dress the color of a tulip.

"Can I come in?"

She didn't answer.

"Rebecca?"

"Yeah," she sighed. "Come on, then." She stepped back
into the hall, allowing him in—closed the door, bolted it and
held her hand toward the staircase. "There's some Fitou I've
just picked up. I expect you'd like some."

Inside, the flat was cool. The shutters were half closed and
a fly lazily circled a fan of brushes upended in a glass jar. "Sit
down—I'll bring it through. Sorry it's such a bloody mess."
She went into the kitchen. Caffery wandered around the studio, looking at the piles of paintings and sketches scattered
around the room. The half-finished painting of Joni still on
the easel. Hair so blond it was near albino.

"Joni not in?" he called.

"Still at the pub."

"What time do you think she'll be back?" He could smell Joni's stale deodorant.

"Who have you come to see, Inspector? Me or Joni?"

"You of course."

In the kitchen Rebecca laughed derisively. "Yeah, sure."

"*Yeah, sure,*" he muttered under his breath, wandering back to the hallway. The bathroom stood opposite, next to it the staircase to Joni's room. To his right the door into the kitchen was closed and on the other side of it he could hear Rebecca washing glasses. He went into the bathroom, locking the door behind him.

It was warm in here. The colors were the hot tropical tones of a holiday brochure—fuchsia-pink towels and aquamarine walls. Black stockings soaked in a bucket in the bath and talcum powder footprints crisscrossed on the bath mat. He switched the tap on full, opened the medicine cabinet and immediately found what he was looking for. Quickly he pulled Rizlas from his pocket, flipped open a paper and folded it around the bristles of a red paddle hairbrush. When he pulled it away four or five silvery hairs came with it. He returned the paper to the little cardboard packet, turned off the tap and went back to the studio.

Rebecca handed him a glass without speaking. She turned away, picked up a stack of paintings from the floor and put them on the table.

"Rebecca?"

"Yes?" She didn't turn to him.

"Did you get my message? Did you hear what I said on the answerphone?"

At first she didn't reply. She pretended to be absorbed with dividing the pile into smaller stacks. Then suddenly she put the paintings down. Her shoulders sagged and she leaned forward on the table. "Yes," she muttered, shaking her head. "Yes, I'm sorry. It's all over the papers too. They're saying—well, they're *suggesting* that that woman in Malpens Street . . ." She waved her hand vaguely in the air, trying to make light of it. "God, they just *love* sensationalizing."

"I meant what I said. You need to be careful."

She paused. Turned slowly to him. Folded her arms, leaned back against the table and looked at him with her head on one side. "He *is* dead, isn't he? Toby? There wasn't a mistake."

"No mistake."

"Then why exactly?" Her voice was low. "And *who*? Who am I supposed to be being careful of?"

"I'd tell you if I knew." When he saw her expression he sighed. "Honestly, Rebecca, I'd tell you. There's not one of us knows for sure what is going on."

"Oh God." She shivered slightly. "I'm so tired. I'm so fed up with being scared all the time. Sick of living in a greenhouse because I can't open a window." She turned back to the table and began sorting the paintings again. "Galleries keep calling. My work's selling out—flying off the walls. They're asking for more and more, and now even *Time Out* wants an interview. *Time Out,* for Christ's sakes. And you know why, don't you?" She didn't look at him and he knew she wasn't waiting for an answer. "Because of the sterling quality of my work? Because I'm the next Sarah Lucas? Because I've added a new word to the lexicon of artistic interpretation?" She shook her head. "No, duh. None of the above. They're only interested because of *him*. Ghouls—the fucking lot of them, a bunch of ghouls. And you think I'm going to get morals over it? No way. No way. I'm as bad as the next. Every intention of exploiting it. I suppose I should be thrilled that it's not all over yet."

As she talked herself through her anxiety, Jack's own tension began to fade. The other doors in London had closed themselves to him for the night—he'd be at the FSS when it opened in the morning, but for now there was nothing left to do. Time to put a full stop at the end of his day. He sipped the wine and let Rebecca talk.

Bliss had recovered from the struggle. He spent the evening waiting for Joni to regain consciousness, twice going into the bathroom to relieve himself, ejaculating into a condom. He congratulated himself on his prudence—he wanted to wait for Joni until she was properly prepared.

It was 10:00 P.M. when he went into the bedroom to get started. He placed his hands under her bottom and, bending at the knees, to save his back, lifted her onto the bed. She dropped down, limp and dry, and now he saw he'd done something bad to her left eye. Even through all the swelling he could see something was wrong. He placed a hand on either side of her face and bent in very close to look. It had taken on an unnatural bulge, and the iris was pointing downward. He prodded the eye experimentally. He'd have to look this up in one of his books later. For now he moistened his finger with spit and tenderly cleaned the dried blood from the side of her nose.

Then he unzipped her boots and placed them carefully in the corner. He pulled off the suede skirt and cut the T-shirt off, letting the big, swollen breasts droop outward.

Experimentally he squeezed one engorged nipple. He had wondered how these new, unnatural things would feel; surprisingly they were quite warm: grained and springy to the touch. He pinched the right nipple between thumb and forefinger and lifted the whole breast, stretching it as far as it would go, a full six inches above her ribs, fascinated by the warm pliancy of the flesh and silicone. "Mmmm." He leaned in and inspected the slightly raised, shiny scar where they cut her to put the silicone in. Good. There would be no need to do too much cutting.

*   *   *

"So . . ." Rebecca had finished sorting the paintings. She was calmer now. She ferreted under the paper and paints and found the corner of a frame, laid it over one of the sketches and squinted at the effect. "Veronica, isn't it?"

Caffery looked up. "Sorry?"

"Veronica. She lives with you?"

"Oh God." He shook his head and leaned against the doorjamb "Yes, yes. I suppose she thought she did."

"What went wrong?"

"Really?"

"Really."

"Me." He smiled. "It was me. I'm a human failure, y'know."

"Mmmm." She was silent for a while, watching him. "It doesn't show."

"You can't tell from looking; it's not visible to the naked eye. But it's there."

"What?"

"An obsession."

"Ah. A woman." She turned back to the painting. "Then I can't blame Veronica."

"No. Not a woman."

"Then it must be Ewan, I suppose."

"Yes—I—" He was taken aback to hear Ewan's name spoken by someone else. "You remember his name."

"Did you think I wouldn't?"

"I thought you wouldn't."

"Well, I did." She put down the frame and began stacking the paintings in small piles, placing them at the end of the table. "And I'm sorry to disappoint you but personally I think it's all crap."

"I'm sorry?"

"It's a crap excuse for not living your life, isn't it? The past. I mean I don't know exactly what happened, but I do know this: by now, being a big grown-up adult and stuff, you're supposed to have let it go—moved on." She dropped the last pile of paintings and turned to him. "Don't you read your American poets? 'Let the dead Past bury its dead' and all that gab."

Caffery stared at her, the glass halfway to his mouth. He didn't answer.

"Oh shit," she sighed, seeing his expression. "I'm so rude to you, aren't I?" She opened her hands and looked around the room as if her own behavior was a mystery, as if the explanation might be tacked up on the wall. "It's like a compulsion. I mean don't you think I was rude not answering that call, for example? And hanging up on you. Don't you think that was unnecessarily rude of me?"

"Yes," he said. "You were rude." He lowered the glass and thought about this for a moment. Then he said, "Did I deserve it?"

Her face softened. "Yes." She smiled. "Yes, you deserved it."

Jack nodded and sighed. "Thought so."

Bliss got irritated when he couldn't lift Joni's hips to remove her knickers, and gave in to his temper again, pushing her roughly onto her side and holding her there with all his force. Then he slipped a pair of his underpants between her teeth, taped over them and sat back down on the bed to look at her.

The Greenwich woman had been tied up here, for almost twenty-four hours. When he'd come to remove the packing tape gag, to replace it where it was becoming soft with saliva, she'd begged him to let her use the toilet. He'd refused and she'd begun crying.

"Please let me go. Please."

But he'd shaken his head, replaced the gag and watched her coolly, until, in tears, she had wet herself. He'd beaten her for it, but dutifully cleaned up the mess. There was blood in it. He believed it meant that her kidneys were struggling with the infection.

"Now." He glanced at his watch. "It's ten-thirty, Joni. I'll be coming in to prep you at eleven. Until then just relax."

Ten forty-five. The studio windows were open, the streetlamps lit the same red as sunset. Passing cars spilled music into the streets. The night and the wine had softened Rebecca; she had unfastened her hair, and her skin was brilliant in the half-light. She sat facing him, not speaking. They'd talked themselves to a standstill long ago—nothing more to say except what was really on their minds.

It was Jack who eventually broke the silence. "I should go," he said, but didn't move.

Rebecca sipped her wine and said nothing.

"It's getting late, I've got an early start tomorrow." He let the sentence hang, waiting for her to respond. "So I should go."

"Yes," she said eventually, putting her glass down. "Yes of course."

They walked down the stairs, Rebecca leading. From two steps above he could see the small indents in the flesh of her shoulders where the ribbon straps of her dress had imprinted and slipped. At the front door she stopped—standing an artificial distance away from him—put her hand on the latch, but didn't open the door.

"Well—" She stared at a button on his shirt, not meeting his eyes. "Thanks for the advice."

"That's okay."

Silence again. Her eyes remained fixed on his shirt buttons and Jack instinctively lifted his hand, holding his fingers over his chest. At the movement her mouth opened. She covered her face and turned away.

"Rebecca?"

"God, I'm sorry." Her voice was muffled.

"Rebecca?" He rested his hands lightly on her shoulders, over the straps, conscious of the dents in the hot skin under his palms. "Maybe we should go back upstairs?"

"Yes." She nodded, not looking at him. "I think so."

"Come on, then."

He tried to turn her but she made a small noise in her throat and caught his right hand, pulling it to her mouth, kissing it, sinking her teeth lightly into his palm, sucking each finger in turn. Jack stood quite still, staring at the back of her head, his heart thumping. She rubbed his finger across her lips, lifted her chin, drawing his hand down her neck, over the dress, and suddenly, unexpectedly, an urge kicked off in him—

"Oh Jesus—"

He turned her to face him, gripped the backs of her thighs and lifted her backward—up and back, so she was resting on the cold hall radiator. He pushed the dress up her thighs and she took a sharp breath, leaning blindly toward him, trying to kiss him, her teeth bumping against his, hands fumbling to help him pull her underwear off, not smiling, but concentrating.

Responding.

Her bare feet scrambled for purchase—found the mountain bike propped next to the radiator and got shaky balance, her foot pressed against the wheel—as Jack braced his feet square on the ground and unzipped himself. Through the fanlight headlights swept across the ceiling, the light shifting on Rebecca's face as he moved inside her. Her eyes were closed, she bit her lips—not stopping him but jacking her hips up against his, matching his rhythm. The bike rocked forward, pedals slammed into his calves, bringing blood that he didn't notice. His focus narrowed—speeded and strained—until every atom of energy and anger and need was isolated in this act and he had forgotten how it had started.

"No," she said suddenly, looking at his face. "No—don't come inside me."

"Jesus!" He thrust himself away, back across the hall—out of control—coming onto his shoes, on the floor. For a moment he stared at her in disbelief, then he put his hand over his face and sank onto the bottom stairs, shaking his head. Breathing hard. "Oh God. I'm sorry, I'm sorry."

Rebecca pushed herself off the radiator and dropped onto the stair next to him, chest heaving, sweat-stained hair stuck to her face. The dress was still hiked up to her waist, plastered against her skin, baring the shadowy notch of her navel.

"I'm sorry. I shouldn't've done that."

"No—it's—" She wiped her mouth and looked sideways at him, her face and neck flushed and sore. "Really—I—it's okay. I could've stopped you."

"I should've used something. I've never done that before. I don't usually—"

Suddenly she covered her eyes, shook her head and started laughing.

"What?" His leg, he saw now, was bleeding—a long, inky trail extended into the trousers bunched at his ankles. "What's funny?"

"Is that what you meant? A human failure?" She opened her fingers and peered out at him, still smiling. "Is that what drove Veronica mad?"

"Oh Jesus," he muttered. "I told you, it's never happened before. I mean it."

"Can you prove it?"

"Yes. I can prove it."

"What—right now?"

"Right now."

"No, seriously—*right now?* I mean, are you sure, can you really?"

"Yes." He looked around for something to wipe the floor, his shoes, his leg. "Yes I can. It's one of my party pieces."

"God." Rebecca sighed, dropping her hands from her face and smiling. "This could be love."

At 11:00 he was ready.

In the bedroom Joni was lying very still. He thought she was still unconscious until he approached and saw her one good eye staring up at him, taking in his scrubs, his mask, his cap. It was only when he produced the scalpel that she responded, bucking on the bed, back arching, head snapping from side to side, little noises coming from her throat.

"Calm down." He put a soft, reassuring hand on her shoulder and pressed her down into the mattress. "Calmly does it."

Joni wrenched her head back and snarled at him from behind the gag.

"Bitch," he said softly, and straddled her. "Shut up now, bitch. I've been good with you, but you're pushing me." He shoved her down onto the bed and Joni became very still under his hands, watching him warily with her good eye.

"Good." He tipped back on his heels and wiped the sweat from his face. "Now, listen. I'm not going to kill you." He bent over and, ignoring the shudder that went through her body, gently rested his face against her neck. "I only want it to be like it was that night. Do you understand me?"

He could tell from the single tear that trickled from her cheek onto his forehead that she had accepted that. She stopped struggling. But to be quite certain, he double-taped her torso to the bed, crossing the tape over her hips; he knew from the Greenwich woman that even unconscious the human body responds violently to pain.

He reached for the styptic pencil.

"This won't take long."

Tongue between his teeth, he painstakingly drew a mark just above the old scar where the new incision would be. Joni dragged in desperate shallow breaths through her nose as he spat on the scalpel and wiped it across his tunic.

"Not much to cut through under here, Joni." He grimaced and the soft flesh bloomed up over the blade like cheese, strained, then relented and split long, like a heavy fruit. A muffled keening sound came from the tape mask. Joni's pelvis jerked frantically against the mattress. There was just a thin smatter of blood scattered amongst the freckles on her belly, nothing much. Bliss bent down to squint up into the new wound. Past the bloody yellow fat, he could see the implants squinting at him from their envelope of meat.

"Lucky," he breathed, and patted Joni's knee. "They've been put above the muscle. Just hold on one moment . . ." He bit his lip and slowly inserted his fingers into the hole, creeping it around, inside the breast.

Joni's good eye widened as his index finger hooked around the silicone bag. Her head thrashed side to side.

"Quiet now. Don't twist." His thumb and forefinger closed on the sack. Confident now, he tugged it. "Easy. Easy." Joni's feet scissored, thigh muscles taut as small drums, as the implant slipped out, drawing an eggcupful of fluid with it.

He gently placed it on her stomach.

"There we are. Easy, wasn't it?" He wiped his hands on his scrubs. "Now let's see. One down, one to go."

Forty-seven

SUDDENLY, without warning, the summer turned its back on England and settled complacently over the Iberian Peninsula. Rain came to London yet again. When Caffery woke, Rebecca asleep next to him, he could smell the change in the air, feel the humidity on his skin. He lay there for a moment, his heart speeding, sensations rushing at him, trying to decide what had woken him. Something in the flat? Joni returning? Or just a dream? He listened hard to the silence for a while, until his heart steadied. Rebecca lay on her side, her right arm flung out over the edge of the bed, her left curled up so the hand was lightly touching the shoulder as if posed for a classical sculpture. Her face was turned from him. He raised himself on his elbows to look at her. She was very still. Still and—

Jesus, Jack, don't do that.

He almost laughed. For a moment he'd imagined she was dead. But her small rib cage rose and fell, and when he put his face very close to her breast he could hear the reassuring, almost inaudible whistle of the air in her lungs, the avian fluttering of her heart.

A dying bird.

He sat up abruptly, got out of bed, went into the kitchen and put his face under the tap. He didn't want to think about Birdman, about what he'd done. Not when Rebecca was sleeping next to him.

He straightened, dripping, the image fading. Joni wasn't back. Last night, before he'd taken Rebecca to bed, he had put the chain on the front door. Joni would have had to wake him to get into the flat. Now he put the kettle on, poured a glass of water and drank it quickly, staring at the photographs on the mantelpiece above the freezer.

Some of the pictures showed Rebecca: dressed in paint-splattered dungarees, paintbrush in hand; or bleary-eyed on a rumpled pillow, hand held out in protest to the lens; another was taken on a pebbled beach, Rebecca in shorts, tongue out, cross-eyed under an outsize floppy hat.

He rested the glass on the ledge and picked up a snap of Joni. She was prettier here than he remembered, probably because she didn't appear stoned. She was clear-eyed, staring into the lens, a cigarette in one hand, her mouth open in midsentence, a finger extended toward the camera as if trying to explain something important, to make a point. Her hair was cut bluntly so that it fell to the shoulders, a low fringe skimmed her brows.

Caffery took the photograph to the table and sat, his elbows on either side of it. Joni stared back at him, trying to *make that point*. He ran his finger across the fringe.

The scars on the victims' heads were a perfect circle, from back to front. Kayleigh Hatch's and Susan Lister's white-blond hair had been cut in a fringe. Caffery traced his hand across his own forehead. On the victims the marks were outside the hairline, below it on the forehead. That was not the natural place a wig would sit. It was too low.

Unless—

Unless it had a fringe. Like Joni.

He jolted to his feet, his heart hammering.

Not Joni now but Joni then—before she had the haircut. Before, Jesus of course, before she had the implants. It's the old Joni he wants.

"Becky?" He kissed her neck. "Becky. Wake up."

Rebecca stirred and woke.

Jack. She thought of him last night: in the hallway, and afterward, in her bed when he'd hit his stride—the things he'd done to her. She sleepily reached out of the sheet, searching for his erection. When she realized he had trousers on and was buttoning his shirt she opened her eyes. "Are you going?"

"I've got to."

"What's the matter?"

"Joni didn't come home. D'you know where she got to?"

"Not home?" She rolled onto her side, rubbing her eyes. "Oh, I don't know—she does that sometimes."

He brushed her fringe from her forehead and kissed her cheek. Her hair smelled of baby shampoo. "Rebecca, let me ask you something about her—it's important."

"Mmm?"

"I am right Joni's got implants?"

Catching the note in his voice, she looked up. "Yes. So?"

"This." He held the photograph out. "When was it taken?"

"That's, I don't know, three years old. Why—?"

"And the implants?"

"God." Rebecca blinked at the photo. "I'm not sure, just after I met her, so maybe six years."

"Okay, listen." He stood, ran a hand across the shirt. Trying to smooth out yesterday's creases. "I need the painting. The one on the easel."

"Why?"

"I'll bring it back."

"Take it. I'm sick of the bloody sight of it." She rolled over and propped herself up on her elbows, looking at him with serious eyes. "Jack, you're not thinking . . . ?"

"No, I—" He paused. "Rebecca, don't look at me like that." He pulled on his tie, ran fingers over it, flattening it against his chest. "There's nothing to worry about." He put his arm around her shoulders and kissed her warm head. "Honestly. Just get Joni to give me a call when she comes in. And you—you be careful, okay? I mean that. If you have to go out call me first. Let me know what you're up to."

Afterward Rebecca sat at the kitchen table, sleepily curling her hair around her fingers, staring at Jack's discarded roll-ups in the ashtray, waiting for a stained two-cup espresso maker to boil. The rain rolled in greasy trails down the window. Her throat was sore and tight.

It wouldn't be the first time she hasn't come home. Nothing unusual, absolutely nothing unusual. She just got a bit out of control after I left the pub and wound up at Adrenaline Village or some scuzzy peyote hideout in Camden. Or she slept it off at someone's place and she'll be back tail between her legs.

Then why's Jack so interested all of a sudden?

"Jesus." She stood up, angry at her tinkering imagination, and went into the studio, casting around for something to level her mind. In the street outside vividly colored umbrellas jostled along: pink, violet and yellow. Tropical-sized raindrops bounced off the roof. She pinned new paper to the drawing board and paused.

He took her picture—he thinks she's in trouble ...

Rebecca put down the drawing pins and, leaving the paper dangling from the board, went to the phone in the hall.

Bliss stood in the bedroom doorway looking at Joni, her head lolling on one side, the pale mucus-colored implants leaving bloody stains on her rib cage. She had been unconscious as he sewed her up and he'd left the implants on her belly for her to look at when she woke. He had slept in another room, determined to wait for the birthday. But Mrs. Frobisher had woken him early, even before the construction work, *clunk-clunk-clunking* around upstairs like an old wooden doll.

She made him nervous—always complaining, always ferreting around and sniffing at him. The birthday party would be a safer, more comfortable event at the bungalow, but he couldn't risk the car journey. Not with Joni bloodied and volatile as she was. He took the phone off the hook and started to blow up the balloons.

Caffery's knife-edge sense of urgency was back. Amedure noticed it when she met him in reception and took the folded cigarette paper from his hands.

"Are you all right?"

"I'm fine."

"What's this you're giving me? You need to fill out a submission sheet."

"Can you match it to the hair from the last PM?"

"Probably. But a submission sheet, please, and this needs to be logged back at Shrivemoor."

"I'm on my way now. How long will this take you?"

"Half a day. Less if you're nice to me."

"Any news on the cement? The trade examination?"

"Ah." She smiled. "I know someone who hasn't checked in with his team this morning. The CCRL've got the results. They phoned them all over to Marilyn Kryotos." But he was gone—hurrying down the steps and pulling car keys from his pocket. "I'll fill the HOLab in for you, then," Dr. Amedure murmured to herself, and went back to the lift.

It was still early, but Betty was already at the Dog and Bell. In the background the Alsatian was barking.

"She went with him from the hospital. You know the one that's always dreaming after her. Him that sits in the saloon bar and drinks halves."

"Malcolm, you mean?"

"That's the one."

Thank God.

"He spent all of forty quid in here yesterday lunch. Bought her God knows how many bottles of Blue Nun and after that she was on the Scotch. By three o'clock I don't think she knew her own name. Why does she do it to herself, Pinky? A lovely girl like that? It doesn't make sense."

You see, Rebecca told herself as she put the phone down, *you bloody paranoiac—it's just Joni being Joni.*

Upstairs she found, amongst the tissues and marijuana seeds tangled in Joni's duvet, the black and silver Kookaï organizer—pages battered and scribbled on, love hearts and smiley faces drawn in ice-cream colors. Joni indexed her friends by their first names. Under "M," next to Malcolm's name she had scribbled one of her little sugar-pink faces. Yawning—a string of black Zs stretching out of its mouth.

Bliss's phone was engaged. Jack, too, was talking—the answerphone picked up. Rebecca silently replaced the receiver and sat in the studio, staring at Malcolm's address and phone number, telling herself it could wait, telling herself to leave it, reasoning herself along a tired old circuit, until she couldn't sit still any longer.

She jumped up and went into her bedroom. "Yup," she murmured, pulling on shorts, a T-shirt, brown dock shoes. "That's you, all right. Never leave things alone, can you?"

In the Jaguar, Caffery had punched out Shrivemoor's number on the Nokia and was listening to the ringing tone. He sat at traffic lights, behind a windscreen misted with rain, the phone pressed to his ears, looking absently at the painting next to him on the passenger seat.

In the background stood Joni, up on the stage, hands raised, head bent slightly down, behind her the stage curtains and pub windows, the Young's brewery crest beveled in the glass. And in the middle foreground, lips slightly parted, head turned in profile to the viewer, a face that made Caffery's blood tingle.

He picked up the paper and tilted it to the window. The face—those bad teeth, curiously spaced, like a child between its milk and adult sets—it was all as familiar as his own hands. *I know you, I know you. I know the voice that comes out of your mouth, I've spoken to you, shaken your hand—*

"Hello? Incident room."

He dropped the painting and sat up. "Yeah, Marilyn, hi, Marilyn."

"Jack—my God, Maddox's having an eppy fit about you. You missed the morning meeting, you big prick."

"I know, I know. Apologize for me. And, Marilyn? Did I get a call from the U.S. this morning?"

"I'm your fairy godmother, Jack, don't forget that. I've been working on it while you were still in dreamland."

"And?"

"It doesn't retail in the south and there's only one developer in London using that batch—Korner-Mackelson. I spoke to their chirpy secretary. They've a site down near Belmarsh, one in Canning Town and one in Lewisham."

"*Lewisham?*" He glanced up at the traffic lights. "Okay. Where in Lewisham?"

"Greenwich border—Brazil Street. Off Blackheath Hill. An old school building. They're developing it into lofts."

The lights were changing. Caffery canceled the left signal and swerved in front of a car. Someone leaned on a horn. "Marilyn? You there?"

"As always."

"Tell Maddox for me, will you, tell him I'm running late. I'm about half an hour away. And, Marilyn? Apologize, okay?"

Today Greenwich reminded her of Paris, with the blue-striped awnings pulled down. Cars splashed the legs of pedestrians, shopkeepers stood looking out of the windows, faces lit by the odd, green, tropical light. She cycled fast, as if her sour anxiety could be pumped out like sweat.

In Lewisham the traffic was heavy. She found Brazil Street easily. The construction workers, sheltering under the scaffolding on the old schoolhouse, waved and whistled at her, riding through the rain in her T-shirt and shorts. She propped her bike in number 34A's carport, next to Bliss's Peugeot. The rain was pattering on the corrugated plastic roof as she rang the bell.

"Yes?" He blinked nervously when he opened his front door and found her standing there. "Yes? What do you want?"

"Joni." She wiped the rain from her face and looked past him into the flat. A solitary green balloon floated like a ghost in the passage behind him. "Is she here? I want to talk to J—"

"Yes. I heard you. W-what makes you think she's here? Eh?"

"I don't know. Sometimes she ends up here when she's had a drink."

"Mmm . . ."

"Look—-" She shook her head, exasperated. "Malcolm, it's important. Do you know where she's gone?"

"Now, Pinky." His tongue worked under the fat lips as if he was chewing something. He pulled his cardigan tight, covering the distended stomach. "You *know full well* Joni's got no time for me."

"Okay." She held up her hands and turned away. His self-pity irritated her. "Okay, I'm sorry. If you see her tell her to call me. It's important."

She was kicking down the bicycle pedal when she sensed that Bliss was still watching her from the doorway.

She looked up. "Yes?"

"I—" He glanced apprehensively out into the street. "I didn't say she wasn't here. I didn't *say* that."

Rebecca frowned. "Sorry?"

"You misinterpreted what I *said*." Bliss stepped back from the door and gestured down the hallway. "She's still asleep. Come in and I'll tell her you're here."

Rebecca slowly pushed the bike back against the wall. *My God, Malcolm, you are the crown prince of weirdos. You really are.*

She walked back to the door, shaking her head.

Brazil Street was a leafy, residential road, lined with dripping plum trees. The semidetached Victorian houses boasted driveways and long, shrub-loaded front gardens. Most of them looked prosperous, garages added, drenched in Virginia creeper and honeysuckle, high-quality secondhand cars parked in front. Caffery left the Jaguar at the top of the street and, tenting his jacket above his head, followed the complex diagram of clay tire tracks to the Korner-Mackelson gates.

Inside the gates, two yellow cement mixers stood like guardian lions, either side of the driveway—beyond them a bulldozer, unmanned, rain streaking the mud on its flanks. The site extended a hundred yards beyond, to the corner of the red brick schoolhouse, where it doglegged and continued almost a third of a mile along the end of the gardens.

He wrapped his fingers around the railings and stared at the laborers huddled under the scaffolding, smoking and drinking coffee from Thermos flasks, waiting for the rain to stop. Just being here, close, maybe touching, the hidden vital circuitry that led to Birdman made his pulse speed. With the evidence from FSS it would be easy to get an order to open the company personnel files, Marilyn could cross-match them, see what HOLMES hit—but in this moment, standing here in the rain, Caffery was the closest anyone had been: nose-to-nose.

The temptation, as always, was to take it into his own hands, act now: not to wait and do it by the rule book. But he knew the line he was treading. He pushed himself away from the fence, went directly ro the Jaguar—socks and shirt damp—unlocked the car door, crawled inside, put the key in the ignition, then suddenly, in one fast movement, flung the door back open and jumped out into the street.

He went straight to a green Polo parked behind the Jaguar and stood for a moment, staring at the windscreen. Then he straightened, turned, looking at other cars nearby, jogging over to stare intently at each one: a Volvo, a Corsa, an old Land Rover.

They had all been parked here for much longer than the few short minutes the Jaguar had. On each the rain had etched an intricate mosaic. Cement dust. Floated here from the construction site and stamped on the paintwork by the weather.

Jack ran a finger along the Polo's door rim, examined it for a moment, his mind racing, then turned and stared back down Brazil Street.

Inside, it was dank, the floors sticky. Almost as if he'd had the heating turned up on this, a humid, early summer day. Bliss stood in the hallway, hands splayed, blocking her entrance to the back of the flat.

"No—in here, in here. In the kitchen." He opened the door.

"It's okay. I only want to speak to Joni." She made a move to pass him. "I'm not staying."

But once again he spread his arms. "Yes, yes—just in here—just go in, go in."

Rebecca sighed. *Jesus.* Shook her head and went in. The kitchen was hot, smelled of sour milk. Condensation ran down the window, welling up under a scattering of dead flies on the sill, making them bob and float. Three chairs crowded around a small table—on top of it dirty dishes, a cup of tea, bowls: all covered in a fine ashy dust. More flies buzzed against the ceiling.

Bliss picked up one of the chairs and began fussing with it, poking his finger into the ripped PVC. "No good, is it—a torn seat. Can't have you sitting on it all torn." Dropping the chair, he rummaged in a kitchen drawer. "Here we are." He turned, holding a roll of brown packing tape, picking at it with dirty fingernails, trying to find the beginning. "I always have trouble with these." He held the roll out to her. "Maybe you could—you know. Fingernails."

Rebecca let out an exasperated breath. "Give me it." She snatched it from him, unpicked the end of the tape with her crumbly nails, peeled away an inch and thrust it back at him. "Now—Joni?"

"Okay! Okay!" He quickly pressed the tape across the tear in the seat, stuffed the roll in his trouser pocket and pushed the chair toward her. "I'm going. I'm going!" Hands up in surrender, he hurried out of the room. She saw his crunched little head pass the frosted glass hatch above the sink and was considering following him into the hallway, geeing him up a bit, when his strange fat-lipped face reappeared at the hatch, his hands scrambling at the glass, making her jump.

"Do you—uh—do you mind?" He opened the glass a few inches, pushed his face into the gap and nodded at the table. "Do you mind? I made a mug of tea for her. It's over there. I forgot."

"Is she awake?"

"Yes, yes. But she'll want tea. The tea, please."

She rolled her eyes. *Just spare me this, Malcolm, for God's sake.* And gave him the mug.

He snatched it. "Thank you. And just those biscuits, I'm sorry, just those biscuits if you don't mind." He wiped his hand across his head. "Joni's a fussy little madam."

"For Chrissakes, Malcolm." Rebecca pushed the packet of biscuits at him. "*Will you please just wake her up?*"

"Of course, of course," he said politely, grabbing her wrist and twisting hard.

Forty-eight

THE HOUSE-TO-HOUSE was being organized at Shrivemoor. The incident room smelled of coffee, freshly laundered shirts and aftershave. Kryotos and Essex were with Maddox in the SIO's room when Jack arrived—hair wet, his suit crumpled. Ignoring their faces, he pulled an *A to Z* map from his desk, opened the Lewisham page. The answer was with him shoulder-to-shoulder—as close as his own pulse. He only needed to point the light in the right direction.

Quickly he scribbled down five names. Every street within a hundred-yard-radius of the Brazil Street builder's site. "Marilyn," he said, rising from the chair and holding the paper up. "Run these through HOLMES and give me the hits—"

He stopped.

The St. Dunstan's fax still lay on the desk from last night, the top page crumpled over. The "Bs":

Bastin, Beale, Bennet, Berghassian, Bingham, Bliss, Bowman, Boyle.

"Jack?"

But Jack's face had changed. His eyes were locked on the address under Malcolm Bliss's name: *34A Brazil Street.*

The face in the painting—the bad teeth. Bliss complaining about the construction work when they'd first met in St. Dunstan's. Jesus—*Jesus*.

"Jack. You with us?"

He looked up. Maddox, Essex and Kryotos were staring at him.

"Are you with us?"

"Yes, I . . ."

"I was just saying you can head up the house-to-house today." Maddox crossed his arms. "Cobble together a questionnaire with Marilyn."

"No." Jack ripped the top page off and shoved it into his pocket. "I need one of the team."

Maddox sighed."Go on, then. Take who you want." He jerked his chin at Essex. "*Him*, I suppose."

Bliss wrenched her toward the hatch, across the draining board, her hipbone slamming against the sink. A teapot clattered to the floor: sprayed cold tea on her legs.

"*What the—?*"

"Shut up," he hissed. "Shut up and don't shout."

"*Malcolm!*"

His warm hands clamped around her arm.

"*What the fuck are you doing?*"

"I said shut up."

And then the tape—*the packing tape, the fucking packing tape that I opened for him*—winding around her wrists. She flung her weight against the sink, rammed her other arm through the small hatch. Fumbled for his hands. Found them. Clawed. Hit. But he didn't flinch.

He's strong. The little bastard, strong—you'd never know it to look. He's trapping you—

Now his pink eyes close to hers, hands fumbling to press a length of tape over her mouth. *No!* She whipped her head away, but the tape got a precarious hold and suddenly Bliss was disappearing—off down the corridor.

Jesus. She twisted the hand violently. The tape contracted and dug deeper into her wrists. *What the fuck is he doing?*

A door slammed. The flat became silent.

Rebecca lay across the sink, breathing hard through her nose, slapped into hyperconsciousness. She swiped away the tape on her mouth. Balled it and flung it in the sink. He'd taped her hand to—she reached through the hatch and felt with her free hand—a pipe: her fingers were curled and taped closed around a water pipe. She hiked a knee up on the sink, hoisting her body onto the draining board. Dishes clattered into the sink. The aluminum bent, boomed back into shape as she moved on her knees toward the hatch.

"*Joni!*" She yelled it down the hallway. "*Joni!*"

Silence.

"*Joni!*"

Silence.

Rebecca dropped her head, panting.

Right, come on, calm down and get this straight. What the fuck is he playing at, the little prick? What the fuck does he think he's doing?

The thought came clean and cold. Drove her breath away.

Oh my God no!

She froze—kneeling there on the draining board in her wet clothes, her eyes wide, knees bleeding, not breathing for long seconds, only her pulse thudding.

Don't be ridiculous Becky—not him, not him, surely not.

And why not him? Joni's not even here. He lied. Lied to get you into his flat.

But Malcolm?

Why not *Malcolm?*

And then came the adrenaline, white-hot, pumping along her system, jump-starting her again. She hauled in a breath.

Twisted her hand frantically, tearing at the tape. Ready to pull her own arm off rather than be trapped here.

You big tough streetwise girl—you fucking idiot—you walked straight into this.

"Keep quiet." It was a whisper, in her ear. "Keep your fucking mouth shut or I'll use this."

DI Basset was sitting behind his desk, his feet stretched out, the chair tipped back a little, his hands lightly clasped over his stomach. He'd been here over an hour, gazing out of the window at people shopping on Royal Hill, reaming out dirt from his nails with a paper clip. He was thinking about Susan Lister and her husband. The DCS had given him a lecture that morning about liaising more closely with AMIP.

On his desk the phone rang.

"DI Basset, CID."

"Please. Please do something, Officer. I'm at the end of my tether with this. There's been screaming and yelling now. I'm not imagining it."

Basset let his chair drop. "Hello? Who is this?"

"Violet, Violet Frobisher."

Rebecca whipped around. Panting, eyes wild, teeth bared.

He stood a discreet foot away—just out of reach—his finger up to his swollen lips. He opened his cardigan and, averting his eyes as if what he was showing her was so indelicate he couldn't bring himself to look, pointed downward to his groin. Reluctantly she dropped her eyes. And there, tucked in the waistband of his slacks, resting like a papoose against his hairless stomach, a dark blue cordless power saw.

He stroked it tenderly, sighing as if it were part of his own flesh.

"I remember your clitoris, Pinky. I've seen your little pink clit."

"*Keep away from me.*" She shrank back. The tap dug into her spine, water dripped down her back.

"If you're good, and keep quiet, later on I'll lick your *clitoris* for you." Through gaps between the pegged teeth his wet bulbous tongue was visible. Like a tomcat tasting the air, scenting a female. He held his hand up, stretched taut, the palm to his mouth, stretched his tongue out until the roots showed, and licked his palm, from the base of his wrist to the bottom of his fingers. "Mmmmm. Little pinky *clitoris.*Would you like that?" He smiled, savoring the words. "Pinky clitoris. *Lovely little pinky clitoris.*"

"Fuck you." She wrenched her hand desperately. "Fuck you."

"No!" Bliss slammed his hands on the draining board. "*Fuck you! Bitch!*" He grabbed the saw from his waistband and squeezed it at her face. "Fucking bitch!"

She recoiled, twisting frantically. The tape on her hand stretched and frayed. Then suddenly she was free. The momentum sent her tumbling off the sink, Bliss shadowing her. She hadn't even caught her balance when the heavy battery handle of the saw came down hard on the back of her neck.

Caffery slowed the Jaguar to a crawl. They crept along Brazil Street.

10, 12, 14.

Past the gates to the schoolhouse. The rain had eased and the bulldozer was moving now, up and down the tracks.

28, 30, 32, 34.

34.

It had been double-glazed and pebble-dashed; graying lace curtains hung in the top windows. There was no front lawn, the driveway had been extended and an ugly carport tacked onto the side. Empty.

"I know him," Essex said as Caffery let the car roll past. A bottle-green Rover was parked in the driveway, half hidden by the low brick wall, and a tall, graying man in a dark suit stepped out, looked into the carport and straightened his tie. Caffery pulled the Jaguar into the curb.

"That's DI Basset. Greenwich CID. Come on."

They hurried back down the street, pulling on their jackets, stopping in the next-door driveway, out of view of the lower windows. Basset had his hands in his pockets and was looking in the window of the ground-floor flat. When he noticed Essex gesticulating from the neighbor's front garden he looked puzzled. Then alarmed.

He hurried over to them. "Jesus H. Christ," he hissed. "I'm not treading on anyone's toes here, am I? I should have checked with you, but it was starting to look as if you weren't going to get to her, and she was driving me nuts over the phone."

"Slow down," Caffery whispered, plucking his sleeve and drawing him farther behind the fence. "Now, what're you saying?"

"It's Frobisher, the one I told you about."

Caffery and Essex exchanged a look. "The one you told us about?"

"Yeah, you know, the one with the neighbor."

"I've lost the plot here," Essex whispered.

"I called you. Remember? Left a message with a Dl, said you ought to check it out? I didn't hear so I just assumed—" He shifted uncomfortably, looking from Caffery to Essex and back again. "Rule number one, eh? Never assume. I take it you know nothing about Mrs. Frobisher and her neighbor? The smells? The leaking freezer?" He stood on tiptoe and shot a look over the fence. "Dead birds in the dustbins and now someone screaming in the flat?"

Caffery closed his eyes and put his hand to his head. "We've got a suspect in 34A. That's this house."

"Frobisher is 34B. His upstairs neighbor."

"And you told our DI—*when*?"

"About a week back. About the time the press were breaking the Harteveld story."

"Fuck." Caffery looked at Essex, who was staring at his shoes.

"Diamond," he said.

"The same," Caffery sighed. "Okay." He straightened up. "What have we got? Have you spoken to anyone in there?"

"No one in."

"You've been in?"

"No, Mrs. Frobisher called about twenty minutes ago, knickers in a twist, said she'd heard screaming. Poor old cow's frightened out of her wits. Didn't want to bother us again because she thought—"

"She thought we were dealing with it?"

"Yes." Basset looked embarrassed. "Shit, y'know the CS's going to love this."

"I'm sorry."

"Can't be helped. Can't be helped." A noise from the house. Basset leaned around the dividing fence and beckoned them to follow. The front door had opened and Mrs. Frobisher stood on the doorstep wearing a blue quilted dress and men's carpet slippers. A tortoiseshell cat weaved around her ankles.

"Mrs. Frobisher." Basset approached, his hand outstretched. "Nice to see you." For a moment she only blinked at his hand, then placed hers in it, looking over his shoulder at Caffery and Essex. "I'm sorry, meet my colleagues. DI Caffery and DS Essex."

She nodded at the two solemn-faced men. "I was making some tea."

"Lovely," Essex said, stepping inside.

The flat was clean but cluttered, magazines piled in corners, a faint smell of food underlying the scent of pine air freshener. The men sat in an annex to the kitchen, on threadbare armchairs, looking at Mrs. Frobisher's rambling collection of ornaments: stuffed toys, a selection of service station mugs, photos of Gregory Peck clipped from magazines and mounted in faux silver frames.

In her kitchen Mrs. Frobisher talked to herself as she matched Blue Geranium cups with striped saucers. She found a crocheted pink tea cozy and opened a packet of custard creams.

"It was yesterday afternoon, about fourish because I'd been watching *Judge Judy* and had just made a cup of tea." She put the tray down. The cat was under the table, its paws placed neatly side by side, eyes closed complacently. "I called Tippy and she was just having a saucer of milk, and then I heard a commotion. He was outside, with a young lady."

"What did she look like, the young lady?"

"They all look the same to me. Blonde. Skirt up to here. Very tiddly, stumbling around in the front. She had a turn on the driveway and he had to carry her inside. Well, I didn't hear hide nor hair of her after that. Didn't think no more of it. Not until this morning, then all of a sudden I heard—" The teacup she was holding trembled slightly. "I heard her screaming. Curdle your blood a sound like that."

"Do you have a key to downstairs?"

"Oh no. He doesn't rent from me. But—"

"Yes?"

"I noticed he left a window open, he was in that much of a hurry to get out."

"Any idea where he's gone?"

"He's got another place, I know that. Somewhere in the country, I believe. Maybe he's gone there. He took the car." She looked at DI Basset. "You said to look at the name of his car."

"And did you?"

She nodded. "A Peugeot. I should have known, my daughter-in-law drives one."

*   *   *

Essex got in through the casement window while Caffery waited outside, in the carport, thinking how sheltered this was, how easy it would be to back a car up to the doorway, open the boot and—

"Jack." Essex opened the door. His face was white. "It's him. We've found him."

Forty-nine

INSIDE THE FLAT, the rooms were dark, the curtains drawn tight, the air sour. They had borrowed plastic freezer bags from Mrs. Frobisher to wear over their shoes and each step peeled flakes of dried matter from the sticky carpets.

"Look at this." Essex stood in the doorway of the main bedroom. "Can you believe it?" Across every inch of the walls photographs had been pasted: Polaroids, snapshots, some torn from magazines. Many were of Joni, but others were taken from Dutch or German porn magazines: showing a child sucking an engorged penis, a woman straddling an Alsatian and in a blurred still, from what looked to Caffery like a snuff movie, an Asian teenage boy strained on a bed, arms and feet tied apart, blood on his thighs.

From a fitted melamine wardrobe came the faint flutter of wings. Essex opened it and the two men stared speechless at the cage. A solitary zebra finch on its perch, feathers wet and clumped. It crouched there blinking silently at them. On the floor, amongst the grit, huddled four corpses, interleaved with maggots.

They moved through the rooms. Essex took a look inside the living room at what was taped to the walls and turned back to Jack—his face white.

"Sick," he murmured. "This man is sick."

Polaroids of the victims in death.

Craw, Wilcox, Hatch, Spacek, Jackson. Raped, mutilated. One showed Shellene Craw wedged in a standing position, like a shop-window mannequin, between the television set and the wall, her eyes open, arms sticking out stiffly.

"The wig," Caffery whispered, nodding at the Polaroid.

Essex came and stood behind him, giving a whistle through his teeth. "You were right, Jack. You were spot-on right."

On the far wall they came face-to-face with a Polaroid of Susan Lister, naked and blood-streaked, bound and gagged, her eyes blackened and swollen.

"Oh, for fuck's sake."

Blurred arcs across the photograph, across her face. A white shape in the bottom corner. Caffery understood. Bliss had photographed himself ejaculating over Susan Lister's broken face.

In the kitchen they found fresh blood on the draining board. Smashed plates on the floor. They inspected the freezer, the array of surgical tools in one of the drawers. In the second bedroom Caffery put his hand on Essex's arm. "Look."

Above the bed a fine spray of blood fanned across the wall like an ornamental headboard. The sheets were blood-stained, and in the center of the mattress a yellowing towel curled around two jellied shapes. "What are they?" Essex approached, cautious. "They're like—"

"I know what they are." Caffery stood and looked at the two implants, the little plug on the underside of one congealed with drying blood and fat. "Joni. He cut them out of her."

*   *   *

The world was dry by the time the blue Peugeot reached Wildacre Cottage. The bungalow lay at the end of an easement which bisected a field of corn, long and mellow and flat, like a blonde girl's wet hair. It was secluded—there was no danger of being observed as he dragged the women, pillowcases over their heads, into the dark bungalow and propped them up in the hallway, against the frosted glass panel at the side of the door.

When the Clitoris had started screaming Bliss's nerves got the better of him. He knew he had to risk the journey. Loading them had been relatively easy—one in the well beneath the backseat and the other in the boot. Covered with anoraks and an old sleeping bag. Though he was agitated, glancing up the street, expecting the police any minute—in practice, on this watery midweek lunchtime, there had been few people interested in stopping to watch an unremarkable-looking man load his car.

The shelter of the carport had helped. That and the fact that both women had been beaten into unconsciousness with the battery end of the power saw.

He went back to the car and took four Sainsbury's carrier bags from the boot, carrying them into the house, the screen door clattering behind him. He muttered to the two women as he unpacked the bags, filled bowls with M&M's and Wine Gums, hung paper chains in the windows and blew up pastel-colored balloons. Telling them this was his birthday, explaining to them his plans for the day. Neither one could hear him but he mumbled on anyway, scratching at his face.

When Essex came out of the flat the rain had stopped. He went into the garden where the cranes of the construction site were outlined against the clearing sky and found Jack standing in the middle of the lawn staring at something in the long grass.

"Jack?"

He didn't respond.

"Jack? What's up?"

Caffery looked around, his eyes blank. Silently he gestured to what lay on the ground.

"What is it?" Essex approached. At Jack's feet, in the wet grass, a bicycle. Painted white and gray. On its side as if it had been thrown there. "A bicycle?"

"Rebecca's," Caffery said quietly. "It's Rebecca's."

He called her flat on the way back to the car. The answerphone picked up. He left a message and called Shrivemoor.

Marilyn answered. "Jack, good. I've just had Amedure on. That hair—it's a match. She wants you to—"

"Marilyn, listen to me. Tell Steve we're onto something—I need the TSG with us. And a forensic search—Quinn, Logan. We're in Brazil Street, PL."

"Okay, okay—hang on." He heard her murmuring to someone. Then Maddox on the line.

"Jack? Where are you?"

"Lewisham. Brazil Street."

"What number Brazil Street?"

"Thirty-four A."

Maddox was silent for a moment. In the background someone was shouting excitedly. Maddox cleared his throat. "Jack, we've got a hit on that address. We've seen it before. Harteveld's phone bill. He dialed someone at 34A Brazil Street twice the morning after Craw went missing and twice the week he topped himself. Logan and Betts are on their way over now."

"It's him, Steve."

"What've you got?"

"Photos, surgical gear, scalpels. The name is Malcolm Bliss. He's running scared. A blue Peugeot. He's got someone with him."

"Oh God." Maddox sounded weary.

"I think he's heading out to the country somewhere. I'll have an address in about ten. I want Territorial Support with us."

"Okay. Marilyn'll get onto op commands. So a briefing at Greenwich in what, thirty minutes?"

"Make it twenty."

Fifty

CAFFERY AND ESSEX were surprised to find Lola Velinor, her handsome black hair tied in a bun, discreet pearls worn over navy-blue linen, sitting in the office at St. Dunstan's. Now they understood that Peace's body had not been left in her front garden by accident.

"You didn't tell me you were in personnel."

"You didn't ask."

"Who's senior?"

"I am."

"And Bliss?"

"Malcolm? Malcolm's my assistant. He's on leave."

"He knew Harteveld."

She cocked her head and frowned. "Yes. I told you that when you interviewed me. So?"

Essex sat at her desk and leaned forward, speaking in soft tones, his head tilted confidentially. But Caffery was impatient.

"Don't give her a fucking life story, Paul. We need an address."

Lola Velinor looked up at him, the planes of her Byzantine face slanted upward, her long eyes narrowed. "I don't have to give you anything, Inspector."

"That's where you're wrong. Section 17, Article 19. I can seize records now if I choose."

"Okay, okay." Essex held up his hand. "Jack, let's do this calmly."

Lola Velinor closed her lips and inclined her head gracefully. Silently she rose and took them into the darkest recess of the office to where Wendy, posted back to personnel, sat as quiet as a mouse, sipping tea, dwarfed by filing cabinets.

"Inspector Caffery!" Wendy stood. "Why don't I make you a nice cup of—"

"Wendy." Lola Velinor's angular jaw worked subtly under the skin. "Give Inspector Caffery all Malcolm's details."

"Malcolm?"

"That's what I said."

"Oh." She turned to the nearest filing cabinet and pulled open a drawer. Her tiny fox face closed and a flush crept up from the base of her neck. "Here." She opened the file. "Thirty-four A Brazil Street, that's Lewisham. And then there's his mother's old place. She died last year, left him a cottage in Kent: Wildacre Cottage. There's the address, the phone number if you need it."

Essex wrote the details down and Wendy blinked at him from behind her thick glasses.

"He used to unzip himself under the desk," she blurted, sitting down suddenly. "If you know what I mean, and rub himself when he was talking to women. They couldn't see on the other side of the desk. But I could." She pulled her handkerchief from her sleeve and pressed it to her mouth for a moment. Her hand was trembling. "Is that why he's in trouble?"

"Something like that," Essex said. "Something like that."

The butt of the power tool had created a small subdural hematoma at the back of Rebecca's head. Blood leaked into it very slowly, giving her moments of drowsiness, some pain if she moved her chin downward. But her thought processes were unimpaired. The moment she woke she knew exactly what was happening.

She lay still at first, eyes closed, constructing a picture of herself and exactly what Bliss had done. He had removed her shorts, her underwear, and using, she guessed, the same packing tape, had bound her legs together from her toes to midthigh. He had left her T-shirt on and positioned her on the floor, on her side, her hands pressed against her stomach. When she wiggled them she realized the fingers were bound too, each one individually taped to separate it from its neighbor.

And Bliss was here. About five yards in front of her face. Slightly to her right. She could hear him and smell him. He was muttering to himself, spinning out a sentence, singsong, ridiculous.

Insane. He is insane, Becky. And you are going to die.

A string of imprecations, seesawing, lilting, comforting, persuading; a one-sided conversation, Bliss following his own perverse loop of logic.

She bent her attention forward, reaching out under his ramblings—searching through the layers of sound to sense the dimensions and temperatures of the room. They weren't in the flat anymore. She knew that from the change in air, from the acoustics. It was quiet here. Only birdsong outside. No trains, no cars, no inner-city rumbling. As peaceful as a childhood bedroom. So the suburbs, then? Or the country? They could be miles from any other houses; and no one knew she was here—

The rambling stopped. Rebecca held her breath and listened hard. When she was sure Bliss had left the room, she opened her eyes and let her breath out.

The room was dim—about the size she had pictured. Sunlight traced the patterns on the closed curtains, large cabbage roses, birds, peacock plumes. Beyond swinging saloon doors, a darkened kitchen. In the foreground, less than two yards from where she lay, six pale pink Lloyd Loom chairs were pulled up neatly next to a bamboo and glass table, on which had been arranged paper plates, a bottle of cherry brandy, party hats, a half-eaten birthday cake. Overhead, whispering and shivering like a crowd of fascinated onlookers—scores of balloons. Posy pink, lavender and sun yellow, jostling for space on the ceiling, tails lifting lazily in the cool air, and Joni—what was left of Joni—propped in one of the wicker chairs. Taped upright with the packing tape, but dead.

Dead? She must be dead—looking like that, she must be—

Bliss appeared from the kitchen, naked and obscene.

Rebecca froze—caught with her eyes wide open. But he wasn't looking at her. Instead he crossed to Joni, humming to himself, lightly fingering his small, leaking penis, cherry red against the soft white thighs. He paused at the table, swigging from the brandy and watching Joni thoughtfully. Then he wiped his mouth, put the bottle down and in one swift move—agile in spite of his build—levered himself onto the table, knelt in front of Joni, caught the back of her head and fed himself into her mouth.

Rebecca lay appalled, paralyzed. Compelled to watch as Bliss worked, pounding at Joni's face, driving himself harder and harder into her.

See? He's not human, you can't reason with him.

Joni retched violently under the assault: her throat convulsed, spasms shuddered across her abdomen as if her muscles were unlatched from their neural system, but still he worked on, squealing softly to himself, his eyes turned inward with lust. When he was finished he withdrew slowly from Joni's mouth, pausing a moment to rest her face in his soft fingers and look into her eyes. Then, nodding to himself, he gently lowered her chin onto her chest, crawled off the table and left the room.

Rebecca didn't move. She lay quite still for several moments.

Then: "*Joni?*" she whispered.

Silence. Joni sat in profile, naked and bruised, her head dropped forward onto her chest. On the table had been placed a slice of untouched birthday cake and a champagne flute. A small paper party napkin was spread on her lap and her hair had been cut into a fringe. Beneath it, where there should have been the natural dips and curves of eye, cheek and forehead, stretched a tender, dappled blood-blister.

"*Joni?*" Rebecca shuffled forward a few painful inches. "*Joni?*"

Joni rolled her head sideways. For a moment she seemed not to recognize Rebecca, then her tongue flickered.

"*Please—*" Her voice was thready, less than a whisper. A tear appeared in her healthy eye. "*Please don't watch.*"

"It's okay." Rebecca licked her lips and hiked herself up on her elbow, wincing at the pain in her head and neck. "It's okay."

She tried to feel for the end of the tape to free her legs, but Bliss had been clever with the neat little tape mittens he'd made for her—when she tore at them with her teeth they only grew tighter. She dropped her hands, panting.

There has to be something. Come on, Becky, there's a way out of this. Everything's there, right there waiting. Think.

Carefully recording any object of use: Next to a gas fire a silver-plated carousel holding fire tongs, poker, a miniature shovel. On the Formica surface of the kitchen, pushed up in the shadows next to the curtained window, a neat wooden knife block. And on the table? She couldn't see properly from this angle. *But knives—have to be some knives, even a fork. Could be to the table and back in twenty seconds. You'd hear him returning.*

A deep breath and she rolled onto her front, balling her face at the pain and nausea. She slammed her hands down on the floor and shuffled her lower body around. A sudden picture of herself, eyes swollen, half naked, broken and bloodied, dragging herself along the floor like a dog crippled by a car: she clenched her teeth, wouldn't entertain the image. The table was only a yard away—she was nearly there. She dragged her legs forward and—

A toilet flushed somewhere. A door closed.

Rebecca froze—heart thumping, eyes wide.

Wendy Dellaney considered herself a loyal person. She was proud of St. Dunstan's reputation. Proud to be a part of it. And *furious,* just *furious,* that Malcolm Bliss had brought more shame to them. She sat at her desk, staring at Malcolm's files, shivering, sipping her tea and taking deep breaths. "I've a good mind to—" She picked up the phone.

"Wendy?" Lola Velinor's head snapped up. "What are you doing?"

"I'm going to tell him exactly what I think of him. He's a dirty, dirty, *nasty* little man."

"No no no." Lola stood and gently removed the receiver from her fingers. "Don't interfere. You don't know how serious it is. Let the police deal with it."

Wendy, with her scared little pinprick eyes, shrank back into the corner, trying to disappear inside her Nightingale print dress. Ten minutes later, when Lola Velinor left to meet the hospital registrar, inform him of the police visit, the incident had been forgotten. Wendy waited till the door closed, then reached for the phone.

Bliss stood over her. Looking at her curiously as if she were a small snail he had found crawling across his living room floor.

"Awake?" he murmured lightly.

"She's dying." Rebecca tried to bend her legs up, get some leverage, but the tape dug into her flesh, cutting the blood supply. She gave up and dropped back, panting. "If you don't stop you'll kill her."

"Yes." Bliss picked thoughtfully at the inside of his nostril. "Yes." He put his hands on his knees and bent in to get a better view of Joni, her head lolling limply against her chest. Then, nodding to himself, he straightened.

"Yes," he said, wiping his hands on his fat thighs. "You're right. Now you. You want it again?"

Shaky, in pain, she held her hand up. "Don't touch me."

"Too late. I already have."

"You're lying."

"No," he said pleasantly. "After I *splattered* you all over my kitchen I fucked what was left. You were unconscious."

Not true.

"Look." He pressed the tip of his penis, wet and distended, between his fingers and smiled. "See? I'm ready. I'll cut your tape off and then you can open your legs for me."

"They know I'm with you. I called them before I came to your flat—told them where I was going. They're on the way."

"Shut up."

"It's true." Her voice trembled but she kept her head up. "First they'll telephone and then they'll arrive at the door."

"I said shut up." He rolled his tongue around his mouth. "Now lie down quietly and—"

Suddenly, shockingly, from the hallway the phone rang. Bliss twitched, his eyes reluctantly flicking to the doorway, and Rebecca saw she had him.

He believed her.

"That's them," she whispered, building on this stroke of serendipity. "That's them on the phone."

"Shut up."

"Go on. Answer it and see." She waved her hand at the door. "It's them. They'll want to negotiate with you—they'll make you think you're safe, but whatever happens they'll get you, Malcolm."

She should have seen it coming, but Bliss was the one with the predator's heart, not she.

"*Shut up, cunt!*" A foot slammed into her stomach.

She rolled sideways, panting, struggling not to vomit. Overhead the balloons shifted, murmuring and bouncing as if they'd like a better view of her struggle. Now she could hear Bliss rummaging in the kitchen drawers, in the drawer that she had earmarked *knives and scissors*. She rolled her eyes to the kitchen and just had time to see—gleaming gently as if it were capable of anticipation—a single, steel butcher's hook protruding from the ceiling, before Bliss came out carrying a length of electric flex and a roll of cling film. He slid a scalpel up the inside of her thighs, splitting the tape.

"*Now open your fucking legs, cunt!*"

In spite of herself Rebecca started to whimper.

Fifty-one

WILDACRE COTTAGE was not a cottage at all, but an ugly precast-concrete bungalow with a red-tiled roof and a generator tacked on the back. It lay above the Thames estuary on the rim of a pine forest in the yellow rapeseed fields due east of Dartford. Out here the air was salty, lines of yew trees, born and grown in the sea wind, fringed the fields, their branches straining inland like harpies' hair. Two miles north, on the other side of the blue estuary, the silent horizon thickened into the sandy-colored slab of Southend.

Caffery stopped the Jaguar in a sheltered lane. He, Essex and Maddox swiveled in their seats, leather creaking, and watched the Territorial Support Group's three armored Sherpa vans pull in, followed by a fire truck and ambulance.

It was Essex who noticed sunlight glinting on a car windscreen beyond them.

"What the—?"

The team Sierra pulled in neatly ahead of the Jaguar. Diamond got out, unsnapping his jacket and pulling cigarettes from his pocket.

"Hey." Maddox opened the door. "What're you doing here? I told you to stay at HQ."

"Am I in the way?"

Caffery jumped out of the car and slammed his hand on the Sierra's bonnet. "He asked you a question. He asked you what the *fuck* you think you're doing here?"

"Detective Inspector Jack Caffery." Diamond ran his hand down his tie and shook the creases out of his shirt as he came around the car, smiling broadly in the patchy sunlight. "You're—what? Stressed? Something personal in this for you?"

"More than a week ago the RG precinct phoned in a tip on Bliss, and you, Detective Inspector Mel Diamond, you dumped it—"

"Oh come on." Diamond interrupted. "I think you're letting your imagination run a bit wild, don't you?"

"Not my imagination. Fact. Now, take the team car up to the top of this road and park it side-on."

"Eh?"

"Stop any traffic."

"Hang on, hang on—"

"You'll stand down when I come and get you."

"Hang on a second here, I'm not a fucking uniform, you know. And you're not my superior, you nasty little prick." He looked at Maddox. "Well? Aren't you going to do something?"

"You heard him." Maddox pulled on his jacket and turned away. "Take the car and get out of my sight."

The Air Support Unit arrived in their black and yellow twin-engined B0105 heliopter, circled the bungalow, flattening the grass, bringing the hot smell of aviation fuel. When it reached the farthest point on its rotation, DI Diamond, standing at the head of the lane under an old oak, could hear the hum of insects again, the crack of the Sierra's engine cooling. He was feeling in his pocket for a cigarette when something caught his eye.

A small man in a stained vest and trousers, a dirty carrier bag dangling from his wrist, he appeared on the lane as if by magic.

"Good afternoon." He fidgeted his hands in his pockets and smiled quickly, showing small, orange-smeared teeth.

"'Ternoon."

"There's quite a police presence, I see. Anything we should be worried about?"

Diamond shrugged. "No. No." He turned to light the cigarette. Straightened and blew the smoke out in a fast thin stream. "Won't take long." He picked a piece of tobacco from his lips and, when he saw the little man was still staring at him, said, "If you'd like to move along now, sir. Back up to the main road. There's a perimeter team from here down to the estuary so keep to this side as you go."

Bliss pottered away, scratching his forehead and muttering to himself. He rounded the bend in the lane and mounted the grass-covered bank, lifting his feet clear of the mud and nettles. Perspiration, more a product of anger than exertion, collected in the crevices of his body.

When the phone—he'd forgotten it even existed—began to ring in the hallway, he knew instantly that the bitch wasn't lying. He did what he had to do to her quickly and neatly. The phone stopped but he continued: dressing and quietly leaving the bungalow before the police arrived. His ears were ringing, his head ached, but he pressed on through the dripping forest, getting himself as far away from the bungalow as he could before he found a damp, grass-covered fosse to crouch in. The rain had stopped and the salt in the air stung his nostrils. He lay on the ground and listened to the police assemble themselves.

Now, only a hundred yards from the Sierra, he hesitated, looked at the sky and sniffed. Up here on the bank, behind the row of tough little hawthorn bushes, he saw he was quite hidden from the lane. It was a simple matter of continuing and taking a bus from the main road. But he knew it was over for him—with Joni's death something had spilled over inside. If he was finished, then what he wanted was to leave his bloody print on this planet. He wanted to *engage*.

He thought of the silent creation in flesh that he'd left in the bungalow. He closed his eyes and smiled. Yes. That was a good start.

Humming distractedly and scratching at his neck, he turned and headed back up the road, until he saw the roof of the gray Sierra to his left. The sun was out, but a few spots of rain fell as he drew level with the car. He slowed, pausing behind a tall, ivy-hung oak. Something of interest had occurred to him. Thoughtfully he chewed his lip, reaching inside the carrier bag to rub the saw blade with the tips of two stubby pink fingers. Below him, from next to the Sierra, rose a thin line of cigarette smoke.

In his black sweater and Kevlar vest, Sergeant O'Shea of the Territorial Support Group, the TSG, was as out of place as a jungle predator in this pretty country lane. His team stood grim-faced, pelvises forward, arms crossed, hands pressed into armpits, watching him pace amongst them.

"Local uniform have done a drive-by, and as of thirteen hundred hours there's been a blue Peugeot in the driveway. We've been trying to establish contact for ten minutes but no one's answering that phone, so our mental health consultant agrees: didn't want it to come to this, but we're looking at a tactical end. We don't know what weapon the target's in possession of; no firearms intelligence—more likely to be blades of some sort, so be aware: necks, hands. Vulnerable. Keep those visors down and stick to the arrest protocol for separating target from weapon. Entry team, I think, looking at it, a staggered MO."

Caffery stood a few feet up the lane, smoking, peering through the hedgerow down at the bungalow. No cars passed, only the helicopter clattered overhead. From time to time he was sure he could hear the telephone ringing.

"Look, Jack." Essex pointed into the distance. Black clouds crowded at the estuary mouth, as if trying to block the entrance. "Talk about bleeding prophetic."

"He's had time to do it, Paul. She might already be . . ."

Essex looked at Caffery's face and bit his lip. "Yes. You need to be prepared."

"Usual radio routine." O'Shea flexed tattooed hands. "Perimeter team keep those check-in calls coming. If it goes belly-up, and you're compromised, you know the radio drill."

Diamond had watched the small man for a while, until he had disappeared down the lane. Then he yawned and scratched his nose, finished his cigarette and dropped it on the tarmac. It had started to rain. He felt in his pocket for the Sierra keys: no point in getting soaked out here, leave that to the heroes. His hand was on the car door when Bliss, sweating now, dropped like wet ivy from the high bank onto his shoulders.

"Hello," he whispered.

Diamond dropped the keys and shot back against the Sierra, gibbering, eyes wide with pain: Bliss had a neat hard hold on his genitals. He hop-skipped along beside him, yellow eyes inches from Diamond's face. "Slowly, slowly, you'll hurt yourself."

"I'm police. Police." He grappled with Bliss's hand, trying to free himself, but the saw whirred to life and made one serene pass across his knuckles, not deep, but enough to tap the wellspring of blood. Diamond screamed, snapping his arms away. "Don't cut me, don't cut me. I'm police."

"Do you promise to keep your hands still? Keep them over your head?"

"Yes, yes yes." Panting, he raised his arms against the tree. "Yes."

"Say it. Say I promise."

"Jesus. Yes—I promise."

"Cross your heart, hope to die."

"Cross my heart and hope to—to—" Diamond started to shake. "What are you going to do to me?"

"Shut up." Bliss blinked furiously. "Just shut up." Spittle formed on the edges of his mouth. He couldn't wipe it away: one hand was tight around the saw's hand piece and one was holding the soft, gristly flesh of the DI's balls and cock. Their eyes were level and Bliss could smell cold terror on the man's breath.

"Look." Diamond was shivering. "I'm a nobody in this. It's not me who brought them down here. They won't even let me near the house. That's why I've been left up here."

"Who makes the decisions?"

"Decisions?" Diamond licked his lips. "Decisions? That'll be our—our—"

"Yes?"

Diamond hesitated, a flicker of realization in his eyes. He calmed perceptibly. "That'll be our DI. Caffery. Jack Caffery."

"Him?" Bliss said, revealing his stained teeth. "Where is he?"

"He's at the bottom of the hill. Shall I show you?"

"That would be nice."

"Will you let me go?"

"We'll see. Now give me your radio."

The rain picked up tempo. It ran down the back of Caffery's collar, soaking into his shoes. The inky clouds had moved across the estuary and seemed to be stacking above the house. The windows remained dark, unopened.

"Answer the phone, you bastard."

He and Essex stood well removed, halfway down the field, radio silent, the squelch down. Caffery had rarely felt this useless. He knew that Rebecca was in the bungalow, and his imagination supplied a list of appalling possibilities. He could just glimpse the TSG entry team, in groups at the end of the easement, pulling on gloves, shouldering the red door-spreader.

Essex turned. DI Diamond stood on the hem of the wood, white and silent, beckoning to him.

"That dickspit. What the hell does he want?" Quickly and quietly he moved to the edge of the trees. "What are you doing down here?" he hissed.

"This way," Diamond whispered, and backed into the woods.

Essex followed. "You're supposed to have stayed on the road."

"This way."

"What happened to your hand? You're bleeding."

From where he lay coiled in last year's leaf compost, Bliss was quick and accurate. In a single movement he had severed Essex's right Achilles tendon with a soft popping sound.

"Jesus fucking Christ." He went down like an old tree, too startled to shout, toppling onto his shoulder, his radio spinning away as he grappled in the blood to gather the ends of the split tendon.

"And the other one." Bliss, eyes watering with excitement, pounced on him, the saw whirring. But Essex was faster than he looked. Grunting, he flipped himself onto his back, pulling his arm behind him in a hard, precise arc, slamming down onto Bliss's spine.

Bliss dropped the saw and rolled over with a tired 'Oof, shocked and winded, into the wet leaves.

"*You piece of shit, Bliss!*" Essex screamed, continuing the roll, pinning Bliss under his bulk. "*You little piece of shit!*"

Grunting loudly, he maneuvered himself until he lay, panting like a beached fish, across Bliss's back. His radio was gone, and he knew the damage done. He knew that his foot was dangling, the muscles, the vessels all open to the air. His only weapon was his weight, enough to keep Bliss down until someone came.

"Diamond," he yelled. "Use my radio, Diamond. All units."

But Diamond was shuddering, holding up his hand. "Bastard cut me," he muttered. "Could've gone straight through an artery."

"*Diamond!*"

"She's dead anyway." Bliss spat into the leaf mulch. "They both are, the bitches."

Essex caught Bliss's shirt above the shoulder blades.

"What did you say, you piece of shit?" But Bliss's face was calm, beatifically serene and silent. Essex rammed his elbow into the pulp of his back. "Did you kill them?" He slammed his elbow down again, ignoring the soft grating of the ligaments in his foot. Bliss didn't flinch. "What've you done, you dickwipe? Have you killed them?"

"Essex?" Caffery knew something was wrong the moment he turned around and saw only empty woods where Diamond had been. He took a few paces to the edge of the trees, his radio at the ready. He paused.

From deep in the wood came a soft, almost inaudible cry. Inhuman. And—intermittently—a brief, unsettling mechanical buzz.

"Essex?" Nothing. "Paul? You all right?"

Silence.

This is all wrong, Jack. All wrong.

Slowly, radio at his lips, he stepped forward. The buzzing dipped and hushed. Fear sucked at his belly.

"Bravo six-oh-two to all units."

He rounded a group of silver birches and stopped.

Diamond leaned against a fallen trunk clutching one arm against his chest, staring at Essex, who lay ten yards into the forest, face frozen and bluish, pinning Bliss to the ground. Bliss had one arm curled behind his back. His lids strained back showing the pink corners of his eyes. Inches away in the leaves the electric saw rotated laboriously, like a tired dog chasing its tail.

"*Jesus*—Paul."

Essex looked up. "He says he's killed them, Jack."

"Okay, hold him." Carefully he started toward them, his hand out. "Keep it calm. Hold him."

But Diamond's arm shot out, gripping his elbow. "I couldn't do anything, I couldn't. Look." He held his hand out. "See the blood—see the color?" His pale mouth quivered. "It's too red. He's gone in too deep."

"Diamond." Caffery rounded on him. Without thinking about it or even breaking step he fractured Diamond's cosmetic little nose in two places. "I warned you."

Diamond went down screaming, hands clamped over his face. "*What the fuck did you do that for? What the fuck?*" and twenty yards away Bliss saw his opportunity.

He pulled the electric saw toward him and, with a slippery, soft-limbed flick, gently brought Essex's right arm down onto it, opening the tender wrist. Blood bloomed, broke and fountained, Essex's mouth opened in a roar.

Caffery jumped forward—"*Paul!*"—but Bliss was quick.

Blinking, concentrating on his intricate operation, he rolled through the screams and bright spray and nestled up to Essex's other hand, neatly drawing the saw across the vulnerable network of blood vessels and tissue. Before Jack could cover the ground, Bliss was up, cannonballing away, painted with Essex's arterial blood. He teetered, slithering in the wet leaves, scrabbled to turn, got his balance and headed back out of the woods, his short arms pumping.

"Paul?" Jack flung himself against Essex, his face hard up against his cold cheek. "Did he get both arms?"

Essex nodded, his eyes screwed up against the pain. Ribbons of bright blood jetted across his shirtfront.

"Diamond! Move it." Jack leaped up, grabbed Diamond by the back of his jacket and dragged him over to Essex. "*Move it!* Give me your hands—"

"Let fucking go—"

"Give me your hands. Put them here." He peeled Diamond's fingers from his bloody nose and fastened them across the big brachial arteries in Essex's armpits. "Press. Press harder." He ripped off his jacket and tie, unhooked his radio and tossed it at Diamond's feet. "Get some compression on those arteries, then radio for help."

Diamond rolled bloodshot eyes to him. "You bastard."

He stood, gripped Diamond's ear and lifted his head. "Do you hear me?"

"Okay, okay. Let go of me."

"Do it." Jack thrust him away and took off after Bliss.

He was about a hundred yards away—where the trees began to smudge into one—a pink and white human flutter hurrying through the rain. He was moving fast. But Caffery was lighter. Stronger and faster. He sprinted through the undergrowth, alone with the sound of his breathing and the dripping of rain in the branches overhead.

He didn't shout. Too much energy. Mud and leaves fountained behind him and he closed fast. Soon he could hear Bliss's breath, see the small arms pumping.

Shit. He could see the black tarmac of the small coast road flashing through the trees. *That's a public road—has it been cordoned? Where's local uniform? The TSG? The hedgerows should be crawling with perimeter backup.*

Up ahead Bliss ducked suddenly under a low branch, shot through the dripping foliage and scrambled into a ditch. He slithered down the bank and was still accelerating when he hit the barbed-wire fence at the bottom.

Essex lay on his side, his face in the leaves, mouth slack-open. He knew he didn't have much consciousness left. Even his bones were cold.

Strange, strange to be so cold in June—

He dropped his eyes to where his hands lay—in front of him, limp on the ground as if they belonged to someone else. Diamond worked at them, making compression pads from the ripped jacket, covering the mess Bliss had made, stopping from time to time to raise bloodied fingers and gingerly touch his own mashed nose. A few feet beyond him Caffery's radio lay on its back in the mud. Maddox's voice, distant and metallic, calling to his DI:

"Bravo six-oh-two, this is Bravo six-oh-one receiving."

The helicopter hovered above the house. The TSG would be going in. *Too late,* Essex thought. *The girls were already dead. Nothing more to be done for them. And Jack was with Bliss. Somewhere in the woods—without a radio.*

"Diamond—" The effort was enormous. It set his head thudding. "Diamond—the radio—"

Diamond didn't respond.

"*Diamond!*"

"What?" He looked up. Angry. "I'm not fucking *deaf,* you know."

"The radio—"

"Yes, *I know.*" He fastened the ends of the cloth around Essex's wrists. "I'm doing my fucking best." He rolled away, grimacing, one hand covering his face, dragged the radio through the leaves and hit the orange override button, throwing a ten-second emergency burst interrupting every channel.

"Bravo six-oh-three to all units. Urgent assistance. Repeat urgent assistance."

Essex, exhausted, dropped his head. A shivering ache crept along his limbs. His vision—his view of the trees, the sky, the fallen branches, of Diamond speaking fast and furious into the radio—bulged, became distorted, as if the air itself were swelling, billowing out toward him. The daylight too, he realized dimly, was changing: growing greener and colder by stages.

Your heart's weakening, Paul, he thought distantly. *You old slob, that'll teach you. Your sodding heart's giving up.*

The momentum slid him onward into the ditch, hands out, the fence rushing toward him. He dug his heels in and his fingers found the smooth wire between the barbs. He stopped inches shy, heart hammering. Instantly he caught his balance and whipped around, panting, ready to fight.

But two yards away, Bliss had not been lucky.

His weight had been taken by the fence; he swayed gently, feet flat on the ground, knees slightly bent, puppet arms lifted. The barbs had stitched into his skin, to his hair, deep under tender ligaments. He made no noise, only blinked once or twice, his expression quiet, intense.

Slowly Caffery lowered his hands. "Bliss?"

No answer.

Jesus, now what?

A tentative step closer.

"Bliss?"

Why isn't he struggling?

Malcolm Bliss's face was patient, serene—only his jaw worked, subtly, as if he was concentrating, working hard on keeping perfectly still. With a shiver of recognition, Caffery understood.

Movement means pain for him. He's trapped.

He let out his breath.

Here it was—trapped and delivered to him. His quarry made flesh. Birdman.

Trembling, he wiped the sweat from his forehead and leaned in, careful not to relax, not to put too much faith in this unexpected switch of luck. Bliss, rigid in his wire bridle, stared docilely ahead as Caffery inspected him, swiftly, precisely, running his eyes across the lattice of barbs, tracking what hurt, why it hurt and what lever it afforded him. He charted countless minor wounds, small but insistent, before he found it—the fulcrum—a single barb, burrowed deep into Bliss's neck. No blood yet, but the pink flesh that rose around it pulsed gently. The carotid artery—ready to be tapped and drained.

"There," he whispered into Bliss's face, resting his fingers on the wire. "*There's* the key."

He drew the wire gently downward, testing where the pain began. Bliss breathed in through his nose, tolerating this childish gesture—closing his eyes patiently, as if this were not pain to be endured, but merely a humiliation doled out by an infantile bully. Caffery released the pressure briefly and twisted the wire in the opposite direction.

"It's the coward's way, Mr. Caffery," Bliss said suddenly, his voice gummy and tight. "The coward's way."

Caffery pushed his face closer. "Have you done it? Is it true? Have you killed them?"

"Yes." Bliss closed his eyes. "And fucked them too. Don't forget that."

Caffery stared at him, his fingers frozen on the wire. Over the treetops the helicopter banked suddenly, away from the bungalow, heading for the road. The clatter grew louder, shaking the ground and springing raindrops from the trees, but Caffery remained rigid, registering nothing above his own anger, staring into Bliss's face, feeling through the opportunity, so swollen and alive with it that his eyes began to water.

And then, abruptly, it was over. Gone.

He breathed out, wiped the sweat from his face and shook his head, heart heavy. He murmured something under his breath, released the wire and without another look at Bliss, climbed slowly back up the ditch.

The helicopter passed. Essex stared up at gray sky beyond shifting silvery leaves. A bird circled, tilting its eye to watch him. His heart followed its cellular instinct and struggled on, pumping the last useless spoonfuls of sap out of the holes in his wrists.

Odd, he thought, *I can't feel the rain on my face. Why can't I feel it landing on my face?*

Twenty seconds later his heart, its inside walls sticky, webby, almost dry, shuddered a little and stopped. The rain came in clear pellets, hard as glass balls bouncing off his open eyes.

The helicopter missed Caffery and Bliss. It passed a quarter of a mile away from the ditch, continuing on, following the road toward the estuary.

Far below, under the tree cover, Caffery had reached the lip of the ditch when something made him pause.

He pressed his temples, as if there were a pain under the skin he could massage away. He turned and stared for several seconds at Bliss, waiting patiently, ornamented in blood and fluid. A bullfinch, attracted by the object tangled in the wire, had appeared a yard away in a sycamore sapling. It was no bigger than an infant's fist. It blinked, assessing for food, head on one side. Caffery stared at it for a long time before drawing a deep breath, slithering down the ditch again, pulling his shirt down over his fingers and taking the wire in his hands.

A thin, vivid spray filled the air—the vessel was pierced. Bliss squealed and jerked; his feet danced—hands jagged reflexively toward his neck. Caffery held his breath, tightened his grip, and the vessel popped audibly, pushing a liquid rope of blood onto Bliss's white neck and hair.

Caffery stood back and watched quietly, absentmindedly pressing his black thumbnail into his palm, as Bliss's vitality emptied onto the ground. The detail that this was a life finishing didn't touch him—instead he felt only light-headed triumph.

Afterward he counted to one hundred to make sure it was over. Then he turned away, straightened his shirt and climbed back up the ditch.

* * *

Sergeant O'Shea's men found Joni's body blocking the narrow hallway. A quick glance told them she was dead. No one could have lived with these injuries; her spine was clearly snapped and a broken bottle had been inserted in her vagina. Quinn went into the bungalow with the camera crew. After twenty minutes she reappeared, grim-faced, to escort Caffery and Maddox inside.

"He's left the other one in there." She shone a torch down the darkened hallway. "In the living room." Quinn stopped and turned to them. "You sure you want to see this?"

"Of course," Caffery muttered. His shirt was wet with rain and blood. "Of course."

Quinn pushed the door open.

There was the smell of a holiday chalet about the room. The blinds were drawn, the furniture upright. Bright flowered cushions were propped on wicker dining chairs. Someone had been having a birthday party, a child's birthday party. Birthday cake was smeared on the table. The balloons bobbing against the ceiling were spattered with blood.

"Here." Quinn stepped into the room. "Turn round and you'll see."

"Where?"

Quinn shone the torch over the saloon doors and up to the kitchen ceiling.

Maddox drew in a breath. "Oh Christ."

She had been suspended facedown, like a tarpaulin swinging above the kitchen. Electric flex was wrapped around her wrists, looped up through a single hook in the ceiling and wrapped back around her ankles. She was naked, except for a sheaf of cling film wrapped around her head and shoulders. Mummified. A thin stripe of daylight shone across blood-streaked thighs.

Quinn put her hand on Caffery's arm. "Forensics, sir."

"No." He stepped into the room.

"Jack," Maddox warned. "Jack. We need forensics in here first. *Jack!*"

Caffery crossed the room slowly, the big muscles in the top of his chest contracting, his body instinctively sealing up its response. Underfoot the lino was tacky. His toes brushed against the metal room divider and he stopped, his hands on the swinging doors.

The grotesque creation twisted slightly, as if touched by a breeze. Under the cling film Rebecca's face was squashed and swollen.

Slowly, minutely, Caffery allowed himself to breathe.

Your imagination, Jack. See, it's not the Goliath you believe. It could never have invented this. And you really believed you wanted to find Ewan. You really thought you wanted to see.

A single pendulous drop squeezed out between a flap in the cling film under Rebecca's nose.

"Becky?" The tear dropped onto the lino. "*Becky?*"

A vein in her neck twitched.

Fifty-two

REBECCA WAS TREATED at Lewisham General. Caffery had refused to let her go to St. Dunstan's. There were CT scans, angiographies, blood transfusions. Ninety-four hours elapsed before the ICU consultants could be sure she would live. As soon as he got the news Jack made the decision he had been pondering. He played God and jury, weighed judgment in a personal court and chose, quite calmly, not to confess to Bliss's killing.

For four days he had been considering his options: disciplinary proceedings, hearings, internal inquiries. A criminal conduct dismissal and an independent trial. He tested these against letting it rest, letting the world go on believing that Bliss had died in the accident before he could be reached.

Now he told himself that this self-preserving choice could, paradoxically, give him a new weapon. He had killed and not confessed—he was now the predator who *knew* his quarry. He could stand upright and invisible in the killers' own amphitheater. The decision made, he surprised himself by adapting quickly. By the time Bliss's inquest rolled around, Caffery was effortless in his lies, nailing the coroner's gaze down as he delivered his neat string of untruths.

Odd how calm you are. Is that all there is to it? Is it really this simple to lie and be believed?

But, seamless as he imagined the change, Rebecca wasn't deceived. She saw immediately that he was carrying something new. She had touched his face on her first day of consciousness and said simply, "*What?*"

He pulled her hand to his mouth and kissed it. "When you're well," he murmured. "As soon as you're well, I promise."

But it was slow; there had been three more blood transfusions before she was out of danger and ten days later she remained too weak to accompany him to the funeral. So he drove alone out to the small Suffolk church and sat parceled into a cold pew next to Marilyn Kryotos, uncomfortable in his hired suit.

Two pews ahead, Essex's mother sat dry-eyed, too bewildered to cry, pinpoint butterfly bows shivering in the netting of her hat. Caffery had found himself embarrassed to see Essex's features so carefully distributed between her and her husband, as if it was a vulgarity for them to show themselves amongst the arum lilies in the nave. He wondered if he would recognize his own face meted out between his parents if he ever saw them again. He wondered what sort of hat his mother might wear to a funeral, and the realization that he had no idea, no sense, made goose bumps rise on his arms.

The canticles began. Kryotos inched forward on her pew next to him, resting her elbows on the prayer-book ledge. She dropped her head.

"Mummy?" Jenna, in a small black velvet dress, black tights and patent button-over shoes, slipped off the pew and clung to Kryotos's leg, staring worriedly up under her hair. "Mummy?"

On Kryotos's right Dean sat quietly, pulling at the collar of his first adult shirt. He was embarrassed. None of them could pretend not to notice the tears darkening the tapestry hassock at Kryotos's feet.

Caffery remembered that feeling: like Dean, staring at his mother's tears falling from under the curtain of hair, feeling her shiver as she prayed, prayed for God to find Ewan.

"It's a crap excuse for not living your life."

The words came with such clarity that he touched his forehead, holding his hand against his face, concerned that others might see his expression.

"You're supposed to have let it go by now—moved on."

Wasn't this, he thought, *what they'd all been saying in their own ways, the women, the girlfriends, over the years?* Maybe they had been justified in their fury, maybe they knew better than he did about what to hold on to, what to allow to drift away. Here he was: thirty-four years old. Thirty-four and he still didn't know how to play the game, the big, important game. As if he hadn't fully inhabited his life but had sat looking the opposite way, watching and planning, trying to make amends, trying to trap the past, while his life played itself out over his shoulder. He could let it go on, continue to scratch at it—rise to Penderecki's bait, allow him to reinvent ways to keep the torment fresh—and trek on, alone and childless in this life. Or—

Or he could choose to drop the battle.

As the minister started the commendation—hushed, gently dipping—Caffery leaned forward very suddenly. Kryotos wiped her nose and looked up.

"What?" she whispered, putting her hand on his arm. "What is it?"

He was staring into midair as if a ghost had risen from the transept up into the fan vaulting.

"Jack?"

After several seconds his face cleared. He sat back in the pew and looked at her.

"Marilyn," he whispered.

"What?" He smelled so clean. She waited while they stirred; all those little life facts that he made her regret. "What is it?"

"Nothing." He smiled. "Something crazy."

*   *   *

After the wake he drove back to London—fast through the flat, sunny Suffolk fields. By the time he got home the day had slipped across to early evening: above the little terraced house the sky was streaked orange.

Jack hadn't been in Ewan's room for more than two weeks. Now he went there without hesitation, throwing all the empty files into a bin-liner, tying it up, carrying it into the street and dumping it in the wheelie bin. He wiped his hands, went back into the house, removed his jacket, found a claw hammer in the cupboard under the stairs and unlocked the back door.

The garden had found its rhythm now July was near. Roused by the summer sunshine, it was blown full with life. Brilliant acrylic-colored flowers dotted the beds, and the *Rosa mundi,* planted by his mother and now in its thirtieth year, stood quietly next to the fence, its sugar-pink medieval blooms unfolded like babies' hands. Jack ducked under the willow, went straight to the old beech and dropped the hammer in the grass at his feet.

Do it. Do it. *If you think about it now you'll waver.*

He rolled up his sleeves, took a deep breath and gripped the lowest plank, levering it up against the trunk. It was weak and rotten. It almost leaped away from the tree, shooting a cloud of lichen onto his shirtfront.

No hesitating.

He carried the wood a few yards along the fence and hoisted it over, letting it drop into the deep undergrowth. He wiped his forehead, returned to the beech and started on the next plank.

The hammer lay unused in the grass and the shadows lengthened. Before long his palms were raw, sweat-streaked, his shirt was covered in moss and a solitary plank dangled from the tree's flank. As he closed his hands on it, taking a step back and bracing himself, something made him pause. A new and uneven element had attached itself to his horizon, changing the evening in the space of a breath.

He released the plank and looked up.

Drawn out of his house by some stale instinct, some old awareness—as if he could smell the change in Jack's intent— Penderecki had appeared in the garden across the cutting. He stood at the fence, in his braces and stained Aertex vest, chewing and scratching the back of his head, his jewel-bright eyes blinking and watching.

Jack took a deep breath and straightened. Ordinarily he would have walked away, or, worse, been drawn in. But now he stood straight and cool, meeting Penderecki's eyes square-on. In control.

No trains passed. No sounds. Reflected in the windows of the terraced houses, bright evening clouds floated above the trees. A seagull, blown off course from the Thames, circled overhead eyeing the two men. And then Ivan Penderecki's eyes flickered.

It was little more than a shadow but Jack saw it.

It meant the scales had tipped.

He smiled. Smiled slowly, his heart rising. He took a step back and in a single move wrenched the plank up from its moorings. He carried it to the fence, paused long enough to make sure Penderecki was still watching and flung it ten feet or more into the undergrowth. Along the "death trail." The last place he'd seen Ewan.

The plank landed, bounced twice, momentarily visible above the grass heads and cowslip, executed one more cart-wheel and came to rest, out of view beneath the green. He wiped his hands and looked up.

Good.

Penderecki's expression had changed.

He hesitated for a moment, tapping his fingers on the fence, lizard eyes lowered, flickering uncomfortably from side to side. Then quite suddenly he hiked up his braces, spat into the cutting, wiped his mouth and, without looking up, pushed himself away from the fence. He turned—his back rigid now, arms stiff at his sides—and walked with scientific precision straight back to the house. Closed the door neatly behind him.

Across the cutting, Jack—dressed in the second mourning suit of his life, sweat darkening the shirt—knew it was over. He dropped his head and stood against the fence, hands linked in the wire, his heart slowing while the evening gathered around him.

Suddenly a commuter train roared by, dotted with city workers late from the office. He looked up, astonished. As if a train were the last thing he had expected to see on a railway line. He stretched forward and watched the train's yellow rump dwindle in the distance. When it had disappeared under the Brockley Bridge he continued to watch the little shimmer of movement for a long time, until he didn't know if he was looking at sky or evening heat or a trick of the light.

He went back into the house, changed out of the suit, showered and drove to Lewisham Hospital.

One

WHEN IT WAS ALL OVER, DI Jack Caffery, South London Area Major Investigation Team (AMIT), would admit that, of all the things he had witnessed in Brixton that cloudy July evening, it was the crows that jarred him the most.

They were there when he came out of the Peaches' house—twenty or more of them standing in their hooded way on the lawn of the neighboring garden, oblivious to the police tape, the on-lookers, the technicians. Some had their beaks open. Others appeared to be panting. All of them faced him directly, as if they knew what had happened in the house. As if they were having a sly laugh about the way he'd reacted to the scene.

Later he would accept that the crows' behavior was a biological tic, that they couldn't see into his thoughts, couldn't have known what had happened to the Peach family, but even so the sight of them made the back of his neck tingle. He paused at the top of the garden path to strip off his overalls and hand them to a forensics officer, pulled on the shoes he'd left outside the police tape and waded out into the birds. They took to the air, rattling their petrolly feathers.

Brockwell Park—a huge, thrown-together isosceles of forest and grass with its apex at Herne Hill station—rambles for over a mile along the boundary of two very different parts of South London. On its western perimeter, the badlands of Brixton—where some mornings council workers have to drop sand on the streets to soak up the blood—and, to the east, Dulwich, with its flower-drenched almshouses and John Soane skylights. Donegal Crescent lay snug up against Brockwell Park—anchored at one foot by a boarded-up pub, at the other by a Gujarati-owned corner shop. It was part of a quiet little council estate, rows of fifties terraced houses bare to the sky, no trees in the front gardens, window frames and doors painted chocolate brown. The houses looked on to a horseshoe-shaped piece of balding grass where kids skidded their bikes in the evening. Caffery could imagine the Peaches must have felt relatively safe here.

Back in his shirt sleeves, grateful for the fresh air outside, he rolled a cigarette and crossed to the group of officers next to the Scientific Support Command Unit's van. They fell silent as he approached and he knew what they were thinking. He was only in his midthirties—not a senior-rank warhorse—but most officers in South London knew who he was. "One of the Met's Young Turks," the *Police Review* had called him. He knew he was respected in the force and he always found it a bit freaky. *If they knew half of it.* He hoped they wouldn't notice that his hands were trembling.

"Well?" He lit the cigarette and looked at a sealed plastic evidence bag a junior forensics officer was holding. "What've you got?"

"We found it just inside the park, sir, about twenty yards from the back of the Peaches'."

Caffery took the bag and turned it over carefully. A Nike Air Server trainer, a child's shoe, slightly smaller than his hand. "Who found it?"

"The dogs, sir."

"And?"

"They lost the trail. At first they had it—they had it good, really good." A sergeant in the blue shirt of the dog handlers' unit stood on tiptoe and pointed over the roofs to where the park rose in the distance, blotting out the sky with its dark forests. "They took us round the path that scoots over the west of the park—but after half a mile they just drew a blank." He looked dubiously at the evening sky. "And we've lost the light now."

"Right. I think we need to speak to Air Support." Caffery passed the trainer back to the forensics officer. "It should be in an air-drying bag."

"I'm sorry?"

"There's blood on it. Didn't you see?"

□ □ □

The SSCU's dragonlights powered up, flooding the Peaches' house, spilling light onto the trees in the park beyond. In the front garden forensics officers in blue rubberized suits swept the lawn with dustpans, and outside the police tape shock-faced neighbors stood in knots, smoking and whispering, breaking off to huddle around any plainclothes AMIT detective who came near, full of questions. The press were there too. Losing patience.

Caffery stood next to the Command Unit van and stared up at the house. It was a two-story terraced house—pebble dashed, a satellite dish on the roof and a small patch of damp above the front door. There were matching scalloped nets in each window, and beyond them the curtains had been drawn tight.

He had only seen the Peach family, or what was left of them, in the aftermath, but he felt as if he knew them. Or, rather, he knew their archetype. The parents—Alek and Carmel—weren't going to be easy victims for the team to sympathize with: both drinkers, both unemployed, and Carmel Peach had sworn at the paramedics as they moved her into the ambulance. Their only son, nine-year-old Rory, Caffery hadn't seen. By the time he'd arrived the divisional officers had already pulled the house apart trying to find the child—in the cupboards, the attic, even behind the bath paneling. There were traces of blood on the skirting board in the kitchen, and the glass in the back door was broken. Caffery had taken a Territorial Support Group officer with him to search a boarded-up property two doors down, crawling through a hole in the back door on their bellies, flashlights in their teeth like an adolescent's SAS fantasy. All they found were the usual homeless nesting arrangements. There was no other sign of life. No Rory Peach. The raw facts were bad enough and for Caffery they might have been custom-built to echo his own past. *Don't let it be a problem, Jack, don't let it turn into a headfuck.*

"Jack?" DCI Danniella Souness said suddenly at his side. "Ye all right, son?"

He looked round. "Danni. God, I'm glad you're here."

"What's with the face? Ye've a gob on ye like a dog's arse."

"Thanks, Danni." He rubbed his face and stretched. "I've been on standby since one o'clock this morning."

"And what's the story on this?" She gestured at the house. "A wain gone missing, am I right? Rory?"

"Yes. We're going to be blowing some fuses on it—he's only nine years old."

Souness blew air out of her nose and shook her head. She was solid, just five foot four, but she weighed twelve stone in her man's suit and boots. With her cropped hair and fair, Caledonian skin she looked more like a juvenile dressed for his first court appearance than a forty-year-old chief inspector. She took her job very seriously. "Right, the assessment team been?"

"We don't know we've got a death yet. No dead body, no assessment team."

"Aye, the lazy wee bastards."

"Local factory's taken the house apart and can't find him. I've had dogs and the territorials in the park. Air Support should be on their way."

"Why do ye think he's in the park?"

"These houses all back onto it." He pointed toward the woods that rose beyond the roofs. "We've got a witness saw *something* heading off into the trees from number thirty. Back door's unlocked, there's a hole in the fence, and the lads found a shoe just inside the park."

"OK, OK, I'm convinced." Souness folded her arms and tipped back on her heels, looking around at the technicians, the photographers, the divisional CID officers. On the doorstep of number thirty a camera operator was checking his battery belt, lowering the heavy Betacam into a case. "Looks like a shagging film set."

"The unit want to work through the night."

"And what's with the ambulance? The one that almost ran me off the road."

"Ah, yes—that was Mum. She and hubby have both been trundled off to King's. She'll make it but he hasn't got a hope. Where he was hit—" Caffery held his palm against the back of his head "—fucked him up some." He checked over his shoulder then bent a little nearer to her, lowering his voice. "Danni. There're a few things we're going to have to keep from the press, a few things we don't want popping up in the tabloids."

"What things?"

"It isn't a custody kidnap. He's their child—no exes involved."

"A tiger, then?"

"Not a tiger either." Tiger kidnaps meant ransom demands and the Peaches were not in an extortionist's financial league. "And, anyway, when you look at what else went on you'll know it's not bog standard."

"Eh?"

Caffery looked around at the journalists—at the neighbors. "Let's go in the van, eh?" He put his hand on Souness's back. "I don't want an audience."

"Come on, then." She hefted herself inside the SSCU's van and Caffery followed, reaching up to grip the roof rim and swing himself inside. Spades, cutting equipment and tread plates hung from the walls, a samples refrigerator hummed gently in the corner. He closed the door and hooked a stool over with his foot and handed it to her. She sat down and he sat opposite, feet apart, elbows on his knees, looking at her carefully.

"What?"

"We've got something screwy."

"What?"

"The guy stayed with them first."

Souness frowned, tilting her chin down as if she wasn't sure whether he was joking or not. "Stayed with them?"

"That's right. Just . . . hung around. For almost three days. They were tied up in there—handcuffed. DS Quinn thinks another twelve hours and one or other of them'd be dead." He raised his eyebrows. "Worst thing's the smell."

Souness rolled her eyes. "Oh, lovely."

"Then there's the bullshit scrawled all over the wall."

"Christ." Souness sat back a little, rubbing her stubbly head with the palm of her hand. "Is it sounding like a Maudsley jobbie?"

He nodded. "Yeah. But he won't be far—the park is sealed now, we'll have him before long." He stood to leave the van. "Jack?" Souness stopped him. "Something else is worrying ye."

He paused for a minute, looking at the floor, his hand on the back of his neck. It was as if she'd leaned over and peered keen-eyed through a window in his head. They liked each other, he and Souness: neither was quite sure why, but they had both fallen comfortably into this partnership. Still, there were some things he didn't choose to tell her.

"No, Danni," he murmured eventually, reknotting his tie, not wanting to hear how much she guessed of his preoccupations. "Nothing else. Come on, let's have a shufti at the park, shall we?"

Outside, night had come to Donegal Crescent. The moon was low and red in the sky.

□ □ □

From the back of Donegal Crescent, Brockwell Park appeared to ramble away for miles into the distance, filling the skyline. Its upper slopes were mostly bald, only a few shabby, hairless trees across the backbone and at the highest point a clutch of exotic evergreens. But on the west slope an area about the size of four football pitches was thick with trees: bamboo and silver birch, beech and Spanish chestnut, they huddled around four stinking ponds, sucking up the dampness in the soil. There was the density of a jungle among those trees—in the summer the ponds seemed to be steaming.

At 8:30 P.M. that night, only minutes before the park was sealed off by the police, one solitary man was not far from the ponds, shuffling among the trees, an intent expression on his face. Roland Klare's was a lonely, almost hermitic existence—with odd tempers and periods of lethargy—and sometimes, when the mood was on him, he was a collector. A human relative of the carrion beetle, to Klare nothing was disposable or beyond redemption. He knew the park well and often wandered around here looking through the bins, checking under park benches. People left him alone. He had long, rather womanly hair and a smell about him that no one liked. A familiar smell—of dirty clothes and urine.

Now he stood, with his hands in his pockets and stared at what was between his feet. It was a camera. A Pentax camera. He picked it up and looked at it carefully, holding it close to his face because the light was fading fast, examining it for damage. Roland Klare had three or four other cameras back at his flat, among the items scavenged from skips and Dumpsters. He even had bits and pieces of film developing equipment. Now quickly he put the Pentax in his pocket and shuffled his feet around in the leaves for a bit, checking the ground. There'd been a heavy summer cloudburst that morning but the sun had shone all afternoon and even the undersides of the long grass were dry against his shoes.

Two feet away lay a pair of pink rubber gloves, large ones, which he slipped into his pocket with the camera. After a while he continued on his way through the fading light. The rubber gloves, he decided, when he got them under a streetlight, were not worth keeping. Too worn. He dropped them in a skip on the Railton Road. But a camera. A camera was not to be discarded lightly.

It was a quiet evening for India 99, the twin-engined Squirrel helicopter out of Lippits Hill air base. The sun had gone down and the heat and low cloud cover made the Air Support crew headachy: they got the unit's twelve fixed tasks completed as quickly as possible—Heathrow, the Dome, Canary Wharf, several power stations including Battersea—and were ready to switch to self-tasking when the controller came through on the tactical commander's headset. "Yeah, India nine-nine from India Lima."

The tactical commander pulled the mouthpiece nearer. "Go ahead, India Lima."

"Where are you?"

"We're in, uh, where?" He leaned forward a little and looked down at the lit-up city. "Wandsworth."

"Good. India nine-eight's got an active, but they've reached endurance, grid ref: TQ3427445."

The commander checked the map. "Is that Brockwell Park?"

"Rog. It's a missing child, ground units have got it contained, but look, lads, the DI's being straight with us, says you're a tick in the box. He can't promise the child's in the park—just a hunch—so there's no obligation."

The commander pulled away his mouthpiece, checked his watch and looked into the front of the cockpit. The air observer and the pilot had heard the request and were holding their thumbs up for him to see. "Good." He noted the time and the Computer Aided Dispatch Number on the assignment log and pulled his mouthpiece back into place.

"Yeah, go on, then, India Lima. It's quiet tonight—we'll have a look. Who are we speaking to?"

"An, um, an Inspector Caffery. AMIT—"

"The murder squad, you mean?"

"That's the one."

Two

THERE WERE MARKS ON the camera casing where it had been dropped and, later, at home in his flat on the top floor of Arkaig Tower, a council block tower at the northerly tip of Brockwell Park, Roland Klare discovered that the Pentax was damaged in other, less visible ways. After wiping the casing carefully with a tea towel he attempted to wind on the film inside and found the mechanism had jammed. He fiddled with it, tried forcing it and shaking it, but he couldn't free the winder. He put the camera on the sill in the living room and stood for a while looking out the big window.

The evening sky above the park was as orange as a bonfire and somewhere in the distance he could hear a helicopter. He scratched his arms compulsively, trying to decide what to do. The only other working camera he had was a Polaroid. He'd acquired that, too, in a not totally honest fashion, but Polaroid film was expensive, so this Pentax was worth salvaging. He sighed, picked it up and tried again, struggling to unjam the mechanism, putting the camera between his legs to hold it still while he wrestled with it. But the winder wouldn't budge. After twenty minutes of fruitless struggle he was forced to admit defeat.

Frustrated and sweating now he made a note of it in the book he kept in a desk next to the window, then placed the camera in a purple Cadbury's Selection tin on the windowsill, where, along with a neon-pink-handled screwdriver, three bottles of prescription pills, and a plastic wallet printed with a Union Jack that he'd found last week on the upper deck of the number-two bus, it would remain, its evidence wound neatly inside, for more than five days.

□ □ □

All prisons in London insist on being informed about any helicopter that passes. It keeps them calm. India 99, seeing the familiar glass-roofed gym and octagonal emergency control room ahead on their right, got on to channel eight and identified themselves to HMP Brixton before they continued toward the park. It was a warm and breathless night; the low cloud cover trapped the orange city light, spreading it back down across the roofs so that the helicopter seemed to be flying through a glowing layer of heat, as if its belly and rotor blades had been dipped in hot, electric orange. Now they were over Acre Lane—a long, spangled, untangled row of pearls. On they went, out over the hot, packed streets behind Brixton Water Lane, on and on, over a warren of houses and pubs, until suddenly, on a tremendous rush of air and aviation fuel—*flak flak flak FLAK*—they floated out into the clear darkness over Brockwell Park.

Someone in the dark cockpit whistled. "It's bigger than I thought."

The three men peered dubiously down at the vast expanse of black. This unlit stretch of wood and grass in the middle of the blazing city seemed to go on forever—as if they'd left London behind and were flying over an empty ocean. Ahead, in the distance, the lights of Tulse Hill marked the farthest borders of the park, twinkling in a tiny string on the horizon.

"Jesus." In the little dark cockpit, his face lit by the glow from the instrument panel, the air observer shifted uncomfortably. "How we going to do this?"

"We'll do it." The commander checked the radio frequency card in the plastic leg pocket of his flying suit, adjusted the headset and spoke above the rotor noise to Brixton Divisional Control. "Lima Delta from India nine-nine."

"Good evening, India nine-nine. We've got a helicopter over us—is that you?"

"Roger. Request talk through with search unit on this code twenty-five."

"Roger. Use MPS 6—go ahead, India nine-nine."

The next voice the commander heard was DI Caffery's. "Hi there, nine-nine. We can see you. Thanks for coming."

The air observer leaned over the thermal imaging screen. It was a bad night for it—the trapped heat was pushing the equipment to its limits, making everything on the screen the same uniform milky gray. Then he saw, in the top left-hand corner, a luminous white figure holding up its hand into the night. "OK, yes. I've got him."

"Yeah, hello there, ground units," the commander said into his mike. "You're more than welcome. We've got eyeball with you too."

The observer toggled the camera and now he could see them all, the ground units, glimmering forms strung out around the perimeter of the trees. It looked like almost forty officers down there. "Jeez, they've got it well contained."

"You've got it well contained," the commander told DI Caffery.

"I know. Nothing's getting out of here tonight. Not without us knowing."

"It's a large area and there's wildlife in there too, but we'll do our best."

"Thank you."

The tactical commander leaned into the front of the cockpit and held up his thumb. "OK, lads, let's do it."

The pilot put the Squirrel into a right-hand orbit above the southern quarter of the park. About half a mile to the west they could see the chalky smudge of the dried-out boating lake, and from among the trees the basalt glitter of the other four lakes. They took the park in zones, moving in concentric circles five hundred feet in the air. The air observer, hunched over his screen, steeled against the deafening roar of the rotors, could see no hot spots. He toggled the controls on his laptop. The ground crews had been easy, hot and moving and outside the trees, but tonight the thermal return was as poor as it got and anything could be hiding under that summer-leaf canopy. The equipment was virtually blind. "We'll be lucky," he murmured to the commander, as they moved on through the rest of the park. "Peeing in the wind." Peeing, not pissing, careful what he said—everything up here was recorded for evidence. "Peeing in the wind is what we're doing."

On the ground, next to the TSG's Sherpa van, Caffery stood with Souness and stared up at the helicopter lights. He was relying on the air unit to crack this—to find Rory Peach. It was an hour now since the alarm had been raised. It had been the Gujarati shopkeeper who had dialed 999.

Most of the Peaches' dole money went on Carmel's Superkings—by the weekend the money had run out and there was usually a tab to be settled at the corner shop. This weekend nobody had paid off the bill so on Monday evening the shopkeeper went down Donegal Crescent to demand his money. It wasn't the first time, he'd told Caffery, and no, he wasn't afraid of Alek Peach, but he had taken the Alsatian with him anyway, and at 7:00 P.M. had rung the Peaches' doorbell. No reply. He knocked loudly but still there was no reply. Reluctantly he continued into the park with the dog.

They walked along the back gardens of Donegal Crescent and were some distance into the park when the Alsatian turned suddenly and began to bark in the direction of the houses. The shopkeeper turned. He thought, although he wouldn't swear to it, he *thought* he saw something running there. Shadowy and wide-beamed. Moving rapidly away from the back of the Peaches' house. His first impression was that it was an animal, because of how furiously and nervously the Alsatian was barking, straining at the lead, but the shadow had disappeared quickly into the woods. Curious now, he dragged the reluctant dog back to number thirty and peered through the letter box.

This time he knew something was wrong. There was junk mail scattered on the hallway floor and a message, or part of a message, had been spray-painted in red on the staircase wall.

"Jack?" Souness said over the roar of the helicopter above. "What're ye thinking?"

"That he has to be in there somewhere," he yelled, jabbing his finger at the park. "He's in there."

"How do you know he didn't come out again?"

"No." He cupped his hand around his mouth and leaned into her. "If he did come out I can promise you someone's going to remember. All the park exits lead into main streets. The little boy's bleeding, probably terrified—"

"WHAT?"

"I SAID HE'S NAKED AND BLEEDING. I THINK SOMEONE WOULD PICK UP THE PHONE FOR THAT, DON'T YOU? EVEN IN BRIXTON."

He looked up at the helicopter. He had another good reason to think that Rory was in the park—he knew the statistics on child abduction: most studies would predict that if Rory wasn't alive he would probably be found within five miles of the abduction site, less than fifty yards from a footpath. Other worldwide stats would tell a more chilling story: they'd predict that Rory wouldn't be killed immediately, that his kidnapper would probably keep him

alive for anything up to twenty-four hours. They'd say that the mo-
tive in an abduction of a boy within Rory's age range would probably be sex. They'd say that the sex would probably be sadistic. If
Caffery had more than a passing knowledge of the habits and life
cycle of the pedophile there was a simple reason: he could reach
back twenty-seven years into his own past and find a mirror image
of this in another disappearance. His own brother, Ewan—the
same age as Rory—had been sucked out of the middle of a normal
day. From the back of the family house. Rory could be Ewan all
over again. Caffery knew he should say something about it to
Souness, he should take her aside right now and tell her, "Maybe
you should cut me out of this—give it to Logan or someone—because I don't know how I'm going to react."

"WHAT IF THEY DON'T FIND ANYTHING?" Souness
yelled.

"DON'T WORRY. THEY'LL FIND SOMETHING." He lifted
the radio and switched on to the helicopter commander's channel.
"Nine-nine." He lowered his voice. "Anything happening up
there?"

Five hundred feet overhead, in the dark cockpit, the commander
moved as far forward as the coms lead, which tethered him like an
umbilicus to the roof of the helicopter, would allow. "Hey, Howie?
They want to know how we're doing, Howie." He couldn't see the
air observer's face, hunched over as he was, his attention on the
screen, the helmet obscuring his eyes.

"I'm struggling. Looks like an effing snowfield. Unless it moves
it just blends in. Has to pretty much stand up and wave at me." He
tried switching so that heat showed black on his screen. He tried
red, he tried blue; sometimes a different color helped, but tonight
the thermal washout was beating him. "Can you give us some
more right-hand orbits?"

"Rog." The pilot nosed the helicopter over, turning in circles,
both he and the commander looking out the right-hand side of the
craft at the dense forest below. The air observer narrowed his eyes
on the screen. He moved the laptop joystick and under the cockpit, in the sensor pod, the gyroscopically mounted camera, deathly
stable, rotated its cool eye across the park.

"What you got?"

"I dunno. There's something at about ten o'clock but . . ."
Without depth perception it was difficult to tell what he was see-

ing on the screen, and every time they got near, the helicopter made the leaf cover shift. He thought he had seen an odd, doughnut-shaped light source, about the size of a car tire. But then the leaf cover shifted again and now he thought he'd dreamed it. "*Scheisse.*" He leaned intently over the screen, moving his head from side to side, flicking the screen from wide field to narrow and back again. "Yeah, maybe get them to have a look at that." He tapped the screen. "Can you see it?"

The commander leaned forward and looked at the screen. He couldn't see what the observer was talking about but he sat back and tuned the radio control into DI Caffery's loop. "Ground unit from nine-nine."

"Yeah, have you got anything?"

"We think we might've got a heat source but we can't quite confirm. Do you want to have a look at it?"

"Will do."

"Right, well, there's a pool, or a paddling pool or something . . ."

"The boating lake?"

"The boating lake—and the forest starts, I dunno, two hundred meters away?"

"Yup—sounds about right."

The commander leaned forward and looked to where the observer held his finger over the screen. "If you could start at that edge of the forest and move in about a hundred yards . . ."

"Rog. Got you."

The commander held his hand flat, instructing the pilot to hover, and the three crew members sat forward, not speaking, only the sound of their breathing in the headsets as they watched the glimmering forms of the TSG, the Territorial Support Group, streaming across the screen in the direction of the heat source.

"Right," the commander muttered. "Let's give them some help, shall we?" He threw a switch and powered up the Night Sun—the gargantuan spotlight dangling from the helicopter's belly. Thirty million candlepower—it could burn through concrete at close range: the ground units followed it like the nativity star, yomping toward it through the trees. But on the screen the observer had lost the glowing, ring-shaped heat source and now he was starting to wonder if he'd imagined it.

"Howie?" the commander said from behind. "Are we in the right place?"

The observer didn't reply. He sat hunched forward, trying to relocate the source.

"Howie?"

"Yeah—I think, but I—"

"Nine-nine from ground units." Caffery came through on the radio. "We're drawing a blank down here. Can you help us out?"

"Howie?"

"I dunno—I dunno. There was *something*." He threw the screen into narrow field once more and shook his head. The noise of the engines and the rotor blades, the heat and the smells were oppressive tonight, and he was having trouble concentrating. On the ground the TSG officers stood looking up at the helicopter, arms open. "Shit," he muttered to himself. "Howie, you sodding idiot." He was going to have to back down. "I—look—I don't know—"

"OK, OK." The commander was getting impatient. "How are we for fuel?"

The pilot shook his head. "About twenty-five percent."

He whistled. "So we need to be going somewhere in about, what? Twenty minutes. Howie? What are we thinking?"

"Look, I—nothing. I imagined it. Nothing."

The commander sighed. "OK, I've got you." He switched to the CAD controller's frequency. "India Lima, we're low on fuel so we're going to slip into Fairoaks for a slurp. I think we've got a no-trace. Haven't we, Howie? Got a clear?"

"Yeah." He ran a finger under his chin strap, uncomfortable. "I guess so. A no-trace. I guess."

"Nine-nine to ground units, if you're clear down there so are we."

"You sure?" DI Caffery sounded tense. "You sure we're in the right place?"

"Yeah, *you're* in the right place but we've lost the source. It's a hot night—we're fighting interference up here."

"Rog, if you're sure. Thanks for trying."

"Sorry about that."

"It's OK. Good evening to you all."

The commander could see Caffery on the screen, waving. He adjusted his headset and switched back to the CAD controller. "That's a no-trace in the open, so we're complete on scene at grid ref TQ3427445, now routing to India Foxtrot." He noted the time on his assignment log and the helicopter banked away into the night.

On the ground below Caffery watched the helicopter disappear across the rooftops, until its light was scarcely bigger than a satellite.

"You know what it means, don't you?"

"No," Souness admitted. "No, I don't."

It was late. The TSG had zoned off the area where the air observer had imagined a heat source, got down on their hands and knees and covered every square inch of it. Still no Rory Peach. Eventually they'd stopped, and Caffery and Souness had finalized arrangements for a specialized search team to come in the next day: a Police Search Advisory team would start at first light in Brockwell Park. There was still an emergency team briefing to get through and search parameters to establish before the night was out and so, at 11 P.M., they drove back to AMIT headquarters in Thornton Heath. Caffery parked the car and swung the door open. "If he's in the park and they can't see him then he's not much of a heat source and he's not moving." In spite of what it meant professionally, part of him secretly hoped, for the boy's sake, that he was already dead. There are some things, he believed, not worth surviving. "Maybe we're too late already."

"Unless," Souness climbed wearily from the car and together they crossed the road, "he's not in the park."

"Oh, he's in the park. I promise you he's in the park." Caffery swiped his pass card and held the door for Souness. "It's just a question of where."

"Shrivemoor" was how most officers referred to this old red-brick building, after the unexciting residential street in which it stood. AMIT's offices were housed on the second floor. Tonight lights were on in all the windows. Most of the team had arrived, called away from dinner parties, pubs, babysitting duty. The HOLMES database operators, the five members of the intelligence cell, seven investigating officers, they were all here, wandering between the desks, drinking coffee, murmuring to one another. In the kitchen three embarrassed-looking paramedics in white-hooded forensic suits—nonce suits, the team called them—waited while the exhibits officer photocopied their boot soles and used low-tack tape to lift hairs and fibers from their clothing.

While Souness made strong coffee, Caffery put his face under the tap to wake himself up and quickly checked his in tray. Among the circulars, the memos, the postmortem reports, someone had left this week's copy of *Time Out*. It was folded open at a page titled "The Artists Who Turn Crime into Art." A photograph of Rebecca—eyes closed, head tilted back, a prison number painted on the center of her forehead where a bindi spot would go.

Rebecca Morant, tabloid totty or the genuine article? You have to be a long way out of the loop not to have heard of Morant, sex-assault victim turned art-world darling. Suspiciously beautiful, the critics found it difficult to take lynx-eyed Morant seriously, until a nomination for the ultracool Vincent award and a shortlisting by Becks confirmed her as a key player in the post YBA pack. . . .

Caffery closed the magazine and placed it facedown in the in tray. *How much more publicity do you need, Becky?*

"Right, crew. Listen up." He used an empty Sprite can to bang on the wall. "Come on, listen, everyone. I know you're all on short notice but let's get this bit done. We'll do it in the SIOs'." Holding the videotape above his head he started toward the office he and Souness shared, beckoning the officers to follow. "Come on, it'll only take ten so you can have your piss breaks later."

The senior investigating officers' room was small—for all the team to cram in, the door had to be left open. Souness stood against the window, coffee mug cupped in both hands as Caffery plugged in the video and waited for everyone to gather. "Right. You all know the basics. DCI Souness is doing the search and house-to-house parameters, so whoever's on the knock come and see her after this. First light, we've got the search team meeting in Brockwell Park so I want everyone ready. SPECRIMs go out as usual, but bear in mind what I'm going to tell you now for holdback on the press bureau. Exhibits, Family Liaison, organize yourselves. What else? We've got primacy but we'll appoint a liaison officer for, I'm sorry to say, the pedophile unit and the risk-management panel at Lambeth and, uh, someone better have a whisper with the child-protection lads at Belvedere, make sure Rory hasn't made an appearance there before. Now . . ." He gestured at the blank TV screen and took a deep breath. "When I show you this, the first place you're going to wonder about is the Maudsley." He paused. At the mention of the Maudsley—the mental-health clinic on Denmark Hill—one or two of the civilian workers had sucked in a breath. He didn't want that: he wanted the team thinking and functioning and not overreacting to the nature of the crime.

"Look," he said, "I don't want you writing him off as a psycho just yet. I'm only saying that's how it looks." He glanced around at the faces. "Maybe that's how it's meant to look. Maybe there's some trail-covering here—maybe he's your common or garden sicko who's trying to throw up a smoke screen, pave his way to an insanity plea if he gets caught. And keep in mind that he's been in play for three days. Three days. That's controlled, isn't it? Have a think about those three days and what they mean. Do they mean, for example, that he knows he's not going to get disturbed?"

Or do they mean he was enjoying himself so much with Rory that he'd decided to stay on for the long weekend?

He pointed the remote control at the video. Donegal Crescent appeared on screen. It was dusk. Beneath the time code a crowd jostled the cordons, trying to get a better glimpse at the little terraced house: blue ambulance lights flashed silently across their faces. Caffery, standing back against the wall now with his arms folded, watched the AMIT detectives out of the corner of his eye. This was the first they had seen of the crime scene and he knew they'd find something terrible about the Peaches' house. Something terrible about its normality.

"This is on the edge of Brockwell Park," he said evenly. "Just to give you some geography, that tower you can just see in the distance is Arkaig Tower on Railton Road, which the divisionals know and love as Crack Heights."

The camera tracked down the path to the doorstep of number thirty and turned to pan across the street, the little scrap of grass opposite, the neighbors' faces shocked white ovals against the evening sky. Any point that could be observed from the Peaches' house could also be a vantage point for a potential witness. The camera recorded everything then swung 180 degrees and faced the house head on. The number 30 in gold screw-on numerals filled the screen.

"All the doors and windows were closed." The camera ran itself around the splintered front door—opened with the Enforcer battering ram—zooming in on an intact lock. "The territorials had to batter their way in. The only thing not locked was the back door—we think it's our point of entry. Watch."

They were inside the house now, the camera flooding the hall-

way with halogen light. Slightly worn wallpaper, a gray cord carpet protected by a heavy-duty plastic runner. Two framed prints
cast long, bobbing shadows up the hall and a child's turbo water
gun lay on its side on the bottom step. Up ahead, at the end of the
hall, a doorway. The tape blurred for a moment, helical scan traces
across the screen, and when the picture steadied the camera had
gone through the doorway and was in a small kitchen. A glazed
terra-cotta chicken eyed the camera beadily from next to the bread
bin, and the checked curtain covering the door wallowed in the
breeze revealing a broken pane, flashes of the darkened yard, a
glimpse of the trees in the park beyond.

"Right. Important." Caffery rested his elbow on the monitor,
leaning over to point at the screen. "Glass on the floor, door unlocked. This is not only the point of entry but also the exit point.
Intruder breaks window and lets himself in—we think this is sometime after seven P.M. on Friday evening." The camera zoomed
through the broken window and out into a small yard beyond: a
carousel clothes dryer, a child's bike, some toys and four over-
turned milk bottles, their contents rancid and yellow. "The intruder
then stays in the house with the Peach family until Monday afternoon, when he's disturbed—at which point he picks up Rory Peach
and leaves through the same door." The camera pulled back into
the kitchen and panned the room, pausing at a set of bloody drag
marks on the doorpost. Caffery tapped the remote control on his
leg and looked around at the silent faces, expecting a reaction. But
no one spoke or asked questions. They were staring at the blood
on the screen.

"The lab thinks his wounds aren't fatal at this point. The received wisdom is that the intruder carried him out of the house—
through this broken fence here and into the woods. He's probably
found a way to staunch the blood flow, maybe a towel or something, because the dogs lost him early. Right." The camera was
moving. "Good, now I'm going to show you where the family were
found."

A woman's face came briefly in and out of shot: DS Quinn, the
crime-scene coordinator, the most experienced CSC in South London. After she and Caffery had orchestrated the video she had returned to the kitchen to ensure that the glass from the break-in was
carefully photographed and removed. Then she had called the Specialist Crime Unit biologists down from Lambeth. While Caffery
was with the helicopter crew, the scientists had come through the

house, dressed in protective suits, applying their specialized chemicals: ninhydrin, amido black, silver nitrate.

"Alek Peach—that's Dad—was found here, handcuffed at the wrists to this radiator, and by the ankles to this radiator. You can tell the position he was in from the mark he's left." Caffery pointed it out to the team—a large dark stain on the shag-pile carpet, stretching between the two radiators in the living room. "He's got a wound to the back of his head so we won't be talking to him for a while. Maybe not at all. And the second place—watch, you'll see it now we're going upstairs—is where Carmel was held."

Carmel, who was now sedated at the hospital, had given something of a statement in the ambulance. Although a cursory examination showed no head wounds it was assumed she had lost consciousness at some point: apart from making dinner at 6 P.M. on Friday, she remembered nothing until she had woken gagged and cuffed to a water pipe in the airing cupboard on the first-floor landing. There she had remained until the shopkeeper had called through the letter box three days later. She hadn't seen or spoken to the intruder, and, no, there was no reason, business or personal, that someone would want to hurt her family. When the paramedics helped her out of the cupboard they angled the stretcher so that she faced the stairs. They didn't want her to turn and see what was spray-painted on the wall behind her.

"And when you see it," he looked around at the faces, "I think you'll agree that, in spite of the heavy traffic through the house, it's what we should keep from the press."

He turned back to the TV. The camera operator was climbing the stairs; the shadows danced across the landing ahead. When Caffery had seen the spray-painting he had instantly recognized it as a tool to weed out false confessions.

The camera wobbled, someone in the hallway said, "Fuck," and then in a louder voice, on screen, "Have you seen this?" Darkness. A brief fumble then a flare of light; the camera aperture closed down momentarily, flinching like an iris. When the image came into focus the detectives in the SIOs' room inched a little closer, trying to read the spray-painted message.

$$\text{♀ HÀZÀ}\rho\text{d}$$

Caffery paused the tape, allowing each member of the team time to bend in and examine it: "Female Hazard." He flicked off the video and turned on the light. "We want this bottomed out by tomorrow—I won't insult your intelligence by telling you why."

In the kitchen at the Fairoaks base the air observer took off his helmet and rubbed his ears. He still wasn't sure what he'd seen. "I'd like to have done that on maximum endurance, y'know."

The commander patted him on the back. "They said we were just a tick in the box, Howie. They don't even know if he's in the park."

"It's a kid, though."

"Maybe when we lift we'll go back, eh?"

But in the time they took to refuel, a traffic officer in Purley had been hit by a car while deploying a stinger. The offender was out of the car and running toward Croydon airfield, so India 99 rerouted to that instead. When his shift finished at 2 A.M. the air observer was finding it a little easier not to think about the hazy white doughnut shape he thought he'd seen among the trees in Brockwell Park.